DAILY
GUIDEPOSTS
2019

Guideposts
New York

ZONDERVAN®

ZONDERVAN

Daily Guideposts 2019
Copyright © 2018 by Guideposts. All rights reserved.

Requests for information should be addressed to:
Zondervan, *3900 Sparks Dr. SE, Grand Rapids, Michigan 49546*

ISBN 978-0-310-35446-8 (hardcover)

ISBN 978-0-310-35460-4 (leather edition)

ISBN 978-0-310-35447-5 (large print)

ISBN 978-0-310-35465-9 (ebook)

Daily Guideposts is a registered trademark of Guideposts.

Acknowledgments: Every attempt has been made to credit the sources of copyrighted material used in this book. If any such acknowledgment has been inadvertently omitted or miscredited, receipt of such information would be appreciated.

Scripture quotations marked (AMP) are taken from the Amplified Bible. Copyright © 2015 by The Lockman Foundation. Used by permission. www.Lockman.org

Scripture quotations marked (ASV) are taken from *American Standard Version*. Public domain.

Scripture quotations marked (CEB) are taken from the Common English Bible. Copyright © 2011 by Common English Bible.

Scripture quotations marked (CEV) are taken from the Contemporary English Version. Copyright © 1995 American Bible Society.

Scripture quotations marked (CSB) are taken from The Christian Standard Bible. Copyright © 2017 by Holman Bible Publishers. Used by permission.

Scripture quotations marked (ESV) are taken from the ESV Bible (The Holy Bible, English Standard Version). Copyright © 2001 by Crossway, a Publishing Ministry of Good News Publishers. Used by permission. All rights reserved.

Scripture quotations marked (GNT) are taken from the Good News Translation in Today's English version–Second Edition. Copyright © 1992 by American Bible Society. Used by permission.

Scripture quotations marked (GW) are taken from *God's Word*. Copyright © 1995 by God's Word to the Nations. Used by permission of Baker Publishing Group. All rights reserved.

Scripture quotations marked (HCSB) are taken from the Holman Christian Standard Bible. Copyright © 1999, 2000, 2002, 2003, 2009 by Holman Bible Publishers, Nashville, Tennessee. All rights reserved.

Scripture quotations marked (JPS) are taken from T*anakh: A New Translation of the Holy Scriptures according to the Traditional Hebrew Text*. Copyright © 1985 by the Jewish Publication Society. All rights reserved.

Scripture quotations marked (ICB) are taken from International Children's Bible®. Copyright© 1986, 1988, 1999. Used by permission. All rights reserved.

Scripture quotations marked (ISV) are taken from the *Holy Bible, International Standard Version.* Copyright © 1995–2014 by ISV Foundation. All rights reserved internationally. Used by permission of Davidson Press, LLC.

Scripture quotations marked (KJV) are taken from the King James Version. Public domain.

Scripture quotations marked (MSG) are taken from *The Message*. Copyright © by Eugene H. Peterson 1993, 1994, 1995, 1996, 2000, 2001, 2002 . Used by permission of NavPress. All rights reserved. Represented by Tyndale House Publishers, Inc.

Scripture quotations marked (NASB) are taken from the New American Standard Bible. Copyright © 1960, 1962, 1963, 1968, 1971, 1972, 1973, 1975, 1977, 1995 by the Lockman Foundation. Used by permission. (www.Lockman.org)

Scripture quotations marked (NCV) are taken from The New Century Version. Copyright © 2005 by Thomas Nelson. Used by permission. All rights reserved.

Scripture quotations marked (NET) are taken from the NET Bible®. Copyright ©1996–2006 by Biblical Studies Press, L.L.C. http://netbible.com All rights reserved.

Scripture quotations marked (NIV) are taken from The Holy Bible, New International Version. Copyright © 1973, 1978, 1984, 2011 by Biblica, Inc. Used by permission of Zondervan. All rights reserved worldwide. www.Zondervan.com. The "NIV" and "New International Version" are trademarks registered in the United States Patent and Trademark Office by Biblica, Inc.

Scripture quotations marked (NKJV) are taken from the New King James Version. Copyright © 1982 by Thomas Nelson. Used by permission. All rights reserved.

Scripture quotations marked (NLT) are taken from the Holy Bible, New Living Translation. Copyright © 1996, 2004, 2007, 2013, 2015 by Tyndale House Foundation. Used by permission of Tyndale House Publishers Inc., Carol Stream, Illinois 60188. All rights reserved.

Scripture quotations marked (NRSV) are taken from the New Revised Standard Version Bible. Copyright © 1989 by the National Council of the Churches of Christ in the United States of America. Used by permission. All rights reserved.

Scripture quotations marked (RSV) are taken from the Revised Standard Version of the Bible. Copyright © 1946, 1952, 1971 by the National Council of Churches of Christ in the United States of America. Used by permission.

Scripture quotations marked (TLB) are taken from The Living Bible. Copyright © 1971 by Tyndale House Publishers, Carol Stream, Illinois 60188. All rights reserved.

Cover and interior design by Müllerhaus
Cover photo by Shutterstock
Monthly page opener photos by Shutterstock
Indexed by Patricia Woodruff
Typeset by Aptara

First printing July 2018 / Printed in the United States of America

Dear friends,

Welcome to *Daily Guideposts 2019*. As another year dawns, we feel privileged you've chosen us to join you on your daily journey of faith. If you're new to *Daily Guideposts*, welcome to the family. If you're a devoted reader of many years, welcome back.

The theme for this year is *In the Shadow of Your Wings,* based on Psalm 91:4, which promises, "He will cover you with his feathers, and under his wings you will find refuge; his faithfulness will be your shield and rampart" (NIV).

What a beautiful portrait of God's constant care, like that of a mother bird protecting her young, providing them a safe place even in the storm.

This year, you may also see these devotions published under the title *Walking in Grace.* We are debuting the *Walking in Grace* name in response to readers who say they prefer the title. Whichever name they appear under, these devotions are sure to bring you encouragement and inspiration throughout 2019.

Our writers share experiences of blessings and challenges, joys and disappointments, of closing chapters in life and starting new ones. Mark Collins writes about leaving a long career in academia. Patricia Lorenz learns about patience after having two knees replaced at the same time. You'll feel like you're there as Kim Henry unfolds the story of the huge fortieth anniversary surprise from her family. You'll remember what it feels like to watch a little child's gleeful discovery of God's creation in the form of a dandelion. You'll smile as you read about Vicki Kuyper choosing between residing in Woe-Is-Me or in Awesomeville. Each day our writers grace our readers with personal confidences and surprising ways of heeding God's voice.

This year, we're happy to welcome several new contributors: Desiree Cole, Lynne Hartke, Erin Janoso, Buck Storm, and Jacqueline Wheelock. And we say farewell to writer Jim Hinch, with our thanks and prayer for God's blessings on him.

We say a different kind of farewell to John Sherrill, who was a long-time contributor to *Daily Guideposts* as well as a best-selling author and a *Guideposts* magazine editor for more than a half century. He died at home on December 2, 2017. His beloved wife of seventy years, writer Elizabeth Sherrill, continues to share her life and wisdom in the pages of *Daily Guideposts*.

This year we have seven special series for you. Pam Kidd relates revelations of grace in "Encountering God in Unlikely Places." Marion Bond West remembers rich times of blessing and learning in "Things My Mother Taught Me." In "Unexpected Grace," Bill Giovannetti takes us on a journey through Holy Week.

In "Praying Through the Psalms," Julie Garmon's meditations remind us that God's Word holds new meaning for us every time we read it. Roberta Messner looks back on her thirty-eight years working relationship with America's heroes, in "Saying Goodbye to My Veterans." And who better than Edward Grinnan to point out the many delightful lessons we can learn from four-legged creatures in "Lessons from the Animals"? Finally, Penney Schwab reflects on the four weeks of Advent as Christmas approaches.

Get ready to meet God each day of this new year and to be reminded that no matter what you are facing—and whether you can feel it or not—you are loved and protected by God and shielded under His wing.

Faithfully yours,
Editors of Guideposts

P.S. We love hearing from you! Let us know what *Daily Guideposts* means to you by emailing DailyGPEditors@guideposts.org or writing to Guideposts Books & Inspirational Media, 39 Old Ridgebury Road #27, Danbury, CT 06810. You can also keep up with your *Daily Guideposts* friends on facebook.com/dailyguideposts.

Going Digital? Especially for You!

Get one-year instant access to the digital edition of *Daily Guideposts* delivered straight to your email. You'll be able to enjoy its daily inspiration and Scripture anytime, anywhere, on your computer, phone, or tablet. Visit DailyGuideposts.org/DG2019 and enter this code: faith2019.

JANUARY

Trust in the Lord with all your heart, and lean not on your own understanding; in all your ways acknowledge Him, and He shall direct your paths.

—Proverbs 3:5–6 (NKJV)

Tuesday, January 1

You have given me greater joy than those who have abundant harvests of grain and new wine. —Psalm 4:7 (NLT)

It's only five hours into the new year and I'm snuggled under a fur blanket in my quiet-time chair. Last night I went to bed at my normal early time, looking forward to these silent moments with God in the wee hours of an untouched year.

The fireplace dances a gentle glow into the room's darkness. In the dim light, my eyes scan the shelves filled with reminders of my abundant life—photos, books, mementos, the comfort of familiar things. I sip my steaming coffee and absorb the beauty of the moon that dazzles white-carpeted ground outside my study window.

I sit with God now and review the year that's passed. We go over its highs and lows, triumphs and defeats, challenges and joys, lessons learned. I breathe deeply of His love and thank Him for another year of life. Our conversation turns to the year ahead. I ask Him what He wants to see, then share with Him my hopes and dreams. I write these things down as if they are a journal entry this same day a year from now and have already occurred. Those pages will become part of my prayers. I tuck them into my Bible, certain that whatever the year ahead holds, He will be with me.

My time with God in the stillness of dawn is precious, priceless, filled with peace and joy no amount of New Year's Eve revelry could have brought. A blaze of orange pierces the horizon, and the first sunrise of this pristine year debuts. I'm filled with anticipation and hope, embraced by the One Who is ever faithful and fully good.

> *Thank You, God, for the best New Year's*
> *celebration ever—my time with You.*
> —Kim Taylor Henry

Digging Deeper: Mark 1:35; Psalm 47:10, 139:9–10

Write it before them on a tablet, and note it on a scroll, that it may be for time to come, forever and ever. —Isaiah 30:8 (NKJV)

New Year's Day my husband's brother passed away. He had spent five years on kidney dialysis, and yet his sudden heart attack was a shock. My husband and I put our life on hold as we went to help his twenty- and thirty-year-old daughters deal with all the could-haves, would-haves, and should-haves. His estate was in disarray. Keys to unknown locks, bills due, credit card payments, bank accounts, burial wishes—everything was a mystery that needed solving.

But I wondered about more than his earthly estate. He was a Christian, but toward the end of his pain-filled life, he estranged himself from family. Had he pushed God away, too? As I cleaned out his closets, I found dozens of T-shirts boldly proclaiming his faith, assuring me he didn't let it go in his heart even as his body failed him. I know he is with Christ, but he inspired me not only to get my own final wishes in order but also to make sure no one has to wonder about my soul.

When I got home, I took out a piece of paper. "I, being of sound mind, hereby commit my heart to Jesus, and I promise to prayerfully follow His teachings until He comes to take me home." I signed and dated it and made it page one in my stack of important papers. I've left room to sign it every year I am able.

Lord, please comfort us when we are left behind to grieve, and bring us closer to You in faith until You come to take us home.
—Erika Bentsen

Digging Deeper: Romans 8:35

Thursday, January 3

And what does the Lord require of you? To act justly and to love mercy and to walk humbly with your God. —Micah 6:8 (NIV)

I didn't choose a focus word for the year—I never have done so. But this year God handed me a word. It started with a sermon on what God requires of us, which inspired me to be more intentional about God's expectations found in Micah 6:8. I began closing my morning prayers by asking God to guide me to act justly in all I do that day, to be kind to all I am with, and to walk humbly with Him all day. Praying this request daily, I soon came to see humility as the key to each aspect— acting justly, being kind, and walking with Him.

The word *humble* kept standing out in my daily readings. I found the phrase "walk humbly with God" in only a few places in the Bible. The Scriptures more often tell us to walk obediently or faithfully with Him.

I started thinking more deeply about the significance of humility to our faith. Until we learn to walk humbly with God, can we:

> Be still and know God.
> Wait patiently for Him to renew our strength.
> Love God with all our being.
> Love others as ourselves.

To walk humbly with God means we must become less so He can become more within us. Only when we walk humbly with Him can His grace extend through us with just actions and kind words.

I'm so glad God pulled my attention to the word *humble*—a focus word I wouldn't have chosen, yet there is not a word I needed to understand more.

Dear God, I get it—to be intentional about what You require,
I must become more focused about being humble in my walk with You.
Help me to do this, Lord. Amen.
—John Dilworth

Digging Deeper: Matthew 23:12; Proverbs 22:4

SAYING GOODBYE TO MY VETERANS
After Retirement Who Would I Be?

When I am afraid, I put my trust in you. —Psalm 56:3 (NIV)

Waiting in the checkout line at Kroger, I studied the shopper in front of me. Early sixties, I decided. About my age. The woman was dressed in skinny jeans and a starched button-down shirt. *I wonder what her story is,* I mused.

"Didn't you once teach at Huntington High School?" the young bagger asked her. "I think I had you for English."

"That was me," she answered. "Until I retired, that is." A tear slid down her cheek. "Until I retired, I was the coordinator of the literacy program."

Was. That word. All too soon it would define me as well.

As I scooted my cartons of yogurt along the conveyor belt, I mentally rehearsed what would come from my own lips in the near future: "I was over the infection control program at the VA Medical Center."

Was. Could there be a sadder word?

My office was located directly across from that of the human resources benefits counselor. The next morning, a guy I'd gone through hospital orientation with back in 1978 trudged over to my desk. "This retirement thing isn't what it's cracked up to be, Roberta," he said. "When are you headed out?"

"Two months," I said.

"Well, let me tell you," he went on, "I've been through births, deaths, divorce, and the military. And retirement is the toughest transition I've ever experienced. I just sit on the porch and think of who I used to be."

All evening long, I rehashed that fellow's words. I was filled with ambivalence. For years I'd looked forward to retirement. But now I wondered what it would hold for me? Approaching change, I turned to the one constant source of strength.

It's time for a new chapter in my life, Lord, but I'm so afraid. Please help me.
—Roberta Messner

Digging Deeper: Isaiah 41:10; John 14:27; Philippians 4:6–7

Saturday, January 5

Praise God, who did not ignore my prayer or withdraw his unfailing love from me. —Psalm 66:20 (NLT)

When a neighbor girl comes by for Saturday breakfast, she predictably sings a mealtime grace she learned at vacation Bible school. It's an old prayer I remember from Girl Scout outings: "The Lord's Been Good to Me." By the end of the song, we've thanked God for "the sun, the rain, and the apple seed"—representing the omelets or pancakes on our plates.

Less regularly, one of us initiates what she calls a "Dear Jesus" prayer: an impromptu petition. With our eyes closed—or not—we talk to God about her family and daily concerns and maybe mine.

One Saturday, toward the end of a Dear Jesus prayer, I lost my focus. Before naming everyone in her family and signing off "thank You" and "amen," I asked her whether she'd finished her homework.

"No, will you help me?"

"OK."

"But…" She paused, as if for effect. "He's waiting for you." This happens sometimes in our communication—a comment I can't quite compute.

"He—who? Waiting for what?"

"Jesus. You didn't finish."

I smiled, shut my eyes, and wound up (or is it "wound down"?) our morning prayer, newly assured our God was in our presence and eager to hear us out.

Dear Jesus, thank You for patiently listening to our prayers, those we articulate in word or song and those that come by delay.
—Evelyn Bence

Digging Deeper: Isaiah 30:18; Psalm 86

"Comfort, comfort my people," says your God. —Isaiah 40:1 (NLT)

One evening, while preparing the following Sunday's sermon, I felt a pain in my chest. At first I thought I was sore from playing tennis the previous night. But as the evening progressed, the pain got worse. I told my wife, but since I didn't exhibit a specific alarming symptom, we decided to go to bed. The pain proceeded to worsen until it became unbearable. Around midnight we went to the emergency room.

About six hours later, the doctor informed us I needed a heart intervention and would be transported to another hospital. The forty-five-minute ambulance ride was surreal. I couldn't believe what was happening to me.

At the second hospital, I was told I needed a cardiac catheterization. There I discovered some of God's angels here on earth. Lori, a nurse of thirty years who came from the Philippines, was a much-needed presence. After several unsuccessful attempts to reduce the pain, she promised she wouldn't leave my side until the next phase of the procedure, and she didn't.

Matthew, a young nurse in his mid-thirties, said, "I'm here to help you get well." His words reassured me God had people lined up to care for me. Coincidently, *Matthew* means "gift of God," and indeed he was. When I was being moved for the cardiac procedure, Mathew promised he would say a prayer for me. This meant the world to me. His and Lori's great care got me through that day.

My stay was less than twenty-four hours, but the impact of the staff remains with me forever. We often think of angels in white robes with wings, but most of God's angels are here on earth, dressed as ordinary people. These nurses were my angels during my time of need. God positioned them to look out for me when I needed it most.

Lord, thank You for the people who come into our lives as
Your messengers of comfort and grace.
—Pablo Diaz

Digging Deeper: Psalm 91:11; Philippians 2:25

Monday, January 7

I in them and you in me, that they may become completely one, so that the world may know that you have sent me and have loved them even as you have loved me. —John 17:23 (NRSV)

Sometimes I go to the live stream site of the International Space Station, HD Earth Viewing Experiment on the Internet and gaze out at the vastness of our universe. Every time I do, I see something different. Today as the sun touched the horizon, a bright horizontal line shot across the screen. By the time the sun sank midway, another line had appeared, only vertical this time creating a golden cross on the screen. When the sun finally disappeared behind the Earth and out of view of the camera, a curved pale blue line was the only image on the screen. It shrank until it disappeared and the screen went black.

At any time, at least a thousand people around the world are watching with me. Throughout the sunset, people bid one an other good night (or good morning) in the comments section of the live stream, signing off until the camera is back in the light. Though I've never commented, I get such a sense of community when on this page. By watching our Earth from a camera in orbit, I feel a wider sense of connection. Somewhere out there under that gaze, a person's life is ending while another's one is beginning. Someone is grieving while another rejoices. There is blossoming, and there are implosions. And life continues to cycle.

Science tells us every element on Earth was formed in a star, that everything that exists originates from stardust. If this is so, then all of those things happening all over the world are also happening to me. If this is so, then my connection is their connection. We are one.

Ever loving and holy God, I am grateful for the tiny moments of awareness that help me see a glimpse into the vastness of all You hold in the palm of Your hand. I am forever in awe of Your works.
—Natalie Perkins

Digging Deeper: John 14:20; 1 John 4:12

They think that they will be heard for their many words.
—Matthew 6:7 (RSV)

There was no point in my even trying out for the open spot in dance class, I wailed to my mother. "Gracie says her dad is friends with the man who owns the school. She says her mother was a famous dancer. She says—"

"Gracie says, Gracie says," Mother interrupted my lament. "You know what this reminds me of? Bobby's bark."

Bobby was our little black cocker spaniel who yap-yapped to the world that he owned our yard. We had one other pet—a lazy black-and-white cat named Domino, who liked to sleep on the front steps in the sun.

Three doors down the street lived a Doberman pinscher, five times Bobby's size and who occasionally came strolling past. Rounding the corner on his patrol, Bobby would stop short. Ferocious bark strangling in his throat, he'd streak for the house, bound up the steps, and stand behind Domino.

The Doberman, hunting instinct triggered, would veer onto the yard. Whereupon Domino stood up, huge and terrible, no longer the gentle pet that spent nights on my bed. Back arched, fur bristling, dagger teeth exposed, he'd emit a fearsome hiss.

At this point in the familiar drama, the Doberman appeared to recollect an errand farther up the street. Long legs sidestepping daintily, he'd continue his afternoon ramble. Domino would sit down and wash. And Bobby, when the bigger dog was out of sight, would resume his rounds, barking as loudly as ever.

In fact, neither Gracie nor I got into dance school that year. But I'd learned a priceless distinction between noise and substance.

Let all my words today, Father, match the reality they represent.
—Elizabeth Sherrill

Digging Deeper: Ecclesiastes 5:2

So in everything, do to others what you would have them do to you, for this sums up the Law and the Prophets. —Matthew 7:12 (NIV)

I noticed the gauges in the cashier's ears and the tattoos that tangled down his arms. He was about the same age as my older sons, and I was glad my boys weren't pierced or painted.

"I only have a dollar and twenty-four cents for gasoline," I said. "I left my handbag at home." The cashier counted my change.

It was dark outside and bitter cold. My husband was traveling, and I'd been late to pick up my son after an out-of-town swim meet. There hadn't been time to stop for gas before meeting the bus. It wasn't until I was at the station that I realized I'd forgotten my purse.

"Here you are," the cashier said. He pressed a receipt into my hand, and I headed into the cold. As I unscrewed the gas cap, I worried we wouldn't make it home. As I pumped gas, the numbers on the pump scrolled past what I'd paid for.

I ran back inside.

"I'm sorry," I said. "I went past what I spent. Somehow it kept pumping."

The young man smiled. "I put some money with yours," he said. "I want you to be safe."

For the first time, I noticed his kind eyes and gentle voice. My soul ached. I'd been so wrong. This person reached into my life with care and compassion.

I once again thought of my same-age sons.

And then of the cashier.

I hoped they would be like him.

> *Lord, forgive me when I don't love as I should—in thought*
> *or in deed. Amen.*
> —Shawnelle Eliasen

Digging Deeper: John 13:34; 1 John 4:11

Surely I have behaved and quieted myself, as a child that is weaned of his mother: my soul is even as a weaned child. —Psalm 131:2 (KJV)

No one was answering my knocks. I stood at the door of an emergency shelter for women and children, as I do each month, caught between feeding a portion of the hungry in my city and getting on with the remainder of the day. Not much of a choice for a Christian, I reasoned, unless she has braved the traffic on a cold January morning and not quite mastered the gift of patience.

I could leave the groceries at the door, I thought, momentarily forgetting the perishables and the fact that the only food some child might have that night could not be left to chance, neither to the elements nor the dishonest.

The warmth of home beckoned me. *It could be hours before someone shows up,* I thought. But I sensed the Lord saying, *Wait.*

Really, Lord? Haven't I done my part by buying and bringing the groceries here? Glancing around at the struggling neighborhood, I suddenly felt chastened. I returned to my car, aware that patience-building was what God wanted to work in me that frosty noonday. I slid under the wheel, and "behaved and quieted myself" as so beautifully spoken in Psalm 131. Within minutes, the lone and likely underpaid staff tore across the yard.

"Here I am! I was just a couple of doors over, getting lunch." A couple of doors over, not hours away. I laughed and unloaded the groceries, knowing I was the one who was richly fed that day on the certainty of God's promptings and the rewards of a patient spirit.

> *Lord, grant me the grace today to simply wait.*
> —Jacqueline F. Wheelock

Digging Deeper: Luke 21:19; James 1:4

From everlasting to everlasting the Lord's love is with those who fear him, and his righteousness with their children's children. —Psalm 103:17 (NIV)

The good thing about having grandchildren is being able to send them home with their parents when the visit is over."

Chuck and I exchange knowing glances. How many times have we heard that maxim? Perhaps life is supposed to be that way, right? But that cliché doesn't apply in our case, since our eight-year-old grandson lives with us full time and has for the past four years.

The person making the statement usually follows with, "They wear us out when they come to visit, and it takes us days to recover."

That part used to apply to us, too. Typically, empty nesters' lives slow down. The pace is no longer hectic, and you can finally take a breath. But when grandchildren enter your lives, with unlimited energy, it's as if your body wakes up and your own energy level kicks up a couple of notches.

And then the next grandparent saying comes into play: "Bet he keeps you on your toes." There is definitely truth to that statement. Not only does the energy level elevate, but so does mental alertness. The mind shifts from autopilot to paying attention to the grandchild's whereabouts and activities. All. The. Time. As mature adults, we are more aware of potential dangers than ever before, certainly more so than when our own children were small. The world is not always a safe place, and now it's our responsibility to protect our grandchild as well as we can.

Another cliché we've heard is, "He'll keep you young." With the elevated energy level and attention awareness we have acquired, perhaps that's true.

At least, I hope so. Being a grandparent raising a grandchild has its difficulties, but staying young is a benefit I didn't expect.

Lord, raising a young child has changed our lives in many ways.
Help us to focus on the benefits instead of the difficulties.
—Marilyn Turk

Digging Deeper: Psalm 103:2–5

So teach us to number our days that we may get a heart of wisdom.
—Psalm 90:12 (ESV)

Thirty years ago, I took my five-year-old son, Drew, to an antique show. We immediately spotted an old mahogany grandfather clock on display. I carefully showed Drew how the brass pendulum swung to make the clock go *ticktock*. Drew was fascinated, and we bought the clock. This tall case clock has been part of our home ever since, tolling the hours each day.

Recently Drew—now thirty-five and an attorney—brought his wife, Katie Alice, and their two small children home for a visit. When Drew's son, Andrew, walked into the living room, I was amazed at how much he looked like his father. This little boy immediately walked over to the grandfather clock, opened the mahogany door, stuck in his hand, and grasped the swinging pendulum. Time literally stopped. Not only did the old grandfather clock grow silent, but it seemed as if life had reversed itself and my son was a child again. The generations flowed together in a moment beyond time, and the room was filled with joy and laughter!

Drew showed Andrew how to make the pendulum swing. Time ticked again, and the hands of the clock slowly moved around the dial. Three generations laughed together and rejoiced in an evolving family tradition of winding the clock.

It is true that time and memories—not money—are our most valuable resources. Spending time with family and friends, creating traditions and memories is what makes life rich. We must all find ways to wind the clock and experience life together, to rejoice with the chiming of each hour.

Father, help us cherish each moment and chapter of life. Amen.
—Scott Walker

Digging Deeper: Ecclesiastes 3:1–8; 2 Peter 3:8

Let no unwholesome word proceed from your mouth, but only such a word as is good for edification according to the need of the moment, so that it will give grace to those who hear. —Ephesians 4:29 (NASB)

"Did you hear? Ellie's coming today."

My heart sank. Facilitating a Bible study at a retirement center was a new and uncomfortable experience for me—way out of my element. Granted, the first few weeks had gone pretty well. But now Ellie, resident spiritual giant, was coming to pass judgment on my theological inadequacies. I'd never met Ellie, but I could see her in my mind's eye. Like the big, rawboned Sunday school teacher of my youth—she'd probably even bring her own ruler to whack knuckles.

Except Ellie wasn't at all what I expected.

Funny, at six-foot-two I'm not a small man. I'm definitely not the nervous type. I've been a deep-sea diver and commercial fisherman. I've traveled the world. In my life I've seen my share of storms. Yet when this tiny slip of an Ellie—eighty pounds soaking wet—took her seat on that folding chair with her little feet not even touching the floor, my palms got sweaty.

Get it over with, man.

I opened the text and fumbled through our allotted forty-five minutes, avoiding Ellie's eyes every time I looked up. When it was over, I shook hands and said a few prayers for people as they shuffled out.

And then there she was—little Ellie staring up with those sky-blue eyes. I braced myself for the critique I knew was coming.

Her face broke into a million lines when she smiled.

"Can I have a hug?" she said.

Have you ever been overwhelmed by grace?

An odd pair, I suppose, but Ellie and I became great friends. You see, that precious little woman managed to show me Jesus with a smile and five little words. She wrecked me with love—just like He does.

Lord, please help me exemplify grace. Let the world see You in me.
—Buck Storm

Digging Deeper: Ecclesiastes 10:12; Romans 14:19; Romans 15:2

Do not judge others, and you will not be judged. For you will be treated as you treat others. —Matthew 7:1–2 (NLT)

Iwas having trouble with a program on my laptop one weekend and resorted to the manufacturer's chat function for assistance. In short order I got a message from a "geek" named Pat, who proved to be very helpful in figuring out my problem (as usual, it was me and not the program). As we were about to sign off, I typed, "Thanks, dude," trying to sound all hip and techie. "Actually, I'm a dudette!" she typed back. "And a grandmother! But that's OK. You're welcome."

I think of myself as fairly enlightened on matters of gender equality and ageism. I'm a boomer who went to college in the mid-seventies, when the world started going politically correct. I want to treat others equally and fairly. And yet I'd made this clumsy blunder, assuming help had come from a millennial who had jumped off his skateboard long enough to solve my problem instead of a grandmother who'd put aside her knitting. And both personas are stereotypes—she could be a skater grandma! Is there no overcoming my unconscious bias?

In our increasingly complex world, some of us tend to default to categorization for simplicity, often revealing our prejudices and pre-conceptions, even our fears. I don't think anyone or any one group is immune to this thinking. Still, the fact that we all do it doesn't mean we should do it.

Jesus teaches us to treat all others as children of God, as individuals deserving of our unqualified love, a command that echoes through the New Testament. In a world so often rent by political and cultural divi-sions, just as His world was, let us follow the example Jesus set forth as He walked this earth, by embracing the "other" as our own.

Today and every day, let me see the world through the eyes of Jesus, treat-ing each stranger with love and respect as a brother or sister in the Lord.
—Edward Grinnan

Digging Deeper: John 8:7; Matthew 22:37–38

Tuesday, January 15

Ye are the light of the world. A city that is set on an hill cannot be hid.
—Matthew 5:14 (KJV)

Before I became a writer, I instructed military personnel on how to teach—presentations skills, lesson plan writing, and evaluation methods. It was a joy to help fearless warriors overcome their fear of public speaking so they could inspire others. I told them, "Risk doing more than you think you can; your students are hungry to hear what you have to say."

But I understood their fear. When I was just beginning to put pen to paper, I struggled to find the confidence and courage to write. It made me feel vulnerable. I bargained with God: *I will write for You, Lord, but let me keep my privacy.*

Two years later I was sitting next to my cousin, who is also my best friend, at a conference attended by over ten thousand women. As a newly published author, my confidence about being a writer was still fragile. But at the conference, I was full of joy. Only the pastor leading the conference, his wife, and my cousin knew me. I embraced my anonymity.

Suddenly I saw the pastor walking in my direction, his hand extended toward me. He was going to introduce me to an international audience. I panicked! I shook my head, silently pleading with the pastor to leave me in peace. He honored my plea.

Recently I've considered what an opportunity I missed to impact the kingdom. Maybe it was because I was raised in the sixties as the only girl in my family. My wonderful parents had their hands full, pushing my four brothers forward while at the same time trying to keep me docile and ladylike.

For years I ignored my failure during that event. But no more, Lord. I'm going to let my light shine!

Lord, forgive my fear. Forgive me for rebuffing You and the pastor.
Use me, Lord! Help me not to fear being a light in this world.
—Sharon Foster

Digging Deeper: John 12:36, 21:17 (KJV); Mark 14:72 (KJV)

What is man, that thou art mindful of him? —Psalm 8:4 (KJV)

This dreary January afternoon, I sit in traffic, basically parked on the interstate outside Washington. A horse trailer on my right creeps ahead. The cement mixer on my left groans forward, then hisses to brake. Now it's my turn to progress a few feet. The five lanes of traffic seem to snake ahead for miles.

Embedded in this grinding glacier of metal, I move toward Florida. My family there expects me at no particular time, so the holdup causes me no distress. Instead I reflect on my anonymity in this mass of humanity bearing license plates from DC, Maryland, Virginia, even Nova Scotia. How many vehicles head south with me? Five hundred? A thousand? Two thousand? Other humans drive and ride in these vehicles, but I know none of them.

And this is only one road in one city of the United States. I try to estimate how many people in other cities on other highways also sit in traffic right now in the US, in North America, in the world. My mind boggles that I share planet Earth with billions of bodies. For the next hour, my mood turns as dismal as the weather: I am an insignificant speck in the universe.

Before I can work myself into an existential crisis, though, grace happens. I remember God has created each driver in His own image and endowed each person in the world with a soul. Incredibly God knows each one of us—each one. Even stuck in traffic and anonymity here on the interstate, I am precious in His sight.

Lord, will I ever understand why You care for us so much?
—Gail Thorell Schilling

Digging Deeper: Matthew 10:29–31; Psalm 139

Thursday, January 17

Fear not, Abram, I am a shield to you. —Genesis 15:1 (JPS)

The Northridge earthquake, whose epicenter was less than a mile from our house, had been pretty terrifying. So when the *New Yorker* published its Pulitzer prize-winning article on the peril to those of us living in the Cascadia earthquake zone, a lot of people here in the Pacific Northwest got nervous. After all, the prospect of a serious quake and perhaps a tsunami was scary. I expected to be one of the frightened.

But, strangely, I wasn't. When my husband, Keith, and I lived in Los Angeles, preparation for a quake was a given. After the Sylmar quake, the earliest one I'd experienced, I learned to keep supplies of water and food, and to anchor pictures to the walls with Velcro. When we moved into our house in the San Fernando Valley, we went further than that. Every piece of furniture taller than I am was strapped to the walls, all the knickknacks were fastened down with museum wax, and we kept a crowbar and a short-handled sledgehammer under the side of our bed.

Those preparations helped protect us when Northridge happened. In spite of the months of necessary repair and recovery, we were unhurt. That experience gave me confidence that God had seen us through, demonstrating to us in unmistakable terms that He was with us when the ground shook and anything not tied down crashed to the floor. I believe that, even if Cascadia were to break loose in my lifetime, as long as I keep faith and prepare, He might well see fit to bring me through again.

> *Please be a shield to me, too, God of Abraham,*
> *just as You were my protector in the past.*
> —Rhoda Blecker

Digging Deeper: Isaiah 48:17; Proverbs 1:33

So, chosen by God for this new life of love, dress in the ward…
picked out for you: compassion, kindness, humility, quiet stre…
discipline. Be even-tempered, content with second place, quick…
forgive an offense. —Colossians 3:12–13 (MSG)

We give great Friday night dinner parties, my wife and I—usually. On one particular Friday last winter, we started arguing mid-afternoon about little things. There were small tensions, topics avoided, slights felt. A couple of hours later, before a single dish made it into the oven, we were arguing about something. Now I don't even remember what it was. But we were both stressed at work, and we were not communicating well about what was going on. We weren't taking the time to listen to each other.

When our guests arrived right on time (why couldn't they have been late this time?), my wife and I couldn't hide the fact that we were fighting. Sometimes that works, but not this time. Three couples walked in the back door, as usual, and stood in our kitchen, looking at our red faces. Our friend Michael spoke for the lot of them and asked, "What's going on?" My wife and I looked at each other (maybe for the first time in hours) and cried.

"How can we help?" someone else said.

My, oh my, good friends are so good. We learned that day that they can bear our burdens with us and make our load easier. Gifts from God.

Help me be a friend today, Lord, and
see the needs on the faces of those I know and love.
—Jon M. Sweeney

Digging Deeper: Colossians 3:14

But the one who looks into the perfect law, the law of liberty, and perseveres, being no hearer who forgets but a doer who acts, he will be blessed in his doing. —James 1:25 (ESV)

My eleven-year-old son, Joey, has amazing hair. It's thick and blond and wavy, and the ends curl out perfectly as if he styled them that way. It's completely unfair, considering that I have thin, scraggly hair that has never curled perfectly, not even once in my entire life.

But alas, Joey's perfect curls tend to get a bit unruly at night when he's sleeping.

Last night, he walked into the kitchen after his shower, his hair sticking out in every direction. "Mom, I have a theory."

"What is it?" I asked.

"Well, since my hair always sticks out everywhere in the morning when I comb it after my shower the night before, I'm thinking that if I don't comb it and just go to sleep with it like this, then I'll wake up and it will look perfect."

Oh, the glory of being young and naive.

Sadly for Joey, his theory didn't work out as planned. He woke up to an even bigger rat's nest in his hair and had to spend a good ten minutes trying to tame the crazy cowlicks.

"It was worth the try, Mom, but I think from now on I'll probably just comb my hair when I get out of the shower." He smiled.

And so my baby learned yet another life lesson: sure, it might seem easier to just let a tangled mess lie, but in the end, it's always better to grab a comb and some conditioning spray and smooth it out before it gets more tangled. Otherwise, you'll wake up with an even bigger mess to unravel.

Jesus, reveal Yourself to me every day so I can wake up with a fresh, clean state ready to honor You. Amen.
—Erin MacPherson

Digging Deeper: Ephesians 4:26; 2 Peter 1:5–8

PRAYING THROUGH THE PSALMS: Just You and Me, God

Blessed are those…who seek him with their whole heart. —Psalm 119:2 (ESV)

One Sunday, our pastor emphasized the importance of having a daily quiet time. *I already do that,* I thought, feeling a little bored. "The book of Psalms is a great place to start," he said. That was not much of a challenge. I've been reading Psalms since I was a child.

"Sometimes I only read a verse or two a day," he added. Oh. "When I slow down and let the Scriptures soak in, God shows me how to pray. "It's not about how many verses you read. It's about listening."

I squirmed in my seat. Lately my morning prayers had felt like busy-work. I would flip through my Bible and scribble the same prayers for the same people. I connected with God in my head but not always in my heart. If my prayers didn't reach my heart, how could they possibly reach His? But something in my pastor's gentle tone—his humility—melted my defenses. He read less Scripture than I did, yet it sounded as though he went deeper spiritually. How was that possible?

The next morning I opened my old Bible—the one full of markings— and turned to Psalm 1. *Lord, show me how to fall in love with You again, through the Psalms,* I prayed.

Reminding myself to slow down, I copied a verse in my journal. Not in black ink like I usually did. But with a purple pen. A royal color. To honor God's Word.

As if the Lord were writing with a golden pen, He drew me to certain verses, sometimes the same ones I'd memorized in childhood. Then He connected my mind with my heart and showed me how to pray the Psalms for people I love.

My prayer time grew sweeter because I finally invited God to join me.

When it's just You and me, God, and I give You all my heart,
You teach me how to pray.
—Julie Garmon

Digging Deeper: Philippians 4:6–7; Ephesians 6:18

Monday, January 21

If anyone wants to sue you and take your coat, give
your cloak as well. —Matthew 5:40 (NRSV)

"Where's our Mahalia CD?" I asked Charlie as I rooted through the CD box. "I love it, and we haven't heard it in ages."

"You're right," he said, searching with me. It took a few minutes to realize this favorite, along with many others, was gone.

At one point, we'd been traveling back and forth between California and Connecticut. We had decided to leave some of our things in storage in California to avoid lugging clothes, records, books, and even jewelry from one coast to another twice a year.

Last year we learned that every single item had been stolen from storage. And situations like this, when we realized something we loved had been taken, always reopened the wound.

This time Charlie said, "We could just order another one."

Yeah, I thought bitterly, *but we can't reorder the bracelet my mother bought or the vase of California shells we collected.* Ignoring my sour face, he wondered aloud, "Do you think whoever has it now enjoys it like we did?"

Huh? I'd never thought about it that way. Did Mahalia end up, eventually, in the hands of a gospel music lover? Are the shells sitting on the shelf of someone who loves the ocean? Is the bracelet Mom gave me around the wrist of a daughter whose mother doesn't care enough to give her a bracelet of her own? Had the Lord perhaps put these items, our "stuff," into the hands of people who need them more than we do? After all, we hadn't even known some of this stuff was missing until we searched for it.

Everything we think we own is really a gift from God. I now think of our California stuff not so much as stolen but as redistributed.

Lord, thank You for helping me focus on the Giver and not the stuff.
—Marci Alborghetti

Digging Deeper: Psalm 9:1–2, 7–8, 13–14

Jesus wept. —John 11:35 (KJV)

Iwas coming out from under anesthesia, and I could see my wife watching over me. Suddenly, I puckered up and cried.

"It's a common reaction to that type of anesthesia," I heard the doctor say to my wife.

I apologized to Sharon for the tears, but then I remembered something I'd learned from one of my college students. She was a rather rough country girl, who sat in the back row and never said a word. After several attempts to reach her, I gave up and left her alone.

One day I was telling the class a hilarious story about my father. Somehow it triggered some deep emotions about my dad, who had passed away at the start of the fall semester. All at once my voice locked up, my face fell, and my eyes blurred. The class grew very still. It took an eternity to find my voice, and then I explained, "My father...passed away...in September. He was...the perfect dad...and I miss him. I'm sorry...for the tears."

I couldn't go on, so I dismissed the class early. I stood there, my head down and hankie in hand, while the students filed reverently out of the classroom. All except one student, who came to my side and put her arm around me. "It's good to see your heart," she said. I looked up to see the country girl, the one I could never reach. "Never apologize for tears," she added.

"I'm glad men are strong," my wife said on the way home from the hospital. "It's an important part of your nature. But sometimes it's good for us to see the little boy inside."

Lord, Your tears were eloquent. Thank You for letting us see Your heart.
—Daniel Schantz

Digging Deeper: Psalm 126:6; Ecclesiastes 7:3

Take my yoke upon you. Let me teach you, because I am humble and gentle at heart, and you will find rest for your souls. For my yoke is easy to bear, and the burden I give you is light. —Matthew 11:29–30 (NLT)

By the time I had both knees replaced on the same day, the left one had been in pain for sixteen years and the right for five. Everyone, including the nurses in the hospital, was shocked I'd chosen to have them both replaced at the same time.

"It's a tough surgery, much longer recovery time than hip replacement. And to do two at once, wow, you're a tough cookie," one nurse said.

But why would I want to go through the long recovery twice?

Life lessons began the minute I woke up in my hospital room, where the wheelchair could not fit through the bathroom door. That meant I had to do my business in a commode right in the middle of the room, often in front of nurses, nursing assistants, or housekeeping employees. I learned humility.

I learned gratitude when I had to ask others to lift my heavy, swollen legs off the bed so I could scoot into the wheelchair or stand up to the walker.

When my neighbor Cindy's husband (a man I had never met) appeared as my nurse one night, I learned to dismiss embarrassment and be grateful for his help to the commode at 3:00 a.m.

When I whined at the surgeon's office months later, asking how much longer the recovery would take, he shot up two fingers.

"Two more months?" I wailed.

"Two years!" he shouted. That day I learned patience.

I'm still working to gain the 110-degree bend in my right knee so I can get in and out of a car comfortably. That is teaching me determination.

Lord, thank You for these new knees but most of all for the humility, gratitude, patience, and determination that came with the surgery.
—Patricia Lorenz

Digging Deeper: 1 Corinthians 15:58; Romans 5:3–5

By awesome deeds You answer us in righteousness, O God of our salvation.
—Psalm 65:5 (NASB)

Not in my wildest dreams did I think I'd be living something out of Psalm 65. It began in the early 1980s when I memorized the psalm in an adult class at church. I chose it for its beautiful imagery—its portrayal of God's abundant joy in His creation.

Thirty years later while I visited my mother, she took me to the "little castle"—a studio apartment add-on in the home of her friends. It was love at first entry. I felt an inner assurance that I would live there one day.

It took five years of trusting God before my husband, Terry, and I arrived. After driving fourteen hundred miles in mid-January, we found ourselves locked out of our dream home! Mom to the rescue—she had a spare key.

The following summer I connected the little castle with Psalm 65. On a wooded mountainside we face west over a beautiful valley. The sunsets "shout for joy"(8). A wide river is "full of water" (9). The forested hills "gird themselves with rejoicing" (12).

Three large fields provide habitat for deer, and elk, and wild turkeys. The "pastures of the wilderness drip" (12) with lush grass hay. The "meadows are clothed with flocks" (13).

The natural world opens before us like God's "holy temple" and I am "satisfied with the goodness of Your house" (4). My soul sings with the psalmist, "You have crowned the year with Your bounty, and Your paths drip with fatness" (11).

I couldn't have planned this. Somehow all those young years ago, God, Who is "the trust of all the ends of the earth and of the farthest sea" (5), placed a hand on my future. He led me to a place I didn't know I longed for.

He brought me to Psalm 65, Idaho.

Heavenly Father, thank You that You do "far more abundantly
beyond all that we ask or think" (Ephesians 3:20). I believe!
—Carol Knapp

Digging Deeper: Psalm 37:3–6, 65; Proverbs 3:5–6

Friday, January 25

Blessed are those who mourn, for they will be comforted. —Matthew 5:4 (NIV)

Outside my office window, the leftover snow and bleak scene mirrored the state of my life. In three weeks my family suffered three unexpected deaths—one each week. The last one was unbelievably devastating, my nephew, my sister Maria's son. My tired heart broke, and I didn't know how to—or really want to—put it back together. Despite it all, I kept going, getting up, getting dressed, and going to work.

I turned inward and tried to make sense of it all. I put on a happy face and tried to feel something other than that deep, fresh grief. I held my breath a lot and tried to care about impending deadlines and responsibilities. I tried to listen on conference calls. I tried to be compassionate when coworkers or friends complained about mundane things like nothing to watch on TV or difficulty finding a dog food that was inexpensive yet healthy.

Grief is like a chrysalis, a heavy coat that fastens itself to you, one you wear and get used to, one that forever changes you—and eventually brings you to a place of ascension—but I wasn't there yet. I was in the darkness of the cocoon. I found myself reflecting the dismal winter landscape and feeling hopeless.

At the grocery store, the tiny greenhouse section called out to me. I purchased an African violet that fit in the palm of my hand. In the midst of soft green leaves, three white flowers bloomed.

I placed the plant in my office beside my computer. Looking at it, I smiled and suddenly realized there was a perfect little blossom for each of my loved ones. Their happy yellow centers shone like miniature sunshine. Each seemed to say, *Breathe. See beauty. Go on.*

> *Heavenly Father, thank You for guiding me through the depths*
> *of my grief to appreciate the blossoming beauty of life.*
> —Sabra Ciancanelli

Digging Deeper: Psalm 61:2; Hebrews 11:1

I will meditate on your majestic, glorious splendor. —Psalm 145:5 (NLT)

I fumble on the nightstand for my watch. It's 5:20 a.m. I close my eyes, then remind myself I can sleep when I get home. Right now we're on a cruise ship, almost to Thomso, Norway. Here, above the Arctic Circle, are sights outside I might not get to experience again. I pull aside the curtain, slide open the glass door, and step onto our balcony.

Vibrant air ensures I'm quite awake now. Craggy peaks rise from deep water. Velvety green lichen and gray stone of timeless mountains blend like melted candlewax into the pewter sea. Jagged snow-dolloped ranges are their backdrop. Sun-infused clouds glow overhead. The ocean expanse ripples as our small ship glides steadily, noiselessly, through the imposing fjord. Millions of years ago massive glaciers inched their way through the earth's granite, carving out the country of Norway and this majestic water path we now travel.

As I absorb the fjord's grandeur and stunning peace, the wind enhances the silence with its song. Though I am but a tiny temporary observer of this slice of God's eternity, I feel grounded and strong. I'm embraced and enthralled by this magnificence He created, here unviolated by human distractions. He speaks to my heart, *Be still and know that I am God.*

I breathe deeply and smile. Yes, I can sleep another time.

Lord, thank You for these moments of awe and
Your regal creation that inspires them.
—Kim Taylor Henry

Digging Deeper: Psalm 46:10, 65:6–8, 96:6

After I go and prepare a place for you, I will come back and take you to be with me so that you may be where I am. —John 14:3 (NCV)

It was one of those Sunday sermons that stirred my imagination. Oddly it was a recommendation for prayer that I'd heard countless times before: when praying, picture yourself talking to your father. My father had owned an upholstery shop, and since Jesus was a carpenter, I decided from that moment on that when I prayed, I'd put Jesus in Dad's shop and talk to Him just the way I had so often done with my father.

The next day I settled into my devotional time, which I do early in the morning. When it came time to pray, I mentally placed myself back in my dad's shop, sitting on the stool and chatting with him. Only I wasn't talking to my dad—I was talking to Jesus. And like Dad, Jesus was busy at work on His latest project, listening intently. I went through my list of concerns, chatting away the same way I had frequently done with my earthly father. In my mind's eye, Jesus listened, nodding now and again as I spoke. I mentioned the book I was currently writing, and sought His wisdom and guidance as I do with all my novels.

Then a strange thing happened—Jesus turned, looked at me, smiled, and said, as clearly as if He'd spoken the words out loud, *Debbie, I have the most wonderful books for you to write…in heaven.*

That experience changed my entire idea of what heaven is like. I will be able to continue doing what I love on this earth, and I am assured that Jesus has prepared a writing space for me when the time comes for me to join Him in heaven.

> *Lord, it thrills me to know there are plots waiting for*
> *me in heaven! Thank You for Your unending gifts.*
> —Debbie Macomber

Digging Deeper: 1 Corinthians 2:9

He used twelve stones to build an altar in honor of the Lord.
—1 Kings 18:31 (CEV)

My breath hung in the January air as I panted and braced myself against the side of the mountain. Even Sunrise, my golden retriever, plopped down on the trail. It was a Saturday morning, and the last few weeks I'd been restless. Normally I have a clear-cut picture of my goals for the year, but not this year.

Earlier this morning, I'd asked God for direction. Glancing out the window, I noticed there wasn't much snow on the mountains. I'd stared at the side of that mountain for years. I wondered what was on top. An hour later, after bundling up like the abominable snowman, Sunrise and I ascended the trail.

The trail was so steep, my clothing so bulky, and the air so cold that I was able to climb only forty to fifty feet before stopping to catch my breath and wonder, *What am I going to accomplish this year?* Each time, I glanced over the view of my valley and dreamed of the endless possibilities.

When I dragged my throbbing legs up the last step to the peak, I glanced at my watch. I'd made the climb in about an hour. I was busy patting myself on the back when I turned and noticed a rock cairn on a knoll. Although it's a common practice for hikers to leave behind one rock on the pile, I wasn't expecting it. A still, small voice whispered in my spirit, "Life isn't about what you accomplish. It's about what you leave behind that honors God." I gasped.

I'd been restless about this year's goals because I was focused on myself and what I wanted to accomplish. I hadn't chatted with God about what He wanted me to do. On the hike down the mountain, I realigned my thoughts and got back on track.

Lord, please share with me Your vision for my life. Amen.
—Rebecca Ondov

Digging Deeper: 2 Thessalonians 1:11–12; 1 Peter 3:15

Tuesday, January 29

We are His workmanship, created in Christ Jesus for good works, which God prepared beforehand so that we would walk in them.
—Ephesians 2:10 (NASB)

I call it being "written in"—in God's "appointment book." Those times I meet up, unplanned, with someone and we have a conversation that encourages one or both of us. Just this week I had three.

One was in the library with a woman I hadn't seen in over a year. In conversing, I learned she had an autoimmune disorder most of her life. My daughter-in-law had just been diagnosed with lupus. This woman buoyed me with an offer to be a listener and mentor for her. I'd gone to the library for a good read and left certain God's "appointment book" contained a whole other reason for my being there.

The second encounter was a phone call from a friend in a serious state of depression. After we hung up, it occurred to me I could do more than promise to pray. I could give her a reason to get out and look forward to something. I redialed, asking, "Where do you want to meet for lunch?" God was giving me an "appointment" worth keeping.

The third meet-up was in the grocery store. This young woman, a friend from church, was facing some uncertainties. We talked of Jesus and how in His own suffering He understands ours. Together we explored the meaning of Philippians 3:10—"That I may know Him and the power of His resurrection and the fellowship of His sufferings." We both left the store enriched by our "appointment."

Nothing is finer than a place in God's daily planner. No matter what else is on my schedule.

God of my surprise, show me where You have me written in.
—Carol Knapp

Digging Deeper: Hebrews 10:24–25; Ecclesiastes 4:9–12;
Acts 8:25–40

Do not be misled: "Bad company corrupts good character."
—1 Corinthians 15:33 (NIV)

I grew up in pristine California suburbs but now live in rural Oklahoma. I prefer where I live now over where I used to live except for one thing: litterers. Trash clutters the roadsides. I can pick it up, but by the next week there's more.

Once, when my girls were little, we stopped for fast food, coming home from somewhere with one of their friends. After eating, the friend threw her trash out the window, and Charlotte and Lulu promptly did the same. I screeched to the roadside and immediately became what the girls called "Mean Mama." Everyone had to get out and pick up not only their trash but also all the other trash in the vicinity. I'm ashamed to say I thought negatively of that little girl and was glad when, not long after—no doubt, chagrined—she stopped wanting to come over.

After that I always preached against littering. Charlotte recently amused us with the story of how, before she left for a high school dance, I subjected her and her date to my littering lecture but not one word against the morally worse behavior one might expect to happen on a teenage date. They'd laughed about that in the car and gone out of their way to litter. She wouldn't say whether they'd done any morally worse behavior. I'm guessing they did.

With this history behind me, I was buying garden equipment in a farm store the other day, eating some free popcorn they give out at the door. Mashed bags littered the aisles, so when I finished my popcorn, I tossed my bag in among them. Just as immediately, horrified at myself, I snatched it back up.

I guess I'm proof that bad company corrupts, despite my most zealous intentions. I'm just glad I didn't do something morally worse!

Dear God, keep me from falling into—or initiating!
—bad behavior I'm prone to with other people.
—Patty Kirk

Digging Deeper: Joshua 23

Thursday, January 31

Keep me as the apple of your eye; hide me in the shadow of your wings.
—Psalm 17:8 (NIV)

On winter mornings I sit on the sofa in the TV room for my prayer time, usually with a blanket over my shoulders. It's warm and cozy, and I feel like I'm shrinking into a cocoon, where I might be transformed into a butterfly or some winged creature that can fly. I can hear the cars go by and the rain or snow pelting outside, sometimes the scrape of a plow or snow shovel. My cell phone sits on the sofa next to me to let me know what time it is—when I'm ready to open my eyes, that is.

One January day when I felt weighed down by too many worries from that age-old list of health issues, financial concerns, and relationships, I huddled under my blanket and dumped my mess of anxieties on God. It was like a game of capture-and-release. I'd catch the worry, thinking, *Yes, God, that is something that's bothering me,* then release it heavenward. *You take it, God. I'm tired of fretting over it.* One by one, I let go of my burdens.

Finally I opened my eyes, checked my phone. Time to face the day. I stretched out my arms and flung open the blanket. It felt like a pair of wings. A verse of Scripture popped into my head: "Oh, that I had wings like a dove! I would fly away and be at rest" (Psalm 55:6). Where would I go? Exactly where I was. God was my refuge, and I'd huddled under my blanket as though in the shadow of *His* wings.

I left the blanket on the sofa to be there for the next day. And the next... and the next.

No matter how far I fly, Lord, You are always with me.
—Rick Hamlin

Digging Deeper: Deuteronomy 33:27; Proverbs 14:26

UNDER GOD'S WINGS

1 _____

2 _____

3 _____

4 _____

5 _____

6 _____

7 _____

8 _____

9 _____

10 _____

11 _____

12 _____

13 _____

14 _____

15 _____

January

16 _____

17 _____

18 _____

19 _____

20 _____

21 _____

22 _____

23 _____

24 _____

25 _____

26 _____

27 _____

28 _____

29 _____

30 _____

31 _____

FEBRUARY

I lift up my eyes to the mountains—
where does my help come from? My
help comes from the Lord, the Maker
of heaven and earth.

—Psalm 121:1–2 (NIV)

Friday, February 1

For the weapons of our warfare are not carnal, but mighty through God to the pulling down of strong holds. —2 Corinthians 10:4 (KJV)

It takes courage to admit we come from families who might have taught us to be mean-spirited, to be liars, thieves, addicts...or even racists.

So I am surprised when Em, a new acquaintance, pours out her heart to me. "My parents worked hard to raise our family and provide for us. But they did teach us that we, as white people, were superior."

I think she expects me to be angry. She doesn't know the heart of compassion the Lord has given me.

She goes on. "It was the culture in the South. They have to be extended mercy." There is pleading in her words.

"Of course. The Lord showed me mercy." She appears surprised by my response.

I come from a family of sharp-tongued people and am grateful the Lord used a courageous friend to bring me truth and to help me bridle my tongue. Because of the mercy shown me, Em's plea sticks in my heart.

Proof of God's love and mercy, I say to her, is that He sends people to tell us the truth. He sent Moses to Pharaoh in Egypt. He sent abolitionists like Frederick Douglass and Harriet Beecher Stowe to warn our nation about the horrors of slavery. He sent Martin Luther King Jr. and Fannie Lou Hamer.

Every day God's love gives us the freedom to hear the truth and to choose to take advantage of the Lord's mercy—and to extend that mercy to others.

Lord, help us to listen with open hearts, to tear down the strongholds in our lives, and to make choices that please You. Help us to love one another.
—Sharon Foster

Digging Deeper: 1 John 1:9; Luke 2:10–11;
Numbers 12:1, 9–13; John 13:34–35

[Jesus] said unto them, Come ye yourselves apart . . . and rest a while.
—Mark 6:31 (KJV)

My daughter Trina tried to work baby Julia's arm into the narrow sleeve of the soft aqua sweater I had knit for her. It didn't fit. Ever gracious, Trina suggested, "Let's take a picture, even of one arm!" She knew I worked for months on this so-called easy beginner pattern. I knitted the panels well but had assembled them wrong. These skinny sleeves would not accommodate a toothbrush, much less a newborn's arms. My creation was a dud. The matching hat matched, all right. It sported holes from dropped stitches and other mistakes. Another dud.

Despite my frustration, I knew enough to unravel the garments in their entirety and reuse the fingerling wool. This took time and produced yarn that looked like a kinky mass of ramen noodles. My knitter friends, however, had taught me the secret of reclamation: soak the kinky yarn in a wash solution to relax the fibers. This, too, took time— about thirty minutes. Next, the wet yarn must be blotted and allowed to air-dry for several hours. More time. Whatever angst I felt at my failures dissipated as the day wore on.

Yet again, my fiber arts were teaching me lessons in humility and patience. Plans might not work out; our best efforts can unravel. Like my yarn, sometimes I just need time to unkink, soak up peace, and rest. It's reassuring to know even Jesus sometimes needed to take time out for rest.

Lord, You teach me profound truths in such simple ways. Thank You.
—Gail Thorell Schilling

Digging Deeper: Psalm 46:10; Isaiah 30:7, 15; Matthew 11:28

Sunday, February 3

PRAYING THROUGH THE PSALMS
Whispering Scriptures in Dark Times
Even the darkness is not dark to you. —Psalm 139:12 (ESV)

It's 4:00 a.m. I'm wide awake.

Several people near and dear to me are struggling. A friend is clinically depressed. My daughter's dealing with infertility. Four friends are going through chemotherapy. My brother is living in a homeless shelter.

Grabbing my journal, I rise from bed and settle into my husband's recliner. I should pray, but my worry is bigger than my faith. I peer out a window of our log cabin. Maybe I'm searching for the moon and stars, for evidence that God's still out there.

I spot a star. Just one star. *I'm here,* God seems to say. *Talk to Me.*

Words don't come, so I open my journal. The pages are covered in Psalms scribbled in purple ink. The verses once brought joy. But this morning, I'm not sure Scripture is enough.

I'm not sure God is, either.

"If I whisper Your own words back to You, does that count as praying?"

The star glitters at me.

"I'll give it a try." I search for my first Scripture. "'Holy is He,' Psalm 99:5."

I pause, praying life and truth will revive my dry, empty soul.

"Lord, You are holy. I can't even pray without You."

I turn the page. "'The heavens are telling of the glory of God,' Psalm 19:1. 'You are the God who works wonders,' Psalm 77:14."

"I can't work wonders. Or create stars. Or bring healing. But I don't have to. You can. You alone are God."

Back in bed, my mind is still. Sleep comes easily.

Lord, the Psalms humble me. Your words calm and restore me.
You are my bright morning star.
—Julie Garmon

Digging Deeper: Psalm 80:19, 87:8

Let the little children come to me…for it is to such as these
that the kingdom of heaven belongs. —Matthew 19:14 (NRSV)

This is the last year we're doing this!" I told Charlie as our godsons made a beeline for the Pokémon cards. Our birthday tradition is to take them to Books-A-Million, where they may each pick out one book and one game or toy. This year RJ had just turned eight and Jett was about to turn seven: too old for me to lure them into choosing meaningful books or educational toys.

At home they showed off their gifts to their mom. As usual all eyes—and ears—were on RJ, who'd already ripped open his card packet to show his mother, and then Jett shrieked. Everyone froze. Jett doesn't shriek. Even when he was a baby, we only knew he was crying if we saw tears, and that wasn't often.

But Jett was shrieking in delight, since evidently, he hadn't realized how many cards were in the tightly wrapped packet. Overwhelmed with this bounty, he tossed his cards in the air and then lay down among them on the floor! This uncharacteristic behavior was hilarious. He looked up and exclaimed, "Marci, this is the best present ever!"

I was struck by his unfettered joy, maybe because Jett and I are alike. I rarely show great emotion, much less joy, but Jett's delight filled me with pleasure at having made his joy possible.

And then I felt a little empty. I realized how seldom I show God my delight in all His gifts. Oh, sure, I pray, "I extol You, I exalt You, I exult in You," but do I show it? Or let myself really feel it? How often do I roll around in the gifts God showers upon me?

I got some strange looks from passing drivers when I took a walk today, occasionally throwing my hands into the air in delight. I couldn't wait for someone to stop and ask why!

Lord, let me rejoice in You always!
—Marci Alborghetti

Digging Deeper: 2 Samuel 22:31–34; Psalm 8

Tuesday, February 5

I saw the people leaving me and scattering. —1 Samuel 13:11 (JPS)

I'm not really a computer person, but because I had a strong online community of friends, I spent a lot of time interacting with my screen. The community was a powerful support to me when my husband, Keith, died, and I was grateful. Every morning, looking on line was part of my routine, as important to me as brushing my teeth and feeding the animals.

Unlike most social media sites, this one was small, alertly patrolled, and ever-ready to help with technical advice and spam monitoring, even though it was not the central business of its owners. I sank into that community with love and depended on it to hold me up. It offered people I could help as well, and that made me feel useful and needed. Then, after many years of vigilant hospitality, the people who hosted the site decided they could not keep it going. The members of the community made plans to scatter to a number of other sites across the internet.

At first, I was upset. I hate change at the best of times, and this felt like a death in my small family. It helped to learn that others in the group felt the same way I did. We discussed options, and slowly our focus crystallized around two or three other sites to try.

Some of the community drifted away, but a core of those to whom I was closest found places—as did I—where we could recapture some of what we had depended on for so long. It was different, but it was better than accepting that the community was permanently gone. I have to keep reminding myself there is only one certainty, and as long as He is there, I can cope with everything else.

> *Thank You, Lord, that You will never leave me or forsake me,*
> *that You will never close Your site.*
> —Rhoda Blecker

Digging Deeper: Psalm 94:22; 1 Samuel 2:2

He that dwelleth in the secret place of the most High shall abide under the shadow of the Almighty. —Psalm 91:1 (KJV)

My oncologist walked into the examining room, devoid of her usual "You're fine." For twenty years she had spoken those soothing words during each of my annual visits, except two. And both those times were painfully etched into my memory.

Handed a brush by the enemy of my soul, I had already painted a dark picture before the doctor entered. *This is the very same room you were in when you got that last "bad diagnosis,"* I reminded myself. So when the doctor said there was a shadow on my X-ray, I leaned my head back onto the chair in resignation, quickly connecting the test results with the proverbial shadow of death.

Here we go again, I thought, my insides threatening to fold.

Settling down a bit, I remembered my commitment to memorizing Psalm 91 a couple of years earlier. Thankfully the very first verse called to mind another kind of shadow, one that comforts, protects, and guides. Three days and two sleepless nights later, after undergoing a more sophisticated scan, I found those words from the Psalms— "He that dwells in the secret place shall abide under the shadow of the Almighty"—taking on new meaning.

"Nothing's there. It was just a shadow," said the accompanying nurse. My calculations had been flawed. I basked beneath the protection of the life-sustaining "shadow" that is always over me. God had given me another chance to reduce my fears and realign my thinking with His precious Word.

Lord, help me to trust You past my own meager ability to reason.
—Jacqueline F. Wheelock

Digging Deeper: Psalm 121:5–8

Thursday, February 7

My times are in thy hand. —Psalm 31:15 (KJV)

It's been ten years this month since my husband, John, and I moved from New York to Massachusetts. Perhaps that's why I've been thinking so much lately about time.

Ten years, when I was a child, was an unimaginable stretch of hours and days. I remember wondering on my parents' tenth anniversary what the world had been like way back when they got married. After all, for me at age five, that event was two lifetimes ago.

Even a single day, to a three-year-old, is a lengthy matter. Our daughter Liz used to ask anxiously when she woke from her afternoon nap, "Is this today?" Were we still going to make brownies, meet her brother's school bus, and go to the park to swing? Or had all that happened and it was a different day? To miss the absorbing events of a whole afternoon would be a huge loss to her!

A whole afternoon... For me today a whole week can slip by in what seems hours. It's a phenomenon we all experience: time moves faster as we age. A weekly chore for me nowadays is filling a pill organizer for the next seven days. I know it's seven: I empty the compartments one by one, Sunday through Saturday. Yet it feels like I'm refilling that tiresome pill holder every other day.

Can it be, I wonder, that the sense of accelerating time is God's gracious preparation for that realm where time overtakes itself in His eternal now? Where we'll experience the timelessness of unending life in the kingdom of heaven?

Remind me today, Father, that hours, short or long, are a gift from You. Show me how to use them in Your praise.
—Elizabeth Sherrill

Digging Deeper: Job 14:5; Daniel 2:21

I will bless the Lord who has given me counsel; my heart also instructs me in the night seasons. —Psalm 16:7 (NKJV)

Eight degrees below zero. Moonlight casts perfect, crisp silhouettes of the trees, right down to the last pine cone and needle, and scatters millions of diamonds across the ice-crusted snow, outshining the stars overhead. The air is shockingly cold and fresh and pure. All is absolutely quiet. No coyotes. No owls. No traffic creeping along the frozen highway in the distance. Not a breath of wind moves. I am caught up in the beauty.

I've got to share this. I pat my pockets and pull off my gloves to retrieve my phone. Cold bites at my fingers as I turn on the camera. The focus icon blinks red. Even with a brilliant full moon it's too dark. A flash won't help. Irritation flares. Then stillness follows. Look. Breathe. Savor. Be. This is for me alone. And it's only for right now. Slowly, I memorize the details in my heart: the colors on the snow, the stark image of the pines. God's creation is much too big to be confined in mere photographs. How often do I rush through moments like this, trying to capture it to be enjoyed later? Sometimes I need to slow down and immerse myself in now. This is when I feel closest to God.

Dear Lord, too often I rush heedlessly through life. Thank You for slowing me down to look around and be near to You.
—Erika Bentsen

Digging Deeper: Psalm 46:10

Saturday, February 9

All the rivers flow into the sea, yet the sea is not full. To the place where the rivers flow, there they flow again. —Ecclesiastes 1:7 (NASB)

It is true that critical decisions shape the direction of our future. But another dynamic is more important. I call this dynamic "Way Leads on to Way."

All of us have made both good and bad decisions. In my teenage years, I decided there is a God Who has a purpose for my life. This has proven a "core belief." Choosing Beth Rushton to be my wife is the most wonderful and wise decision I made in early adulthood.

However, I have made some boneheaded decisions, too. My decision not to seriously study during my fun-filled freshman year in college resulted in academic probation. Sometimes the train runs off the tracks. Yet bad decisions do not define us if we trust that the "God of another chance" is still leading us.

How many young adults make vocational choices that do not fit them? How many marriages end in divorce? How many life dreams dim? Yet God's desire for our lives cannot be thwarted if we continue to follow Him. Our evolving "river of faith" will always flow to the ultimate sea. Our river may flow over rough terrain and circuitous routes, but God is not limited by our poor navigation or circumstance. He is faithful in enabling our personal river to flow to the sea. Way leads on to way.

Father, amid my good and bad decisions, may I not doubt that my river of faith will flow to the eternal sea. Amen.
—Scott Walker

Digging Deeper: Lamentations 3:22–26.; Psalm 23;
Mark 1:16–20; John 21:8–17

Come and hear... let me tell you what he has done for me.
—Psalm 66:16 (NIV)

Sharing my faith is easy... at church, with my family, or when a close friend asks. But when a nearby university invited me to participate in a panel discussion on how to be successful in business, I was surprised when I found myself struggling. As I prepared a list of the five factors that had been most helpful to me, an was item missing. It was the one that had been most important to me—seeking God's guidance. How could I make the point relevant to the audience in a concise but impactful way? How would it even go over at a state university?

I asked God for His insight, and a training course I'd attended for beginning supervisors came to mind. During the final hour of that program, the most senior and respected supervisor in the organization outlined what he had found necessary to be successful. Although I forgot his name and most of what he said, I clearly remember his last point: "Every day you will face challenges and difficult situations bigger than you.... Be sure you take time to pray." His words came at the time in my life when I felt the most insecure and was searching deeply to develop my faith. Those words in that moment, coming from someone I looked up to at work—not at church or at home or from a friend—were especially poignant to me.

Only because of insights from seeking God's guidance were the other items I had listed even significant to me. So at the end of my comments, I told the story of the supervisor and how his last bit of advice helped throughout my career. He is the only leader at work who ever reminded me to pray. Because he shared his faith, I had a story to tell.

Thank You, God, for those who boldly share their faith. Build our courage to do the same wherever You open a door! Amen.
—John Dilworth

Digging Deeper: Mark 5:19; Psalm 92:4

Don't be impatient. Wait for the Lord, and he will come and save you!
Be brave, stouthearted, and courageous. Yes, wait and he will help you.
—Psalm 27:14 (TLB)

On a warm, sunny February day in Florida, I was visiting Sawgrass Park. Walking on the boardwalk above the natural Florida ferns, oaks, and swampy areas, I came upon a ten-foot alligator and about twenty little ones from six inches up to two feet in length. That big old mama gator did not move an inch, nor did she even open her eyes as I stood on the boardwalk just three feet above her. Mama gator looked so peaceful and content, surrounded by her numerous babies from different litters. Some had been born just a month earlier, others a year or two earlier. I felt perfectly safe, because the boardwalk has a three-foot-high railing of vertical boards on both sides.

When I texted my twelve-year-old granddaughter, Adeline, who lives in California, about my gator encounter, she replied, "Oh, I would never be able to go anywhere like that if alligators were there." I reassured her it was perfectly safe because of the enclosed boardwalk and that I would take her there when she came to visit to see for herself.

Adeline attended an art school in downtown Oakland, where she often navigated on her own by public transportation. To her, it's nothing. To me, with my small-town upbringing and small-town life now, I would be uncomfortable trying to find my way around in a big city like Oakland by myself, especially at night. After my conversation with Adeline, I understood that each of us has fears that can easily be evaporated by taking on the world and perhaps holding hands with the one I love while I experience something outside my comfort zone. Oakland, here I come!

Father, You gave us an amazing world with incredible adventures
and creatures and places to experience. Be with me and calm
my heart as I step out to explore Your world.
—Patricia Lorenz

Digging Deeper: 1 Chronicles 22:13, 28:20

Through wisdom a house is built.... By knowledge the rooms are filled with all precious and pleasant riches. —Proverbs 24:3–4 (NKJV)

Yesterday at a used-book sale, I couldn't resist buying an old dog-eared book imprinted with gold lettering: *Springs in the Valley* and then the staid name Mrs. Chas. E. Cowman. Opening to a random page and seeing the distinctly decorated capital letters that initiate every entry, I recognized it as a companion volume to a devotional of 365 readings—*Streams in the Desert,* which graced our family bathroom throughout my childhood and beyond.

Reading that devotional compilation, just a page a day, helped set my life on a faithful course. An introductory Bible verse focused my attention. Selected anecdotes in various settings modeled how to be loving, hopeful, brave, steady, and true. Kindly exhortations guided a day's compass. Pithy quotations rooted in my mind.

The Cowman books—already classics in my youth—are over eighty years old, forerunners to collections by new encouraging voices. I no longer contentedly read the same devotional year upon year until its binding disintegrates. The *Daily Guideposts* annual now provides me and so many others with fresh inspirational stories and challenges.

And yet today I'm drawn to the yellowed pages of my book-sale find. A winter entry includes a striking quotation attributed to Abraham Lincoln: "The strength of a nation lies in the homes of its people." A previous reader has underlined the nouns. I read the line again. The tattered book, the fond memories of Mrs. Cowman's work, and the presidential assertion that ties strength and nation to homes—they draw out my morning prayer....

Lord, thank You for the elements of my residence and its routines that have buttressed me spiritually—as a child and even now as a contributing member of my community.
—Evelyn Bence

Digging Deeper: Psalm 1:1–3; 1 Timothy 4:11–16

Wednesday, February 13

Happy are the kind and merciful, for they shall be shown mercy.
—Matthew 5:7 (TLB)

My mom could be quite a handful, which I have come to see as a blessing as the years go by. But I did not always appreciate it when she was alive, especially after her Alzheimer's diagnosis. The news came as no surprise to her children. We'd seen our tough, sharp-witted mom change. But she was not about to take Alzheimer's lying down. "There's nothing wrong with me!" she insisted, even after she side-swiped a cop, denied doing it, and blamed it all on him. Eventually my brother and his wife moved her to a sweet little house on the property next to theirs with a lit path between the two houses so she could visit when she wanted, which occasionally happened at 5:00 a.m. when she thought it was 5:00 p.m.

One thing we couldn't do was make her eat properly, especially after she nearly burned the house down making tuna salad (don't ask). So we arranged for a senior Meals on Wheels program to deliver her food. At first she wouldn't let them in the house. "This is ridiculous," she said. "I know how to eat!" She offered to help them deliver meals to "people who really need them." Ultimately, she relented—except she simply hoarded meals untouched in the fridge in case she had hungry visitors. When we told the volunteers this, they somehow got Mom to eat. I still don't know how they did it, but she admitted the food was "pretty good, considering."

Mom had many loving caregivers, a lot of them volunteers, in her last years. I don't know what our family would have done without these earthly angels. Today I say a prayer for them, for all whose commitment is rooted in love and service.

Loving God, so many do Your work on earth. May You bless
them as they minister to others, especially those who cared for Mom.
—Edward Grinnan

Digging Deeper: Matthew 18:33; James 2:13

God loved the world so much that he gave his one and only Son so that whoever believes in him may not be lost, but have eternal life.
—John 3:16 (NCV)

I must admit I have a romantic heart. Not only do I write romances; I read them, too. A certain kind of plot gets to me every single time. In the story, the very instant the hero meets the heroine, he knows in his heart of hearts that she's the one for him. Instant, spontaneous love. Nothing and nobody will stand in the hero's way of making that woman his own. He would run into a burning building for her, stand in front of a bullet for her, and love her beyond and above anything or anyone. And as you would expect, in the end of the story he sweeps her off her feet. What woman in her right mind could resist such a hero?

Not I, for sure, and not a lot of other romance readers, either. Because I'm a writer, I wanted to know what it was about these stories that captured my attention every time. I devoured these books, reading for hours on end, swept away in my favorite fantasy. I felt it was important that I understood what attracted readers to these stories.

It didn't take me long to figure out the answer. The hero in these stories is a picture of Christ. Like the heroes who pursue their heroines in romance novels, Christ relentlessly pursued *me*. He knows me better than anyone, and loves me despite all my flaws and foibles. He even loved me enough to suffer pain and grief beyond human understanding to save me.

My hero is Jesus, the Lover of my soul.

Thank You, Lord, for pursuing me and for Your continual, unconditional love.
—Debbie Macomber

Digging Deeper: Romans 8:39

Friday, February 15

My soul clings to you; your right hand upholds me. —Psalm 63:8 (ESV)

"Samuel, you're on my toes," I say.

My fifteen-year-old son blushes and apologizes, and I wonder how we've gotten to this place. Samuel will attend his first high school dance tonight, and he needs to learn to slow-dance. As we move over the worn wool rug in our living room, I catch our image in the mantel mirror.

His height matches mine.

Sam and I have danced miles on this rug. When he was a babe, I swayed as he slept. As a toddler, he stood on my feet. Later, we cut loose until breathless laughter took us to the floor. Now it's time for the dance lesson. Until this day, Sam has danced only with me.

Oh, the letting go!

It seems to me motherhood is a process of release. There's one last time for a babe to nurse. We run beside our little ones as they wibble-wobble away on two wheels. We kiss sweet, warm cheeks at the Sunday school door and bid farewell over and over as our children grow and go. A child's life is an opening of a mother's hand.

So often, I think of Hannah (1 Samuel 1). She cried out to the Lord for a child and promised, if God would hear her prayer, to return him to the Lord for service. God provided, and Hannah honored her word. When her Samuel was still small, she took him to the temple to live with and learn from Eli the priest.

She opened her hand.

Sam steps on my foot again, and I'm charmed by his smile. He shakes his head, and we dance through one more song. When we finish, he is visibly uncertain. Unsure. "Will I be okay, Mom?" he asks.

"Yes," I say. "You'll be just fine."

We both will.

My hand will open tonight, but my son will remain in the Lord's hand.

Thank You for holding my children in Your hand. Amen.
—Shawnelle Eliasen

Digging Deeper: Isaiah 41:10; 1 Samuel 1:27

I discipline my body and keep it under control, lest after preaching to others I myself should be disqualified. —1 Corinthians 9:27 (ESV)

We have a puppy.

We rescued Zeke about six months ago, after we lost our beloved fifteen-year-old golden retriever, Jack. We heard from a friend that there was a litter about an hour away, and I convinced my husband to take the day off from work just to look.

Of course, we all know what "just looking" means when it comes to puppies.

I knew right away Zeke was my boy, because he ran up to me and pulled on the string from my sweater.

"He practically chose us!" I gushed to my husband.

On the way home, my little buddy found more things to chew on. It was adorable.

Until it wasn't.

The nine-pound puppy turned into a sixty-five-pound puppy that had some, let's say, "self-control issues."

I figured out pretty quickly that if I wanted my house—and my sanity—to survive, that puppy was going to need some discipline. What seemed like "too small to hurt" problems had quickly grown to be destructive.

Isn't that how life goes sometimes? A teeny-tiny problem quickly grows out of control when we ignore it.

But it's never too late to pull it back, to exercise a little bit of self-control and hire a trainer to teach a new dog some old tricks.

> *Father God, show me the trouble spots in my life before*
> *they become destructive. Amen.*
> —Erin MacPherson

Digging Deeper: 1 Peter 1:5–7; 1 Corinthians 10:13

Sunday, February 17

Are not two sparrows sold for a cent? And yet not one of them will fall to the ground apart from your Father. —Matthew 10:29 (NASB)

Last Sunday when my wife, Beth, and I returned home from church, I opened the front door and was greeted by a discordant chorus of baby bird chirps. In our fireplace I found five baby chimney swifts, whose nest had disconnected from our interior chimney wall and crashed to the hearth floor. The nestlings were not injured. But what do you do with five helpless baby birds?

Gathering them in a wicker hanging basket, we hung the basket on the outside chimney wall, hoping their mother would find and feed them. But there was no such luck. The next morning, I did not know what to do.

I called our veterinarian, whose assistant told me about a wonderful lady in our community who rehabilitates injured birds. I called her and discovered she is also a nurse and physician's assistant. I explained what had happened, and she replied, "I'll be right over after work to take them home with me. Working with baby birds takes experience, and I'll be glad to help."

Wow! This woman helps sick people all day and, out of goodness and compassion, drives to my house to rescue injured birds. I believe she is "living in the image of God"! Her actions humble me and inspire me to love all that God has created.

Father, help me to help You respond to the needs of all
Your creation. Amen.
—Scott Walker

Digging Deeper: Matthew 6:26; Isaiah 40:11

SAYING GOODBYE TO MY VETERANS
Leaving a Legacy
Therefore encourage one another with these words.
—1 Thessalonians 4:18 (NIV)

When my former coworker spoke the words "who I used to be," I froze in my chair. Part of the reason I feared retirement was Dad. When my father left the railroad, losing his identity was so difficult for him, he actually became suicidal.

As the days wore on and I completed work projects, I called on the heavens. "Help me to know that what I've done in my job has really meant something," I prayed. I dreaded saying goodbye to my veteran patients and their dear ones. But I also longed to leave a legacy.

One afternoon at work, our new medical center director, Mr. Nimmo, stopped by. "I'm learning you have quite a reputation, Roberta," he said. "It goes beyond your role in infection prevention. Rumor has it, whenever you teach a class, you always tell great stories about your experiences with veterans."

I smiled. My motto was always this: "When in doubt tell a story." I'd found it was the shortest distance between two hearts.

In the nearly forty years I worked with veterans and their families, I cared for soldiers of the Spanish American War, World Wars I and II, the wars in Korea and Vietnam, and more recent conflicts.

Mr. Nimmo continued, "I'd love for you to help me collect a book of veteran stories, Roberta."

Before our conversation ended, I told him of my plans to retire. I also promised to stay on a little longer to help compile those stories.

Lead me to the stories You want told, Lord.
—Roberta Messner

Digging Deeper: Hebrews 13:16, 10:24–25

SAYING GOODBYE TO MY VETERANS
The Powerful Instrument of Self

Whatever you do, work at it with all your heart. —Colossians 3:23 (NIV)

Our medical center director, Mr. Nimmo, emailed over twelve hundred hospital staff about our idea to write a book about caring for veterans. My phone rang off the hook. I arrived at work early and left late to listen to sagas that spanned decades. There were so many terrific, close-to-the-heart tales that had never before been shared. I loved each and every one.

One harried day, I sandwiched an interview with Rita, an HR specialist, between two classes I had to teach. Rita told me about the time she was asked to be with a gravely ill patient on her lunch break as part of our hospital's No Veteran Dies Alone initiative. "I held the dying veteran's hand and sang the old hymn 'Farther Along,' like I'd once done for my own father," she told me. While her effort was a tad off-key, Rita noticed the veteran's facial muscles relax, and she detected the slightest tug of his lips. As sick as he was, he was trying to smile!

Rita prayed over him, "Father, one of Your soldiers is coming home. Please welcome him and ease his journey." The next day when she learned the man had passed on, it occurred to her that she'd worried her gestures weren't enough. But when she gave everything she had, that was enough.

Rita's story made me think of a day when I was changing a dressing on an HIV patient who had no family. He asked, "Could you stay with me just a few minutes more, nurse?"

I took off my gloves and squeezed his hand. The simple gesture of removing that barrier meant everything to him. Like Rita, I discovered that when we offer ourselves, it is everything to the recipient of that gift.

The stories of others and my own are helping me face retirement with
joy, Lord. You already know that, don't You?
      —Roberta Messner

Digging Deeper: Deuteronomy 6:5; 1 John 3:18

Keep awake—for you do not know when the master of the house will come. —Mark 13:35 (NRSV)

The place where we stayed this past February in New Hampshire had a great indoor pool. We invited our friend Jon to bring his young son, Axl, over.

Axl shed his hoodie, boots, and sweatshirt before the pool door even closed behind him. An hour later he'd exhausted his dad and my husband, who both collapsed on chairs. I sat at the edge of the pool, and Axl paddled over.

"Marci, aren't you going to swim with me?"

"You know, honey, I don't have my suit on under my sweats."

"Couldn't you go put it on?"

"Well, Axl, I didn't really plan to swim today."

He regarded me with clear blue eyes for a long moment. "But why not? You knew I'd be here."

That night I thought about how my caution and pragmatism constrain me from other wonderful opportunities. How often do I say to God, *No, I'm not prepared today?*

Lord, I don't have time to gaze at Your daffodils breaking through the winter-ravaged earth.

Father, I'm not dressed to stop at church and visit You.

Jesus, I don't have any small bills for the Salvation Army collector outside the store.

How often do I make excuses when God invites me, "Come in, the water of life I give is warm, and after all, you knew I'd be here"?

Lord, open me to Your Presence and invitations every moment of my life.
—Marci Alborghetti

Digging Deeper: Luke 9:46–48; Psalm 5:11–12

THINGS MY MOTHER TAUGHT ME: Supper Guests

Contributing to the needs of God's people, pursuing the practice of hospitality. —Romans 12:13 (AMP)

My husband, Gene, and I knew about the tragedy. He felt we should have Don over for supper and some measure of comfort. His wife had just taken her life. I thought there was nothing we could do. I was putting our supper on the table when there was a desperate pounding on our back door. When Gene opened it, dear Don practically fell into his arms. As Gene helped him into a chair at the table, a kitchen memory slid into my heart.

Mother had worked late and walked home, then cooked supper and washed out a few clothes by hand. No washing machine. The kitchen smelled good with whatever she made but also because Mother had hired a man named Happy to paint our kitchen—a sea green. I loved the smell of paint and the color. When we sat down, she said matter-of-factly, "Happy, come down off that ladder and wash your hands at the sink. You must be hungry, and we'd love to have you join us." Happy came down off that ladder in two hops. He was a very short man, and his nose and chin nearly touched. Not many teeth. He got ignored a lot around town. He and Mother talked, mostly about life and losses.

I put food on Don's plate and filled his glass with sweet iced tea. Put a fork in his hand. As I hugged him, I whispered, "Eat."

He stayed for several hours. We sat in the living room and listened and listened. Gene prayed, and we held him. God's love showed up.

Don came back again and again. Sometimes for food. Most often for a bit of temporary comfort.

> *People sometimes say it feels good in our home, Lord.*
> *Please remain, and let us encourage those in need.*
> —Marion Bond West

Digging Deeper: 1 Peter 4:8–10; Hebrews 13:1–2

When all these things begin to happen, stand straight and look up!
For your salvation is near. —Luke 21:28 (TLB)

One day, I rode my bicycle over to the neighborhood next to mine. With its beautiful condos, winding roads, and lots of trees, I thought it would be the perfect place for a leisurely ride. But every ten or twenty yards was a big speed bump across the road, put there by the condo association to keep cars from speeding through the neighborhood. I was trying to concentrate on my riding, since it was the first week I was back on my bike after knee replacement surgery nine months earlier. But every few yards it was up, down, bump, bump. I began to hate those speed bumps.

I kept my face down toward the pavement as I thought about how my life felt like one giant bump after another ever since the surgery. Healing had taken much longer than I expected. Walking more than a mile was still painful. Even biking caused pain with each downward pedal.

My neck hurt as I kept my eyes glued to the road, watching for those speed bumps. When I reached for my water bottle, I looked up and to my amazement saw a whole beautiful world in front of me. Between two condo buildings, I could see a patch of the intracoastal waterway. People were walking their dogs. Huge hibiscus bushes were in full pink bloom. American flags hung on a number of homes. It was nearing the end of February and people were lounging at the outdoor pool. Neighbors waved and smiled. I chuckled at the twelve-mile-per-hour speed limit sign. I stopped obsessing about the speed bumps and concentrated instead on what was up at eye level—all the good things life offers.

Jesus, hold my head high and take every bit of negativity out of me. Help
me to be positive, happy, and grateful for all that is in my world.
—Patricia Lorenz

Digging Deeper: Numbers 11:1–25; Deuteronomy 1:21

Saturday, February 23

I have loved you with a love that lasts forever. And so with unfailing love, I have drawn you to myself. —Jeremiah 31:3 (CEB)

It's Carol's favorite part of the Metropolitan Museum, the long corridor of prints and drawings. Whenever we go to the museum—one of our favorite spots in New York City—she always stops in that hall. Because these works on paper are fragile and shouldn't be exposed to too much light, the exhibition changes constantly. I suppose that's why Carol likes it. Always new things to see.

That Sunday, Carol was away, enjoying a reunion in the Colorado mountains with her college roommates. I dropped in at the Met by myself after church, thinking this time I could hurry past all those works on paper and go straight to the paintings I prefer. Then I paused. Maybe I'd see something here she'd like.

My eyes were drawn to a brilliant watercolor. A scene of Alpine mountains, like the mountains where Carol was staying, and a blue sky reflecting in a placid lake. A stunning Turner watercolor. I remembered how art critic John Ruskin said of landscapes like this one that it was as though a hole had been cut into the wall where they hung, breaking through to nature. This hole could have gone all the way to Colorado.

I took a picture with my phone. "What passes for mountains here in New York," I keyed in, texting the image to Carol.

My way of saying, *I love you. I miss you. I appreciate the beauty you have gotten me to see.* I'd gone to one of her favorite corners of the city and seen something she would have enjoyed.

Love expands your world. You come to see color where you thought you were going to just see black and white.

> *Thank You, Lord, for my loved ones who help me to*
> *understand Your greater love.*
> —Rick Hamlin

Digging Deeper: Romans 12:9; 1 John 4:7

Come unto me, all ye that labour and are heavy laden,
and I will give you rest. —Matthew 11:28 (KJV)

Steam billowed, momentarily clouding my view as I lowered myself into the hot water swirling around my legs. I sat down and leaned back against a comfortable spot on the river's bank. Finally situated, I looked up at the hillside across from me. A herd of elk grazed at its crest. Snow flurried, and way overhead, a bald eagle soared, riding the air currents above Yellowstone National Park.

Around me, other soakers reclined near where a large hot spring flowed into the otherwise icy waters of the Gardner River, earning the place its Boiling River nickname. What an unlikely spot of respite from winter's cold, it seemed. Here we all were, in our bathing suits, sitting in a river. In Montana. In February.

I remembered reading that the animals also knew to seek out the heat of the park's geothermal features when winters got serious. Near areas where hot water flowed up from the depths of the earth, the steam warmed them and snowpack was less deep, or absent altogether, making grazing—and their struggle for survival—a little easier. As I relaxed into the river, a cold wind made me grateful for the water's warmth and the relief it provided—for me and for all God's creatures that came here seeking refuge.

Help me be more aware of Your generous gifts of refuge, Lord,
especially those that might be found in unexpected places.
—Erin Janoso

Digging Deeper: Isaiah 28:12; Jeremiah 31:25

Do not withhold good from those to whom it is due, when it is in your power to do it. —Proverbs 3:27 (NASB)

My mother-in-law has been matriarch in the family for nearly fifty years, having married my husband's father, a widower, when they were in their mid-forties. Margaret, who did not have children, acquired three daughters and a son. And eventually nine grandchildren and twenty-nine great-grands. Beloved by us all.

Entering her ninth decade, she encountered health problems, twice landing in the hospital. We weren't certain she would recover, but she did, both times transferring to a rehabilitation center to gain strength to return to her home.

During Margaret's second rehab stay, our daughter, Tamara, gave birth across town. She and her husband, Rich, named their baby girl Bethany Margaret. The baby was just two hours old when they left the birthing center. Tamara was exhausted, but she made a special stop on the way home.

She and Rich walked into her grandmother's room, holding a bundle. They gently handed over their gift to her as she sat in her wheelchair, saying, "Meet Bethany Margaret." My mother-in-law said it was the greatest moment of her life. The precious baby she cradled carried her name.

The whole family felt uplifted by this generous act of love. Happy for the birth, for the parents, but most especially for the joy of an old woman for whom there were still surprises, still great moments.

The Bible encourages, "So then, while we have opportunity, let us do good to all people, and especially those who are of the household of the faith" (Galatians 6:10). Tamara saw opportunity, and she turned it into something extraordinary. For all of us.

> *Friend, if we are to "do good to all people," we have millions of opportunities. Where do we begin?*
> —Carol Knapp

Digging Deeper: Philippians 2:3–4; Exodus 20:12; Luke 6:38

And there was evening, and there was morning—the first day.
—Genesis 1:5 (NIV)

Patches of snow glowed blue, reflecting the dark cobalt sky. Sunrise, my golden retriever, bounded along the trail ahead of me. Although I only wore a fanny pack holding basic survival gear, I felt as if I were carrying the weight of the world. *Lord, help me unwind.*

My body felt tight and stiff with each step. Even my breathing was shallow. I'd just completed a major project, one I'd been working on for years. The last few months I'd worked brutal hours, before and after my day job, to meet the time line. Tonight after I finished, even though it was dark and cold outside, I decided to celebrate by taking a short hike in the Sapphire Mountains.

Huge snowflakes lazily danced on the breeze as I neared the faint outline of the gigantic boulders on the bluff. My boots crunched through the fresh snow, and I felt the weight of my world melting away. I paused in wonder as the snowflakes coated the ground, the pine trees, the boulders, Sunrise, and even me with a glittering coat.

A strange thought drifted through my mind. Years ago a Jewish friend of mine told me their day begins at sundown, with evening first, then morning. How profound. A new day is starting right now, this evening, washed by the snow so fresh and clean with not a track in it. This is how I'm supposed to end each day. I'm not to carry the day's projects to bed and wait till morning to start over!

While hiking out, I made a pact with myself. From now on, each evening before bed I will lay down my life and start the new day without a track in it—and I'm not going to wait days, months, or years to do it.

Lord, thank You for showing me how to unwind. Amen.
—Rebecca Ondov

Digging Deeper: Matthew 6:34; Leviticus 23:32

Wednesday, February 27

Commit thy way unto the Lord; trust also in him. —Psalm 37:5 (KJV)

This can't be happening!" I was in one of the busiest seasons of my work in wealth management when I got the dreaded "blue screen of death." My computer had crashed. I was frantic, thinking about the possibilities of information lost. I worked hard to serve my clients. Their well-being mattered to me. Having their accounts at my fingertips, every hour of the day, was of uppermost importance.

My hands trembled as I sent out a quick, desperate prayer, "God, how can I serve the people who are counting on me if my screen is blank?"

My assistant, Jeannine, appeared in my office seconds later. "I've got a call into our information technology team," she assured me.

For the next few hours, I struggled to be productive. I made phone calls to my clients, but it was hard to make any progress without the sophisticated systems I relied on. I left that evening with a pleading prayer for the tech guys who were now in charge.

Early the next morning, I found two young men in my office in full hustle mode.

"Good morning, Brock. I'm Adam," the youngest introduced himself. "Sorry for the trouble, but we'll have you fixed up soon." Adam pointed to several large boxes next to my desk. "We've replaced everything," he said. On my desk were three screens, larger and crisper than the two I'd had before. The other young man spoke up. "Brock, I'm Bill. We've put together a new system for you with a much faster processor." He smiled proudly. "This baby will hum!"

Later, sitting alone, surrounded by the best technology available, I remembered other disasters that, like my blank screens, had turned into blessings. In the middle of it all, God always stands strong, waiting for us to stand back and put Him in charge of our reboot!

Father, with total trust I commit my days to You.
Thank You for being there even when my screen is dark.
—Brock Kidd

Digging Deeper: 1 Peter 5:7

The memory of the righteous is a blessing. —Proverbs 10:7 (ESV)

My son, Henry, burst through the front door and announced, "My school bus will be the last one to ever cross Madalin Bridge! It's true!" he said. "The bus driver said so." Lasts are always bittersweet. You wouldn't think a person could be sad and sentimental over a bridge, but this almost-hundred-year-old bridge that stretches over Stony Creek has played a large role in my life.

I've literally crossed this bridge a thousand times. Years ago my sister Maria held my small hand and pointed out that the town never fixed the dam that broke. The day after she died, I looked at what was left of the crumbling stone wall, feeling just as broken.

For many years I trekked over the bridge every single day to go to the candy store, piano lessons, or church, or to jog to the river—the list is long and tracks my entire life. My father used to drop a stick on one side, and we watched our little makeshift boat disappear underfoot and reappear on the other side, a trick I later shared with my sons.

My son Solomon and I walked over the bridge tonight, the last night before the barricade is put in place. We took turns taking each other's picture standing on it. I touched the rock edges and thought of the long walks and many worries that bridge carried me over—from high school tests to grieving losses—and then the happy times of pushing newborn Henry to show him off to the neighborhood.

"Goodbye, bridge," I said, patting the old stone wall. "You served us well."

Heavenly Father, guide me to see change as a blessing, a bridge that connects our beautiful memories to gifts the future holds.
—Sabra Ciancanelli

Digging Deeper: Psalm 112:6; Ecclesiastes 8:10

UNDER GOD'S WINGS

1 _____

2 _____

3 _____

4 _____

5 _____

6 _____

7 _____

8 _____

9 _____

10 _____

11 _____

12 _____

13 _____

14 _____

15 _____

16 _____

17 _____

18 _____

19 _____

20 _____

21 _____

22 _____

23 _____

24 _____

25 _____

26 _____

27 _____

28 _____

MARCH

Every word of God is pure; He is a shield
to those who put their trust in Him.

—Proverbs 30:5 (NKJV)

You can make many plans, but the Lord's purpose will prevail.
—Proverbs 19:21 (NLT)

M y wife and I helped my son move to Michigan for a new job. I planned to get a good night's rest so I could drive the first five hours and he would drive the last. I got to bed on time but woke up at three in the morning and couldn't get back to sleep. I eventually decided to stay up until it was time to leave.

I had every intention of completing my shift. My plan was simple and feasible; at least I thought it was. Shortly into the trip, my eyelids became heavy, and I realized my plan wasn't going to hold up. I gave the wheel to my son, who took control and drove us safely to our destination.

This experience got me thinking about how often my plans take a backseat to God's purpose for my life. That is not to say I don't plan, but things don't always pan out the way I expect. For example, I have worked at Guideposts for over fifteen years. When I started here, my plan was to stay for two years and then go on to be a pastor in New York City. God had other plans.

It's only natural and wise to make plans, I know. But my plans and God's purpose for me don't always align, and I'm glad they don't.

God's purpose is always better.

Lord, lead our planning, but let Your purpose prevail in our lives.
—Pablo Diaz

Digging Deeper: Proverbs 16:1; Romans 8:28

Saturday, March 2

I have composed and quieted my soul. —Psalm 131:2 (NASB)

In March 1968, my mom gave birth to twins. When she came home from the hospital, she placed a baby boy in my lap and handed the second baby to my sister. A powerful, topsy-turvy bond began that day, as if I were this boy's mother instead of being his eight-year-old sister.

Fifty years passed, and sometimes the love I felt for my brother still extended beyond safe, healthy boundaries. He lived in a homeless shelter. No matter how hard I tried, I couldn't piece the puzzle of his life back together.

The shelter manager assured me he appeared healthy and happy, but I wasn't satisfied. When I visited, I found him waiting in line for a bed. "You're getting older. This'll get harder. Come home with me. I don't know what to do next, but—"

"Thanks. I'm fine."

I almost said, "No, you're not. Stop saying that." But I spotted an undeniable emotion in him—one that made no sense to me.

Contentment. My brother was content, and I was a mess. I buried my face in his strong shoulder. "I love you."

He hugged me. "Love you, too."

With that encounter, my understanding turned upside down.

When I considered that perhaps he possessed what matters most, my brother/son became my teacher. Despite his circumstances, it seemed he'd found peace.

Maybe daily he trusted God to quiet his soul—something his mother/sister couldn't do for him.

Father, You alone quiet our souls.
—Julie Garmon

Digging Deeper: Psalm 125:2, 126:3

And what does the Lord require of you? To act justly and to love mercy and to walk humbly with your God. —Micah 6:8 (NIV)

I love the Bible study I attend each week, so when a session clashed with my carless niece's need for a ride to the grocery store, I debated what I should do.

Our group was deep into the Gospel of John, and I knew tonight would add a wealth of knowledge straight from the mouth of the disciple Jesus loved. What was more, the never-miss lecturer would, as always, be riveting in her summary. Taken as a whole, the experience promised to be exhilarating and supply me with that burst of spiritual energy I so craved each Thursday as we marched toward John's unique unfolding of our Savior's crucifixion and resurrection. I didn't dare miss one episode, I told myself. Or... did I?

The question popularized a decade or so ago powered its way into the debate: "What would Jesus do?"

When He was on earth, Jesus loved to discuss the Scriptures, and so do I. But in the final analysis, Jesus loves my niece more. And so do I.

Perhaps like the Jewish rulers who called for the death of their Savior while refusing to enter Pilate's judgment hall "lest they should be defiled," sometimes we confuse our conviction to follow God with our own law-driven self-righteousness. What the Lord has always required of us, then and now, is to "act justly and to love mercy and to walk humbly with God."

Dear Jesus, help me to always be mindful of what You truly want me to do, and help me do it with the humility that You desire.
—Jacqueline F. Wheelock

Digging Deeper: John 18:28, 19:31

Monday, March 4

Yours, O Lord, is the greatness and the power and the glory and the victory and the majesty, for all that is in the heavens and in the earth is yours. Yours is the kingdom, O Lord, and you are exalted as head above all.
—1 Chronicles 29:11 (ESV)

On the first day of my internship, the judge gave me a tour of the courthouse, starting with a new courtroom. Its ceiling arched in a modern curve. The back of the room was lined with rows of comfortable seating. The doors opened and closed soundlessly. Then the judge took me to the historic courtroom. "We don't use this courtroom as much as the newer ones," he said. The room was dark when we entered. It smelled antique—like old books and wood polish.

The judge flipped on the lights. The walls were dark-paneled cherry. The benches were tall and straight like Puritan pews. High above, metal chandeliers sported stars and shields. "This is my favorite courtroom," he said. "It has a gravity to it. When people are in this room, they know important things are happening. The room demands respect." The comfort of the modern courtroom might lull an audience into complacency, but this room certainly wouldn't.

The courtrooms made me think of my prayer life. God wants me to be comfortable praying to Him anyplace, anytime. But sometimes I get too comfortable. Sometimes I treat prayer more like texting a friend than conversing with the Almighty. *Thanks for this meal. Let this test go well.* Not every prayer needs to be the knees-on-the-floor kind. But it's a problem when I forget to have proper respect for the Creator of the universe. It's wrong to mistake the supernatural for the just plain natural.

As we left the courtroom, the doors swung shut, and the sound echoed. Nobody would dare slip out of that courtroom during a hearing. Nor should they. Their full respect is deserved.

> *Lord, help me to remember the gravity of prayer.*
> —Logan Eliasen

Digging Deeper: 2 Chronicles 20:6; Psalm 147:5

Thank him! Bless his name! Because the Lord is good. —Psalm 100:4–5 (CEB)

I was sitting with friends, shortly before Ash Wednesday, when I noticed most of them had long, beautiful fingernails. "How I wish I had nice nails!" I said, showing my short, brittle ones. "Yesterday I broke one folding laundry and another loading the dishwasher."

Susan was wearing gloves but took them off to display strong nails. "Yours could be like mine," she said, "if you oiled your hands six times a day and wore gloves." I was mortified. Cancer treatments had caused Susan's skin to peel in an extremely painful way. Touching anything with her bare hands hurt, and she had to wear soft, cushiony socks and oversize shoes to walk without pain. But she graciously accepted my apology and said, "I guess we each need to count our own blessings."

Her words hit home. Too often I dwelled on negatives: low crop prices and high expenses, grandchildren struggling with career choices, occasional aches, and the survival of our tiny church. So for Lent I decided to spend at least five minutes daily praising God for blessings. I was thankful for the three inches of rain, a boon for growing wheat; for overall good health; for granddaughters, Haylee and Natalee, ours through adoption; and for the joy of celebrating Easter with my church family.

Forty days and at least a hundred blessings! But the best blessing of all was the report that Susan's treatments were working and we would have many more years of friendship.

Thank You, gracious Lord, for "strength for today and bright hope
for tomorrow, blessings all mine and ten thousand beside"
("Great Is Thy Faithfulness", Hope Publishing Company 1951).
—Penney Schwab

Digging Deeper: Deuteronomy 28:2–7; Psalm 103:1–5;
1 Thessalonians 5:18

Wednesday, March 6

Do not worry, then, saying "What will we eat?" or "What will we drink?" or "What will we wear for clothing?" —Matthew 6:31 (NASB)

I look forward to Lent and to the discipline of fasting from a habit as a way of putting myself in a penitential frame of mind. But a recent spring of hardship had me thinking in new ways of what it means to "give up" something for Lent.

My dad was preparing a pot of coffee and asked if I wanted a cup.

"No, thanks," I announced to him and to Mom, who was sitting with me at the kitchen table. "I've given up coffee for Lent!"

You could say I had already given up a lot that season. Strapped for cash, I'd recently taken a new, lucrative job in Cleveland, 150 miles away from my husband and our struggling business in rural Ohio. A week earlier I had moved in with my parents, who lived closer to my new job. Weekdays, I lived with them; weekends, I made the long drive home to my house and husband in Ada. I was surrendering a lot.

My mom reminded me of this, shortly after my dinner table announcement. "Please rethink what you're doing," she said. "You have enough to worry about with this new job and new lifestyle without adding the stress of no coffee!"

I didn't think of giving up coffee as another source of stress. It was supposed to act as a way to renew my reliance upon God.

Nor did I think of my recent hardships as stand-ins for Lenten disciplines, as if I didn't have to give up coffee because I'd already "given up" my husband and home. But I could put my situation to a similar use. I could fast from worrying about it. For worry has no place in penitential disciplines and no currency in God's economy.

> *God, I give everything to You—even my worry over*
> *what will happen to me if I give everything to You.*
> —Amy Eddings

Digging Deeper: Psalm 31:5, 7; Matthew 24:36–38

Be strong and take heart, all you who hope in the Lord. —Psalm 31:24 (NIV)

I heard a woman on *Wheel of Fortune* say one of her dreams was to run with the bulls in Spain. I thought she was crazy. I made a list and posted it on Facebook. "Things I Will Never Do: wear false eyelashes, run with the bulls, skydive, smoke anything, get a tattoo or a face-lift. Everything else is up for grabs, especially after regaining my courage and getting back on my bicycle today."

I'd taken my first bike ride in ten months. The last time I'd tried to ride, the pain in my knees was so bad I had to get off and put the bike away after two blocks. The next month, I had both knees replaced. Double knee replacement surgery is extreme, the recuperation long and difficult. After eight months a bad pain in the back of my right knee still kept me from bending it more than ninety degrees. But after hearing that woman say she wanted to run with the bulls, I decided it was time to get back on my bike and hope for the best.

The first few times I pushed down on the pedals, it was scary. My back tensed up. My hands clenched the handlebars. The bike wobbled. I winced in pain every time my right knee had to push down. I was terrified I would fall down when it was time to get off the bike. But I kept going. And going. Around the block. Around the block again. I went farther, around two square blocks this time. The pain behind my right knee lessened. I practically shouted prayers of thanksgiving. I rode for two and a half miles before stopping. The next day I did two and a half miles again. Day three, almost five miles. Every day more miles.

Lord, when I'm fearful of scary or uncomfortable endeavors,
give me courage to do them anyway. Thank You for the push.
—Patricia Lorenz

Digging Deeper: Acts 4:28–30; Job 14:7–12

For by me your days will be multiplied, and years will be added to your life. —Proverbs 9:11 (ESV)

William, our older son, was turning thirty, and his girlfriend, Karen, had asked thirty of his friends and family members to celebrate him with emails and letters.

Trying to figure out what to send, I dug through a box of old photos and memorabilia. There was a picture of Will, when he was barely one, sitting in my lap as I played the piano. And a school photo of him, the only third-grader in a tie. Another picture showed him, in junior high, wearing those huge balloon pants he was only allowed to buy after he promised he'd be the one to wash them.

But what really made me smile was an email I'd printed out and saved, something he sent me from boarding school for my birthday. It was full of sentiments one could only imagine coming from a sixteen-year-old. How his friends thought I was cool "because you picked us up at the Phish concert," how dumb my jokes were but "you always act like yourself." The best line was at the end: "Dad, if you were my age and you went to school here, I would hope that you would be a good friend of mine."

The bonds that tie a family together are many, but the value of not just thinking nice things but also saying them—or putting them in an email—cannot be emphasized enough. Of course our loved ones are special. Telling them so is doubly special.

For Will's thirtieth I would try. He'd mastered the art at age sixteen.

Give me the words, Lord, that will make my loved ones' hearts sing.
—Rick Hamlin

Digging Deeper: Ephesians 2:10; Psalm 16:11

Hasten to my aid, O Lord, my deliverance. —Psalm 38:22 (JPS)

I shouldn't have inhaled. I'd just gotten off the treadmill and drank some water, but I was still breathing hard from the exercise, and suddenly the water went down the wrong way. I could cough, which I did. Then I tried to take a breath and discovered my throat had closed. I could not get air in.

Except for my dog and cat, I live alone now, so I was on my own. The last time something like this had happened, I was in college, and even though a lot of people were around then, no one had been any help. I'd had to get the lettuce leaf out of my windpipe by myself, and I would have to save myself now.

I kept thinking that if I passed out, I was done for, and there would be no one to take care of my pets, so I really had to breathe. I remembered that one of my husband's doctors told us that when he had trouble breathing, he panicked, which made his throat muscles spasm. He learned to relax when things got tough, and so could I.

My usual way of calming myself was to take a deep breath, but that was clearly out of the question. There was time to think just one word: *Help.* My lungs were burning from the coughing and the effort to get air. I managed to pull in a very small breath before my throat closed again. The small breath gave me enough hope to be calm for a split second and take in even more air. That first big, cold inhalation was all I needed to convince me everything would be all right, even though I kept coughing for quite a while.

> *Thank You, God, for the ability to think of You,*
> *even when I can think of nothing else.*
> —Rhoda Blecker

Digging Deeper: Psalm 70:2; Isaiah 55:6

Sunday, March 10

Though I walk in the midst of trouble, you preserve me against the wrath of my enemies; you stretch out your hand. —Psalm 138:7 (NRSV)

I worry. What if there's a long line and we miss the beginning of the show? What if it rains? I don't so much fret as sweat about the health of my kids, the happiness of my marriage, the future of the company I work for. Only when I looked into the life of Francis of Assisi did my perspective begin to change.

One day Francis was traveling on foot with a friend. Noticing Leo was bothered by the cold and freezing rain, Francis said, "What do you think is the source of joy?" Annoyed, Leo walked more briskly. Francis spoke again a few minutes later, "There's no joy in great theology!" For two miles, this went on. Leo walked, ignoring Francis; Francis talked to his friend, who pretended not to listen.

Finally Leo stopped, spun around, and said, "So what's the source of joy?"

"When we arrive," Francis said, "our cloaks drenched by rain, our bodies shivering with cold, and we knock at the door, if our host says, 'Wait outside awhile'—if we bear all of this with patience, kindness, and love, we will be brimming with joy."

Now I practice replacing my worries with faith. I try fasting on special days, especially this time of year. I focus on any discomfort I experience and realize its unimportance. By making my perspective shorter, looking ahead less often, and living each moment more fully without worry, I become a part of God's larger perspective and learn to accept that with joy.

You, God, are my hope today.
—Jon M. Sweeney

Digging Deeper: 1 Thessalonians 5:5–6

SAYING GOODBYE TO MY VETERANS
Prayer: The Most Important Gift

Devote yourselves to prayer, being watchful and thankful.
—Colossians 4:2 (NIV)

I wondered if what I did day after day in my role as an infection preventionist actually mattered in the grand scheme of things. One afternoon, Dalene, who works with sight-impaired veterans, stopped by my office. She told me of the time a veteran became severely despondent because he was blind and felt he was a burden. More than anything, he wanted to live on his own.

Dalene earmarked an entire day just for the two of them, and they checked out apartments together. They finally found one that met his living and financial needs. As a result of having his own place, the veteran was energized to help other blind vets. The experience taught Dalene that if she was attuned to small assignments, the masses would take care of themselves.

I remembered a situation with a similar theme.

One day I was challenged by a homeless Afghanistan vet who was bicycling across the country and became lost to follow-up. "This is an impossible situation, God," I prayed. "I'll never find this veteran."

I documented the veteran's plight and reached out to a number of health departments in states where it was believed he might be headed. The following Saturday morning, the young veteran called my cell phone. He went on to receive the needed treatment at a VA facility two thousand miles away from me. A single assignment affected a greater whole when I made prayer part of the equation.

I'm seeing that prayer is a part of every little thing, Lord. Keep me trusting You every step of this life-changing journey.
—Roberta Messner

Digging Deeper: 1 John 5:14, 15; Mark 11:24

Tuesday, March 12

Let us run with perseverance the race marked out for us. —Hebrews 12:1 (NIV)

Whenever my dreams are frustrated, I think about Christian novelist Fyodor Dostoyevsky. Fyodor's dream was to write, and the mountain of obstacles in his way make my setbacks look like molehills.

The first obstacle was his tyrannical father. Born in Russia in 1821 to a wealthy serf-owning family, Fyodor "of course" would become an officer in the tsar's army. A nobleman's son become a lowly writer? That was his father's reaction when the youngster showed him an early composition. The man tore up the handwritten pages, then sent his son off to a regimented boarding school and from there to a military college.

When Fyodor was eighteen, his father was found dead on his estate, murdered for his cruelty, people said, by his serfs. Free to leave school at last, Fyodor joined a secret group of writers working to liberate the serfs. Reported by the tsar's spies, Fyodor was sentenced to four years of hard labor in Siberia.

It wasn't the backbreaking work or the cabbage-and-cockroach soup he minded most—it was the absence of pen and paper. No way to write down the powerful sentences continually forming in his head. His prison term over, he was transported to a military outpost even deeper in Siberia to spend more "wasted" years in another pen-and-paperless wilderness.

But when he finally began writing the books that made him perhaps the greatest writer of all time, he did what many people do after long holding on to a dream. He used the frustrations, delays, and roadblocks, to enlarge the dream. The prisoners he was thrown among, the bullying guards, the illiterate soldiers, became his windows into the world he opened for all of us to see.

> *When my small plans are thwarted, Father, don't let me miss*
> *the larger opportunities You may be offering.*
> —Elizabeth Sherrill

Digging Deeper: Hebrews 10:36

She gave this name to the Lord who spoke to her: "You are the God who sees me." —Genesis 16:13 (NIV)

He was considerably younger than I was and handsome in a hipster kind of way. When he smiled and laughed at my jokes, it didn't feel fake or dismissive. When I spoke, he looked me straight in the eye and really listened to what I had to say. He not only listened—he asked questions. Thoughtful questions. Then he gave me a coupon for a free latte the next time I dropped by.

OK, so this great guy worked the drive-through at a coffee shop. I know it's part of the brand to be kind to customers. Even the lids of the cups proclaim how "awesome" you are. But for a single woman living in a very couple-centric world, simply being acknowledged as a fellow human being is something I no longer take for granted. This brief interaction was the highlight of my morning.

It was also a gentle kick in the khakis. I walk by people every day but all too often don't see them for who they really are: divine works of art. It's so easy for me to get caught up in my own life, in errands and plans and my little homemade dramas. Yet the more I focus on myself, the less I see others—really, truly see them.

I strive to see people through God's eyes, to recognize every individual as valuable, full of potential, and dearly loved. To do that takes intentionality. Intentionality takes prayer. Prayer turns up the volume of God's Spirit in my life. It allows me to hear God's whisper more clearly. Then God can help me focus forward, beyond my own little life, so I can more clearly see the living, breathing masterpieces all around me.

Dear Lord, thank You for seeing me inside and out, every minute of every day. Teach me how to see those around me in the way You do.
—Vicki Kuyper

Digging Deeper: Genesis 16:1–16

Thursday, March 14

From everyone who has been given much, much will be demanded.
And from the one trusted with much, much more will be expected.
—Luke 12:48 (NCV)

My parents were generous people. They were raised during the Great Depression and knew the power of giving, which they passed along to me. It became important that I, too, be an example to my children and grandchildren. Over the years, I've practiced this in several different ways. When my grandchildren were young and celebrating a birthday, instead of purchasing them another toy or gift they didn't need, I let them choose a gift for a child in a Third World country. Many organizations have catalogs, and I loved the way my grandchildren mulled over the pages in search of the perfect gift. As a result, children around the world have a barnyard of chickens, a goat, and even a camel, all of which have deeply enriched their lives as well as those of my grandchildren.

Recently I decided to use my grandchildren's birthdays as occasions to sponsor a child for a year, and not just a random child but a child born the same day. This way the grandkids will be able to form relationships with those children, exchange letters with them, and become involved in their lives. My hope is that this impresses upon my grandchildren how blessed they are and that they come to realize that with those blessings come responsibilities. We have been given much, and from us much is expected.

Father, we are generous because You have given us so much.
Help us always to remember that.
—Debbie Macomber

Digging Deeper: Luke 12:48

Delight yourself in the Lord, and He will give you the desires and petitions of your heart. —Psalm 37:4 (AMP)

Now that I'm old, I so want to remember my childhood. My best childhood friend, June, and I played together daily. My mother arranged for June's mother, Flora, to care for me while she worked. June and I played in the house together, shared a pair of skates—each of us wearing only one—played Monopoly on her living room rug, and swung on the glider. Our dogs—Dixie, a spitz, and Chris, my fox terrier—adored each other, too.

June and I have reconnected lately to relive those fun-filled days. June and Don, her husband, stopped by our home one glorious day. They were traveling cross-country in a van. She brought a scrapbook, and we sat close together at my dining room table, turning pages and squealing at the photographs and memories.

We've both given birth to fraternal twin sons, and both of us are writers. Along life's way, we each decided we must have an intimate relationship with God to make it.

I received an email from June recently: "I've discovered Mother's old diary. I'm transcribing it. Here's a chapter. More to follow."

I read slowly, moving my lips, clinging to each word as though it were a piece of candy:

The year 1944 was a war one—our streets were paved with asphalt and gravel by men working on the WPA. June and Marion Bond stayed close, watching the process of tar and gravel and bringing samples of the same to the washtub on their pants. These two were a team! They loved to dress up in long dresses, old hats, and high-heeled shoes and parade the street. Halloween would find them in costume and masks, visiting from door to door with a request for tricks or treats...[*]

Only You, my Father, knew how I longed to recapture more of my childhood!
—Marion Bond West

Digging Deeper: Matthew 6:33; Psalm 20:4
[*]"Kissing Kin, by Flora Janie Bond Fowler, Memories 1944".

Saturday, March 16

*May the God of peace… equip you with everything good that you may
do his will, working in us that which is pleasing in his sight.*
—Hebrews 13:20–21 (ESV)

Waiting for neighbors at a strip mall, I sat on a sidewalk bench
when a commotion overwhelmed the scene. A wailing woman,
accompanied by a barista on break—bless her—took a seat facing me.
The older woman was inconsolably lonely, missing her homeland, her
deceased mother, and the siblings and church congregation she'd alien-
ated. Hearing her complaints, I gingerly asked if I could pray for her.
"It doesn't help," she said. "It doesn't bring my mother back." I prayed
anyway, for the Comforter to come. Having her attention, I took exag-
geratedly deep breaths, hoping she'd follow my lead.

Soon my preteen neighbor left her family in the store. Scooting
beside me, she gaped. "What's wrong with her?" We whispered. Holding hands, she and I prayed again. I admit I now prayed with dual
intent: to appeal to God for calm amid the storm and to model prayer
as a coping mechanism.

Over the next half hour, the drama subsided. Was it an answer to
prayer? As the barista rushed back to her post, another young stranger,
appropriately bilingual, eased in, listening, soothing, and offering
hope. I stepped away and returned several times. ("Why is your family
taking so long? Don't wander out of sight.") We were back at the bench
when the woman, no longer distraught, hugged me *thank you* and left.

Will my young neighbor catch my vision for her and turn to God in
times of distress? I don't know. But she obviously listens to my lessons.
Riding home, she sternly lectured me: "You're not supposed to talk to
strangers."

God, equip me well as I endeavor to be an emissary of Your peace.
—Evelyn Bence

Digging Deeper: John 14:25–27; Matthew 11:25–30

Teach us to number our days, that we may gain a heart of wisdom.
—Psalm 90:12 (NIV)

Despite being Irish and redheaded, I'd never paid much attention to Saint Patrick's Day. It felt crammed between Valentine's Day and Easter, so I skipped right over it. I'd planned to do the same this year, as I hurried past the greeting cards covered with leprechauns and four-leaf clovers.

But what if…?

Turning around, I trailed my fingers along the green cards.

In 2015, our daughter Katie remarried and became a stepmom to a beautiful little girl named Rilynn, who's now five and in kindergarten. Our only grandchild. I'd sent her cards for Valentine's Day, Christmas, and her birthday. But never for Saint Patrick's Day.

I found a grass-green card with an image of a little girl on the front.

Inside the card was plenty of room for me to draw a picture and write a short note.

After sketching a stick figure, I added long, wavy hair and colored it sunshine yellow just like Rilynn's.

I wrote a Scripture—something to bless her long after Saint Patrick's Day passed.

Using my best penmanship, I printed this:

"You made me bold with strength in my soul," Psalm 138:3 (NASB).

God put His strength in you. He makes you bold.

Grandpa Rick and I love you SO, SO, SO much.

Love,

Grandma Jewels

Addressing the envelope, I decided to add Scripture to every card I send her from now on. We never outgrow His Word.

> *Father, as Rilynn grows up, help her gain a heart of wisdom.*
> —Julie Garmon

Digging Deeper: Psalm 85:11, 124:8

Monday, March 18

You are the salt of the earth. But if the salt loses its saltiness, how can it be made salty again? It is no longer good for anything, except to be thrown out and trampled underfoot. —Matthew 5:13 (NIV)

New Yorkers don't typically speak to one another on the subway or public buses. We rarely even make eye contact. We push our bodies into crowded trains until we're snug as kittens, but never do we say "good morning" or "have a great day." This was the case one normal day on the New York City subway as I sat playing with my phone. Everyone silently had their heads down—their noses in books or screens, or just looking at their shoes.

A group of friends broke the silence, entering a subway car at the next stop. They laughed and joked, changing the seriousness in the atmosphere. One friend had a speaker for his smartphone and played ABBA's "Dancing Queen," one of my favorite songs. The friends all sang, and the rest of us lifted our heads and smiled at the scene. By the chorus, others were singing along, too, including myself. The friends danced, and I moved my shoulders as I belted out the rest of the song. The group stayed for three more songs, surprising unsuspecting passengers who boarded the celebration train. Strangers smiled at one another, singing and dancing together like longtime friends. The group got off the train at the next stop and took their joy with them.

The train car went silent again. We looked around with shy smiles now, then slowly put our heads back down into our phones and books.

Lord, help me to spread joy in this world that is often cold and full of pain and strife. Let me be an example of Your love, peace, and joy, and remind me how desperately this world needs it.
—Karen Valentin

Digging Deeper: Romans 15:13

My bed shall comfort me. —Job 7:13 (KJV)

Every night, after I've nodded off at least twice while reading, I turn off my bedside lamp, wriggle down under my covers, and roll onto my left side. As I burrow into my pillows, I always sigh, "Thank You, God, for my bed."

Now, there's nothing remarkable or high-tech about my bed: no memory foam, no firmness number, no expensive mattress or box spring. In fact, it's just a double-platform bed with a budget mattress. Nor does my bedding feature high thread counts, genuine down, or exotic fabrics, though I am pleased with the puffy coral comforter I found on sale. No, my bed fits nicely into the "basic" category. I am grateful to have its comfort, because I haven't always had it.

Nearly twenty years ago, I moved to New Hampshire to help my elderly parents and slept on a bed at their place. When I finally moved into my own apartment, I invested only in a mattress, which I put on the floor. I would move back to Wyoming after my parents no longer needed me, so why buy a bed frame? After two years, however, I knew I would be needed for quite some time, so I bought a golden pine bed frame and moved off the floor. But when the opportunity to travel emerged, I gave up my apartment and bed altogether for four years. My bed went to my son's apartment in Boston, while I alternated between helping the folks, house-sitting, and traveling—and slept in a total of forty-one beds.

I've been reunited with my bed for several years now. To me, it's not just a bed—it's a cozy blessing.

Dear God, thank You for my bed!
—Gail Thorell Schilling

Digging Deeper: Job 33:15; Isaiah 57:2

Wednesday, March 20

Where were you when I laid the earth's foundation? Tell me,
if you understand. —Job 38:4 (NIV)

Recently I read of a prehistoric baby bird that fell into tree sap in ancient Burma and died. The sap turned into amber and preserved the bird's body. Scientists found this rare specimen and concluded it was ninety-nine million years old. This is amazing!

Large numbers make my mind go blank. I cannot comprehend the magnitude of their meaning. I can conceptualize one hundred years and even one thousand years. But to understand that one million years is one thousand years experienced one thousand times awes me. To think of a bird preserved in amber for ninety-nine million years is beyond my grasp.

As a university professor, I often talk about millions and billions of years. But seldom do I pause to marvel at the immensity of what my words attempt to express. Numbers are often a symbolic representation of a much deeper truth beyond human comprehension. To put it another way, the more we know, the less we know.

We spend our entire lives seeking truth and understanding. But our exploring should always lead us to a place of profound mystery, reverence, and awe. God is beyond time and measurement. But Jesus teaches us that God is also love. And ultimately our lives are unified within this eternal dimension of love.

Father, help me to seek truth with all of my mind, soul, and strength.
But may I never forget that You are holy and a compassionate mystery
far beyond my understanding. Amen.
—Scott Walker

Digging Deeper: Job 38:1–41, 42:1–6; Psalm 8;
1 Corinthians 2:7; 1 Timothy 6:16

(Source of the newspaper article about the bird preserved in amber:
Ben Guarino, "Stunning Fossil Reveals Prehistoric Baby Bird
Caught In Amber," Washington Post, June 9, 2017.)

Behold, I am doing a new thing; now it springs forth, do you not perceive it? I will make a way in the wilderness and rivers in the desert.
—Isaiah 43:19 (ESV)

We took our puppy, Zeke, to the beach for spring break. He loved the sand, the freedom to run free, and the wind blowing his tennis ball much farther than it does in our yard at home.

But the water? He wasn't about to go in. Instead he stood at the edge of the waves, whining at the great expanse of ocean, jumping backward each time an unruly wave came close to his feet.

Day two dawned, then day three and day four, and still Zeke hadn't touched the water.

Then, on day five, a seagull swooped down right in front of him, causing him to forget his fear for just a moment. He dived after it and splashed down on his side in the churning water.

He appeared dazed for a minute. He looked back at me, and I said, "It's OK, Zekey-boy. Go on in!"

And so he did.

He dived headfirst into the deeper water, jumped over the waves, and swam. It was a messy doggy-paddle at first as he tested out his skills, but minutes later he was smooth and sleek in the water, swimming fast enough to catch up to my kids, who played in the surf.

Of course, he loved it.

On day six, Zeke sprinted down the beach and into the surf.

When we got back home, he ran from the car and jumped straight into our swimming pool.

What had been a huge fear was now his greatest joy. He just had to find the courage to dive in and see if he could float.

Heavenly Father, give me the courage to push beyond my fears and dive headfirst into the promises You have for my life. Amen.
—Erin MacPherson

Digging Deeper: Ezekiel 36:26–29; Isaiah 42:10

Friday, March 22

Make you a new heart. —Ezekiel 18:31 (KJV)

To say I was grumpy would be the understatement of the year.

It was my son Harrison's last spring break with us before he would leave for college, and we wanted to make it his best. Because he loved to ski, my wife, Corinne, and I sacrificed to the hilt to pull off a ski trip to Colorado.

It seemed a daunting task with Harrison, plus two young girls and five-month-old David, but somehow we made great memories and pulled off the week without a hitch...until the day we were supposed to return home. It was snowing, and our morning flight was canceled, which meant we would miss our connection from Denver to our home in Nashville. There were no available flights home for two days.

My grumpy attitude overshadowed the elation of our family time together. I was angry and wanted to get my family home. Corinne calmly took my hand and whispered, "Time to make lemonade out of lemons." Soon Harrison joined the adventure, good-naturedly calling his girlfriend in Nashville to cancel their weekend date. He and Corinne hatched a plan, and soon we all checked in to a hotel with an indoor pool in downtown Denver.

After a lengthy swim, Harrison delighted the girls with his next suggestion: "Let's go bowling!" Corinne even found a movie we all enjoyed, with baby David cooperating by sleeping through the entire show.

The lemonade turned out to be a perfect antidote to my grumpy attitude, and even now it's the Denver stretch, the unplanned part of our last spring break with Harrison, that most stands out.

"Harrison, don't you wish we could go back to Denver?" his younger sister asked not long ago. He answered with a smile that said it all.

> *Father, in every setback and every situation, turn our hearts*
> *toward the good You have waiting.*
> —Brock Kidd

Digging Deeper: Isaiah 7:15; Job 34:4

He who was seated on the throne said, "Behold, I am making all things new." —Revelation 21:5 (ESV)

Maybe I shouldn't have suggested she come," I told Michael that evening as we unpacked our suitcases at the cabin. His grandfather had died a month earlier, and we invited his grandmother to join the family in Branson for spring break. But everything reminded her of Pap Pa.

At Branson Landing, Mam Ma walked to the dock and gazed at the water. "Pap Pa and I came here before," she mused, a faraway look in her eyes. "The river was decorated with Christmas lights. It was breathtaking."

We attended the evening performance of *Joseph* at Sight & Sound Theatres. Mam Ma confided she'd seen it last year. "Pap Pa was feeling good. A group of us came."

During dinner at Mel's Hard Luck Diner, she regaled us with escapades of Pap Pa and his siblings when they vacationed here together. Branson had been a treasure trove of memories during their sixty-seven-year marriage.

That evening, we had a fierce air hockey tournament. Mam Ma laughed as we all failed to beat our daughter, Micah. The next day brought sightseeing and more reminiscing. I worried that the trip and all these memories might be upsetting her.

The morning we were to leave, I worked up my courage. "Was it bad timing for you to accompany us so soon?"

Mam Ma's green eyes shone with love. "Oh no, shug. It's good to get my mind off my grief."

"But everything reminds you of Pap Pa."

Mam Ma paused. "I'm going to have grief for a long time, but it gives me joy to make new memories with you three."

Lord, thank You for the gift of experiencing joy
even in times of deep sorrow.
—Stephanie Thompson

Digging Deeper: Isaiah 65:17; Matthew 5:4

Sunday, March 24

The joy of the Lord is your strength. —Nehemiah 8:10 (NIV)

My husband, Lynn, and I have an ongoing disagreement these days about JOY. At Christmastime my sister gave me an outdoor decoration: three huge separate letters, each with a spear to sink into the ground, to spell out the word JOY. I happily set up the decoration in a garden off our back patio, where I could see it from the kitchen window. Big, bright, white letters during the day and letters that shine through the darkness of night. I love it.

The disagreement? My husband's recurring question: "So, when can we take down the JOY sign?" Usually he adds some annoying reminder that it isn't Christmas anymore. Duh.

I've been responding with future dates: "I need JOY until I finish this project in a few weeks." Or, "I need JOY until the siege of gray weather is over." Or, more recently, "I need JOY until Easter." But as Easter draws nearer and he reminds me of my promised end to JOY, I've come up with a whole new defense that clarifies my need for ongoing JOY.

"JOY isn't just a Christmas word. It's a prayer word I need to remember every day. Besides," I add, assuming this will address his concern, "they are LED lights that hardly use any electricity." At least I think that's what I read on the box.

He just turns away, which is code for, "I don't agree, but let's table the discussion for now."

So that's where JOY stands at our house. Right where I can see it out my kitchen window. For now.

Lord, thank You for a Christmas word that reminds me
"JOY" can shine through the darkness all year long.
—Carol Kuykendall

Digging Deeper: John 16:19–24

Do not worry about tomorrow, for tomorrow will bring worries of its own. Today's trouble is enough for today. —Matthew 6:34 (NRSV)

I was working hard on memorizing lines and lyrics. I'd been cast as Sister Mary Clarence in the musical *Sister Act* and needed to know my part as soon as possible. The problem was that the songs all seemed to consist of lists: take me here and take me there, look at this and look at that, bless this and bless that. The faster I tried to memorize, the more mixed up the lyrics became, as I confused repeats and reprises and jumbled them up into one giant mess.

Frustrated, I looked for help. I searched online, asked friends for memorization tips, and suggested to God that the lyrics just be placed in my head. Nothing seemed to help. Finally I paused. *This is not gonna happen this way,* I thought. *I've got to be a little more patient with myself. It will come.*

And sure enough, as I became more patient, breaking the scenes and songs down into smaller pieces—or as Anne Lamott puts it in her classic book on writing, taking it "bird by bird"—I got more right than wrong. By opening night, the entire book—script and score—was committed to my memory. While I am so grateful to God for the incredible opportunity, Sister Mary Clarence was one of the most difficult roles I've ever had to memorize. She will forever go down in my book as the Patron Saint of Lists!

God, I am grateful for Your presence in this challenge. I know
You are there for all challenges, both great and small.
Though I seemed to want You to be a genie who grants wishes,
looking back, I am thankful You gave me the space to challenge
and push myself in new and exciting ways.
—Natalie Perkins

Digging Deeper: Matthew 6:25–34

Tuesday, March 26

Give to everyone who begs from you. —Luke 6:30 (NRSV)

March is stressful when your spouse is a CPA. Kris works late and throughout the weekend. One night we were eating dinner, trying to relax, when my phone buzzed. I listened to the garbled voice mail: it was ADT, something about a phone on the table in my office, call this number.

I called and listened to a stranger's weird explanation. His wife had driven an Amish couple to get their taxes done and left her phone in Kris's waiting room. They saw it through the window from the street and called the posted security service, who—I surmised as the man spoke—must've called the emergency number: mine. The man wanted us to drive out and get it for them.

I pressed the phone to my stomach and explained everything to Kris.

"Can't they come tomorrow during business hours?" he asked.

"What if it were my phone?" was my automatic response. My phone: daughter emergencies.

We left our dinner, changed clothes, and drove to Kris's office.

The couple was older, nice. Kris got the phone while the wife—wearing her pajamas under her coat, I noted—explained her job of driving Amish people to doctors' offices, appointments, and emergencies. She gets lots of business. Waits in waiting rooms, often for hours. Other clients call while she waits. Her job—and her clients' lives sometimes—depends on her phone.

It struck me afterward how easy that simple directive "do to others as you'd have them do to you" makes it to do the right thing even when you don't want to.

You think, *What if it were me?* Then automatically, you're doing what is right.

Lord, help me hear others through my stress.
—Patty Kirk

Digging Deeper: Luke 6:27–36

At least there is hope for a tree: If it is cut down, it will sprout again, and its new shoots will not fail. —Job 14:7 (NIV)

A crust of snow froze my fingertips. I knelt in my mother's garden, using an ungloved hand to dig into the white left behind by an early spring storm. Looking closely at the dormant ground, I wondered, could it have survived? I doubted it.

Yet...there! Just breaking through last year's brown deadfall was the brilliant green of a dozen brand-new French sorrel leaves.

French sorrel is one of my favorite garden plants. Among the first to poke above the soil after winter's cold, its tart, lemony leaves pack a refreshing punch. But in my own Montana garden, thousands of miles from where I knelt in the Virginia snow, a vole infestation had devastated my perennials. I'd tried everything to stop the invaders, but they defeated me at every turn. One of the most disheartening casualties was my sorrel bed. As the last of my carefully tended plants wilted and died, cut off from its roots, I'd sadly resigned myself to starting over from seed in the spring. But during this visit home, I remembered the root slips I'd shared with my mom years before.

And here they were! Life where I'd expected to find none. Little did I know that, far from my own garden, in this place that once also nurtured me, my sorrel had been spreading and growing strong, rootstock to restore what was laid low.

Thank You, Lord, for rooting me in Your love, and reminding me that—even when life deals out blows—through You, I'll have the strength to bounce back and flourish once more.
—Erin Janoso

Digging Deeper: Daniel 4:15

Thursday, March 28

See whether I do not open all the windows of the heavens for you and empty out a blessing until there is enough. —Malachi 3:10 (CEB)

During a bone-dry March, raging wildfires destroyed over five hundred thousand acres of pastureland in the Red Hills of Comanche and Clark counties. A man died, and several homes and barns were reduced to cinders. Hundreds of cattle died. Ranchers had to destroy hundreds more that were too seriously injured to survive. Horses, dogs, birds, and wild animals were lost. Wildlife habitat was destroyed. Fencing, which costs ten thousand dollars per mile to build, was ruined for miles and miles.

Recovery will take years. The true cost of the fire might never be known, and not every ranch and business will survive. But something remarkable happened in the aftermath of the fire. Prayers went up, and help poured in. Volunteers of all ages and faiths came from Kansas and around the nation to clear damaged property so rebuilding could begin. Four-H clubs, veterinarians, and individuals took in orphaned calves to bucket-feed. Huge truckloads of hay rolled in from as far away as Wyoming and Illinois. Churches, businesses, and individuals donated money.

I wanted to assist, but I couldn't dig through rubble or build fence. I prayed and added a check to the larger donation our church mission committee made. But that was insignificant for such overwhelming need! Then a friend involved in the recovery efforts put my mind to rest. "Every gift helps," he said. "Every volunteer, every sack of feed and roll of wire, every dollar, and especially every prayer."

Loving God, thank You for prayers and gifts large and small that restore the faith and lives of those who suffer devastating loss.
—Penney Schwab

Digging Deeper: Job 42:11–12; Isaiah 43:1–2; Romans 15:5–6

I praise you, for I am fearfully and wonderfully made. Wonderful are your works; my soul knows it very well. —Psalm 139:14 (ESV)

A flash of white zoomed down the walnut tree and across the lawn. I stared at it from the dining room, trying to figure out what I was seeing—a white rat? No, the tail was wrong. Big and bushy, it moved like a squirrel. A white squirrel? Watching closer, I yelled for Tony or the boys to get a second opinion. *What the heck is it?*

The boys came first. They looked out, said, "Yeah, I see it, a white squirrel," and walked away.

I tried to tell them the uniqueness of the situation, that it isn't every day you see an albino squirrel. I told them I've been on this earth for decades and it's the first one I've ever seen and, if I were a betting person I'd say I'm not likely to see another.

Tony came to the window. His eyes widened. "That's something," he said.

I watched the squirrel run up and down an oak and then disappear in the knot of a maple. Nature's anomalies feel sacred. Their differences calls out the beauty in everything around us. Their existence seems to say, *I'm special, but everything else is, too. Look, look at that crow, hear the way his call sounds like "mama-mama." And that tree over there, towering over the house, that started as a seed. The dandelions, yellow now, will later give children pause to blow on them and wish.*

All day long that little white squirrel helped me see the extraordinary in the ordinary, and I am blessed to be a witness.

Great Creator, the world is filled with so many wonders. Forgive me if I forget to notice and thank You for today's "white squirrel," a heavenly messenger to call out the miraculous all around me.
—Sabra Ciancanelli

Digging Deeper: Genesis 1:1–31; Psalm 50:2

Saturday, March 30

Jesus, lifting up His eyes and seeing that a large crowd was coming to Him, said to Philip, "Where are we to buy bread, so that these may eat?" —John 6:5 (NASB)

When my friend Steve asked if I could spare some monarch caterpillars and milkweed for his second-grade class, I eagerly agreed. "We're studying the life cycle of the butterfly," he explained. "I've got a small habitat in the classroom. It'll be a great science lesson."

The next morning I snipped branches of milkweed from my garden, carefully placed tiny caterpillars in a cardboard box, and dropped them off at his school. A few days later, I received a text message from him: "Caterpillars devoured all the milkweed! Send more!"

The next morning, I walked out to my garden to cut more milkweed. But only tall green stalks, stripped bare of leaves, were left. *Oh no!* I thought.

I texted Steve: "Milkweed all gone! Caterpillars ate everything left!"

A few minutes later, he responded: "I told my students we didn't have enough food for the caterpillars. One chimed in, 'Jesus'll feed 'em! Just like He fed all those people with those loaves and fishes!'"

"Sure hope so!" I texted back.

At work that day, I called the local plant nurseries. Everyone was sold out of milkweed. I was discouraged. It didn't look like I'd be able to give the students more food for their caterpillars.

That afternoon my friend Beth stopped by. "Hey, I was at the garden shop across the lake," she said. "They had a few pots of milkweed." She shrugged. "Not sure why, but I bought them for you. I figured you could use them."

I smiled broadly. "I sure can! And so can some second-graders who are getting a great science lesson. But the biggest lesson is for me," I said, giving her a hug, "a reminder that Jesus is indeed our great provider!"

Thank You, Lord, for caring for every living thing, both great and small.
— Melody Bonnette Swang

Digging Deeper: Matthew 14:19; Genesis 22:8

You will pray to him, and he will hear you. —Job 22:27 (AMP)

Late, as usual, I strode past the snowbanks through the church door, leaving my husband, Charlie, to find a parking space. I'd planned to make my Lenten confession today, and nothing was going to stop me. Not the foot of snow, dumped by a blizzard the day before, that canceled everything. Not the fact that I was unfamiliar with the church or priest and couldn't find either as I whirled around looking for the confession booth. Eventually Charlie wandered in and wondered where to sit while waiting for me and the Mass scheduled to start after confessions.

I gestured impatiently at the empty church. "Anywhere," I hissed at him. I added in frustration, "They better not have canceled confession today!"

Sliding into a nearby pew, Charlie nodded toward a corner behind me. "Maybe she knows."

An older woman knelt there, reading a prayer book. Normally I would not have interrupted her, but I didn't have time to worry about that. I walked swiftly toward her, whispering loudly, "Excuse me, is there confession this evening?"

She looked up and answered softly, "Yes."

"Where?" I asked plaintively. "I'm new here."

"Yes," she said in the same soft voice, "I've noticed that."

She paused a moment to let that sink in, and sink in it did. With it, my arrogant, selfish spirit deflated, and I thought I heard God chuckling, *Were you really going to confess with that attitude?* The woman rose from her prayers. "Come. I'll show you."

She led me back to the entrance of the church, where the priest sat in a small confession room with the door half-open, welcoming. I'd blasted right past it when entering the church. She smiled before returning to her prayers. She had, indeed, shown me.

> *Lord, thank You for reminding me to seek and approach*
> *You always with a humble spirit.*
> —Marci Alborghetti

Digging Deeper: 1 Chronicles 16:8–12; 2 Chronicles 6:21–24

March

UNDER GOD'S WINGS

1 ______________________________

2 ______________________________

3 ______________________________

4 ______________________________

5 ______________________________

6 ______________________________

7 ______________________________

8 ______________________________

9 ______________________________

10 ______________________________

11 ______________________________

12 ______________________________

13 ______________________________

14 ______________________________

15 ______________________________

16 _____

17 _____

18 _____

19 _____

20 _____

21 _____

22 _____

23 _____

24 _____

25 _____

26 _____

27 _____

28 _____

29 _____

30 _____

31 _____

APRIL

Ah, Sovereign Lord, you have made
the heavens and the earth by your
great power and outstretched arm.
Nothing is too hard for you.

—Jeremiah 32:17 (NIV)

Whoever gives to others will get richer; those who help others will themselves be helped. —Proverbs 11:25 (NCV)

Lessons in generosity come in many forms, and one day I had an idea brewing in my head for such a lesson. At Easter each year, Wayne and I fill plastic eggs with coins and candy. Even though most of our grandkids are in their teens, they still love our little egg hunt. This past year I added a twist to the day. After everyone had gathered their candy and opened their eggs to collect the cash inside, I announced I had a surprise for them. I handed each grandchild a fifty-dollar bill.

"Cool, Grandma."

"Wow."

I knew I would get comments of appreciation and looks of awe. But I had a catch. "Two things before you take this money. It comes with stipulations."

They stared at me, wondering what was next.

"The first stipulation: you have to give the money away, and second, you have to tell me what you did with it."

I expected them to groan and complain. Instead, they were excited and eager. Several of the grandchildren sent the money to the Third World children I sponsor for their birthdays. Jaxon, six years old, purchased birthday gifts for foster children. Bailey gave her money to a homeless teenager she had befriended at school. When she shared her story with me, she had tears in her eyes and thanked me for giving her the opportunity to help others.

Tremendous power is in generosity, and I'll forever be grateful to my parents for passing this lesson along to me.

Father, I have learned I can never outgive You.
—Debbie Macomber

Digging Deeper: Hebrews 13:2

Tuesday, April 2

For your steadfast love is before my eyes, and I walk in faithfulness to you.
—Psalm 26:3 (NRSV)

My husband, Charlie, and I have had a really challenging year. We're dealing with issues around aging—ourselves and the people we love—including finances and problems with our condominium. All normal stuff, but when it comes in wave after wave, it's challenging to cope.

Naturally I've been praying a lot. Maybe too much, at least when it comes to petitioning the Lord. I've noticed my prayers are centered on asking, sometimes begging, the Lord to heal this, forgive that, help that one, protect this one, or fix the other thing. All necessary prayers, certainly, but also very much focused on our needs and our situation.

I'm trying to break out of that pattern, choosing to spend more time just being with God silently. This is uncomfortable for me, honestly, but each time, it becomes a bit easier.

I'm also trying to focus more on others, especially people I don't really know well. On my daily walk, I try to notice anything unusual in the houses I pass. One usually fastidious elderly householder still has her holiday wreath up in April, so I pray for her health and mobility. Noticing a police car outside the house of a family with teenagers who have been in trouble before, I pray for their safety and for their parents. Passing a yard covered with newly blooming hyacinths, I thank the Lord for the person who planted them.

I find I like praying for people I hardly know. Not only does it take my mind off of, well, me, me, me, but it also helps open my heart to others, to really search for and see what others are experiencing. I've seen pain, joy, hope, and fear, all as I pass by the homes of my neighbors. It has given me a better, more comforting sense of God's presence, not just in my own life but in all our lives.

Lord, expand my horizon so I can see, just a little, of what You see.
—Marci Alborghetti

Digging Deeper: Proverbs 14:21, 30; Isaiah 57:14–16

I was in prison and you came to visit me. —Matthew 25:36 (NIV)

"A lways tell the truth." Growing up, I must have heard these words from my father a thousand times. A private detective, he devoted his life to uncovering truth.

His first effort was on behalf of a thirty-nine-year-old man named Clarence Boggie. Clarence was convicted of bludgeoning a lonely old man to death in a city he swore he'd never set foot in. When my father learned of his case, Clarence had already spent thirteen years of a life sentence in Washington's Walla Walla State Penitentiary.

Clarence was a skilled lumberjack. But by Great Depression year 1935, most Northwest lumber mills had closed. Clarence joined thousands of other unemployed men roaming the streets of Portland, Oregon. One day he was arrested for a murder that took place 130 miles away in Spokane, Washington.

Tried and convicted quickly, Clarence decided his only hope was an appeal to one of Washington's two senators, its governor, or the President of the United States. For thirteen years Clarence wrote to them all, again and again. The replies, if they came at all, were routine turndowns with rubber-stamped signatures.

Within weeks of getting involved in Clarence's case, my father uncovered a pattern of false witnesses, suppressed evidence, and a city rushing to close a sickening crime. His efforts became a classic study, leading eventually to the freeing of many framed for murder.

Why start with Clarence Boggie? Because of his answer to my father's first question: "What kept you sending those letters year after year with never a reply?"

"It's how I was raised," Clarence said. "Mother told me, 'Always tell the truth, and leave the result to God.'"

Father, help me cherish the truth in everything I say and do.
—Elizabeth Sherrill

Digging Deeper: Isaiah 58:7; Hebrews 13:3

Thursday, April 4

Do not be afraid or discouraged, for the Lord your God is with you wherever you go. —Joshua 1:9 (CSB)

How are you feeling about your last week living in New York City?" a colleague asked. I was standing by the elevators near our office, about to make a coffee run.

"It's tough," I said, "but I've missed my family."

A month earlier, my husband, Zach, and I had decided to move home to Kansas. I came to the Big Apple eight years prior, hoping to become a successful journalist. But over time God spoke to my heart. My desires had changed. It felt as if God was nudging me to go home and love on my family.

"Do you have a job lined up? A place to live?" my colleague asked, just as the elevator arrived.

"Not yet," I said, stepping in. "We'll be staying with my parents for a short time and then see what happens." I waved before the doors closed.

I'd always prepared for the future. This time I was counting on God alone.

Once outside, as I waited to cross the street, the sun peeked around a skyscraper. The golden light flooded John Street.

This wasn't the first time I'd seen a sunrise in Manhattan, but it felt like it.

During these last days in New York, I caught myself living more in the present. I was still crossing the same intersections, looking at the same skyscrapers, and getting off at the same subway stations, but now these scenes felt more precious. My heartbeat thumped loudly in my eardrums as I stood at that intersection. But I could still hear Him, whispering, "What's next is good. Wait and see."

> *Father, Your voice is the first voice I ever heard,*
> *before I was even born. I'd follow it anywhere.*
> —Desiree Cole

Digging Deeper: Ecclesiastes 1:3–8; Philippians 4:6–7

The church offered earnest prayer to God for him. —Acts 12:5 (CEB)

This isn't a voice you've heard recently," my late-evening caller said. Although it had been months since we'd seen each other, I immediately recognized the voice of Carol, my dear friend since high school.

"Is everything all right?" I asked.

"That's why I'm calling," Carol replied. "Something very strange happened." She explained that her daughter just telephoned from a remote area in China, asking her to check on my sons, Patrick and Michael. "Denise hasn't seen either of them in thirty years, but she dreamed they were in danger and woke up with a strong urge to pray for them. She's continuing to pray and wants me to make sure they are safe and well."

"As far as I know, they're fine," I said, "but I'll text you as soon as I talk with them." Thankfully both boys were in good health and couldn't remember any recent close calls, although they were extremely grateful for Denise's concern and prayers.

I was thankful, too, but also puzzled. Could Denise have been mistaken? This certainly wasn't a miracle story of answered prayer. Or was it? Only God knows whether tragedy—physical or spiritual—might have happened if Denise hadn't listened to God's voice and prayed fervently for two men, from halfway across the world, who were practically strangers.

Lord, thank You for those who intercede for others in prayer.
Thank You for those who share concerns. And please,
fine-tune my spiritual ears so I may also be receptive to
Your voice and willing to act whenever You call.
—Penney Schwab

Digging Deeper: Psalm 91:9–11; Acts 10:30–33; James 5:16

Saturday, April 6

He cuts off every branch in me that bears no fruit, while every branch that does bear fruit he prunes so that it will be even more fruitful.
—John 15:2 (NIV)

The doorbell rang. A man stood on the porch, holding a box of roses for my wife, Pat. In our community, the Lions Club takes orders for roses early in the year. When Rose Day Saturday arrives in April, I am always surprised.

After bringing the roses to the kitchen, I grabbed and filled a vase with water, stirred in the packet of plant food, cut the stems, and nestled each bud within the greenery. Pat, coming in from shopping, exclaimed, "It must be Rose Day!" "Yep...I forgot, too...they're for you," I said.

Later, Pat trimmed away the leaves and shortened the stems. "I liked them just the way they were," I remarked. "Only making a few adjustments...wait and see," she responded. More annoyed than amused, I returned to cutting the grass. By the time I came back inside, the roses were out of my mind and I was surprised anew. With the excess greenery cut away, the velvety red blossoms were fully visible rather than hidden like Easter eggs. And Pat had come up with more surprises, too—a single rose in a small vase on my desk and another arrangement with three roses in our bedroom.

The pruning produced three stunning displays and got me thinking about where I need to do some cutting. I can start by working on my desire for control and allowing others' creativity to enhance my day. They were Pat's roses, after all. I can cut out sharing too many opinions, to better understand what my friends think. I also need to prune out the self-focus that keeps me from seeing the needs of others I walk by each day.

> *Dear God, help us cut out the dead branches in our lives.*
> *Guide us to find the ones we don't see. Amen.*
> —John Dilworth

Digging Deeper: John 3:30; Luke 13:9

PRAYING THROUGH THE PSALMS
Never Stop Praising God

Praise God in his sanctuary. —Psalm 150:1 (NIV)

A few years ago, my husband, Rick, and I found a church closer to home. Soon we discovered something unusual. Every Saturday night at 9:15 since the church was established thirty years ago, the congregation has been invited to attend a prayer meeting.

"Want to go?" Rick asked.

He'd gone to church as a child, but not like I did. My family showed up "every time the doors opened." Sunday mornings, Sunday nights, Tuesday night visitation, and Wednesday night youth. Maybe an extra night seemed like a treat to him. Not to me.

"I want to see what it's all about," he said.

I already knew. Dread filled me for the boredom ahead.

A few hours later, we entered the dimly lit sanctuary. A tingling sensation covered me, as though this night might be different.

After we sang a couple of songs, the pastor prayed, "Lord, put us under the waterfall of Your words." I imagined a beautiful scene— God's voice raining over us like manna from heaven.

He reminded us that Israel forgot to thank Him for His faithfulness.

When I closed my eyes to thank Him, holy murmurings filled the sanctuary as everyone around me praised God for great things He'd done. Years of memories returned—times He'd proven His faithfulness.

"Lord, twenty-five years ago, I was afraid to have another baby, but You created Thomas. Two years earlier, we'd buried his infant brother. Last week, You provided a job for our daughter Jamie. In 2004, You set our daughter Katie free from anorexia."

I could've praised Him in the sanctuary all night long.

> *Father, "Your faithfulness continues through all generations"*
> *(Psalm 100:5).*
> —Julie Garmon

Digging Deeper: Psalm 135:1–3, 150:2–6

Monday, April 8

Watch and pray, lest you enter into temptation. The spirit indeed is willing, but the flesh is weak. —Matthew 26:41 (NKJV)

I'd never met a crossword puzzle I didn't like. Not to say I'd be able to finish each one, but I wasn't about to let one go untried. It got to the point that if I found a puzzle, I dropped what I was doing, put things off, or pretended to listen to someone, in order to work on it. That's why when I announced I was giving up crosswords for Lent, my husband raised his eyebrows and wisely said nothing.

I placed a Bible beside my half-completed book of crosswords on a shelf in the back room to remind me of Jesus's forty days of temptation. I continued bringing home the free classified ads, which I only get for the puzzle inside, but I dutifully stacked them by the Bible. *Whom do you serve?* I asked myself whenever I found an excuse to wander near my growing puzzle collection.

Not only did I resist temptation during Lent, but by the time Easter came, I didn't miss the puzzles like I thought I would. In fact, I felt freed up to do other things. I realized I'd been serving them like a god, wasting so much time on games.

Although Easter is long past, I'm in no rush to work crosswords again. I might eventually, but I doubt I'll crave them like I did before. I didn't realize how addicted I'd become. This lesson in Lent has changed me. Christ won a victory over death, and I've won a victory over my weakness. It might be only a small thing, but if I do enough small things, they add up to something big. Praise the Lord, indeed!

Thank You, Lord, for opening my eyes. You alone have transformed a sacrifice into a blessing. Hallelujah!
—Erika Bentsen

Digging Deeper: Psalm 71:1–5; Mark 14:38

Since our friendship with God was restored by the death of his Son while we were still his enemies, we will certainly be saved through the life of his Son. —Romans 5:10 (NLT)

I don't like the line in that song," my husband said on the way home from Sunday morning service.

"Which song?" I asked. His comment was so out-of-the-blue. My husband is one of the most positive people I know, rarely criticizing anything.

"The one about Jesus's resurrection," he replied. "It says, 'He arose with a mighty triumph o'er His foes.' That's not what happened. We were all His foes, because our sinful nature puts us at enmity with God. In spite of that, Jesus loved us enough to die for us. So when He arose, He wasn't triumphing over us. He was triumphing for us."

"Wow." I agreed, "You're right."

I never in a million years would've thought of those lyrics the way my husband did. I guess the writer of the hymn had the same human perspective I and many others were likely to have. The resurrection could have been the ultimate "so there!" moment. Jesus would have been completely justified if, upon exiting the tomb, He'd triumphantly declared, "See? I told you I was the Son of God!"

But that's not Who Jesus is. Instead, the resurrection was the most un-"I told you so" moment in the entire history of the world. In His crucifixion, Jesus took what we deserve instead of giving us what we deserve. In His resurrection, Jesus rejoiced with us that death was defeated. He didn't see His glorious resurrection as a triumph over those who put Him in the grave, because no one had the power to put Him there; He chose to go. The triumph was over death, sin, and our separation from Him. We were God's enemies, yet He died for us!

As the lyrics to another old hymn say, "I scarce can take it in."

Lord, I praise You that Your thoughts are not my thoughts!
—Ginger Rue

Digging Deeper: Isaiah 55:8; Luke 6:35

Real wisdom, God's wisdom, begins with a holy life and is characterized by getting along with others. It is gentle and reasonable. —James 3:17 (MSG)

My husband, Gene, and I squabble at the dining room table when income tax time rolls around. For months he spreads out endless stacks of paper, all over the table and every piece of furniture in the dining room. He "arranges" it on the floor, too. I usually stand with my hands on my hips, whining.

This year I screamed, "I hate clutter!" Gene shouted, "Don't lecture me!" We were arguing so loudly we almost didn't hear the doorbell. "You get it!" he ordered. "I can't be disturbed."

"Of course, Your Majesty," I snarled, then jerked the door open forcefully and looked down.

"Hello, Mrs. Marion. I'm selling these pictures I drew." Her voice was so tender I had to lean way down to hear the little six-year-old girl from across the street.

I immediately lowered my voice and breathed more regularly. "Hi, Mary Beth. Come on in and tell us about your pictures."

"Thank you." She sat in a chair Gene pulled out for her, feet dangling. "Someone we know in another state has a very sick dog, and my sister and I are sending a contribution."

Gene made room on the table, and she spread out the bold, happy pictures.

"They are beautiful," I murmured, near tears. Gene reached into his pocket and pulled out more than the dollar she asked for each picture. We made our selections.

"Thank you both." The child smiled endlessly.

"Thank you, honey." Gene beamed—the real Gene.

I hugged her—the real me.

> *Thank You, Jesus. Little children still show us the way.*
> —Marion Bond West

Digging Deeper: Galatians 5:22; Colossians 3:12

All who are victorious will be clothed in white. I will never erase their names from the Book of Life, but I will announce before my Father and his angels that they are mine. —Revelation 3:5 (NLT)

M aybe this year," I mused as I looked at the healthy green leaves in our waterfall flower bed. Heavy rains on Maundy Thursday produced profuse purple blooms in our backyard iris garden, but the ones in the front still hadn't budded. I hoped they'd resurrect soon.

I collect irises from friends. Double-blooming purple from Marge. Petite lavender ones from Bonnie. Yellow from Nana. Those I'd planted in the front yard were from Marinan, Mom's best friend. She'd thinned hers and shared some with me months before she was killed in a car crash. It had been two years since I replanted them. I had no idea what color they were and worried I'd planted them too deep. Would they ever bloom?

I missed Marinan, so it was important to have a remembrance. Besides an affinity for irises, we shared a love of God. She often focused on Jesus by putting herself second. She even planned her funeral to glorify Christ rather than mourn her earthly death.

Up at dawn for Easter services, I walked past the front window and spied a single white bloom in my flower bed. My heart soared. Marinan's iris! It was just like her to give me a sign on Easter morning.

After church, I surveyed the simple, white iris. How could it be? So many blossoms, yet only one bloom. I counted the buds. Holy chills ran down my back. Surrounding that single white flower were twelve buds on this Resurrection Sunday.

Marinan's iris proclaimed the Easter message: He is risen!

God, I praise You for the miracle of Easter.
—Stephanie Thompson

Digging Deeper: Roman 6:4–5; Matthew 17:2

Friday, April 12

Lord, your love reaches to the heavens. —Psalm 36:5 (NCV)

It was Easter, and the family gathered to celebrate the resurrection of our Lord. The big meal was over, and the dishwasher loaded. While the family was occupied with grandkids racing hither and yon, and some adults napped, I took a well-deserved break and settled into my most comfortable chair, taking the chance to hold our sleeping four-month-old grandson, Mason Dale Mihai Macomber. As many know, little in life is more relaxing than holding a sleeping infant.

Our son Ted met his wife at a conference for those who had recently experienced the loss of a loved one. Ted was attending after the death of his brother Dale. There, he crossed paths with Irina, who had lost both parents within a short amount of time. After this chance meeting, they fell in love and were married within eighteen months. Mason is their first child.

As our new grandson slept contentedly in my arms, I thought about how much joy this precious baby had brought back into our lives. Suddenly I experienced the most peculiar sensation that someone was with me, someone invisible. Nothing like this had ever happened to me before. Someone was reaching out to me from across that great chasm on the other side of life. I never had the opportunity to meet my daughter-in-law's family, but I knew with every fiber of my being who was standing close by my side in that moment. With my spiritual eyes, I recognized the woman instantly: Irina's mother, Pepa Laura Dogaru. She spoke to me, from one grandmother to another. She reached out in love and whispered in my heart, *Love him for the both of us.*

And I do.

Thank You, Lord, that love reaches to the heavens and back.
—Debbie Macomber

Digging Deeper: Luke 11:9–13

I praise and honor the Lord. —Exodus 15:2 (CEV)

Although I braked my blue Subaru at the stop sign, my thoughts whirled with distress, totally unaware of Peter*, who sat in the passenger seat. He was a dignified, white-haired World War II veteran I'd picked up to bring to church.

It was a few days before Good Friday, and my town's storefronts brimmed with Easter bunnies—but nothing of the true meaning of the holiday. *Oh, God, my heart grieves when I see how some have forgotten You. What can I do?*

I accelerated, and we passed the post office. Peter asked, "Why is the United States flag flying at half-mast?"

I frowned and shrugged. "I missed the news."

Intently, Peter looked at me and mused, "I wonder what would happen if Christians flew the flag at half-mast from Good Friday until Easter."

Peter's question challenged me. I'd never thought of Jesus as a national hero. He is the King of Kings, and He died for us. Would I fly the flag at half-mast?

On Main Street we passed rows of stores with Easter Bunny banners flapping in the breeze. Instead of whining about what others were doing, I could choose to do something. Ideas flooded my mind. Why not plan ahead and choose not to shop on Good Friday or Easter Sunday? Why not fly a Christian banner at home? Why not "opt out" of Easter commercialism? Peace flooded my heart as I took up Peter's challenge. Instead of going along with the masses, I'm going to show my allegiance to God and honor Him for His ultimate sacrifice.

> *Lord, give me creative ideas of how I can honor You in a visible way during the Easter holiday. Amen.*
> —Rebecca Ondov

Digging Deeper: Psalm 145:1–21; Daniel 4:34–35

*Name changed

UNEXPECTED GRACE: Loved Anyway

A very large crowd spread their cloaks on the road, while others cut branches from the trees and spread them on the road. The crowds that went ahead of him and those that followed shouted, "Hosanna in the highest!" —Matthew 21:8–9 (NIV)

I hadn't played tennis in decades, but my teenage son dragged me onto the court. Jonathan loves tennis. He can't put his racquet down. He's usually either on the courts at school or pounding a ball against the side of our house. "Come on, Dad. Let's play." "I have to warn you, I'm pretty good." Visions of glory days past danced in my head. Blistering serves. Dominance at the net. Unbeatable forehand. Quick feet. "Just don't cry when I beat you," I said.

Two minutes into our match, he said, "I'll start out easy on you."

"No way! Just give me a while." Well, "a while" wasn't enough. Age and time off had taken their toll. I wasn't as good as I remembered. I could barely run to the net. It was funny and a little sad. I was more rusty than I'd realized.

Jonathan tossed some friendly trash talk my way. "I guess you're not as good as you think you are." "Just for that, you're walking home," I joked.

But I thought about his gibe, as we walked to the car. God whispered His grace that day. I thought, No. I'm not as good as I think I am, but He loves me anyway.

The very next day, it struck me for the first time that Palm Sunday was also "Cloak Sunday." Crowds spread their cloaks on the ground in addition to palm fronds. God whispered a reminder to me. Just as Jesus trampled those garments, so He trampled my own self-righteous garments. No, I'm not as good as I think I am. But my Savior stooped to love me anyway.

Lord, never let me forget that I'm not as good as I think I am
but that You are always better than I can even imagine.
—Bill Giovannetti

Digging Deeper: Isaiah 61:10

UNEXPECTED GRACE: Rescuing Joy

He noticed a fig tree in full leaf a little way off, so he went over to see if he could find any figs. But there were only leaves because it was too early in the season for fruit. Then Jesus said to the tree, "May no one ever eat your fruit again!" —Mark 11:13–14 (NLT)

I caught two fish on one cast," my brother told me. We were each on the road, my brother driving home to Chicago while I drove to work in California, and were catching up by phone.

"What do you mean?" I said.

"Check your phone."

My brother had texted me a picture. He was holding up a thirty-three-inch northern pike. "Wow! How did you catch him?" I asked. "When I felt a hit," he said, "I started reeling in. A good-sized fish. Then, I got a second hit. Only this one was huge." I was confused. "So, two hits?"

"Yep. The first hit took my lure, a largemouth bass. But while I reeled him in, the northern pike grabbed the bass and wouldn't let go. I guess you could say he died of stubbornness."

Our conversation ranged to other topics. I shared how busy I was, how many projects I had my hands in. "Sometimes I feel the days and months just racing by," I said.

"It's an occupational hazard," my brother said. "Sometimes being a pastor can be more about the job than about God."

That grabbed my attention. "Maybe you're too busy, like Martha," he said. "Just hang with Jesus, like Mary. Don't let your joy and peace die because of stubbornness."

Our call ended, and I finished my drive to work, planning to slow down my hectic pace.

Lord, may Your grace and peace inside me shape
my life in the world outside me. Amen.
—Bill Giovannetti

Digging Deeper: 1 Samuel 16:7

Tuesday of Holy Week, April 16

UNEXPECTED GRACE: Joyful Sacrifice

For they all put in out of their abundance, but she out of her poverty put in all that she had, her whole livelihood. —Mark 12:44 (NKJV)

The red-capped bird caught my eye as it flew to the scraggly pine. I'd seen that woodpecker plenty as it knocked away at the barren tree through the rainy winter. What I hadn't seen was the perfectly round hole he created high at the top. He hopped up the trunk and disappeared into the hole.

Excited peeping filled the air. Father bird was feeding his hatchlings. I couldn't see it, but I imagined him carefully feeding each one. His head reappeared in the hole, and he flew off to the south. The little birds protested but eventually quieted down.

I was continuing my chores when my teenage daughter walked by. I told Josie about the birds. I pointed out the round hole, just in time to see the mother woodpecker arrive. She hopped up the trunk and disappeared. Her offspring chirped their excitement.

It was a great moment to share with Josie. She was excited. "I so wish we could see the baby woodpeckers." Mother's head appeared in the hole, and she looked around for a bit and flew away to the north.

Then father bird returned, hopped inside, fed his excited brood, and flew away. Mother bird repeated the cycle. And on and on it went. It was endless. They gave their all.

I smiled at Josie. "Now you know what parenthood feels like."

"I'm just glad you're not feeding us worms," she quipped. Josie went to do homework, and I went on to my chores. As I contemplated the great blessing of home and family, the shirt on my back and the pillow every night for my head, I felt a lump form in my throat. I whispered a prayer to my Savior, thanking Him for the profound sacrifice He made to care for me so well.

Gracious Lord, You gave Your all to care for me, and I am ever grateful.
—Bill Giovannetti

Digging Deeper: 2 Corinthians 8:9

UNEXPECTED GRACE: Invisible Grace

*But as many as received Him, to them He gave the right to become
children of God, to those who believe in His name: who were born, not
of blood, nor of the will of the flesh, nor of the will of man, but of God.*
—John 1:12–13 (NKJV)

I t was a difficult season in my life and ministry. I wondered why God
felt so far away. Had He forgotten me?

During that season, our family visited Chicago with some friends.
We bought pricey tour bus tickets to see the sights. The ticket agent
explained how it worked. "Ten red double-decker buses keep circu-
lating along the same route," she said. "They stop at a dozen tourist
spots." She slid a map over the counter to show the attractions at each
spot. We could get on or off any bus at any stop, visit the attractions
for as long as we liked, and then catch the next red bus to the following
destination. As the buses rolled, knowledgeable tour guides pointed
out fascinating features of the city's architecture and history. It was a
fantastic way to see a lot of sights in one day.

We weren't sure who loved it more—the kids or the adults.

The ticket agent emphasized one point, however. "Be sure you're on
the last bus by five p.m.," she said. "You have unlimited on-off privileges till then. But if you miss that last bus, you'll be stuck walking back
to where you started."

"So the buses just keep rolling along," I said, "with or without us."

"Sounds like God's plan," my friend Pastor Todd said. "When we
think He's absent, His plan still rolls along. Whether we see Him or
not, He's still working His plan."

Just what I needed to hear. Even when I can't see His hand, I can still
trust His heart.

Father, teach me to trust Your loving heart even when I can't see Your face.
—Bill Giovannetti

Digging Deeper: Romans 8:28

Maundy Thursday, April 18

UNEXPECTED GRACE: Soaring Protection

Going at once to Jesus, Judas said, "Greetings, Rabbi!" and kissed him.
Jesus replied, "Do what you came for, friend." Then the men stepped
forward, seized Jesus and arrested him. —Matthew 26:49–50 (NIV)

W e carried cushions and lawn chairs from the lanai, through the
house and into the garage. We were vacationing on Hawaii's
majestic Big Island as a rare hurricane bore down on us. The state
issued warnings to bring small items inside to keep them from blowing
away and causing injury.

The blue skies and gentle breezes gave no indication of the storm
about to hit.

We continued our vacation. The pool. The beach. Lunch. A few
clouds skittered by, but the skies stayed sunny. By dinner no rain had
fallen, and only a few wind gusts kicked up sand at the beach.

I asked "Uncle Greg," who ran the surf shack, about it. "What happened to the hurricane?" "Oh, it hit the island," he said, "but on the other
side. It's still whipping up storms over there. On this side, the mountain
protected us."

He was referring to Mauna Loa, which, when measured from the
seabed, is the tallest mountain in the world. Its massive bulk dominates
the skyline from anywhere on the island.

The mountain protected us. Those words stuck with me all day. I
thought of how the mountain of God's grace protected me from the
storms. From life's trials. Even from my own failures and wrong choices.
I had a Savior Who would call me "friend," even on my worst day ever.

That night, I told my family what Uncle Greg had said. We thanked
God for the mountain of His love in Christ Jesus that protected us all
our lives.

Thank You, Jesus, for the mountain of Calvary's grace that protects us
from the storms of life—and even from our own bad choices—forever.
   —Bill Giovannetti

Digging Deeper: Psalm 121

UNEXPECTED GRACE: The Depths of Love

When Jesus had received the sour wine, He said, "It is finished!"
And bowing His head, He gave up His spirit. —John 19:30 (NKJV)

I guess it's truly riverfront property now," John said.

We were standing on his back deck, looking down a steep drop to the swollen river below. "You promise this thing is stable?" I said.

A careworn smile creased his face. "According to the geological engineers, it is. At least for now."

John's home, high above the Sacramento River, had suffered a mudslide. What had been a sixty-foot-wide backyard vanished overnight. Unusually heavy rains, for months, were the culprit.

"I'm at peace with it," he said. "Everything is the Lord's anyway, right?"

His spirit inspired me. We walked inside. Over coffee, John explained that the engineers said he had to drive concrete anchors deep into the earth to prevent the whole house from falling in. It would cost as much as his house was worth. Insurance wouldn't cover it. It was more than he could afford.

Then my dad had an idea. "Why don't you move the house?" They did some research. It was affordable, and John already owned the lot next door. They had a plan, and everything was in the works. I asked how he was handling it.

I'll never forget John's answer. "God has already given me Jesus, the cross, and my salvation. If He never does another good thing for me, He's already given far more than I deserve."

I drove home that day, singing my thanksgiving to a Savior Whose whole world collapsed that He might give everything for me.

Lord, anchor my soul to the bedrock truth of
salvation through Calvary's love. Amen.
—Bill Giovannetti

Digging Deeper: Romans 5:6–8

UNEXPECTED GRACE: Coming Home

They returned and prepared spices and fragrant oils. And they rested on the Sabbath according to the commandment. —Luke 23:56 (NKJV)

The tiny puppy felt lighter than a bird. She snuggled immediately against my chest as I carried her to the car. Black eyes blinked from her furry white face. Love at first sight.

It was a busy time for my family, so a trip to Hawaii from a Northern California airport had offered a much-needed break. I flew back alone, one day early, to pick up little Pippy from Southern California. I would return to pick up my wife and kids at the airport that night—a ten-hour round-trip before the four-hour trip home.

I looked at Pippy in the carrier beside me. She whined and scratched to get out. Did she need a potty break? Would she settle down? She missed snuggling with her siblings. Now all she had was me and a very long drive. I whispered a prayer for wisdom and strength. I needed it more than I realized. Little did I know an accident ahead would stop traffic cold for almost three hours.

As we inched along the highway, I had an idea. I reached over and picked her up. She was as light as a feather, small as a bundled pair of socks. I gently set her behind my neck, between my back and the car's headrest. Pippy snuggled in, enjoying the sights out the window. She had found her happy place, nuzzled against the skin of my neck. Soon, I heard the sweet sound of gentle puppy snoring.

She rested. My heart, too, rested. Traffic came to a stop, and there was nothing to do but wait. And look forward to introducing Pippy to a family filled with anticipation.

So we waited and inched our way four hundred miles to the airport—Pippy, the puppy-turned-neck-warmer, and me, a guy who just needed to breathe.

When the road ahead is long, teach me, Father, to snuggle into Your love.
—Bill Giovannetti

Digging Deeper: Matthew 11:29

Say to the whole congregation of the people of Israel, "Come near before the Lord, for he has heard." —Exodus 16:9 (ESV)

On Sunday morning, rushing to my car, I clipped a handful of purple azaleas. *They're past their prime, but they'll have to do,* I thought. Over several decades, I'd come to anticipate the congregational participation of my church's Easter service. Upon arrival, it was always hard to miss a barren wooden cross—about three feet high, covered with chicken wire—in front of the altar. At the appointed time, while singing hallelujah hymns, children and adults brought forward cut blossoms—from yards or floral shops—to "flower the cross." Old rugged boards were typically transformed into a beautiful, structured, multicolored bouquet that adorned the sanctuary throughout the liturgy.

But this year new leadership changed things up. The flowering took place after the recessional and at the outdoor altar, as a prelude to the egg hunt. *Come, ye children.* Most of the adults held back or headed to coffee hour. Not I. I wanted to be part of this—though by now my wilted azaleas represented age and decay more than vibrant life. *Should I bow out and let the children decorate without me?* As if to answer my question, I caught sight of a dandelion in a sidewalk crack just ahead. For this moment, it wasn't a misplaced weed but a fresh addition to—an affirmation of—my contribution. I plucked the yellow flower, approached the garden altar, and slipped my few stems into open spots in the wire. As I stepped back from the cross, the sight of the colorful collective inspired my Eastertide prayer. . . .

Lord, at Your cross and resurrection altar, You welcome all of us and our hallelujah gifts—even the most humble.
—Evelyn Bence

Digging Deeper: 1 Corinthians 15:3–10

Monday, April 22

UNEXPECTED GRACE: Fill My Heart with Hope

He is not here; for He is risen, as He said. Come, see the place where the Lord lay. —Matthew 28:6 (NKJV)

Our old pickup bounced across the grassy field. My son, in the back of the truck with our fishing gear, loved it. The little pond ahead glistened in the sun, promising a memory. A picture-perfect day at our favorite fishing hole. Seconds later, the wheels were spinning, the truck leaned hard to the right, and we floated to a stop in the middle of a field on a thousand-acre ranch, miles from anywhere.

Both tires on the right side had sunk in mud up to the car frame. It turned out the rancher had dug a trench and filled it in, and steady rains had made the softened soil quicksand. We were suctioned in, but I was concerned. We trekked up to the rancher's house and rang the bell. Soon, Mr. Shoup was trying to yank me out with his tractor.

The pickup didn't budge. We pushed and pulled, and spun the wheels. But the tires were buried and weren't getting out. The Shoups graciously lent me a spare vehicle, and Jonathan and I drove home. We talked about feeling stuck yet keeping faith with God. My son sensed my concerns. "Don't worry, Dad, you'll get it out." He had more faith than I did. That was Friday.

It wasn't until Sunday afternoon that my buddy Gary followed me to the ranch. We shoveled. Hours later, his giant truck yanked me out of the mud. Sweet, mud-splattered victory.

Jonathan and I created a memory that weekend. Not about fishing but something better—trusting God, Who brings life out of death.

> *Father, may the promise of Your Son's resurrection*
> *always fill my heart with hope.*
> —Bill Giovannetti

Digging Deeper: Romans 8:11

By My great strength and outstretched arm, I made the earth, and the people, and animals on the face of the earth. —Jeremiah 27:5 (HCSB)

It was the men's workday at church, and I was working in the garden. I know next to nothing about plants. But I love a garden in spring, the tulips trembling in a cool breeze, the lilacs spreading their intoxicating fragrance, and the cherry trees dripping blossoms on the ground like snow.

"You need to trim the old leaves off to make room for the new shoots," my friend instructed me as I knelt over these shrubs that needed a haircut (if I were a true gardener, I'd be able to tell you their names). I clipped away and thought of what Jesus said about pruning: "He prunes every branch that produces fruit so that it will produce more fruit" (John 15:2). Wasn't that what I was doing? Didn't I need to do some pruning on myself? Get rid of that callous thought, cut out that self-defeating monologue, dig my roots deeper into the nourishing ground of faith, trim back anger and resentment.

No wonder God planted the first man and woman in a garden. It's a richly satisfying place to be. The next day, Sunday, we sang one of my favorite hymns: "All things bright and beautiful, all creatures great and small, all things wise and wonderful, the Lord God made them all." We sang as we marched around the garden, blessing it. But the blessings work both ways for anyone who lingers in the wonders of God's creation.

I thank You, Lord, for the beauties of Your creation.
May I be a good steward of it.
—Rick Hamlin

Digging Deeper: Psalm 89:11; Acts 4:24

Wednesday, April 24

SAYING GOODBYE TO MY VETERANS
Looking for the Supernatural

Jesus looked at them and said, "With man this is impossible,
but with God all things are possible." —Matthew 19:26 (NIV)

To garner more enthusiasm for our medical center's book project, I shared staff memories in the classes I taught on patient-centered care. In my research on the power of personal stories, I'd learned our brains are more active when we're hearing or telling stories, and that doing so actually releases endorphins, the body's feel-good chemicals.

As I closed my talks, I told of a nurse, Julius, who once tended a veteran at a West Virginia community hospital. The man had cancer and was given only six months to live. Depressed about his recent news, the veteran said to Julius, "Tell me something good, son." Julius is from Nigeria, not Appalachia, and he wanted to say the right thing to bond with his patient from a vastly different culture. He took a chance at sharing his faith. Cupping his large black hands around the veteran's smaller white ones, he raised them toward the sky. "I respect the medical profession, sir, with all that is within me. Still, I have to share a little secret. You're in good hands with God. He's the only One Who really knows your future."

Years later, Julius was making rounds when a veteran's family nearly ran him down. "You were giving my grandfather his chemo at the other hospital, and you told him a secret," they said. "That he was in good hands. Every day after that, the two of you agreed that God, not the medical profession, was Papaw's source. Well, those words became his prayer, Julius, and I have to tell you: Papaw didn't die in six months like that doctor predicted. He lived five wonderful years."

> *Thank You for reminding me of Your supernatural*
> *touch in veterans' health care, Lord.*
> —Roberta Messner

Digging Deeper: Mark 10:27; Luke 18:27; Jeremiah 32:27

Do not merely listen to the word, and so deceive yourselves.
Do what it says. —James 1:22 (NIV)

It was the grunt that got my attention, and then a small, panicked whine brought me face to face with any parent's nightmare: my almost-two-year-old's head was stuck in a railing at the theme park. We'd come to Disney prepared. A five-to-two adult-to-child ratio provided plenty of hands to deal with snack, diaper, and nap needs, and yet no one had noticed Jake was stuck. I tried to bend the wrought-iron bars. Jake cried out as the bars scraped against his temples.

"I have lotion!" a mom behind us called out, likely remembering the old butter-the-heads trick of getting kids out of crib rails and stair railings. I was debating the merits of this when I realized a dad behind me had been repeating himself in a low, calm voice since the panic started.

"Turn his shoulders, and push him through," he said again. When he caught my eye, he explained, "The biggest part of him is already through. Just turn his shoulders and push, then lift him back over the railing." He gestured to his family—seven little boys sat quietly. This guy had seen some stuck heads.

We turned Jake's shoulders and, sure enough, he slipped right through. Later as we relived the moment, I realized we'd all heard the dad repeating himself, but no one had tuned in because his voice was so calm and steady. We chose instead to listen to other, louder voices of help and our own panicked thoughts.

Now that Jake isn't stuck in the railings, it's easy to recall that God often speaks to us in a low, level voice—ones we have to listen to in order to hear. I know now to listen for that voice not only in others (thank you, kind dad of seven!) but also in my heart.

Lord, help me tune out the noise that drowns out Your voice.
Let Your words be my guide today and always.
—Ashley Kappel

Digging Deeper: Proverbs 16:20; Psalm 116:1–2

Friday, April 26

My Lord God will wipe away the tears from all faces.
—Isaiah 25:8 (JPS)

The day I walked into the bathroom and found L. E. on the rug in front of my sink, rather than the rug in front of Keith's sink, I realized she had finally become my cat. For three years after Keith died, I thought it was a lost cause. I knew she was grieving Keith from the first, and since I, too, was grieving, I hoped we could comfort each other, but she stubbornly refused to acknowledge it as a companionship of loss. She clung to her memories—lying pressed against his slippers in the bathroom or sleeping on his side of the bench at the bottom of our bed—without seeming to understand I would cuddle and pet her just as I petted Anjin, the greyhound.

L. E. always seemed far more aloof than she had ever been with Keith. She never meowed at me, never curled up in my lap on the sofa. I felt she wanted me to leave her alone, so I did. I had to be patient. Every so often, I tried to play with her, but she just walked away, tail in the air.

In the beginning of the fourth year, Anjin had to have her teeth cleaned, and that involved my taking her to the vet early in the morning and returning home without her. The house seemed so empty. My dog's comforting presence following me around or pressing up against my side was not there, and I missed it. The emptiness reminded me of missing Keith.

For the first time in a long while, I cried and hugged L. E. because I really needed her. Later that afternoon, she moved to my side of the bathroom. Even after I brought Anjin home, L. E. stayed by my side.

Thank You for reminding me that reaching out,
to You and to others, can bring rewards.
—Rhoda Blecker

Digging Deeper: Ezekiel 16:8; Exodus 6:5

Do not forget the things your eyes have seen or let them fade from your heart as long as you live. Teach them to your children and to their children after them. —Deuteronomy 4:9 (NIV)

I want to have a hundredth birthday party for Dottie," I casually told my husband, Lynn. He looked at me strangely, probably because my mother, Dottie, had died thirty-three years ago. So I hurried to defend my idea.

"Some of her grandchildren and all of ours don't know her. I want them to know her."

Dottie's birthday was a few weeks away, so I created the vision for this extended family party. I made invitations and soon more than forty people said they'd come. I rented a tent so we'd have plenty of room for the twenty-plus kids to run around. I planned the menu, pulled pictures out of old photo albums to make poster collages, and scoured area grocery stores for yellow daisies, her favorite flowers.

The late-April date seemed doable in a tent, but a slushy spring snowstorm surprised us the day before the party. So we canceled the tent and moved lots of furniture out of our main living area to squeeze in more tables and chairs.

We ate her favorite foods and told stories about her sense of humor, fierce determination, and family loyalty. We topped the evening off with heaping plates of her strawberry shortcake. It was a great celebration.

The next day, our three-year-old granddaughter Genesee came back with her mom to help us clean up. She scooted a chair over by some of the pictures and climbed up.

"There's your mommy," she told me. "I like Dottie."

Lord, thank You for the families You give us that help us know where we came from and who we are, from generation to generation.
—Carol Kuykendall

Digging Deeper: Psalm 102:18; Luke 1:48–49

Sunday, April 28

Let us keep our eyes fixed on Jesus, on whom our faith depends from beginning to end. —Hebrews 12:2 (GNT)

My jogging route has some paved roads, but mostly it's a zigzag of rocky dirt switchbacks through scraggly woods.

Dirt roads are best for bird-watching—especially, I've noticed, if I look straight ahead into the trees as I approach a turn. Somehow, though I hear birds all around me and sometimes see them shoot from one side of the road to the other, I rarely glimpse any in the trees beside me as I jog past.

I've pondered this phenomenon for years. Is it just physics—the turn of the road, pinching two clumps of perches into one to reveal twice as many birds? Or is it biology? Is the crook of a road somehow safer for birds, so they prefer to perch there?

Today I got my answer. I was jogging along, peering vainly into the woods ahead for the pair of phoebes I always see there—whose conversation I was hearing—and I stopped to fish a pebble out of my shoe. When I stood back up, those phoebes were in the trees beside me.

They probably perch as often there as in the trees before me, I realized. Not seeing them there was a problem of my perspective. Typically, to locate a bird, you have to see it move. I can't miss a bird flying through the stationary trees in front of me, but from my jogging perspective, the trees I pass appear to move, making the birds' movement harder to see.

That reminded me of Peter walking out to Jesus on the Sea of Galilee. Looking straight ahead, he saw Jesus beckoning him to come. Seeing the wind-tossed waves though, he sank. Matthew ascribes his loss of footing to fear, but Jesus accuses Peter of doubt. In the movement and noise of the waves, Peter could no longer discern Jesus waving, perhaps calling, in the distance.

Help me keep my gaze on You, Lord.
—Patty Kirk

Digging Deeper: Colossians 1:1–4

See, I am doing a new thing! Now it springs up; do you not perceive it?
—Isaiah 43:19 (NIV)

The texts came in at twenty-minute intervals: a photo of the George Washington Bridge, a tree beside the Hudson River, the view of New Jersey. My thirteen-year-old was scootering along the bike path that runs the length of Manhattan. Stephen is not athletic, but he loves being by the water.

"Don't go so far you can't make it back," I texted him. Thinking ahead is not an adolescent forte.

"I'm fine," came the reply.

"Did you really go the whole way?" I texted later, amazed. This was not like my son at all. He was at an age where life was all about video games and trying to get out of homework. I looked up the distance: thirteen miles.

"I'm going to come back, too!" my son replied.

That seemed a bit much. "Do you have a MetroCard if it gets dark or rains? Take the subway home if you get tired," I cautioned.

"I'm fine."

Over the next two hours, more pictures pinged on my phone as my son documented his way back. As far as I knew, he had no cash and hadn't taken a water bottle. It was possible he didn't really have a MetroCard. But since he was sending regular updates (when did this sense of responsibility emerge?), I shrugged and made a big supper.

The sun had set by the time Stephen arrived home. He was happy, tired, and understandably proud of himself. He ate (a lot), showered, and fell asleep quickly. The next weekend he did it again.

> *Lord, people change, often for the good, even*
> *when we're not noticing. Thank You for that.*
> —Julia Attaway

Digging Deeper: 2 Peter 3:9

Tuesday, April 30

He has made everything beautiful in its time. —Ecclesiastes 3:11 (NIV)

Our cat, Kirby, is always getting into trouble. This time he almost killed himself swallowing a spool of thread. The emergency vet said we saved his life by bringing him in. He took X-rays and kept him overnight for observation.

The next morning Kirby came home, ears-back and angry, confused and exhausted. We were told to keep him isolated, monitor the litter box, and return immediately if he was sick to his stomach.

I stayed awake all night with Kirby beside me. I watched odd movies that only seem to play in the wee hours of the morning and prayed my way to sunrise, trying not to think of a dire outcome.

The next morning Kirby went in for a follow-up visit. The vet was optimistic the thread would pass on its own. If not, Kirby would need immediate and expensive surgery.

By the fourth day, I worried the operation might need to happen. The entire afternoon, I prayed, "Please, please help him."

Right before bed, I went into Kirby's sequestered room. I combed the litter box as I'd done a hundred times. This time, the thread was there, the evidence, the source of my anxiety. I hugged Kirby and kissed him. *Phew!*

> *Thank You! Thank You! Heavenly Father, the next time*
> *I get myself all stressed out, I'll remember that*
> *litter box... and try to have faith in Your perfect timing.*
> —Sabra Ciancanelli

Digging Deeper: Lamentations 3:25–26; Ecclesiastes 3:1

UNDER GOD'S WINGS

1 _____

2 _____

3 _____

4 _____

5 _____

6 _____

7 _____

8 _____

9 _____

10 _____

11 _____

12 _____

13 _____

14 _____

15 _____

April

16 _____

17 _____

18 _____

19 _____

20 _____

21 _____

22 _____

23 _____

24 _____

25 _____

26 _____

27 _____

28 _____

29 _____

30 _____

MAY

Trust in the Lord forever, for the Lord, the
Lord himself, is the Rock eternal.

—Isaiah 26:4 (NIV)

Wednesday, May 1

And he said: "Truly I tell you, unless you change and become like little children, you will never enter the kingdom of heaven. Therefore, whoever takes the lowly position of this child is the greatest in the kingdom of heaven. And whoever welcomes one such child in my name welcomes me." —Matthew 18:3–5 (NIV)

"*M*ama, Mama—stop! Quick!"

I white-knuckled the brakes on my bike's handlebars, my heart lurching into my throat. The tires locked, skidding on the roadside gravel. Breathless, I turned. "What? What is it!" I asked my four-year-old, who was seated behind me in her little bike trailer.

"I saw a dandelion," she said. "I *have* to go sniff it!"

My fear rushed out of me, annoyance taking its place. *A dandelion! Good grief.* The way she'd yelled, I thought something terrible had happened. I glanced at my watch. At this rate, we'd never make it to our appointment on time. But, seeing her hopeful expression, I couldn't say no. "OK," I said. "Go sniff it." Joyfully she clambered from the trailer and bounded over to the flower growing at the curbside. When she turned back to me, her eyes alight and her nose yellow with pollen, the dandelion was clutched in her small fist.

"For you, Mama," she said, holding it out to me, a happy smile stretching across her sweet face. My heart melted. Indeed.

Thank You, Lord, for my child, who reminds me daily that we are surrounded by beauty and simple opportunities for joy.
—Erin Janoso

Digging Deeper: 1 Peter 2:2

I love those who love me, and those who seek me diligently find me.
—Proverbs 8:17 (ESV)

My youngest two boys were yo-yo wild. Wooden yo-yos. Plastic yo-yos. Aluminum yo-yos. Yo-yos with gears. Gabriel and Isaiah stood in sunlight, a string length apart.

"See? Rock-the-Cradle," eight-year-old Isaiah said. His hands held a string triangle, and his green Duncan whooshed through the center.

"Watch me," ten-year-old Gabriel said. "I can do The Elevator." With a flick of the wrist, his bright blue yo-yo sailed up and down a doubled-over string.

Smiles broke bright and wide. Theirs. Mine. I encouraged my sons and admired their determination. Yo-yo tricks aren't for the faint-spirited. Tricks like The Eiffel Tower and Hop-the-Fence demanded a price. Time. Patience. Recently an antique glass lamp. But what spoke to my spirit was the boys' perseverance. They yo-yoed in between chores. At recess. They did Walked-the-Dog while I walked our yellow Labrador.

My boys' example lends itself to my spiritual life. I want to live in the fullness of God's grace. I want His love to penetrate every decision, outlook, perception, action, and reaction. I want the Spirit to direct my words and desires. When I'm intentional about seeking the Lord, fruit flows. I'm more patient. Peaceful. Forgiving. When I'm too busy, when I don't pursue Him with passion, it's just as evident. I criticize, complain. I trade daily bread for daily grind and wonder why I'm weary.

"Mom," Isaiah said, "give it a try!" He placed his yo-yo in my hand. I slipped the string around my finger, raised my arm, and let it go.

It floundered. My boys giggled, and I considered a simple truth: perseverance pays.

Lord, let me persevere in passion for You. Amen.
—Shawnelle Eliasen

Digging Deeper: Jeremiah 29:13; 1 Chronicles 16:11; Psalm 119:10

Friday, May 3

When anxiety was great within me, your consolation brought me joy.
—Psalm 94:19 (NIV)

I woke up from a dream, my heart beating fast. It took me a few seconds to realize I wasn't in Brooklyn anymore. I was back in Kansas, at my parents' house.

The week before, my husband, Zach, and I moved back home after eight years. Most of our friends expected us to stay in New York. So when we announced we were coming home, many of them had questions. It was confusing to explain why we were giving up our life there, but the answer was clear between God and me. I know He put in my heart that longing to return home.

In my dream, I had run into friends from high school at a coffee shop.

"What are you doing here?" said one who was behind the counter.

It was hard for me to maintain eye contact with her. She handed me a cup of coffee, and I sat at a table. More friends sat around me at other tables. They whispered to one another and looked at me. Finally one got up and came over. "Why did you give up your dream and move back home?" I woke up before I answered her.

I got dressed and met my dad in the kitchen.

"I was thinking about something this morning," he said, as I poured a cup of coffee. "I want you to know you don't have to explain to anyone why you moved back home. I'm happy you're here."

It was a comforting message I know was sent directly by Him.

Father, I'm grateful for Your showing me
Your heart when I need You most.
—Desiree Cole

Digging Deeper: Isaiah 41:10; Proverbs 29:25

LESSONS FROM THE ANIMALS: Loving Shelter

Are not five sparrows sold for two pennies? Yet not one of them is forgotten by God. —Luke 12:6 (NIV)

This chilly spring day, I optimistically liberated my Weber grill from its winter spot on the back porch for its yearly scrubbing. Gracie, my golden retriever, watched me with considerable anticipation. The Weber is like an altar to her, offering grilled steaks, chicken, burgers, and hot dogs, feasts from which she is never excluded. I yanked off the protective covering and tossed it in the yard to be hosed down. Then I lifted the top of the grill, only to be taken by surprise: birds had built a nest in the kettle, since abandoned, though I detected flecks of shell.

Amazing. They must have gotten in through the vents in the bottom, which I had neglected to close for the season. What diligent work to establish such a haven. And clever. I've had bears and raccoons attack my garbage cans, but never the Weber. It was a good place for a mama bird to hatch her young.

I lifted the nest remnants off the grill and put them on top of a woodpile. Gracie raised her nose and sniffed. Animals are so curious!

So was I. I Googled "bird nests" and learned nests come in many forms and are made with an incredible array of materials. There is almost nowhere that some bird species won't find a place to nest. Except a Weber grill. I couldn't find anyone else reporting that phenomenon, though one man said he'd found a nest in the bumper of a vintage car he stored in his garage.

This felt like a blessing, a sweet reminder of divine providence. The Bible says God watches over even the birds. Even those that nest in my Weber grill.

Father, thank You for this reminder. You bless all creatures, from the birds of the sky to the humans like me who are sometimes used to shelter them.
—Edward Grinnan
Digging Deeper: Matthew 10:29

Sunday, May 5

The Lord replied, "If you had faith the size of a mustard seed, you could say to this mulberry tree, 'Be uprooted and planted in the sea,' and it would obey you." —Luke 17:6 (NRSV)

I've heard seminary is nicknamed "cemetery" because, once exposed to the academic side of faith and religion, many completely question their faith by graduation. I graduated from seminary in May 2015 with different beliefs than I'd entered with—as well as a whole slew of questions. I was amused that the degree I earned was called a Master of Divinity because I would hardly say I'd mastered anything, much less the divine.

My father held a graduation reception for me in Indianapolis when I was home preaching for the ninetieth anniversary of the church where I grew up. My uncle Jerome stopped by before the party, to drop off a gift for me: a thin silver necklace. Dangling from the chain was a small glass circle with a mustard seed in the middle. "Oh my goodness," I exclaimed. "This is perfect!" It was the perfect reminder that God does not expect me to have all the answers. God has space for my questions and wrestlings. I only need faith the size of a mustard seed. I immediately put the necklace on and hugged my uncle, considering he generally only came to church for weddings and funerals. "I can't begin to tell you how much this means to me. It really is perfect."

"Of course it is," he said with a wink and a smile. "I know what I'm doing!"

I'm not much of a jewelry person, but I never take that necklace off.

God, thank You for the reminders of Your presence during periods of certainty and of doubt. I know You are big enough to hold them both. Thank You for accepting all of me, just as I am.
—Natalie Perkins

Digging Deeper: Luke 13:19

For the Lord Almighty has purposed, and who can thwart him? His hand is stretched out, and who can turn it back? —Isaiah 14:27 (NIV)

I've always been in awe of my father because Dad could do anything. In 1947 he built his beautiful home and lived there for 70 years until the day he died in his living room at age 98 in 2017. During those years he took care of all repairs and improvements. Throughout his life he designed and built hundreds of things, from go-carts to an outhouse on wheels for the annual outhouse races, to shelving for our homes and beautiful wooden boxes for storage.

Me? I can't build or fix much of anything. I can't do math or science. I've never balanced my checkbook. Never made a piecrust. All I can do are write and paint. Definitely a right-brained soul and definitely not nearly as talented as Dad. I've wondered if I've really even fulfilled my purpose in life.

Then one day I read that purpose comes from any of four elements: passion, mission, vocation, or profession. In other words purpose means you love it, the world needs it, you're great at doing it, or you're being paid to do it.

When I thought about my writing and painting, I saw that those two activities give me purpose. The world needs writers and painters, although I'm not vain enough to think it needs my work. But because those are God's gifts to me, I'm at least able to make some money doing them.

Now when I get a little wistful seeing someone who is talented in so many areas like my dad, I remember my purpose. Doing something I love on a daily basis is such a blessing. I'm determined to step back and just admire the purpose of all those I meet.

Thank You, Jesus, for helping me see that the life You give each of us is filled with purpose. Help me to keep using the gifts You give.
—Patricia Lorenz

Digging Deeper: Psalm 17:3–7; Isaiah 23:9; Ephesians 3:10–13

Behold, he cometh with clouds; and every eye shall see him.
—Revelation 1:7 (KJV)

My friend Jenna wants to learn the names of the birds in her area, so I sent her a field guide. But she complained she couldn't see the birds. So I wanted to send her some binoculars.

"No," she said, "I already have two pairs. I can't use binoculars. Everything doubles."

"They're probably out of collimation," I said.

Next time I visited, I checked. Sure enough, one pair was cross-eyed. The other was fine, though.

I eventually got her to try. Sort of. She squinted through them for a second, then jerked them back down and gave up.

I remembered my own first attempts to use binoculars took effort. Now I'm a pro.

"I'll teach you," I told Jenna, starting right in. "The thing is, you can't use them to search. You have to already know where to look."

But the whole subject of binoculars made her mad. She still can't see the birds.

I thought of my unhappy atheist years and the believers—my sister, her husband, eventually members of the Bible class my husband and I attended—who schooled me in how to see God. Where to look. How to focus my gaze. It made me so mad that God's existence was clear to them but not to me.

Miraculously, their patience seared through my resignation, and everything finally made sense.

"Just keep trying," I told Jenna. "Someday it'll all come together."

Father, I'm so glad I see You now! Help me help others, too, to see You.
—Patty Kirk

Digging Deeper: Acts 17

You have not received a spirit that makes you fearful slaves. Instead, you received God's Spirit when he adopted you as his own children. Now we call him, "Abba, Father." —Romans 8:15 (NLT)

My husband and I are blessed with two children through the miracle of adoption. One day my daughter Joelle was commiserating with me about spring's fierce allergy season. We both suffered, along with many others in our middle Tennessee region, with fierce allergy symptoms—the sneezing, itchy noses, and watery eyes an abundance of allergens had spurred.

"My allergies have been so bad, Mommy," Joelle said. "I have to go to the school nurse for my allergy medicine every day now." Without thinking I responded, "Mine, too, Joelle. This year my allergies have been the worst they have ever been. You probably inherited those bad allergies from me." A few moments later, I pondered my response. There was no way Joelle could have "inherited" anything from me, much less her allergies. Since she was adopted, we do not share any genes or biological traits. If she inherited allergies or other genetic pre-dispositions, it is through her biological family.

After processing this, I smiled at Joelle. "Sweetie, I actually forgot you were adopted. As a matter of fact, I often forget you were adopted. In my mind, it's as if I gave birth to you and Christian."

Joelle and her brother Christian are my children now, and their adoption gives them the same privileges, inheritance, and access to me that my biological children enjoy.

When I became a Christian, God adopted me into His family. I now enjoy an inheritance of joy, eternal life, and a true sense of belonging. It makes me wonder: a I so fully His child that He "forgets" He adopted me? I believe He does.

Lord, thank You for adopting me as Your beloved daughter
and blessing me with an eternal inheritance.
—Carla Hendricks

Digging Deeper: Romans 8:18–25; Galatians 4:1–7

Thursday, May 9

Be joyful in hope, patient in affliction, faithful in prayer.
—Romans 12:12 (NIV)

Our son Paul's relocation for his new job in Detroit was a big adjustment for Elba and me. Throughout his life, he always lived with or near us and the family. Now we have come to accept that chatting via FaceTime, text, or telephone are our only means of communicating with him, besides the rare visits in person. But these limiting forms of communication were hard to accept at first, when he became very ill soon after moving. It all started when he felt fatigued and was unable to complete his weekly workout routine. Soon after, he was experiencing constant stomach pains. He saw a doctor, but no answers were forthcoming. His condition worsened, and this went on for weeks. My wife and I felt helpless, as we were so far from him.

We soon realized, given the distance between us, all we could do was pray. We placed his name on the Guideposts prayer list and asked friends and family to keep him in their prayers. As we prayed, we took comfort in remembering how we turned to God when Paul was born. The doctors told us he had only a 50-percent chance of survival because of medical issues. When he underwent his first surgery a few days after birth, we prayed. We prayed again for surgeries two, three, four, and five. It's the only thing you can do when your son's life is in the hands of doctors.

Prayer got him and us through it then and again this time. While doctors prescribed medications and Paul waited for the meds to take effect, we continued to pray. After eight weeks, Paul was finally back to normal. Sometimes praying is all we can do, and it is always enough.

Lord, when we are afraid or concerned and feel powerless,
we can always pray. Thank You.
—Pablo Diaz

Digging Deeper: Genesis 25:21; Matthew 7:11

After it his voice roars; he thunders with his majestic voice, and he does not restrain the lightnings when his voice is heard. —Job 37:4 (ESV)

Thunder booms. Sheer energy fills the air. Dark for day time, but no rain yet. Distant rumbles are punctuated with deep vibration like a drumbeat—a heartbeat, an earth-beat perhaps—and I'm struck by how amazing the world is. I think we forget its amazement sometimes, most times, watching TV or reading of the many tragedies that befall us. We forget about things like heartbeats and love, nature and all its wonders, and awe-inspiring phenomena like lightning and thunder.

The spring my sister died, a rare and endangered flower appeared out of nowhere all around the tree trunks of our yard. I researched and discovered how precious they were and couldn't for the life of me figure out how or why they grew and thrived. The synchronicity of their appearance, timed exactly one month after my sister's sudden death, seemed like a sign somehow, more than just a coincidence.

The rain pelts the tin roof, rattling a calming hum. It grows louder and louder until it seems the whole house is an instrument of heaven's music. The rare flowers have yet to appear again, but there are more gifts to see and hear.

In every blooming flower, every clap of thunder, every downpour, I feel God. I tell these things to my sons, who are now too old to hear it, too distracted by handheld gadgets, texts, and video games. I pray that someday they'll discover it for themselves.

I think that's part of the magic—God's presence can't really be pointed out by another. It happens the way you fall in love, uniquely yours to stumble upon, to discover deep in the crevices of your heart, right where it has always been.

> *Heavenly Father, thank You, thank You,*
> *thank You for this beautiful and amazing life.*
> —Sabra Ciancanelli

Digging Deeper: Psalm 77:18; Jeremiah 10:13

Saturday, May 11

Let me hear in the morning of your steadfast love. —Psalm 143:8 (ESV)

B rittany, my daughter-in-law, was going away with her mom for the weekend. She asked me to check on her ninety-one-year-old grandmother. "Will you visit Mimi at the assisted living center and tell her we love her?"

"Sure! I love Mimi, too."

Two days later, I found Mimi eating lunch in the cafeteria. The room felt alive with love...until I spotted a woman sitting at Mimi's table. The woman shifted in her chair and looked down.

Lord, help her feel loved. Like Mimi. I've probably prayed an impossible prayer, but what if she has no one? Father, help this woman feel Your love.

A pianist across the room played a hymn, her slender fingers dancing across the keys: "Love lifted me! Love lifted me!"*

Everyone joined in, except the poor lonely soul sitting at our table.

Lord, please.

"When nothing else could help, love lifted me!"

When we finished singing, the pianist stood and studied each face. "If you don't feel loved today, know that you are." She touched her heart. "God loves you. I do, too."

The woman nodded, shiny tears pooling in her brown eyes, the weight of loneliness lifting.

Lord, these words carry wonder-working power: "God loves you."
—Julie Garmon

Digging Deeper: Psalm 109:26, 117:2
*"Love Lifted Me," James Rowe, 1912, Public Domain

Wisdom is with the aged, and understanding in length of days.
—Job 12:12 (ESV)

Four-generation girls' night!" my daughter Kate shouted as she jumped into the car and buckled in next to her cousin in the back-seat. My sister hopped into the front seat, and we swung by my mom's house, where we picked up my eighty-nine-year-old grandmother and my mom.

We went to one of those paint-your-own-sign places. My daughter picked a turquoise sign with sparkling glitter as an accent. My mom picked muted cream with a Bible verse.

And my grandma? She picked a stencil with the words *Amazing Grace, How Sweet the Sound.* Written in hot pink, of course.

But soon Grandma had a confused look in her eyes. Her canvas was blank. She had no idea how to even begin.

The one who cared for us all so well for so long, the one who was so capable, the one who was so vibrant and quick to begin was now…blank.

Her once strong, vibrant mind was an empty canvas.

I walked over to my grandma and helped her pick up the brush. I held her hand in mine, and we painted together. Up, down. Down, up.

"Look how pretty this is, Grandma." My sister laid a hand on her shoulder and pointed to the hot-pink paint.

My grandma looked up with sparkling eyes. "I painted it all by myself, you know."

"Yes, Grandma, you did. And it's beautiful."

Father God, thank You for the wisdom of generations,
for Your amazing grace revealed through those
who came before us and those who will come after. Amen.
—Erin MacPherson

Digging Deeper: Proverbs 13:1; Leviticus 19:32

Monday, May 13

SAYING GOODBYE TO MY VETERANS
The Shortest Distance Between Two Hearts

*That is, that we may be mutually encouraged by each other's faith,
both yours and mine.* —Romans 1:12 (ESV)

During the talks I gave on patient-centered care, prior to my retirement, a nurse who works in an outpatient clinic lifted her hand. "It's no surprise to anyone here, after twenty-five years, I'm a bit burned out," she said. The auditorium crowd chuckled in recognition. "But after hearing all of this today, I know I can go back to the trenches and do it again with passion. These stories have reawakened something inside me."

Over the past few months, I'd witnessed how veterans who were no longer in their prime had, through stories, inspired and taught an entire VA staff what patient-centered care is all about. Like I did, they had health issues and personal doubts. But that didn't stop them.

Since the first cave paintings were created, telling stories has been one of humankind's fundamental methods of communication. And the greatest love story of all time is most certainly the Bible. Stories are the shortest distance between two hearts. They help us understand one another and even ourselves.

The heart most transformed by our medical center's endeavors was mine, however. I knew I would never stop telling veterans' stories, even after retirement. For I am a VA nurse. There is no "was" to my story.

I'm not at the end of anything. It's a whole new beginning.

*You are the greatest storyteller of all time, Lord. Thank You
for showing me the power of sharing stories in today's world.*
—Roberta Messner

Digging Deeper: Mark 16:25; 2 Timothy 1:8

Those who are gracious to the poor lend to the Lord, and the Lord will fully repay them. —Proverbs 19:17 (CEB)

I've heard all the arguments against giving to beggars on the streets and have probably made a few myself: "They'll probably use the money for drink or drugs," "They need work, not a handout," "You only encourage their shiftlessness by giving to them."

At the same time, the words of Christ ring in my ears: "Give to those who ask, and don't refuse those who wish to borrow from you" (Matthew 5:42). So I keep a few loose bills in my pocket, or I have an energy bar handy in my briefcase, and if someone asks, I give. But I make a point of looking them in the eye, asking their name, and telling them I'll pray for them. "God bless you" is the standard response.

Okay, I can even be cynical about that. They're just saying that. They don't really mean it, I tell myself. They're just trying to soften me up. Maybe so. But I'm not sure how many times you can say, "God bless you," without the words catching in your soul.

Not long ago I gave to a beggar on the subway. "God bless you," he said. I turned back to the psalm I was reading that day: "Don't let the oppressed live in shame," it said. "No, let the poor and needy praise your name" (Psalm 74:21).

That was good enough for me. The two of us were working in tandem, giver and receiver, praising God's name together.

> *God, don't let my cynical heart prevent me from seeing*
> *You in unexpected places.*
> —Rick Hamlin

Digging Deeper: 2 Corinthians 9:7; Matthew 25:40

Wednesday, May 15

Lord, it is good for us to be here. —Matthew 17:4 (NIV)

My son John's orientation session for his first job was in the middle of the Bronx, a considerable schlep from home. Like many New Yorkers, we don't have a car, and I knew he'd be nervous going by himself, so I offered to accompany him. We looked up the bus schedule and decided on a time to leave that left ample wiggle room. We walked eight cold blocks to the bus stop and just missed a bus. I didn't worry, for the schedule said one would arrive every eight minutes. Unfortunately, twenty-five minutes passed before the next bus arrived, and by then it was rush hour. The bus crawled, the minutes sped, and by the time orientation started, we were still two miles away in traffic at a standstill.

John took his stress out on me, of course. That was mostly OK. I'm Mom, it was his first job, I'd come along because I knew he'd be anxious, and better that he got testy with me than with his new employer. It was good to be there, better than if he were alone.

John called in and was instructed to get off the bus a stop earlier—one we'd just pulled out of. Thus, when we finally disembarked, we had to backtrack half a mile. I exhorted John to hurry, and he answered with a rude retort. I'd suddenly reached my limit.

"I'm going home," I announced, sharply. From where we were, John could get where he needed to be. I strode back toward the bus stop and was so angry I walked right past it. I kept walking, full tilt, before my annoyance waned enough for me to realize my fingertips were numb. I decided to hop a different bus home, then stared out the window and prayed.

Lord, thank You for making legs good for walking alongside others when they are stressed and for helping me walk away when my own stress spikes.
—Julia Attaway

Digging Deeper: Psalm 4:4

Therefore encourage one another and build each other up.
—1 Thessalonians 5:11 (NIV)

A tale of two women: the first was my friend Honey, who died a few years ago. We called her Honey because she was so sweet. Always a kind word. Always a smile. Generous with love, she blessed people everywhere she went. I miss her every day. The second is an acquaintance we'll call Mara, the name Naomi chose in the book of Ruth because it meant "bitter." I'll change the name here to protect the not-so-innocent, for Mara is one of the most bitter people I've ever met. Never a kind word. Never a smile. Just sour remarks and bad attitude.

I ran into Mara the other day at a doctor's office. My heart sank upon seeing her. I braced myself. "You've put on weight," she said. That one didn't hit the mark, so Mara tried again: "I heard..." She then assured me that "everyone" in town was saying a completely horrible thing about me—something I couldn't imagine anyone would ever even think. She almost had me before I realized I was letting her get my goat. I recovered and said, "I'm sure you must be mistaken. I can't imagine anyone saying something so unkind and untrue." I pulled a book out of my bag and pretended to be absorbed in it until my name was called.

I hid my anger and hurt until I got home. How could anyone be so mean? *Lord, why did I have to run into Mara again?* Then I looked at the photo of Honey on my dresser. It's from when she was a young girl, her smile beaming. I remembered one day sitting outside with her in the oppressive humidity and ninety-plus-degree weather. She never complained about the heat. Instead, when a breeze finally blew, she proclaimed, "Thank You, Jesus, for the breeze to cool us off!"

Oh, the little choices we face moment by moment!

Lord, let me be a Honey and not a Mara!
—Ginger Rue

Digging Deeper: James 3:10; Ephesians 4:32

Friday, May 17

Holy brothers and sisters, who share in the heavenly calling,
fix your thoughts on Jesus, whom we acknowledge as our apostle
and high priest. —Hebrews 3:1 (NIV)

Springtime in Idaho. A few of us went into the woods to shoot pistols. An array of firearms were laid out on a wide table. A couple of the guys had impressive collections.

Not Burt. Burt wasn't the collection sort.

A quiet, unassuming man, he wore old jeans, boots, and flannel. His thick, gray beard and sun-lined face were a throwback to a simpler time.

Burt took in our soda-can war. At length, he pulled an old five-shot revolver from his back pocket.

Five shots. Five bullets found their targets. The old pistol went back into his pocket.

"Used to be a saying," he told me later, "keep a wary eye on the man who only shoots one gun. He most likely hits what he aims at."

What Burt said that afternoon stuck with me. With today's information overload and new winds of doctrine every other week, it's easy to lose focus.

I'm called to a one-gun walk. It's simple. It's good. No need to detour even a foot off this beautiful, narrow path.

My destination, my target—eternal communion with the Lover of my soul. And with His Word, arm in arm with Jesus, I'll hit what I'm aiming at every time.

Lord, blind me to the distractions of this world. Let my eyes find only You.
                        —Buck Storm

Digging Deeper: Hebrews 5:10, 6:20

For God hath not given us the spirit of fear; but of power, and of love, and of a sound mind. —2 Timothy 1:7 (KJV)

I'm too old for this."
    My stage fright was ratcheting up. No matter that the rehearsal had gone off without a hitch, my promise to lead praise and worship service the next day had me as nervous as a first-grader summoned to the chalkboard. What on earth made me agree to do this in the first place? I asked myself.

I paced my bedroom floor, tested my voice. No question I loved to sing—I bombarded my husband's ears daily with songs of praise. Still, a nagging voice said, *This is organized worship. No room for an old woman's erratic creaks and squeaks.* Should I wait another month or two? Perhaps when allergy season was over, I'd have a bit more confidence.

It was too late. I had promised Doris, the praise and worship coordinator, and I had promised God.

Realizing I had forgotten to ask Doris what the theme Scripture was for the next day, I trudged to my office to send a quick text message. I reached for my cell phone, and it blinked a message from the energetic young woman who faithfully plans our worship: "Forgot to tell you." I could almost hear the perpetual upbeat laugh in Doris's voice. "The theme Scripture for tomorrow is 'For God has not given us the spirit of fear; but of power, and of love, and of a sound mind.'"

I smiled at the message, equivocation vanished. I was ready to sing to the glory of God. He had spoken, and it was time to obey.

Heavenly Father, help me today to walk in
Your glorious strength and not my imagined failures.
    —Jacqueline F. Wheelock

Digging Deeper: 1 John 4:18; Psalm 27:1; Luke 1:74

Sunday, May 19

Do you have eyes but fail to see, and ears but fail to hear? —Mark 8:18 (NIV)

Late yesterday afternoon, the sky's impressive show—gray puff balls tinged with mauve—drew me out of the house. Walking along a ridge, I focused exclusively on the heavenly light, heralding sunset. *Thank You, Creator God.*

But then a persistent, familiar sound drew my attention to the lower residential street. Could it be? Yes. I saw a schoolboy dribbling a basketball. Once I'd engaged a second, aural sense, I heard a chorus of birdcalls—brash crows and lyric songbirds. And then? Katydids portending seasonal change. Tracing my steps back home, I stopped for a good look at low-lying, late-blooming roses I'd missed earlier.

The blossoms reminded me of a Sunday visit to the National Cathedral. I had anticipated seeing the bishop's rose garden in full bloom. But an unexpected sensuous delight overwhelmed that afternoon: I'd happened upon a rarely completed full-bell peal, a sequence of tolls—more than five thousand variations—that lasted three hours.

For an hour I sat near the roses, reading a book, enjoying the sounds. Eventually it was hard to ignore a carload of tourists swarming the roses. They animatedly pointed toward, touched, and with great fanfare smelled the blossoms. Before long, the scene sank in: they were talking with their hands. Sign language. *They can't hear the bells! They are savoring what they can experience!* With an expanded gratitude for the full array of senses, I approached one bush, then another, and drew fragrant roses to my face.

And yesterday, finishing my walk, I breathed deeply....

Thank You, Lord, for making us sensuous beings.
Help us delight in Your world using all the senses You give.
—Evelyn Bence

Digging Deeper: Deuteronomy 33:13–16; Psalm 89:11–18

Do what the Lord wants, and he will give you your heart's desire.
—Psalm 37:4 (CEV)

The diesel engine of my Dodge truck rumbled as I drove Interstate 90 toward home. My heart was satisfied from spending the last few weeks in Minnesota helping my elderly father move so he could put his house up for sale. It was Sunday morning, and I needed to be back to work on Monday. But I was tired from the trip. *Lord, I could use a vacation right about now.*

As the miles of prairies rolled past, I daydreamed. There was no chance I could get any time off from work after being gone all these weeks, but if I could take a vacation, what would I do? Instantly I relaxed, as I imagined myself hanging my feet off the end of a dock. Wouldn't it be fun to rent a cabin and hang out for a weekend?

The highway wound through snowcapped mountains. If I were to rent a cabin, where would I like to go? Without hesitation, in my mind's eye I could see the vast expanse of Flathead Lake rimmed by rocky peaks. *Keep dreaming, Rebecca. A cabin on Flathead Lake would cost several hundred dollars a night. Well, that's not in the budget.*

I drove past a signpost announcing an exit and glanced at my fuel gauge. It was time to pull over. As I parked at the gas station, my cell phone chimed, announcing a text. Glancing at it, I smiled. It was from Betsy, a longtime friend. It read, "I'm living in a cabin on Flathead Lake, and it'd be fun if you could come up next weekend and stay."

Tears rolled down my cheeks as I texted back, "Of course!"

While I fueled the truck, I chatted with God. *How could I forget You? With You all my dreams are possible.*

Thank You, Lord, for surprising me … with my dreams come true. Amen.
—Rebecca Ondov

Digging Deeper: Psalm 20:4; Matthew 11:28–30

Tuesday, May 21

The moment we get tired in the waiting, God's Spirit is right alongside helping us along. If we don't know how or what to pray, it doesn't matter. He does our praying in and for us, making prayer out of our wordless sighs, our aching groans. He knows us far better than we know ourselves.
—Romans 8:26–27 (MSG)

Please don't tell my five-year-old this little secret of mine: the best way to get her to eat carrots instead of potato chips is to—while she watches—peel a carrot, chop it into sticks, set them on the counter, and say, "Now, don't eat all my carrots!" It's predictable. As I turn away, pretending not to notice, she grabs them with a giggle, runs away, and only returns in time to show me she is consuming the very last one.

If only I could use a similar technique to get her to clean her room!

I pondered my technique the other day, realizing God has similar knowledge of me—my faults and my opportunities for doing better. There's no question God knows what I'm up to. He knows me inside and out, better than I even know my five-year-old. Better than I know myself. God knows I do one thing when I know I should do another. God knows what motivates me, both good and bad. God doesn't trick me, but He *knows* my heart!

Don't eat from that one tree, God said to Adam and Eve (and to me), but then we did it and still do. God knows. He looks lovingly, waiting and knowing what's best for us. And when I come back each time, after doing (or not doing) what I know I should have done or not done, God knows how to turn it to good.

I come to You today with all my weaknesses.
Thank You for turning them into strength.
—Jon M. Sweeney

Digging Deeper: Jeremiah 29:12

Hatred starts fights, but love pulls a quilt over the bickering.
—Proverbs 10:12 (MSG)

One day my son Jeremy brought me a five-week-old orange kitten he'd found screaming in the woods, high in a tree. She was tiny, beautiful, helpless, and hungry. I carried her around like a baby—even rocked and sang, "You are my sunshine." I named her Sunshine.

She grew into a giant creature—a super cat from another planet, with keen wisdom and a will of iron. She bit and scratched me daily. I scolded her loudly, "No! Bad!" Undaunted, she stood on her mighty hind legs like a boxer, punching and scratching me. She roamed our house like a wild beast of prey, hiding in obscure places to jump out, startling my husband, me, and my two indoor cats. Sometimes when I tried to rock her, she glared at me with wide amber eyes, then stuck out a giant orange paw and slapped my face.

I called my aunt Lillian, a fellow cat rescuer, and she told me, "Mannie, you don't know what she had to go through to survive or what her mama taught her. She has feral genes. Poor little thing."

That very day, I whispered to Sunshine, "I love you. Always will." I kissed her face several times. She seemed to like my face on hers. So we butted heads often. Softly. Sometimes she initiated it, her eyes closed. Her scratching and biting didn't suddenly stop. But she relaxed and even snoozed on the back of my husband's chair, while he bravely read.

Now she sleeps with us nightly, waiting patiently for me to tuck her in underneath the soft blanket.

She's learned to purr.

> *Oh, Father, teach me how to love unlovable people,*
> *who've most likely been hurt.*
> —Marion Bond West

Digging Deeper: Ephesians 4:2; Galatians 5:3

You... tell me where to stop and rest. —Psalm 139:3 (TLB)

My husband, John, and I had been on the road for six weeks and were missing friends and familiar routines. That morning we were in a remote corner of West Virginia, following a winding, unnumbered highway called Mud River Road.

"Let's stop at the next Starbucks," John joked.

"That's not funny!" I groaned, staring gloomily at endless cornfields.

And then... uncannily, unbelievably, as the road rose I seemed to see a green sign with the familiar Starbucks mermaid. The huge sign was real, and we soon saw it had not been erected for the sparse traffic along Mud River; far below, at the bottom of the hill, was an interstate. The man behind the counter had the name Venu embroidered on his apron. We took our grande lattes to a pair of overstuffed chairs.

Before long Venu came over and introduced himself as the manager of this store. "Where are you folks from?" he asked.

"New York," John told him. "And you?"

"Dallas," Venu said.

"Dallas!" John said. "My mother grew up in a little town just north of there. Sherman." "I know Sherman," Venu said.

"My grandfather owned a cotton-gin factory there," John went on. "His name was on the redbrick wall in yellow bricks."

"Hardwicke," Venu supplied.

What were the chances, we asked ourselves an hour later, of meeting an immigrant's son, in West Virginia, who knew a favorite landmark from John's childhood in Texas? No chance at all, we decided. But in the loving care of God for two homesick travelers, every chance in the world.

> *Remind me, Father, that in You we are always home.*
> —Elizabeth Sherrill

Digging Deeper: 1 Chronicles 22:9

I have given you authority to trample on snakes. —Luke 10:19 (NIV)

Being that it was rattlesnake season, when snakes leave their hibernation holes in the warming temperatures of spring in the desert, we left the dog at home and were extra vigilant during our late-afternoon hike on South Mountain near Phoenix, Arizona. While some religious groups handle snakes to prove authority over reptiles, I prefer a wide swath around the creatures, especially rattlers.

We were four miles away from the car on the Bursera Trail when I came up and over a small hill, a few steps behind my husband, Kevin. He did not see the camouflaged, dusty body of a two-foot diamondback stretched across the trail.

"Snake!" I yelled at the same time Kevin heard the warning rattle.

"Where?"

In a slow-motion dance with danger, Kevin jumped right at the same time the snake moved right. Still unsure of the snake's location, my husband hopped left as the snake moved left. Adrenaline pumping, he leaped with both feet in the air. The snake struck at the same moment, missing the bottom of my husband's size-twelve hiking boots by inches.

Finally at a safe distance, we watched the rattlesnake slither off the trail to hide under a creosote bush. Flicking its black, forked tongue, the diamondback shook its eight-section rattle, black-and-white zebra bands prominent on its checkered brown body, while we gulped an air of relief.

"Thank God," Kevin breathed.

"Yes," I agreed. "Thank God."

> *Jesus, when I am not even aware of danger,*
> *You watch over me and those I love.*
> —Lynne Hartke

Digging Deeper: Psalm 18:35–36, 32:7; Nahum 1:7

Saturday, May 25

They seized Simon from Cyrene, who was on his way in from the country, and put the cross on him and made him carry it behind Jesus.
—Luke 23:26 (NIV)

How's your family doing?" inquired a longtime friend I hadn't seen in ages. I paused to consider a suitable reply.

"Better than we were, but a long way from well," I said, slowly. "We're millimetering our way forward." I gave her the two-minute synopsis of the past six months.

"Is there anything I can do to help?" she asked when I was through.

I smiled and shook my head. "Not at the moment. But thanks."

I believe in accepting help for the simple reason that Jesus did. When the Roman soldiers commandeered Simon of Cyrene, our Lord could have protested, "No, no! I can do it myself!" Besides, I am always honored to be able to help others, so who am I to deny someone else the opportunity to be Christ's hands on earth?

My family has been the recipient of more goodness and kindness than almost anyone I've ever heard of. We have received groceries and food, frequent flier miles for emergencies, rides to hospitals, and even tickets to see the musical *Hamilton*. The blessings don't necessarily negate the difficulties, but they remind me that light shines in the darkness.

As it turned out, the friend who inquired about my family emailed a week later, wondering if I could talk to her friend whose son was struggling with deep anxiety. This was an act of service I could easily do: help someone carry a cross with which I was familiar. I contacted the friend-of-the-friend immediately, and we met up for coffee that week. As we parted ways, she thanked me and said, "This was so helpful. I feel better knowing I'm not doing this alone."

Father, thank You for each and every person
who has ever made my life easier.
—Julia Attaway

Digging Deeper: John 1:5

For You have been my help, and in the shadow of Your wings,
I sing for joy. —Psalm 63:7 (NASB)

I was on my way to a church in Iowa and realized I was lost. From the rearview mirror, I could see the grain elevator, where I was supposed to turn. Sometimes the view through the mirror is clearer than the view through the windshield.

When I started my career as a college teacher in 1968, it was hard for me to see God at work in my life. I lived in a state of confusion, most of the time. Now that I'm at the other end of life and looking back, I see clearly the presence of God in my life at every turn.

Who guided me through the maze of course plans and procedures new teachers face? Someone wiser than I was.

Often I worked three jobs to get us through financial drought, but showers of blessings always arrived just in time.

I traveled over a million miles on weekends, serving in churches, without a single, serious accident. Trust me, I am not a five-star driver.

Hardest was midlife, when our daughters went off to college and I felt lonely. I almost lost my way, but God firmly pulled me back to the main road.

Now I am coming up on old age, and the road is lined with warning signs: Disability Ahead, Beware of Loneliness, and Watch Out for Grief.

I should be terrified, but instead I feel a sense of peace that God will temper these trials with mercy, as He has done in the past.

You were there all along, God, but I didn't recognize Your hand at work.
Now I know You can be trusted to help me to the end.
—Daniel Schantz

Digging Deeper: Psalm 31:3, 139:7

Memorial Day, Monday, May 27

Greater love has no one than this: to lay down one's life for one's friends.
—John 15:13 (NIV)

Standing aboard the USS *Missouri*, where the treaty was signed ending World War II, our tour guide remarked, "You are experiencing today the beginning and end of World War II." The *Missouri* is docked near the USS *Arizona*, which is resting where it sank during the Japanese attack on Pearl Harbor.

I had spent the morning at the USS *Arizona* Memorial. The smell of oil still leaking from the sunken ship drew me deeper into that moment of history. I heard stories of the attack and scanned the names of the 1,177 sailors and marines who died on the *Arizona*. The short distance separating the two ships does not capture the magnitude of sacrifice made between these two historical bookends. Some lost their lives at the start, others during the journey, and still others served throughout the war and returned home. For me, each became a hero the moment he or she pledged to defend and protect our nation no matter the cost.

Today we observe Memorial Day, established to honor those who died in military service. In our township all heroes are honored, living or deceased—veterans, active military, firefighters, teachers, police officers, coaches, mentors, medical professionals, family members, and friends—with a flag placed in each of their names on a "Field of Heroes." Walking among hundreds of flags, reading the tributes and honoring their contributions, fills my soul with an indescribable gratitude.

Join me today in honoring all of your heroes. And at 3:00 p.m.—the national moment to pause—remember especially the sacrifice of those who gave their lives so we can fly the Stars and Stripes.

Dear God, we give thanks for all who laid down their lives in service to our grateful nation. Thank You for Your great sacrifice, Lord, that gives us hope for eternal reunions with each one. Amen.
—John Dilworth

Digging Deeper: Mark 10:45; John 3:16

Pray in the Spirit on all occasions with all kinds of prayers and requests.
—Ephesians 6:18 (NIV)

Ever since Mom taught me "Now I lay me down to sleep," prayer has become deeply ingrained in my daily life. Sometimes I pray silently, for example, when admiring the natural world or before meals alone. Sometimes I pray aloud—"Thank You, God! That driver missed me!" Sometimes I write praises, thanksgivings, and petitions in my journal. Perhaps singing prayers best satisfies my soul. Didn't Saint Augustine claim that whoever sings prays twice?

However much I enjoy private dialogue with God, I'm increasingly aware of the connectedness I derive from group prayer. So when my globetrotter friend Lois planned to visit Jerusalem and offered to leave my very own prayer in a crevice of the Western Wall, I agreed. She tucked the slip of paper in her purse and duly followed through on her mission. Of course, I knew God could hear my prayer just as clearly from her dining room table, but knowing my prayer had joined those of millions of the faithful strengthened my feeling of community...and God's presence.

I consider other tangible forms of corporate prayer that bring me closer to God. Dozens of times I've lit candles in churches in Europe, to remember loved ones and connect with other pilgrims. Scores of votive lamps flickering together burn more brightly than a single candle. Airport chapels rarely have candles, due to safety concerns, but often these tranquil oases provide smooth prayer stones: pray for an intention, then place it in a container with other prayers. The mystery of group prayer draws me closer to God and also those who love Him.

What a gift, Lord, to know You hear us. Always.
—Gail Thorell Schilling

Digging Deeper: 1 Timothy 2:8; Psalm 122:6; 2 Chronicles 6:21

Wednesday, May 29

Those who seek me find me.... My fruit is better than fine gold.
—Proverbs 8:17, 19 (NIV)

N o matter how awful my day has been, there are always some gifts of beauty in it, however small. Every night I review my day and ask God to help me find them, and He always does."

When I heard those words from a friend who's battling a serious illness, a memory rose and settled gently on my mind.... I'm about eight years old. My grandpa stands next to me at a large backyard metal tub filled with water. He reaches into a bucket of deep brown creek-bottom mud and places some in his gold-mining pan and in mine. He drizzles water in and expertly circles his pan, swirling the liquid into and through the mud, patiently showing me how. I try it. Sure enough, within a few minutes, the sludge gives way to fine black sand amid which tiny golden nuggets sparkle.

My friend's comments remind me God is our expert gold miner. No matter how dirty or dark our days, they hold nuggets of beauty, of God's wonders—gifts of life as it is meant to be. He helps us sift through the muck and mire of even our worst and most difficult times, revealing specks of splendor. We can pick out those bits of loveliness, treasure them, and throw the mud away.

Thank you, my friend. The next time my day has seemed muddy and bleak, I'll do some gold-panning with our God and discover nuggets worth more than fine gold.

Thank You, Lord, that even our darkest days contain the shimmer of Your wonders. We need only seek, and with You we will find.
—Kim Taylor Henry

Digging Deeper: John 1:5; 2 Peter 1:19

How excellent is thy lovingkindness, O God! —Psalm 36:7 (KJV)

A dog on my running route scares me. When I first saw him, he barked menacingly from a far-off yard, then came after me.

Without knowing any better, I did what's supposed to work against bears. I raised my arms and yelled, "Go away!" It worked. The dog growled and lunged after me a ways but eventually slunk back home.

So it was that I was yelling, arms raised, the other day. An SUV swerved backward up the drive and a sweet-faced teenager leaped out.

"Oh, Bill won't hurt you," she said, tugging him by his collar into the SUV. "He just likes to act all big." Bill still growled as I jogged off.

The girl must've told her dad about our encounter, because when Bill surged up from the ditch the next day, a man jumped from the SUV.

"Get in, Bill," he snarled. This time, Bill obeyed.

As I ran off, the man leaned out the SUV window to echo his daughter: "He won't hurt you."

"He sure acts like he will," I said. I was mad.

"It's 'cause you flinch is why," the man said, sneering.

The whole two miles home, I snarled my way through what God might be telling me through Bill and his owners. *Turn the other cheek? Hate is tantamount to murder?*

I settled on this: People can be mean. I'm mean sometimes. But God isn't. If He were, I'd be a Bill—obedient, perhaps, but perpetually hostile. As soon as I thought it, my own hostility lifted.

Father God, thank You for Your kindness!
—Patty Kirk

Digging Deeper: Isaiah 63

Friday, May 31

Do not neglect to show hospitality to strangers. —Hebrews 13:2 (ESV)

Yesterday was frustrating! While I was driving on the interstate to Atlanta, traffic was diverted to a narrow road because of highway repairs. Slowing to a crawl, miles of cars stacked up into a single lane. Just at this moment, the fuel pump in my old Suburban finally quit working. Barely able to coast to the shoulder of the road, I carefully stepped out of my car and gazed at the endless line of stalled traffic and angry drivers. Suddenly a window in the car idling next to me rolled down, and a young man spoke to me with very limited English. He said three words: "You need help?"

I looked at his old, dilapidated car and saw a young father with three small children. They were speaking Spanish. He smiled and pointed toward the one available seat. Relieved, I hopped in and soon learned this small family immigrated from Mexico. They were working in Georgia during the peach season, seeking to put down roots and make a living.

After a few minutes, we came to a service station. As I thanked him for his kindness and help, he insisted he would wait with me until I called a tow truck to rescue my Suburban. He offered me his cell phone, and I arranged for repair service. As I returned his phone, he smiled again—that universal language—shook my hand, and drove off with a delighted grin. I knew, in that moment, God had spoken to me and said, "You, too, need to be a good neighbor!"

> *Father, I thank You for a stranger who chose to be my brother.*
> *May I follow his example. Amen.*
> —Scott Walker

Digging Deeper: Isaiah 58:7; Matthew 25:31–46; Romans 12:3

UNDER GOD'S WINGS

1 _____

2 _____

3 _____

4 _____

5 _____

6 _____

7 _____

8 _____

9 _____

10 _____

11 _____

12 _____

13 _____

14 _____

15 _____

May

16 _____

17 _____

18 _____

19 _____

20 _____

21 _____

22 _____

23 _____

24 _____

25 _____

26 _____

27 _____

28 _____

29 _____

30 _____

31 _____

JUNE

If we are unfaithful, he remains faithful, for he cannot deny who he is.

—2 Timothy 2:13 (NLT)

Saturday, June 1

He will cover you with his feathers, and under his wings you will find refuge; his faithfulness will be your shield and rampart. —Psalm 91:4 (NIV)

During my many months of recovering from double knee replacement surgery, I had days when my normally happy mood gave in to depression. I hated taking pain meds, hated not being able to walk as fast as I used to, and hated feeling old.

A letter from my then-ninety-seven-year-old dad arrived: One evening while Dad was sitting in his oversize recliner, he explained, a windstorm knocked the power out. Dad's recliner was powered by electricity, and there he was, in the far back position, unable to get out. He'd broken his back a couple of years earlier and still felt the disabling effects from that.

"With no electricity I was stuck," Dad wrote. "After one and a half hours in the chair, I finally shifted my weight down to the lower end, which tipped the whole chair forward, and I was able to twist my body onto my hands and knees. In total darkness I crawled to the desk and found my flashlight. The power didn't come back on for two and a half hours."

Inspired by that letter, I did water aerobics, sitting on a noodle, so I wouldn't have to jump up and down while my knees healed.

I put a thick pillow in the driver's seat of my car, so I could get in and out more easily.

If God could give my elderly father the strength, patience, and determination to get out of that chair and find the light, God would surely help me through my long recuperation. I just had to think creatively.

Heavenly Father, thank You for my father, who, up until he passed away at age ninety-eight, continued to inspire and remind me of the infallible protection we have under Your wings.
—Patricia Lorenz

Digging Deeper: 1 Corinthians 12:3–11;
Deuteronomy 32:39

SAYING GOODBYE TO MY VETERANS
The Mystery of Faith

Faith is confidence in what we hope for and assurance about what we do not see. —Hebrews 11:1 (NIV)

One evening as my retirement grew near, I telephoned my older brother, Robert. He is a hospital chaplain and knows a lot about what God's Word says about certain issues.

"The closer my retirement gets," I said, "the shorter I am on faith. Is there any life event with more unknowns and less options?" I cataloged my worries: Would I have enough money to get by? Would there be enough structure to my life? Would I discover meaningful activities?

"I even fret that I can't be creative at home like I've been at the hospital," I admitted. "You know creativity is one of my deepest joys."

Robert chuckled at that one. "You'll be creative anywhere, Roberta. You're involved in so many pursuits, and you always have a project or ten going. You won't believe all you'll get into once you have time to call your own."

He went on to explain that faith wouldn't be faith if I felt it in advance. "You have to trust God first, and then faith follows. You'll find every age and life stage is the best place to be. I promise."

My work years, which had stretched on seemingly forever, were coming to a fast close. But in this new faith journey, I had dear family and friends, and especially God, to count on.

In faith, I depend on You, Lord, for this new chapter of my life.
—Roberta Messner

Digging Deeper: 2 Corinthians 5:7; Hebrews 11:6; Mark 9:23

Monday, June 3

Some give freely, yet grow all the richer; others withhold what is due, and only suffer want. —Proverbs 11:24 (NRSV)

I had to look up her email in my address book. It had been that long since I'd sent Kimmy an email or communicated with her at all. We'd had a falling-out the previous year over a political disagreement and both said things we regretted. Or at least I had. I sent her an apology the next day, which she acknowledged. That was the end of the discussion and, it became clear, the friendship. Over the next few months, I made a few half-hearted overtures, but she did not respond.

I decided to forgive and forget. But recently, I've been thinking about how good I am at forgiving and forgetting, especially the forgetting part. I find it much easier to let a difficult relationship go than to mend it. Forgiving is so much easier if I don't have to think about fixing. When I study the handful of relationships scattered in my wake, I guess others feel the same way. Maintaining long-term friendships can be challenging.

Last weekend, I heard a sermon I couldn't get out of my mind. Instead of the usual line about God's unconditional love for us, this visiting priest had a different message. "I don't think it is always easy for the Lord to love us," he said, as people in the church, including me, sat up and paid close attention. "I think there are days He really has to work at it."

Gulp. What if, instead of working at loving me when I'm at my worst, God were to decide to forgive...and forget?

Kimmy came to my mind immediately. She used to attend this church with me on special occasions. I'd start my effort with a small thing. I began my email, "Hey, Kimmy, do you remember when we..."

> *Loving Father, Who never forgets me, teach me to do the challenging work of loving others.*
> —Marci Alborghetti

Digging Deeper: Job 34:12–15; Psalm 6:1–5

We do not look at the things which are seen, but at the things which are not seen. —2 Corinthians 4:18 (NKJV)

I don't know about God," a friend said. "How can you believe in something you can't see?"

I didn't know how to answer at first. Then the lyrics from a Christian song popped into my head, prompting my reply. "Do you believe in wind?" I asked.

"Of course wind is real." My friend looked at me like I'd lost my mind.

I said gently, "But you can't see wind."

"Sure you can."

"Not really," I said. "You see the flag it waves or the leaves it stirs in the trees or the destruction left behind in a storm. But you can't see the wind itself. You can only see what it does and feel it when it touches your skin, right?"

"I guess so."

"That's how God is. I don't have to see Him. I can see what He does and feel Him at work in my life. He can't be any more obvious to me."

My friend was quiet for a long time. "I hadn't thought of it that way."

"He's really there," I said. "The more you practice seeking His presence, the more places you'll find Him. I promise."

(In case you're curious, the song that came to mind was "Feel It" by TobyMac with Mr. Talkbox.)

> *Dear Lord, please forgive us when we are tempted to doubt.*
> *Just as leaves are stirred by unseen winds, stir our hearts*
> *with the breath of Your very real presence.*
> —Erika Bentsen

Digging Deeper: John 3:8; Hebrews 11:1–3; 1 Corinthians 13:12

THINGS MY MOTHER TAUGHT ME: How to Fall
We've been thrown down, but we haven't been broken.
—2 Corinthians 4:9 (MSG)

Running to answer the phone, I continued reading my iPad and then—oops. I was falling, still holding my iPad, wearing glasses.

The corner of the wooden ottoman struck my shin hard. Down I went like a felled tree.

In a split second, I recalled something my mother told me when I was a child. She'd come home from work at the bank, and we were eating supper. Just the two of us. That was our family.

"Mannie." She smiled, pulling biscuits from the oven. "Have I ever told you how to fall?"

"What, Mother?"

"You know, honey. As in down. Boom!"

I must've looked stunned.

"Today I fell down all those steps at the post office." She beamed.

I saw them mentally. Maybe twelve concrete steps that ended at a concrete sidewalk. Supper forgotten, I asked, "Did anyone call an ambulance? Did you see a doctor?"

"No, baby. I'm okay. First of all, when you know you're falling, don't be afraid. No panic. Relax. Think something like, *Okay, so I'm falling.*"

As I fell now, her words flashed through my mind.

I landed flat on my face. But I stood up, walked over to my chair, and sat down. Dabbed at a little blood on my leg and the side of my nose. Applied ice packs. No scars ever developed. Or pain. Actually my back, which usually aches, felt stronger.

Days later I told Mother, pretending she was alive again, "I did it, Mother! You were right. In everything you ever told me."

Father, help mothers encourage children, however they may fall in life.
—Marion Bond West

Digging Deeper: Isaiah 43:2; Joshua 1:9; Deuteronomy 31:8

LESSONS FROM THE ANIMALS: Always Loved

I say, "Loyal love is permanently established; in the skies you set up your faithfulness." —Psalm 89:2 (NET)

G racie, no!"
My young golden retriever was trotting into the living room, a dish towel in her mouth. She'd captured it from the handle on our fridge. She stared at me, uncertain she was ready to surrender it. "Gracie, drop!" I said, my voice firmer. Another second or two of deliberation, then she dropped the purloined towel gently on the floor and proceeded to her bed, where she curled up and sighed.

Gracie loved putting things in her mouth. It was a habit my wife, Julee, and I were determined to curb. A few minutes later, my dog's cold, wet nose nudged my hand. Julee, coming into the room, said, "I heard you scold her. I think she wants to make up."

"Maybe she wants to play or something," I said.

"Maybe that's what she wanted in the first place. She was just trying to get your attention."

I fought off a pang of guilt. She nudged my hand again, and I put my arm around her. Julee was right, though. Gracie needed reassurance. We were her family, and she needed to know everything was all right. Do dogs feel and think, much like we humans do? You bet they do.

"Get your ball," I said to Gracie. She leaped up, tail wagging excitedly, went to her toy box, and, after clearly thinking it over, picked out her favorite ball. We were off to the park. Mission accomplished, from my dog's point of view.

Father, how often I seek Your reassurance when I feel
I have failed You! It is the enduring grace of Your love
that reassures me I am never forsaken.
—Edward Grinnan

Digging Deeper: Nehemiah 1:5

Friday, June 7

I found that wisdom is superior to folly as light is superior to darkness.
—Ecclesiastes 2:13 (JPS)

By the time I learned my friend Gayle's husband was in the hospital, he'd already had three seizures for which the doctors could not identify a cause. When I visited him, he seemed to know what was going on, and I was heartened. Gayle told me later he didn't remember I'd been there.

The next time I spoke with her, she said he was "a thousand percent better," but the time after that he'd been delusional and thought he was in prison rather than the hospital. It went on like that for days. He'd improve, then lose all the ground he seemed to have gained. Once his physical condition stabilized, he was moved to a rehab center, where the seesaw nature of his still-undiagnosed illness continued. Gayle told me that while the underlying cause of the seizures was not known yet, the doctors agreed on the result: Gayle's husband had dementia.

I watched helplessly as Gayle tried to cope with the situation, and slowly it dawned on me that, even in my pain over my husband Keith's death, I had been given a great blessing. I didn't notice it at the time because I was too focused on the fear of losing him, but now I was really aware of it. Keith had been completely Keith, as sharp and warm and funny as he'd been all the time I'd known him, until the last few hours of his life. I imagined the pain if I'd had to watch him vanish slowly, and for the first time I thanked God for keeping him whole and keenly aware, up to the very end, that I loved him.

Forgive me, Lord, for being so late in recognizing Your kindness.
—Rhoda Blecker

Digging Deeper: Ecclesiastes 9:9; Deuteronomy 34:7; Psalm 92:5

Come and hear, all who fear God, and I will tell of what He has done for my soul. —Psalm 66:16 (NASB)

It was so good to reconnect with JoAnn. We hadn't seen each other since high school.

"I remember you quoting the lyrics from a song by Blondie, and thinking, *We don't have the same tastes*," she said, looking back at how our friendship had faded. "That's when I felt we were going in different directions."

She told me of her marriage—"We met in a Bible class"—and of their subsequent divorce. "We're still good friends," she said.

She spoke of the death of her mother and of more recently her father, a gloomy and fierce man who had frightened me and her. JoAnn said he softened as he got older and sicker and needed her help—help she found the courage and grace to give. "By the time he died, I was able to honestly tell him I loved him," she said. "I had my head on his chest when he passed."

She told her story with no sense of bitterness or regret. She was at peace.

She had mentioned a Bible class.

"Can I ask," I ventured, "what role your faith has played in getting you through all this?" I wondered if this was appropriate to ask, given how we were now, despite a few shared years of childhood, utter strangers.

"I never would have made it without it," she said. "I trust God completely. He's my Protector, my Comforter, my Guide. I may not have had that kind of father on earth, but I do in heaven."

I nodded, buoyed by her conviction. Her trust renewed mine. Our disparate paths merged again in that moment, through her willingness to be open and honest, to have high praise ready on her tongue.

Lord, may no embarrassment or fear of what other people may think keep me from giving credit where credit is due: You are my Rock and my Salvation!
—Amy Eddings

Digging Deeper: Psalm 135:3; John 17:18; Acts 10:43–44

Sunday, June 9

ENCOUNTERING GOD IN UNLIKELY PLACES
The Criminal

One God and Father of all, who is... in you all. —Ephesians 4:6 (NKJV)

When I was twelve years old, I read a remarkable story called "The Bishop's Candlesticks." The story captivated me, as I read about Jean Valjean, a dark, filthy ex-convict, who is welcomed by a hospitable bishop. A meal is offered. A bed is made. But in the night, Valjean steals the bishop's silver and slips out into the darkness. Apprehended nearby, Valjean is shackled like an animal and marched back to the bishop's house.

"Ah, here you are," the bishop greets him. "How is this? I give you the candlesticks, too, which are of silver like the rest. Take them now."

Redemption thus comes to this man made despicable by an unjust world, and he becomes the transformed hero of Victor Hugo's enduring novel, *Les Miserables.*

I thought it would be nice to know someone like that bishop, who so purely shows the love of God. Someone who finds good in the untouchables of our world. Someone perfect.

Years fly by, and I look at that old bishop differently. He becomes not some holy apparition, but a mirror reflecting the face of God, which he discovers deep within the soul of Jean Valjean. The glow, I finally discover, has never been who the bishop is, but a reflection of what he sees in others.

I smile fondly at my twelve-year-old self, the girl who thought there were perfect people in the world. The girl who already knew herself well enough to know she could never be one of them. Thank God for the bishop. His lesson is simple: God waits in the faces of everyone we meet. Look and see. Find perfection in the seeing, not the being.

Father, let us acknowledge the humanity in others as we seek
and find Your face in theirs.
—Pam Kidd

Digging Deeper: Ecclesiastes 11:5; Psalm 86:15

The Lord is good; his steadfast love endures forever,
and his faithfulness to all generations. —Psalm 100:5 (ESV)

I'm heading out to help Opa in his garden, Mom."
Will, my five-year-old, had on a pair of too-big shorts, a stained T-shirt, and a black leather belt. Into the belt he had tucked a variety of tools, including my good kitchen spatula, a screwdriver, and a toy bow and arrow.

I followed him outside, watching as he walked next door to where my dad was planting flowers in his yard.

He tapped my dad's shoulder, and my dad turned around and smiled. He carefully took Will's hand, helped him pull the spatula out of the belt, and showed him how to dig a hole in the wet earth.

I wanted to scream, "That's my spatula!"

I wanted to tell my dad he didn't have to let Will help him, that the job would take twice as long, and that Will would likely break flower stems and tear the petals off his geraniums.

I wanted to call my little boy inside, to have him do something age-appropriate or educational or less messy.

But then I saw Will's eyes. Eyes that looked at his grandfather with admiration. Eyes that begged for more. More time, more love, more mud.

I knew then that God was giving my son just a glimpse of the always-patient, always-tender, always-gentle love He has for us. A love that includes us, that pulls us in even if we are likely to botch it up.

A love that takes the time to show us how to dig in the mud.

And holds our hands as beautiful flowers grow out of the mess.

Lord, thank You for the legacy of love that carries
from generation to generation. Amen.
—Erin MacPherson

Digging Deeper: Psalm 78:6; Deuteronomy 4:9

He had compassion on them, because they were harassed and helpless.
—Matthew 9:36 (NIV)

The teenager in the apartment two doors away was raging again. The police were by a month earlier, though, of course, we hadn't asked why. Now the girl was home again, and the conflict got more intense by the minute. It echoed through the hallway with terrifying ferocity.

My children sat glued to the sofa, wide-eyed. "I don't hear sounds of violence," I said, tentatively. Elizabeth and Stephen nodded, mute. I wondered, *Should we call 911? Wait for the argument to pass? What if things turn violent?* I had no idea what to do. I was suddenly reliving the experience of having to call 911 on my son John during a violent outburst years before. I hoped my kids were not affected as viscerally as I was.

I sent Stephen and Elizabeth off to their bedrooms, where it would be quieter, and after talking with each of them, I returned to the living room. The argument down the hall had abated. And then it took on new intensity.

The squawk of a walkie-talkie told me police had arrived. From the nature of the shouting, it seemed the mother had called 911. Chaos reigned for another twenty minutes as EMTs struggled to get the thrashing teenager onto a stretcher.

When all was quiet, I talked again to my deeply unsettled kids. I searched my frazzled brain for ways to fill the now-awful silence, and then I put my tension to work baking gingersnaps. I left a container of cookies by my neighbor's door with an anonymous note: I'm sorry you had such a horrible morning. Leaving the gift unlabeled was the second gift: it allowed the rattled mother to wonder which neighbor had been kind rather than worry about who was judging her.

Lord, in the midst of fear, set my heart to compassion.
—Julia Attaway

Digging Deeper: Matthew 7:1

Forget not to show love unto strangers: for thereby some have entertained angels unawares. —Hebrews 13:2 (ASV)

I pass two feed mills when I run, so I frequently encounter loud, diesel-huffing eighteen-wheelers hauling hopper-bottom trailers of grain to be ground as well as round-sided feed trailers bound for local livestock operations.

I should be grateful for them, since they dribble grain along the road and richly amplify the bird population. I'm not grateful, though. Whenever a big truck passes, its noise, stench, and lurching sloth make any birds I might see vanish. If I wait for the birds to return, another big semi invariably approaches and scares them away before I can record what I saw on my eBird app.

The other day, after a feed truck scattered the sparrows, it jerked to a stop beside me. The driver rolled down his window and hung himself over the side to speak to me.

"You Ms. Kirk?" He had to yell to be heard over the truck's roar.

"Yes?" I yelled up, hoping I'd successfully transformed my eye roll into a squint.

"Had you way back in seventh grade. Gave you hell, so you probably don't remember me." He told me his name—I didn't remember him—and hung himself down even farther to put his warm hand in mine. If he hadn't been so high up, I'm sure he'd have hugged me.

"Been thinking that was you. Wasn't sure, though," he said, after we exchanged news. "Now I'll be sure to wave at you all the time!"

His rosy face and unexpected warmth filled me with goodwill for days after that run.

Father, I'm so self-centered and mean. I'm sorry.
—Patty Kirk

Digging Deeper: Revelation 14:6–7; Hebrews 13:1–3

Thursday, June 13

I praise you because I am fearfully and wonderfully made; your works are wonderful, I know that full well. —Psalm 139:14 (NIV)

Gravel crunched underfoot. The tired muscles in my legs burned, begging me to stop. "Almost there," I puffed, willing myself to keep going. I was only out for my short morning jog, but for some reason, today it seemed like a marathon. "Come on, body, cooperate!" This shouldn't be so hard. I should just admit it, I am more lumbering beast than runner.

This negative dialogue played like a loop in my head until I rounded a corner and a glimmer caught my eye. What is that? Stopping short, I looked down and saw the sun's light twinkling off the wet surface of a small, brilliantly purple stone. Picking it up, I marveled at its beauty. How could something so extraordinary become mixed in with all that regular old gravel? Slipping it into my pocket, I looked forward to sharing it with my four-year-old. "Treasure," I knew she'd call it.

When I arrived home and retrieved the stone, I was surprised to find it had transformed. As it was dry now, its shine was gone. It had become just a dull gray pebble with a slight purplish hue. "Watch this, though," I told my daughter as we held it under the kitchen faucet. The moisture once again revealed the stone's splendor. Thinking about how critical I'd been of myself just a few moments earlier, I wondered if, seen through God's eyes, my ordinary, less-than-perfect self also sparkled. I smiled. Who would've guessed I could have so much in common with a little stone wet from the dew?

Thank You, Lord, for the reminder that all Your creations
are wonderfully made—including me.
—Erin Janoso

Digging Deeper: Revelation 15:3

While bodily training is of some value, godliness is of value in every way, as it holds promise for the present life and also for the life to come.
—1 Timothy 4:8 (ESV)

I contorted my hand in another attempt to lure an F chord from the depths of my guitar. The cool steel strings bit into my fingers. I strummed. The sound that issued from the instrument was warped and unbalanced. I'd been at this for an hour, trying to perform motions that were natural for me last summer. During the busy school year, there had been no time for music. Now my fingers were stiff. Their once-calloused tips were soft. It would take time and practice to relearn songs I had once mastered.

As I changed the position of my fingers and strummed again, I thought about something else I hadn't practiced during the school year: spending consistent time with God. I started the school year with good intentions. I attended weekly Bible studies and scheduled prayer time assiduously. But school dominated my life. What should have been the most important parts of my days sometimes disappeared between classes, homework, extracurriculars, and my job.

Without taking time for regular spiritual exercise, my life was off-key. My deficiency affected my attitude and actions. I became accustomed to grumbling about my schedule. I was impatient with others when they used up my time. My fingers weren't all that had stiffened—my heart had as well. I settled my instrument into its case and opened my Bible where its red-ribbon bookmark trailed out.

Ready to stretch. Ready for God to change my tune.

Lord, help me to be intentional and consistent about walking with You.
—Logan Eliasen

Digging Deeper: 1 Peter 2:2; Luke 2:52

Saturday, June 15

The very hairs of your head are all numbered. —Matthew 10:30 (NKJV)

My aversion to numbers began early. In fact, my earliest memory of counting went like this: "One, two, three, infinity."

That's because my dad used to say, "I'll count to three. One, two…," and we immediately did whatever he ordered, because we assumed the world would end if he ever got past three.

In grade school we learned multiplication tables. (By *we*, I mean not me. I struggled. I still struggle.) In high school we learned atomic weights of the periodic table, which I only understood periodically. Then I became a taxpayer: a collection of numbers and check boxes. My favorite question on Form 1040 is "head of household?"

You're supposed to check *yes* or *no*, but I have three daughters. I tried to write in, "Well, it sure ain't me," but the box was too small.

Jesus didn't seem to have much use for numbers, except to make a point. When asked how much we should give to the government, His cagey answer was something like, "Well, render what's appropriate, but your question misses the point." How many times should we forgive our neighbor? This time Jesus was seemingly specific: "I do not say to you up to seven times, but seventy times seven."

I don't think He meant 490. I think we're supposed to forgive our neighbor to infinity or until the world ends—whichever comes first.

Despite knowing the right answer, I still struggle with this particular problem.

Lord, the calculus of Your wisdom is both easy and easily forgotten:
forgive us as we forgive others.
—Mark Collins

Digging Deeper: Acts 27:34

Seek ye first the kingdom of God, and his righteousness; and all these things shall be added unto you. —Matthew 6:33 (KJV)

I was enjoying a rich discussion with my son, Johnny, one I didn't want to end. Pat and I were going home to Ohio the next morning following a great visit. Before heading to bed, I said, "Mom and I pray for you each day...the prayers we think you need." Then I asked him, "How would you like us to pray for you?"

Pausing, he said, "Pray that I will find fulfilling days, become an effective supervisor, and gain wisdom." I hadn't quite expected something so specific. Johnny, excited to be a new supervisor, was already experiencing how the drama of managing others can sometimes sidetrack a day.

While I prayed for Johnny that night, I thought of a small card tucked inside the Bible I take along whenever I travel. Inscribed on the card are words from Matthew 6:33: "Seek ye first the kingdom of God." My dad gave me the card when I was about Johnny's age—new in my career, not yet married, and filled with concerns. I had lamented about some fears to Dad and Mom during a visit home. Before going to the airport, Dad handed me the card, saying only, "You might like to have this." I read it, thanked him, and put the card in my Bible.

Now my prayer for Johnny is that he seeks first God each day. As he does, he can be confident he will grow in wisdom and find God's guidance to deal with all his needs...now and those yet to come. In doing this, he will become more effective in his work and enjoy fulfilling days!

Dear Lord, as I pass to my son this card with the wisest words
ever given to me, help me—like my dad—limit my words
so Your words speak to him. Amen.
—John Dilworth

Digging Deeper: Jeremiah 29:13; Psalm 9:10

Monday, June 17

Even to your old age and gray hairs I am he, I am he who will sustain you. I have made you and I will carry you; I will sustain you and I will rescue you. —Isaiah 46:4 (NIV)

My boys silently worked with construction paper as I sobbed. I had just gotten the call from my sister in Florida telling me my father was bleeding internally after surgery, and they didn't think he would make it. My six-year-old made a small black covering for my eyes—like a Zorro mask—to catch my tears. My seven-year-old made two hearts, one with my picture on it and the other with my father's, whom they called Papa. I wasn't crying because I thought he might die. No, I was already mourning his certain death before it came. He would not survive this; the doctors gave little hope. I cried myself to sleep, knowing I would wake without a father.

But morning came, and he was still alive. I had given up hope, but my father had not. He's never been one to give up, even as an impoverished child with bare feet and an empty belly. He didn't give up at age ten, when his father died, but instead worked hard to earn money to take care of his family. He never gave in. How did I ever believe he would give up now?

I flew out as soon as I could to be with my parents. "He's like Superman," the doctor said, amazed by his recovery. We were soon able to take him home, and I snuggled next to him on the couch, holding on tightly to a man who never let go of hope.

> *Remind me that You have the last word in all matters, God.*
> *No matter how hopeless the situation, I can hold on to hope,*
> *knowing all things are possible with You.*
> —Karen Valentin

Digging Deeper: Matthew 19:26

You make known to me the path of life. —Psalm 16:11 (NIV)

I love to walk the fields around our home, but the grasses covering them had grown thick and knee-high. While we don't have lots of snakes on our land, I'm still wary when I can't see where I'm walking. It wasn't quite time for our annual mowing, so my treks into the pastures dwindled, then disappeared, until my husband, David, surprised me by mowing tractor-wide paths through the dense grasses. I could now walk without fear, so I followed the paths, delighting in the purple, orange, and yellow wildflowers along the way. A red-winged blackbird perched on a fence post. From a thicket, two deer leaped and bounded away. Several red-tailed hawks soared overhead.

Enjoying these mowed trails reminded me of when I was young and my father mowed paths through tall grass in our backyard. I pretended they were rooms and hallways of a big house. I felt happy and secure playing inside those boundaries.

Paths make me feel safer. They tell me, *This is the way that's best.* They help me circumvent dangers I might otherwise stumble upon. When hiking, I prefer to take prepared trails rather than create my own, which could lead to perils I'd rather avoid. Paths lead me to my destination. Without them, I can be fearful or get lost.

David and my father aren't my only path makers. I have a loving shepherd Who leads me in paths of righteousness for His name's sake. I will fear no evil.

Thank You, Lord, for preparing the way and pointing me to it.
—Kim Taylor Henry

Digging Deeper: Isaiah 30:21; Psalm 23:3, 25:4–5

God made him who had no sin to be sin for us, that in him we might become the righteousness of God. —2 Corinthians 5:21 (NIV)

The river draws me. I walk down and sit at the water's edge. The serenity pulls me.

Inside I'm not serene. I feel rejected and left out. I cringe to think that I wrestle with such feelings, but I do. There's a circle of women I want to belong to, and I tried. I gave it my all. In the end, there was no acceptance. No inclusion. No favor.

I wasn't enough.

I pull blades of grass through my fingers and wonder why some friendships flourish and others fail. Is it chemistry? Timing? Is it a gift of God's grace when relationships work and possibly providential protection when they do not? I ponder. I feel the sun on my face. I breathe deep. As I do, I feel God's gentle Presence. As I sit, He reminds me He's here.

The town across the river has quaint buildings with white steeples and red-brown brick. Today the river acts as a mirror, and the town's reflection stretches over the water's surface. The image is unmarred. Defined. Perfect. Pure.

The simple-strong beauty speaks to me. I understand that the Lord looks at me and decides I am enough. He accepts me with sacrificial love. When He looks at me, He doesn't see shortcomings. He sees only the glorious, flawless reflection of Jesus.

Suddenly, I hear the heartbeat of grace. I feel the pulse of God's passion.

I am fully pleasing.

I am loved.

Lord, thank You for reminding me that I'm valuable. Amen.
—Shawnelle Eliasen

Digging Deeper: Romans 5:8; 1 Peter 1:18–19

You can make many plans, but the Lord's purpose will prevail.
—Proverbs 19:21 (NLT)

Thud! I looked up from my book to see what had hit the door in my study. Spotting nothing, I got up and looked down through the full glass pane. A tiny bird stood there, head cocked, looking dazed and confused. Other than that he seemed fine, so I returned to my book. A bit later I checked again. The bird was gone but had left a large swatch of droppings. It had obviously been frustrated that its intended path was blocked. Perhaps the droppings were its form of protest, voluntary or involuntary.

How many times have I flown straight into a figurative glass wall, been knocked down, and stood dazed and confused? How many times have I left my share of protest droppings to show my frustration at not getting to do what I'd planned, at not being able to pursue the path I'd chosen, at things not working out the way I'd hoped?

That little bird had no idea why we'd placed that glass door where we did. I'm sure he couldn't even see it and didn't know what had hit him. But it did its job, keeping the bird from pursuing a path into our house, where it's not in his best interest to go.

God has put invisible barriers in my path many times, knowing that while I won't see or understand, hitting those barricades is what's best for me. He also knows that other than looking a bit dazed, confused, and frustrated, I'll be just fine—far better than if I'd succeeded in following my own plans.

> *Lord, when things don't go my way, remind me to look for Yours.*
> —Kim Taylor Henry

Digging Deeper: Proverbs 16:1, 16:9, 20:24

Friday, June 21

I know that there is nothing better for people than to be happy and to do good while they live. That each of them may eat and drink, and find satisfaction in all their toil—this is the gift of God. —Ecclesiastes 3:12–13 (NIV)

Smile!" I called out, likely for the twentieth time that day. We had finally arrived at Disney World, and the day was already filled with memorable moments: an airplane ride, a bus trip, and now the kids were seeing the Magic Kingdom castle for the first time.

I was unable to take picture. "Storage almost full," read my phone.

"Shoot," I said. My husband, Brian, agreed to get pictures during the day, and with that, I put my phone away.

It sounds simple, but that moment was vacation-changing. I was no longer trying to capture each moment. Instead I soaked in the looks on my kids' faces as they experienced carousels and ice-cream bars. I left my phone in the hotel the rest of the time.

I don't consider myself phone-addicted, but I tend to pick it up if it's around, so having a week in which I could fully be in the moment with my family on vacation was an incredible gift. I could see God send this gift my way so I wouldn't miss out on the moments while trying to capture each and every one on camera.

The memories from that trip are clear in my mind, augmented by pictures grabbed by the grandparents and Brian. Believe it or not, I'm actually in some of them! Now when we go on vacation, I empty my phone's memory, but I also remember to step away from my cell so I, too, can enjoy giggles over an ice-cream bar and wave as the parade goes by.

Lord, thank You for every single reminder to be in the moment, in every moment of my life. Thank You for giving me a life of joy amid daily toil.
—Ashley Kappel

Digging Deeper: Ecclesiastes 8:15; 1 John 2:15

Consider how the wild flowers grow. They do not labor or spin. Yet I tell you, not even Solomon in all his splendor was dressed like one of these.
—Luke 12:27 (NIV)

I need to mow the lawn today," said my husband, Chuck, seated at the breakfast table.

"Don't cut the flowers!" said our young grandson, Logan.

"Flowers? What flowers?" I asked.

Logan pointed. "Those little purple ones."

Chuck and I followed the direction Logan pointed. Long, slender weeds had sprouted throughout the yard, each topped with tiny lavender-color flowers.

"Those are weeds," said Chuck.

"But they're pretty," insisted Logan.

We let the matter drop, and the conversation shifted to other subjects. Later that day, before Chuck mowed the yard, Logan came to me with his arms behind his back.

"Grandma, I have a surprise for you," he said, a satisfied look on his face.

"Oh? What is it?" I smiled, wondering what might appear before me. You never know when a little boy has a "surprise" for you.

He brought his arms around and held out a bouquet of the weeds with the purple flowers.

"See? Aren't they pretty?" he said with conviction.

"They certainly are. Thank you for my pretty flowers."

And they were. The little boy who gave them to me thought so, and his gift made them beautiful.

Lord, help me see the flowers instead of the weeds in Your creation.
Thank You for a little boy who sees the beauty in both.
—Marilyn Turk

Digging Deeper: Song of Songs 2:12; Genesis 1:11–12

Sunday, June 23

The grace of the Lord Jesus Christ, and the love of God, and the fellow-ship of the Holy Spirit, be with you all. —2 Corinthians 13:14 (NASB)

I haven't lived the day fully until I've had what I call "creative thought." This surprising way of thinking can startle me with its clarity, as happened one winter morning.

I sat before dawn, reading my Bible, three lit candles on the hearth representing the Trinity of God—Father, Son, and Holy Spirit. One candle was about to burn down, and I put it out. As I stared at the remaining two, I thought, *If I had to choose only two of the three—Father, Son, and Holy Spirit—whom would I leave out?*

I considered Jesus—the Son—and His presence in my life as Savior and Friend. The One Who died to forgive sin. Who rose from the grave to show the power of life over death. Who promises to "prepare a place" in heaven for me.

I contemplated the Father—Creator and Sustainer of all life and beauty in the world. The One Who so loved His creation that He sent the Son to redeem it. Who is filled with such holiness and light that no darkness can touch Him.

I dwelt on the Holy Spirit—Counselor and Comforter—the One living in me because of my faith in Jesus. The One Jesus promised to us when He said He would not leave His followers "as orphans" after He was no longer physically present on earth.

There was no way I could subtract from God. I felt new love and joy for the Trinity, and for Jesus's words: "But the Helper, the Holy Spirit whom the Father will send in My name, He will teach you all things" (John 14:26).

Precious Father, Son, and Holy Spirit, how I need Who You are.
     —Carol Knapp

Digging Deeper: Isaiah 9:6; John 1:1–23

I give thanks to you with all my heart, Lord. I sing your praise before all other gods. —Psalm 138:1 (CEB)

I loved eating carrots as a kid. The crunch in my teeth, the sweet taste on my tongue, the noise of the chewing inside my head, the bright orange color when I held them in my hand. Some adult always claimed, "Carrots are great for your eyes," or, "Carrots are great for your teeth," as though that's why I ate them.

If anybody had asked, I would have said, "I eat carrots because I like them."

Who ever said the things that are good for us have to be hard or come as the result of great struggle or simply taste yucky? Think of that old expression, "the carrot, not the stick," about how people are motivated by rewards rather than threats or punishment. My experience has shown that to be true. Praise, thankfulness, enthusiasm, kindness— they are all carrots, not sticks.

Take the Psalms, for instance. They're full of praise and thanksgiving, establishing a right relationship with God. Of course they're good to say and sing. But don't think for a moment God expects us to recite them because He needs all that praise. On the contrary, God likes us to praise Him because it's good for us. It feels good. The words taste sweet in our mouths, nourishing, crunchy, and satisfying. Irresistible.

Like munching on a handful of carrots.

Oh, Bread of Life, we feast on You and
can never stop singing Your praise.
—Rick Hamlin

Digging Deeper: Psalm 8:1; 1 Samuel 2:1–2; Revelation 4:8–9

Tuesday, June 25

The tongue can no man tame; it is an unruly evil, full of deadly poison.
—James 3:8 (KJV)

A student from the middle school where my son Chase teaches posted a video to social media. In it she and her friends giggled while sharing racial slurs and threats. The event reminded me of a story about my father.

It was a beautiful summer afternoon. I was a preschooler, jumping rope on the sidewalk next to my home while my beautiful mother watched me. She was the family's librarian, disciplinarian, and conscience. She talked about civil rights and the systematic mistreatment of the Navajos on the Arizona reservation, where she and my father taught during my first year of life.

My less-outspoken father left for work in St. Louis while it was still dark. He usually didn't return home until dusk, but that day he arrived early. My father walked to the sidewalk to join us.

Smiling at my mother, I sang as I jumped in time.

"Acka, backa, sodie cracker, acka, back boo!

If your daddy chews 'tobacca,' he's a dirty—"

The song ended with a slur.

The smile left my father's face. He spoke quickly, quietly, but firmly to my mother. "I don't ever want to hear her sing a song like that again." Uncharacteristically, my mother simply nodded. That was it.

It would be more than a decade before I understood the word's meaning, but my father's reaction made it very clear that cruel epithets and slurs would not be tolerated. Stopping cruelty requires prayer, and I pray each of us finds courage to resist injustice.

Lord, give us the courage to speak the truth with love,
embrace kindness, and resist evil.
—Sharon Foster

Digging Deeper: Ephesians 4:15–16;
Matthew 22:36–40; Luke 6:31

I am overwhelmed with joy in the Lord my God! —Isaiah 61:10 (NLT)

Sunrise, my golden retriever, ran wild, chasing her tail and splashing in the water of the irrigation ditch, which ran on my little farm. Sweat trickled down my back from the hot afternoon sun. I grumbled as I scooped a shovel of mud out of a ditch. *How am I going to get everything done?* At least I had gotten the car cleaned out that morning.

Over the next hour, I opened headgates and redirected the water across my field. Sunrise played exuberantly while I grumbled about everything. When it was time to go, I commanded my muddy dog to swim, in order to wash off, before I loaded her in the car. But just as I opened the back hatch to my Subaru, that clean dog spotted a mud puddle. She dived in it, rolled, bounded into the car...and shook. Mud flew everywhere. The car I'd spent an hour cleaning was now a disaster zone.

I stomped my foot and screamed at my happy dog. "Out! Get out right now!" Sunrise hopped out, wagged her tail, and I slammed the hatch closed. "Look at the mud you shook all over the car!"

A still, small voice in my spirit said, *Not unlike the muddy thoughts you've shook all over your day.* The blood drained from my face. I'd let my mind whirl with negative thoughts. I giggled when I dreamed up the solution. The next time those thoughts jumped into my mind, I needed to stomp my foot and command them to get out—and slam the hatch closed. Then choose to be filled with joy, like Sunrise.

I patted Sunrise's head. "Go wash up. We're going home."

Lord, show me how to focus my thoughts on Your blessings. Amen.
—Rebecca Ondov

Digging Deeper: 2 Corinthians 10:5; Joshua 1:7–9

Thursday, June 27

PRAYING THROUGH THE PSALMS: For Emotional Healing

Shut down debilitating self-criticism. —1 John 3:19 (MSG)

While studying Psalms, I found notes I'd scribbled in my Bible. Next to Psalm 68:19, I'd written, "6.27.94. Quit school." It was one of the worst days of my life. When I graduated from high school in 1978, Daddy said I was "college material." But I didn't pursue a four-year degree. Instead I got married.

On June 27, 1994, the day I wrote the note, I was a young wife, college student, and mother of three. The children and I were at our neighborhood pool when I realized I couldn't balance motherhood with studying. Feeling like a failure, I loaded them still in their bathing suits into the car and drove straight to the campus to withdraw from classes. I was the high school salutatorian who couldn't cut it. In the registrar's office, with Thomas on my hip and his sisters behind me, I felt covered by a cloud of shame. Convinced I'd disappointed God and ruined His plan for my life, I cried all the way home. Over twenty years later, I still cringed when anyone said, "Julie, where'd you go to college?" I needed emotional healing, but not having a degree was my deepest, darkest secret.

Months after finding the note in my Bible, I attended a Christian speakers' conference. The leaders instructed us to choose a gift bag. Each contained a different surprise.

When I peeked inside my green bag, my heart went *thumpity-thump*. It seemed God Himself had chosen this particular gift specifically for me: a giant pink eraser with "For Big Mistakes" printed on it. Holding the eraser, I mentally erased years of shame—shame He never placed on me. For so many years, what I considered a colossal mistake became part of His perfect plan for my life.

Father, "The lines have fallen for me in pleasant places; indeed, I have a beautiful inheritance" (Psalm 16:6). Thank You for forty years of marriage, three children, and the precious assurance of being in Your will.
—Julie Garmon

Digging Deeper: Isaiah 54:4; Psalm 25:2

Give to him that asketh thee. —Matthew 5:42 (KJV)

The flight attendant passed through the cabin during my flight from Dublin to Boston, gathering leftover pence and pounds for a relief organization. We passengers were encouraged to donate our spare change. After all, United Kingdom currency would be useless back in the States.

I hesitated. Finally I donated a plastic bag with a few coins but decided to keep the bulk of them—and they were bulky—as souvenirs of my visit to London and friends in East Anglia. Besides, I wanted to show them to my granddaughter. I transferred my half pound or so of souvenirs into my wallet and strained to zip it closed. The wallet attached safely to a clip inside my shoulder bag, and I forgot about it.

The next day, severely jet-lagged, I tried to resume my normal routine: drive to the gym, stash my shoulder bag in the car trunk, and swim. I finished my laps and opened the trunk to discover that, although my shoulder bag was there, my wallet was gone. I felt rising panic prickle in my chest. Frantic, I pawed through my truck, the car seats. I rushed home to check my room, my suitcases. Nothing.

I should mention that the zipper on my well-traveled shoulder bag had worn out months ago. I used the bag anyway. Now I noticed the inside clip had sprung. The extreme weight of my souvenir coins must have torn the wallet loose from my bag. It had fallen—who knows where—taking useless coins along with my IDs and 350 dollars in American cash.

I learned a hard lesson from this. Had I been more generous with piffling coins, the needy and I would have both benefited.

Dear God, forgive my selfish ways.
—Gail Thorell Schilling

Digging Deeper: Matthew 10:8; Deuteronomy 16:17

Saturday, June 29

Your life is a journey you must travel with a deep consciousness of God.
—1 Peter 1:18 (MSG)

Tony, the boys, and I walk the sandy path, our arms filled with towels, shovels, buckets, and a cooler. We've packed as light as possible for the long walk from the parking lot to the ocean. With every step, fiddler crabs scatter and disappear in nearby holes. The air is rich with life, salty ocean, and seaweed baking in the sun.

Ahead, beside the path, is something. We walk close enough to see it's a loon, its eyes closed, curled as if it is peacefully asleep. "What do you think killed it?" Solomon asks.

"It looks like it just died," Henry says, and it does.

We're about halfway to the point, a tucked-away Wellfleet, Massachusetts, heaven of sorts, with the curious name of "the Gut." This hard-to-get-to destination is worth every step, even in overcast and drizzle, but today is a perfect blue-sky day with a relaxing breeze, just right for wading in tide pools.

We round the bend, and the entrance is in sight. The boys run ahead. They stop, read something, and fall to their knees, defeated. "It's closed!" they yell. A sign explains the point is the current home of endangered nesting birds, and the beach is closed for their safety.

We sigh. We argue that the sign should be at the parking lot. We strain our necks to maybe see the ocean over the dune. We can't.

We turn around and head back, once again frightening fiddler crabs inside their holes. We revisit the loon Henry is positive died of old age. We talk about getting an ice cream on the way to a different beach, one that's close to the parking lot, and it seems a small family miracle we've managed to go with the flow.

Heavenly Father, help me remember times like this when plans change and I feel like I'm backtracking. Help me enjoy the journey.
—Sabra Ciancanelli

Digging Deeper: Genesis 1:20; Psalm 13:5

Jesus said to them, "Follow me! and I will make you become fishers of men."
—Mark 1:17 (ESV)

Forty-five years ago I was a young man unsure of my vocational future. However, what I did know was that I wanted to help people. By this time, my college grades had proven I was not destined to be a doctor. So, with a sense of hesitation, I decided to go to seminary. My father was a pastor, and I did not want to be a "pious preacher." I hoped there might be other options to choose from.

During my first semester at seminary, I had the good fortune—or providence—to take a course on contemporary people of faith whose lives have changed the world. I was assigned to study Dag Hammarskjold, former secretary-general of the United Nations. Fourteen years prior he was killed in an airplane crash while interceding in a political conflict in northern Rhodesia.

Late one night, while reading Hammarskjold's personal journal titled *Markings*, I was jolted by his words: *I don't know Who—or what—put the question. I don't know when it was put. I don't even remember answering. But at some moment I did answer Yes to Someone—or Something—and from that hour I was certain that existence is meaningful and that, therefore, my life, in self-surrender, had a goal.*

I was jolted awake! I realized I had at least said "yes!" to striving for a spiritual purpose. I did not know how, when, or where. But I knew I had said "yes!"

None of us can see the future. But we can say "yes!" to living a life of goodness each day. This is all that matters.

Dear God, help me say "yes!" today and to follow You! Amen.
—Scott Walker

Digging Deeper: Mark 1:16–20; Luke 9:23–25; Psalm 25:4–5

UNDER GOD'S WINGS

1 _____

2 _____

3 _____

4 _____

5 _____

6 _____

7 _____

8 _____

9 _____

10 _____

11 _____

12 _____

13 _____

14 _____

15 _____

16 _____

17 _____

18 _____

19 _____

20 _____

21 _____

22 _____

23 _____

24 _____

25 _____

26 _____

27 _____

28 _____

29 _____

30 _____

JULY

*Do not let your hearts be troubled. You
believe in God; believe also in me.*

—John 14:1 (NIV)

*Jesus answered them, "My Father is still working, and
I also am working."* —John 5:17 (NRSV)

Only my husband, Kris, knows how to operate his elaborate
espresso machine, so he always makes our breakfast. Nothing
fancy (besides the coffee): for himself, bacon and eggs and two espressos and, for me, bran cereal and a gigantic café latte.

While Kris cooks, I play solitaire on my computer. I like to "just win
once" before beginning the day.

I don't always win before leaving for work. Sometimes I turn on my
computer to a slew of work emails, so I can't even try. But usually I
can claim a victory, thanks to my brother, Larry, teaching me how to
control-Z my way backward through the game whenever I'm losing.

Why is sorting random cards into columns so satisfying? I recently wondered. Thinking it through, I decided I like something about making
disorder into order. It's why I like writing—shuffling random experiences into stories and essays that help me make sense of an event
or topic. And teaching writing—helping students sort their ideas into
interesting stories and compositions. And cooking—rearranging the
mess in the refrigerator and pantry into healthy, good-tasting meals.

God is the original reorganizer. Out of formlessness, He created our
whole universe. He's still at work making our chaos into order. Surely
we humans, made in His image, inherited that desire to organize the
mishmash around us into something good.

I pervert that creative urge by wasting it on games instead of, say,
cleaning my house. But I'm fundamentally equipped, inclined even, to
do God's kind of wholesome, creative work, if I only would.

Creator-God, shape my creative urges into good creations!
—Patty Kirk

Digging Deeper: Genesis 1–2; John 4:1–18

Tuesday, July 2

His unchanging plan has always been to adopt us into his own family by sending Jesus Christ to die for us. —Ephesians 1:5 (TLB)

Shea Cacoria Kuyper!" Two-year-old *Sheila Victoria* Kuyper enthusiastically bangs her "judge's gavel," announcing her presence to the family and friends who've gathered. My newly adopted granddaughter has not only a new last name but also a new middle name—chosen in honor of me. And what an honor it is!

Sheila's four-year-old sister, Laverna (Lula), stands nearby as the younger one holds court. They're both wearing their Team Kuyper T-shirts paired with bright pink tennis shoes, the official family uniform for this special day. Balloons, stuffed bears, official paperwork, applause, and a smattering of joyful tears are all part of the adoption celebration. In less than fifteen minutes, two sisters who've been in the foster care system for almost two years will officially have a "forever" family.

But there's a flip side to the adoption celebration. In the hall outside the courtroom, right before the proceedings begin, a stranger unexpectedly calls out, "Laverna?" Sweeping Lula up into her arms, the woman says, "I'm your mother!" Lula and Sheila don't recognize her, but she certainly recognizes them. I can't help imagining this woman searching the face of every two- or four-year-old girl she passes on the street every day in hopes of seeing her children. Although it's a seemingly random encounter, I feel this moment is God's gift to her—a quick hug, the reassurance her girls are OK, and a chance to say goodbye.

Every happy adoptive family begins with the story of a family in crisis, including yours and mine. Our invitation to become God's children came at a cost—Jesus's sacrifice on the cross. It's at the heart of our own adoption celebration.

> *Dear Lord, I want to be a child who follows in her Father's footsteps. Please teach me how to love You, and others, well.*
> —Vicki Kuyper

Digging Deeper: Romans 8:22–23

After this I beheld, and, lo, a great multitude, which no man could number, of all nations, and kindreds, and people, and tongues, stood before the throne, and before the Lamb, clothed with white robes, and palms in their hands. —Revelation 7:9 (KJV)

Summertime has always meant corn on the cob, barbecue, swimming, and fireworks. I'd been counting down the days to July Fourth, anticipating the fantastic light displays that come.

I was like an excited toddler as my daughter and I made our way to the shopping center and found a place to park where we could see the light display. Even before night fell and the fireworks began, there were so many people to observe. I marveled at God's display.

A middle-aged European-American couple flew two large flags from the back of their truck. A Latino family was parked next to us, and a gaggle of Asian children ran back and forth behind us. They were soon joined by some African-American children, all laughing with delight. All of them, all of us American. I smiled as I watched everyone, imagining what America's founders might think of this celebration.

They were immigrants, who founded a nation on Native American land, forging roads and erecting buildings with the labor of enslaved Africans brought to America. There was never a time when our nation was not diverse. Despite our stumbles and setbacks, we are learning to respect and even enjoy one another, to coexist.

When the fireworks began, we oohed and aahed with our neighbors. The flashes, all the colors, the people. I giggled with joy and clapped my hands, thankful for the display.

Lord, we stare in amazement at the beauty You have created.
Help us to love and appreciate every soul.
—Sharon Foster

Digging Deeper: Revelation 7:9–17; Leviticus 19:34;
John 17:20–23

Independence Day, Thursday, July 4

It is God himself who has made us what we are and given us new lives from Christ Jesus; and long ages ago he planned that we should spend these lives in helping others. —Ephesians 2:10 (TLB)

I love coincidences. My sister-in-law, her husband, and their firstborn all have the same birthday: March 17. The chances of something like that happening must be a million to one.

Another coincidence was revealed to my friend Abby when her daughter was experiencing a rough time in her marriage. Abby pulled out a greeting card from her stash to send to her daughter. The words on the card were a Bible verse: "Be still and know that I am God" (Psalm 46:10). As Abby read the verse, she wasn't sure it applied. She sent it anyway. That weekend, during the Sunday Mass Abby attended, the priest delivered a sermon entirely centered on that very verse. As Abby left the church, the choir sang a song that also contained those words. Abby's daughter was moved, and the verse helped her considerably. It was certainly more than just coincidence.

July Fourth also has a special coincidence. John Adams and Thomas Jefferson, the only signers of the Declaration of Independence to become presidents of the United States, died within five hours of each other on July 4, 1826. Five years later, the next former US president to die was James Monroe, who also passed away on Fourth of July, in 1831.

Coincidences are interesting and fun. However, I believe God has a hand in everything. Because when coincidences happen, they make us take notice of things that often change lives for the better.

Lord, today on July Fourth, keep me aware that coincidences are Your way of waking me up to the fact that You are right here guiding, inspiring, and encouraging me to keep plugging away.
—Patricia Lorenz

Digging Deeper: Exodus 34:5–6; Psalm 31:6–8

The people who trust the Lord will become strong again. They will rise up as an eagle in the sky; they will run and not need rest; they will walk and not become tired. —Isaiah 40:31 (NCV)

I was born into the Adler family during the baby boom years following World War II. Six cousins arrived within a few short months of one another. Adler is a German name that translates to "eagle," and all six of us have soared together over the years. We grew up alongside one another, attending the same church and schools. Our families vacationed and spent holidays together. When my husband, Wayne, and I were married, my cousin Linda served as my maid of honor. We six were as close as siblings. Entering adulthood, we moved away and spread out in different directions.

This last Fourth of July, I decided it was time for us all to get together again, and I invited my cousins to a mini-reunion at our home. I decorated our patio in red-white-and-blue with American flags. My cousins and I sat around, talked, and laughed for hours, recalling events from childhood as we shared stories of growing up as Adlers. How fortunate we were to be part of a close family!

After everyone left I wandered about the house and grounds to do a quick cleanup, and I saw something unusual in the front yard. I went to investigate, and what I found brought chills down my spine. Sticking straight up in the yard was an eagle feather. To me, this was a sign that my mom, dad, my aunts, and uncles had been watching over us, letting me know they too had enjoyed the get-together.

Dear Lord, although raised in the Adler family here on earth,
I know my eternal family is in heaven. Thank You.
—Debbie Macomber

Digging Deeper: Psalm 18:32

Saturday, July 6

LESSONS FROM THE ANIMALS: Life Is Good!

Titus not only welcomed our appeal, but he is coming to you with much enthusiasm and on his own initiative. —2 Corinthians 8:17 (NIV)

I'm sure I've learned more from my dogs than they have ever learned from me. Love, acceptance, loyalty, compassion, empathy. These are all qualities they have deepened in me. Dogs have taught me to be a better human being. And Gracie, our golden retriever, yet again showed me something I could use more of in my life.

If Gracie could take a personality assessment test, she would be an off-the-charts extrovert. Every dog she sees she greets joyously. One day we arrived at Chelsea Dog Park at an off time, and only one other dog was there—mature, stately Nico.

I've known Nico for years. If ever a dog took himself seriously, it's Nico. He's a big shepherd mix with a somber gaze. Nico stood astride one of the rocks in the park. Gracie bounded up and gave him a playful nudge. He backed off indifferently. She tapped his nose with her paw. Nico bared his teeth. Not a threat, just a mild warning. Gracie took flight, tail and ears flying, buzzing Nico like a dive-bomber. Nico growled. Gracie got down in a play crouch and gave a little bark, which translates, "C'mon, let's play."

All at once Nico lunged. Gracie tore off. Nico and Gracie played for a whole hour, while I thought about Gracie's persistence, exuberance, and confidence she could break through Nico's reserve.

At this point in my life, am I still an unfettered optimist? Or am I Nico? Probably a question that never would have occurred to me if not for Gracie. I know for sure how I want to answer.

Lord, You send many angels to teach me how to live with joy
and exuberance. Thank You for Gracie and all my dogs.
May I be worthy of their wisdom and companionship.
—Edward Grinnan

Digging Deeper: Hebrews 13:22

If we confess our sins, he is faithful and just and will forgive us our sins and purify us from all unrighteousness. —1 John 1:9 (NIV)

My pastor preached today from the first book of John. John was a disciple who lived and walked with Jesus during His time on earth. John wrote about many things, including the importance of a forgiven life. "Sin can push us away from God," Pastor Steve said. "Fellowship with God comes through forgiveness and properly dealing with our sins."

It was a timely message for me. Lately when I settle in for my night-time prayers and reflection, I list the things I am grateful for. Most recently I've had quite a list. Yesterday I discovered monarch caterpillars munching on my milkweed. I saw a bright blue indigo bunting in the bird feeder. And I received the news my son is having his first baby boy. The list goes on and on.

I realize now that I'd been skimming over the more challenging parts of my life, not taking moral inventory of my days. I reflect on my daily thoughts and actions to see if perhaps I did not respond as best as I could have in a situation that deserved my care. If not, I plan to ask for forgiveness and make amends.

Pastor Steve's message was clear. We shouldn't "wait to do anything that breaks fellowship from God."

By not acknowledging my shortcomings and certainly not correcting them, I was missing out on opportunities for personal growth. I decided that night and those that followed to begin my prayers with my grateful list, then reflect on where I had fallen short with God and others and ask for forgiveness. That Sunday sermon was a careful reminder that my shortcomings push me away from God. Away from Him is never where I want to be.

Forgive me when I fall short of Your goodness, Lord.
—Melody Bonnette Swang

Digging Deeper: Colossians 1:13–14; Isaiah 1:18

Monday, July 8

SAYING GOODBYE TO MY VETERANS
Facing My Replacement

Therefore do not worry about tomorrow. —Matthew 6:34 (NIV)

I'd just attended a staff meeting in which everyone seemed to be talking about the future. A future I wasn't going to be a part of due to retirement. Shortly after that meeting, I received an email announcing that my replacement had been chosen.

I fingered the lace edging on the collar of my blouse. *You'll soon be as disregarded as a scrap of heirloom lace in contact with a moth, Roberta.* I simply wasn't prepared for the spectrum of emotions I would face at the end of a thirty-eight years career caring for America's veterans.

My replacement nurse's name is Maggie. I know her as an accomplished ICU nurse. She is brilliant, beautiful, and has a darling personality. I know she also has the energy necessary to juggle the multiple roles and responsibilities of the job. *But will she adore my veterans?*

I struggled with the thought. Mostly because of people like Charlie, a ninety-something World War II patient who had a horribly painful bone infection from a shrapnel injury inflicted during combat. Charlie always arrived alone to the clinic. He needed abundant TLC.

Was Maggie up to the task? Would she listen to all of his stories?

Maggie would likely exceed me on many levels, for she is younger and ready for a new challenge. I decided to send her a big bouquet of flowers in a decanter I'd purchased at an estate sale and was saving for someone special. I'd also share secret tips for mastering the job and give her a top-notch orientation. To passionately mold a newbie is to believe in tomorrow.

Before I knew what was happening, my feelings followed my actions. I fell in love with Maggie and prayed for her to do well. Most important, I knew she would adore the veterans I so loved.

I see now, Lord, that in Your plan, no one really replaces another.
Each of us makes a one-of-a-kind contribution.
—Roberta Messner

Digging Deeper: John 14:7; Joshua 1:9

He is the Rock, his works are perfect, and all his ways are just.
A faithful God who does no wrong. —Deuteronomy 32:4 (NIV)

My husband, Charlie, introduces himself at the beginning of every phone call. "Charlie Duffy calling," he says, and then explains why he's calling. He does this whether he's calling a close friend, a doctor's office, an insurance company, or the computer service technician in India.

It's always kind of driven me nuts.

It seemed a bit arrogant to me, as if the person on the other end should sit up straight, drop whatever he or she is doing, and acknowledge the honor of receiving a phone call from Charlie Duffy. Indeed, when I heard him introduce himself, I occasionally muttered under my breath, "Like they care."

I've always assumed the people I'm calling are not thrilled to hear from me, particularly if I have a problem to resolve. I am keenly aware that I am consuming precious time in their busy days. I figure the sooner the call is complete, the better. Consequently, when I make a call, I am formal, perhaps even a little brusque and defensive.

I had a wake-up call the other night after our evening prayer. As usual I came to God with formal words of praise, thanks, and petition, wondering if I was getting it right. Charlie, on the other hand, approached God with great familiarity, expecting to be heard. We were facing a problem at our condominium, and he presented it to God. Charlie's prayer was, "God, please, please, please, please, *please* help us!"

After prayer time, Charlie was cheerful, wondering what we'd eat for dinner, while I moped around, still worried. I realized I needed to change my heart and my words.

"Hi, God, Marci calling…"

> *Lord, help me remember that You always*
> *recognize my voice and are ready to listen.*
> —Marci Alborghetti

Digging Deeper: Deuteronomy 33:26; 1 Samuel 2:1–3

Wednesday, July 10

THINGS MY MOTHER TAUGHT ME: Big Little Things

The Lord directs the steps of the godly. He delights in every detail of their lives. —Psalm 37:23 (NLT)

When I was seven, my mother took me to the Samuel Elbert Hotel in Elberton, Georgia, to have my portrait made by Olan Mills. We stood in line with others waiting. The hall carpet was maroon with yellow swirls. I whispered to Mother as she leaned down to hear me, "Look at that little girl behind us. She has Shirley Temple curls."

Mother glanced back at the adorable child. "Oh, Mannie, I know what we forgot. A ribbon for your hair! I'm going to run across the street to Woolworth and get you one. Be right back!"

Stealing glances at the child with the huge blue bow in her bobbing curls, I waited. As the line moved up, I glanced back to look for Mother. She came, hurrying down the hall, speaking to friends. From a small brown bag, she pulled out a pink hair ribbon already tied into a bow. She knelt down, smiling, and placed the bow in my straight brown hair.

"Now you just smile for the man, baby. You are beautiful."

I still have the picture in the frame she used. A rather plain child with a pink ribbon in her hair—smiling big-time. It was such a little thing. Seemingly.

My friend Bobby had been hospitalized. I wanted to take her something. A little thing that might mean a lot.

Right then I looked out the window at my miniature pink rosebush. Twelve tiny buds were just starting to open. I cut them and arranged them in a small milk glass vase, then hurried to the hospital that late afternoon.

"Oh, Marion. Pink roses from your very own yard. Put them where I can see them. How beautiful." Bobby beamed.

Help me remember, Jesus, that little things mean a lot.
—Marion Bond West

Digging Deeper: John 14:26; Psalm 25:9

Pray for each other so that you may be healed. The prayer of a righteous person is powerful and effective. —James 5:16 (NIV)

As a working mom of four, I seldom have time to pamper myself. So I was really excited to get my eyebrows threaded and shaped. When I entered the salon, my senses were immediately awakened by the essential oils permeating the room. I took a seat and relaxed while waiting to be serviced.

Ten minutes later, a young woman approached and apologized for my wait. But I was unbothered. It had been calming to sit still for a moment with no agenda or to-do list to check off.

She went on to thank me for being patient and explain that her delay was because her father had called with horrible news: his doctors discovered a cancerous tumor. At that point no one knew how aggressive the tumor was or his next steps of treatment. Her father lives in her home country of Iran, far from her current residence in Nashville, Tennessee. She had no idea when she would be able to visit him.

I expressed my deep concern and empathy for her situation. I, too, have walked the road of aging, ill parents living far away. After she finished my eyebrows, I asked if I could pray for her. She asked if I was Muslim, and I said, "No, I was in fact a Christian." She smiled and said, "Oh, I have so much respect for Christians and for Jesus. Of course you can pray for me."

I took her hand and prayed for her father's health and the peace of God. With tears in her eyes, she thanked me.

It was amazing to me how much my purpose had changed. I'd entered the salon hoping to have my needs and wants met but left having shared my heart with someone in need of prayer.

Lord, thank You for opportunities to pray for others,
friends and strangers alike.
—Carla Hendricks

Digging Deeper: Ephesians 6:18; Philippians 4:6; John 5:14–15

Friday, July 12

May these words of my mouth and this meditation of my heart be pleasing in your sight. —Psalm 19:14 (NIV)

As I walked across a parking lot at the mall, I ran into a friend I hadn't seen for a while. In the midst of catching up, she mentioned a mutual acquaintance had recently accomplished something noteworthy. "So well deserved for such a kind person," she added.

Instead of echoing her words of praise, I wanted to say something unkind. This person had wounded me years ago, and I wanted to challenge that "kindness" description.

In that instant I faced a familiar choice: to say what I wanted to say, or not. When faced with this situation, I've been trying to pause long enough to think before spilling words from the tip of my tongue. I've done that before and almost always later regret that choice.

In that parking lot, I paused long enough to access that place deep inside me where the better response lives. The place in my soul where Jesus's love shapes my love for others and gives me the words I'll be thankful I said as I remember this conversation later.

"Nice," I finally said. "Good for her."

As I walked away, I doubted my friend noticed my pause moment. But I'm pretty sure she would have noticed if I'd chosen to say something unkind.

Lord, there's power in a pause moment, and when I stop to invite You into that moment, You give me what I need to make the righteous choice.

PS: I know I need to talk to You about letting go of old wounds.
—Carol Kuykendall

Digging Deeper: James 3:9–12

ENCOUNTERING GOD IN UNLIKELY PLACES
Pink Hair and a Baby

My thoughts are not your thoughts. —Isaiah 55:8 (NIV)

What kind of mother dyes her hair pink? I asked myself as I walked in the park. My eyes followed her as she pushed an infant in a rickety umbrella stroller. About ten feet behind, a little guy not older than three tried with all his might to keep up.

Driving home, a memory caused me to make a sudden U-turn. I saw my own mother, age four, trailing her mother, dragging a suitcase away from a train station. Two miles from home, my mother with two baby sisters in tow, had been abandoned by their father.

Back in the park, the trio was huddled together on a park bench. I hurried into the food court on the opposite side of the street, emerging with a sack of bananas, bottled water, milk, cookies, and food bars.

My heart sank. They had disappeared.

Wait, what was that up ahead? A shock of pink hair!

I was a bit nervous as I approached them. But the mother, to put it mildly, was relieved. She was gracious, and her smile of appreciation was priceless. The father had promised to pick the three of them up hours earlier, but he never came.

She filled the boy's sippy cup with milk and cuddled him as the baby slept. His favorite food, she shared with me, was bananas.

We visited awhile. I lent her my phone, and she called a relative who was happy to rescue them.

I hugged her as I left.

So, here You are, God, I thought as I softly touched her pink hair. *Here You are.*

> *Father, You used pink hair to allow me to make a painful memory*
> *right and to show me Your smile in a young mother's gratitude.*
> —Pam Kidd

Digging Deeper: 1 John 3:20; John 7:24

Sunday, July 14

PRAYING THROUGH THE PSALMS
Lord, You Are My Lifeline

My heart overflows with a good theme. —Psalm 45:1 (NASB)

When I began praying through Psalms, I wasn't sure which version of the Bible to use. Several were stacked in the wicker basket beside my bed. Finally I settled on my New American Standard translation—the one I'd had since childhood, full of markings, with its maroon cover falling off. Holding it in my lap, I felt eight years old again.

But strangely, verses I'd memorized as a child seemed like long-ago, far-away nursery rhymes. Sad. I remembered quoting them at church when I was in elementary school. After I grew up, though, something happened. I stopped reciting my verses to make sure I wouldn't forget them.

This had to change. As I inched my way through my Bible, each time a verse tugged on my heart, I wrote it down. Soon I'd filled a notebook. I wanted to carry it with me at all times, but it was the size of a three-ring binder.

I shopped until I found the perfect journal—pink, leather, and small enough to fit inside my purse. With the same determination I'd had as a child, I condensed my life verses and carefully printed them on the lined pages:

Our help is in the name of the Lord (Psalm 124:8).
You made me bold with strength in my soul (Psalm 138:3).
Even darkness is not dark to You (Psalm 139:12).
You are the God Who works wonders (Psalm 77:14).
How lovely are Your dwelling places (Psalm 84:1).

Now I take my pink journal everywhere I go—to the grocery store, the dentist's office, and even on the streets of downtown Atlanta. And I was wrong! The words I'd memorized in elementary school never left me. They're still alive and well. When I speak them, they rise up, full of hope, from deep within my soul.

You, O Lord, are my hope, my trust...from my youth (Psalm 71:5).
—Julie Garmon

Digging Deeper: Psalm 96:1, 104:5

They say, and do not. —Matthew 23:3 (KJV)

I was walking to the sandwich shop and heard a long honk from the parking lot across the street. As my eyes followed the sound, I saw a furious lady leaning out her car window. She was shouting obscenities and making rude hand gestures at an elderly gentleman who, it seemed, accidentally backed out in front of her. She was at least a car length away from the gentleman who was backing up, and it was entirely possible her car had not been visible to him. I couldn't help thinking she must have felt she had a right to take "her half out of the middle" as she traveled through life. That sense of entitlement was in her display.

I was amazed at the depth of her anger. Why didn't she simply stop and allow the man to exit his parking spot? Instead she continued to lean on the horn until he pulled back in and waved apologetically to her. He smiled and mouthed, *"I'm sorry,"* as she screeched by and shook her head in disgust.

As she pulled away, I noticed a glowing cross sticker on her rear window, an advertisement to everyone that she was a Christian.

"False advertising," I said out loud. But then, just as quickly, I had to ask myself, how many times have I "said and done not"?

I made my way to the shop and decided to strengthen my resolve to try my best to be who I say I am.

> *Father, following Your way is not an easy job.*
> *Give me the wisdom to stay on Your path.*
> —Brock Kidd

Digging Deeper: James 1:8; Luke 6:46

Tuesday, July 16

If I rise on the wings of the dawn, if I settle on the far side of the sea,
even there your hand will guide me, your right hand will hold me fast.
—Psalm 139:9–10 (NIV)

I wanted to run away. Life was getting out of control. The burdens were weighing me down.

Texts and calls to a son who lived out of state went unanswered. My imagination went to the worst-possible scenarios. Is he in trouble? Sick? Hurt?

Another son was upset about a relationship gone bad.

And we had our grandson, Logan, to care for. The day-to-day challenges of raising a young child wore on my husband and me. I couldn't share my distress with my husband, though, because he was having his own issues with our situation. There really wasn't anyone I could talk to, except God. But I wondered if He remembered me, since my prayers seemed to be going unanswered.

I couldn't run away from my problems, so I opted for a walk instead— someplace I hadn't been before, a place where I wouldn't see any neighbors who required conversation. I took off away from my home and walked past familiar streets, not knowing where I was going. After I'd walked some distance, I turned down a street I hadn't been on before and headed toward the bay that surrounds the area. Seeing a vacant lot, I crossed it to the shore, where I found remnants of an old pier. I sat by the water and talked to God. Soon the tears flowed. Is God listening? Does He even know I still exist?

The water's gentle, rhythmic lapping on the small beach calmed me, and peace washed over me. I lifted my eyes to the sky and heard the reassuring words of God in Psalm 139:9–10. He did remember me.

Dear Father, thank You for not forgetting me
and for caring about my concerns.
—Marilyn Turk

Digging Deeper: Isaiah 41:10; Deuteronomy 31:6

We do not wrestle against flesh and blood, but against the rulers, against the authorities, against the cosmic powers over this present darkness, against the spiritual forces of evil in the heavenly places. —Ephesians 6:12 (ESV)

The fish was tiny. Like, maybe if I rounded up, I could say it was three inches long, but it was probably more like two.

Regardless, my five-year-old son, Will, had reeled it in all by himself. "Take a picture, Mom!"

Will held the line up in front of his face, the fish squirming on the line. I grabbed my phone and snapped a picture before my husband unhooked it and tossed the fish back into the stream.

Later that evening, we looked through my pictures on my phone and found the one of Will with his teeny, tiny fish. Only now the fish looked huge. The angle of the phone had changed the perspective, making it so the fish looked like it was a foot long at least.

I shared the picture with Will. He was amazed. "Wow, that fish I caught was huge!"

I decided we needed to talk about perspective, how sometimes something that's really tiny seems huge when you look at it from a certain camera angle or distance. likewise, something really big can look tiny if it's far away.

"So we can't always believe things are just like they look, right, Mom?" Leave it to a five-year-old to have spiritual insight beyond that of an adult.

I pulled him into a hug. "That's right, buddy. Many things in our world look or feel huge even though they are actually tiny. And other things appear to be tiny but are really huge."

"I think I'll just tell everyone I caught a medium-size fish, then, Mom." Then he ran outside to play.

Jesus, give me discernment to seek out the big things in life—those that really matter—and to toss aside the tiny things, even if they seem huge. Amen.
—Erin MacPherson

Digging Deeper: Colossians 1:9; 1 Corinthians 2:11

Thursday, July 18

By this everyone will know that you are my disciples, if you love one another. —John 13:35 (NIV)

I was flying home from a family vacation and also getting an earful. A woman a few rows back had some frustrations to air about her job. And air them, she did. Loudly. Though she was talking to her seatmate, I imagine at least a quarter of the passengers on the plane could hear her as clearly as I did.

Like many employees, she felt too much responsibility was placed on her. She criticized her boss and coworkers. Things we've all heard or maybe even said at one time or another—just maybe not so boisterously and in a cramped space filled with strangers.

At some point in her rant, the woman revealed her profession: she was in ministry! "I say all this with love and exhortation," she added. My heart sank.

I couldn't help cringe at the example she was setting for all the passengers in earshot. Did she really think adding a claim about "love and exhortation" at the end of her comments was edifying? Was this her churched-up version of adding "no offense" at the end of an offensive statement? I was sad to think of how many fellow passengers might run in the other direction from church after overhearing this minister. She definitely wasn't making Christianity sound appealing.

But what about me? Do onlookers see the fruit of the Spirit in my life? Or am I more like this woman on the plane than I'd care to admit?

Message received, Lord. It's sometimes hard not to give in to frustrations. Help me to build up, not tear down.
—Ginger Rue

Digging Deeper: Philippians 4:11; Ephesians 4:1–3

Since we died with Christ, we know we will also live with him.
—Romans 6:8 (NLT)

I had been busy most of the morning in meetings before I noticed the blinking red light on my phone indicating I had a voice mail. The sad, unfamiliar voice I heard was the daughter of my dear friend and former colleague Florence. "Mom passed away. She had you on the list of people for me to call," she said. Six months earlier, Florence was diagnosed with terminal cancer. We spoke several times between the diagnosis and her passing.

Our last conversation was about three weeks before she went home to be with the Lord. During this chat, we took a trip down memory lane and talked about funny stories from the past. Florence had a wonderful sense of humor. We recalled a Guideposts event that took place many years ago. I was wearing a pink tie with my blue suit, and a woman approached me and said, "You are wearing a Donald tie." I didn't know what she meant.

Florence was nearby, so I said, "This lady just told me I am wearing a Donald tie. Did she mean Donald Duck?" Florence burst out into laughter and said, "No, a Donald Trump tie." I knew she really wanted to say, "No, dummy, it's a Donald Trump tie." I was clueless about the tie label, but her reaction made me laugh. And we never forgot that moment.

Florence brought a spirit of joy into every conversation. Even when she knew death was knocking at her door, she never lost her joy and love for the Lord. I was comforted as I remembered how she received the news when she was first diagnosed. She told me, "I'm ready to go home. I was blessed to live this long. I've had a good life. The Lord has been good to me."

> *Lord, may You be our solid Rock in life and death.*
> —Pablo Diaz

Digging Deeper: Romans 8:38; Revelation 21:4

Saturday, July 20

Be kind to one another, tenderhearted, forgiving one another, as God in Christ forgave you. —Ephesians 4:32 (ESV)

I'd had an aching and restless heart all day. A family member casually said a hurtful thing, and I felt blindsided and attacked. I work with words all day, every day. I struggle to find the right ones, spend hours arranging and rearranging them, and so it seems I reexamined the hurtful words with an editor's eye. I analyzed the insult, turning it this way and that, searching for motivation, questioning word choice, and nitpicking the perceived offense. I deconstructed and reconstructed the affront a dozen times before I realized I was worsening the situation.

I called a friend and felt my anger rise as I went into great detail about what was said. I shooed away advice to simply let it go and found an excuse to hang up.

I turned to prayer but still rehashed the whole miserable, hurtful ordeal, complaining and complaining until I had worked myself up again.

When the restlessness didn't go away, I turned to cleaning. I scrubbed the kitchen cabinets and stove, and when that didn't help, I filled a pail with water, got on my hands and knees, and washed the floor.

The day was half over, and my heart still felt tarnished. My mind raced with thoughts that were making me sick, so I put on my sneakers and went outside for a run. The air was cool. My pace quickened. Up one hill and down another, my breath grew fast and even. I lost myself in the pace. In the pace, I found peace. Right there, in that moment— my aching heart soared a little. I stopped in my tracks and took a deep, long, clearing breath, and a heaviness lifted, just enough for my heart to begin to mend.

Heavenly Father, forgiveness isn't easy. Guide me to heal my wounded heart, to stop focusing on things that hurt and instead lead me to Your comfort and love.
—Sabra Ciancanelli

Digging Deeper: James 5:16; Luke 6:27

Come! Let's bow down and worship! Let's kneel before the Lord, our Creator! —Psalm 95:6 (NET)

When we sing in church, I hate making claims that I'm doing something I'm not: shouting hallelujah, raising my hands, bowing my head. I feel so uncomfortable. Here I am, in church for Pete's sake, and I'm lying.

Just do it, part of me says. *Cry out! Lift your hands! Dance!*

But my other parts are too embarrassed. Or proper. And by the time I get this far in my thinking, it's too late anyway—we're singing about something else.

So I was standing in church last Sunday, and, while singing the hymn, I found myself making the claim that I was kneeling.

I've never been a kneeler. Except in my Catholic childhood, when postures of worship were mandated during Mass and when my parents oversaw my bedtime prayers.

These days, I pray in whatever position I happen to be in: lying in bed, standing before a classroom of students, sitting coffee in hand with colleagues, or staring at the computer screen reading some desperate piece of news. I never kneel to pray.

But you should, Adviser Me coached as I sang the song's lie.

What's so holy about kneeling? Rational Me demanded.

The answer that filled me, as I stood, wanting to kneel but not, was this: I only ever kneel to garden or play with small children, tasks God gave us in the beginning. Till the soil! Produce good children!

To kneel is to accept God's assignment, I realized then. Kneeling is saying simply, "I'm willing."

> *Creator God, help me kneel to Your will and plan.*
> —Patty Kirk

Digging Deeper: Luke 1:26–38; Romans 14:11–12

Monday, July 22

As he thinks in his heart, so is he. —Proverbs 23:7 (NKJV)

First day of my child's science camp, and chaperones gathered outside for orientation. The camp's goal was for students to believe in themselves by mastering various challenges.

"They'll practice problem solving, teamwork, communication, conflict resolution, and leadership," explained the director. "So will you."

Ugh! I had no interest in challenging myself. I rolled my eyes as we walked to the first activity: sticking a tomahawk into a stump.

"Like throwing a football," the director explained, hurling the hatchet into the target on the first try. "Two sticks per team. Same person can't make both."

A Boy Scout den mother went first for our group. Standing twenty feet away, she sank her hatchet on her fifth attempt. I waved two team members ahead of me, hoping one would have success. No such luck.

Reluctantly, I grabbed a handful of tomahawks from the metal box. The first sailed completely past the stump. My cheeks burned.

Finally, I hit the target! Our team jumped, cheered, and headed for the next challenge.

"It didn't stick," called the director. I turned. The tomahawk lay in the dirt. Round two.

I watched my teammates each throw with one hand while holding several tomahawks in the other. *That's it!* By taking more than one, I was subconsciously cueing myself for failure.

My turn. I grabbed one, closed my eyes, took a deep breath, and channeled my inner quarterback. Extending my left arm straight in front of me, I bent my right elbow close to my head. The tomahawk sailed to the bull's-eye, and this time it stuck!

Lord, my challenge is overcoming negativity. Help me believe I can do all things—even throw a tomahawk into a stump—through You.
—Stephanie Thompson

Digging Deeper: Luke 1:37; Philippians 4:13; James 1:6–8

Can any one of you by worrying add a single hour to your life?
—Matthew 6:27 (NIV)

O n occasion I become fixated on a problem, fear, or issue and can't release that thought or emotion. Such fixation only distorts my perspective and weakens my health.

Today as my wife and I were vacationing at the beach, I woke up worried about our golden retrievers we left at home (with a house sitter!). I was also concerned that I had a nagging headache. Two hours later I'd made the headache worse by stressing about the pain, and I had certainly not helped my uneasiness about my dogs!

One of my counseling professors, Dr. Wayne Oates, called such unproductive worrying "stinking thinking." And that is right! Much anxiety is counterproductive and unhealthy, not helpful. To be blunt, "It stinks!" Why stay around the stench of our obsessive-compulsive worries?

I often talk to God about my anxieties, during my prayer time. I ask Him to help me let go of fear, prioritize what really deserves attention, and avoid "stinking thinking." It is amazing how prayer helps me do this. Soon, God's Spirit usually places another person's needs before me that are more important. Then I am free to move beyond my problems and help God actually address the needs of others.

To overcome "stinking thinking" takes more than our strength and willpower. It requires asking God to give us the "mind of Christ" and calming presence of the Holy Spirit.

> *Father, I lift my needs and fears to You today.*
> *Help me release them to Your care.*
> —Scott Walker

Digging Deeper: Proverbs 3:5–6; Matthew 6:25–34;
Romans 8 26–39; Philippians 4:6–7

Wednesday, July 24

Do everything without grumbling or arguing. —Philippians 2:14 (NIV)

I gasped when I saw the line of people wrapped around the building. My son Brandon's friend signed up for this free swim event, and his mother suggested we go. I reluctantly took Brandon, annoyed that he'd miss gymnastics training with his team.

"Excuse me," I said to a worker outside. "We're supposed to meet our friends, who are already inside." The lady whisked us into the building so we could share the same time slot with our friends. Brandon was taken down to the locker room with a group of other children. Parents went into the balcony of the Olympic-size pool. Hundreds of kids sat around the pool, waiting.

"I thought this was just going to be an open swim," I said.

"Nope," my friend clarified, "it's a big race, one group after the other."

We waited and waited in the stuffy heat as more children filled up the space.

"When are they going?" I complained. "This is ridiculous! Had I known they were just going to sit there for over an hour to do one lap, I never would have come." I continued to complain under my breath until it was Brandon's turn to swim. He swam the whole length of the pool, which I'd never seen him do, and was given a medal like all the other kids. I huffed out of there, annoyed I had wasted a whole day. I was certain Brandon was equally annoyed. But when he came out of the locker room, his face beamed. "That was so awesome!" he exclaimed. "Did you see me swim? Look at my medal!" "That's incredible," I said, not wanting him to know how negative I'd been all day. "I'm glad you had a great time."

Lord, forgive me when I complain and grumble.
Thank You for those who lead by example of positivity
and thankfulness. Help me to be that kind of person.
—Karen Valentin

Digging Deeper: Matthew 18:9

Whatever you did not do for one of the least of these, you did not do for me.
—Matthew 25:45 (NIV)

The temperature and humidity both neared a hundred. After wandering this small, dusty town in Vietnam for several hours, I just wanted to get back to the comfort of our cruise ship. I pulled the remainder of my local currency from my pocket. Just under five US dollars. It was my last day in Vietnam, and I decided to buy additional gifts for my grandchildren.

As I approached a vending cart of trinkets, I passed a man, who was weathered and dirty, with no legs, begging. I'd seen so many beggars that I'd grown calloused, even cynical. I looked away. As I scanned the items for sale, I sensed the man's presence. He'd moved closer. "Money, money," he said. The vendor shooed him away and accepted the last of my currency for the gifts I'd chosen. I left, never looking back.

I've since felt haunted by my decision to ignore this man. I'm certain my grandchildren would have appreciated far more my giving him the money than they did the trinkets I bought. And what about other things I could have done for him, but didn't? I could have looked into his eyes, smiled, or even offered my hand. He couldn't help his condition. What must his life be like, day after day, begging, being ignored, treated like a nobody? He has a heart and a soul! I could have made his day with even that small amount of money and an acknowledgment of his humanity. I'd failed. I felt spoiled, ashamed. For the first time I thought about this man as a person, what he might have been thinking and feeling. But it was too late.

Lord, I'm sorry for ignoring a human in need.
May I never forget the lesson I learned.
—Kim Taylor Henry

Digging Deeper: Ephesians 4:32; Proverbs 14:31;
Matthew 25:41–45

Friday, July 26

The light shines in the darkness, and the darkness can never extinguish it.
—John 1:5 (NLT)

I walked out of the sweltering reception hall and into the summer night. It wasn't any cooler outside, but here—away from the people and the noise—I could finally breathe.

The door behind me opened, then clicked shut. "Are you OK?" my friend Becca asked. Her words were simple but heavy with understanding. Becca came to the wedding from Chicago to be my plus-one. She was one of the few people who knew how difficult it was for me to watch Kaitlyn walk down the aisle.

"I'm happy for her," I said, loosening my tie. "It's just we had something once, and I let go of her. I can't stop wondering how things would have turned out if I had chosen differently."

She nodded. It was all I needed. I didn't want her to tell me the right girl was waiting for me, or that Kaitlyn and I never would have worked out. I just needed a friend to be there and to understand.

"The stars are beautiful out here in the country," she said. "You can't see them like this in the city because the lights drown them out. This backdrop of darkness makes them shine."

Her words spoke a deeper truth. Darkness makes the light stand out. This ache would someday make the joy of my own wedding that much sweeter.

"Thank you," I said, staring at the sky. I took a deep breath. Together we stepped out of the darkness and into the glow of the reception hall.

Lord, thank You that the darkness only makes the light brighter.
—Logan Eliasen

Digging Deeper: 1 Peter 5:10; Romans 8:18

Whatever you ask for in prayer, believe that you have received it, and it will be yours. And when you stand praying, if you hold anything against anyone, forgive them, so that your Father in heaven may forgive you your sins.
—Mark 11:24–25 (NIV)

M y friend John is an ordinary guy. He does his work, loves his wife, and doesn't want to be noticed. He still subscribes to the daily newspaper. It lands in his driveway just past the begonias. I most often see John when he mows his lawn every Saturday morning, all summer long.

But John is more than ordinary to me now. You see, John's two kids graduated from college and moved to other parts of the country a few years ago. He did his job raising them, together with his wife, Margaret. Then he heard about the kids without families at the group home across town, the ones whose parents had to give them up because of bad decisions they made along the way. "I need to do something to help," John said to me one Saturday when I stopped by.

And that's what John and his wife did. They adopted a teenage boy—a boy with plenty of problems, both of the ordinary and extraordinary kind. But that's why John is more than ordinary to me now. Several Saturdays later, he told me about his decision to help. "I asked God what I could do," he said, "and this is a work of love that God gave to me."

Show me, Lord, what I can do to be extraordinary this week.
—Jon M. Sweeney

Digging Deeper: Mark 4:30–32

Sunday, July 28

*Jesus said, "Let the little children come to me and do not hinder them, for to such belongs the kingdom of heaven." —*Matthew 19:14 (ESV)

One summer afternoon, the grandparents came into town and we headed to our favorite restaurant, which sits beside heavily trafficked train tracks—a toddler's dream come true!

My two-year-old, Jake, could hardly eat lunch he was so excited. He watched from inside the restaurant as a few trains zipped by, then practically leaped from his seat when it was time to go sit on the platform and watch them up close.

The trains that come through don't stop here. They zip through at a somewhat alarming rate, even from our safe spot on the platform.

Jake wasn't prepared for the noise the engines made or the shrill shriek of whistle as the kindhearted engineer tooted the horn.

He turned to his sister, Olivia, who had covered her ears. She jumped up and ran to him, putting her hands over his ears instead. Of course her ears were now bare. Olivia had been here before and liked her ears covered when the trains passed, but it was Jake's first time. She looked back at us, pained by the noise, until Poppa put his hands over her ears. Olivia motioned to her grandma, KK, to put her hands over Poppa's ears.

Brian and I laughed at the little ear-covering train we had going on there on the train's platform—all because Olivia was willing to put Jake's comfort above her own. There are people who stand frozen from inexperience or fear, and those who leap to action, doing what they can to help others. I'm thankful for Olivia's willing spirit and God-given empathy, and her willingness to share those gifts with her little brother.

Lord, help me raise good-hearted, kind children who are tuned in to the needs of those around them. It would be my honor and my life's greatest work.
—Ashley Kappel

Digging Deeper: Colossians 3:12; Lamentations 3:32; Psalm 103:13

When you meet together, sing psalms, hymns, and spiritual songs.
—Ephesians 5:19 (CEV)

I turned the ignition key. The engine of Dad's van purred. Then the low-tire light glowed on the dash. I groaned.

Over the last few months, I'd helped my elderly father plan his move from Minnesota to the town where I live in Montana. We were 430 miles into our 1,425-mile trip, parked at a gas station in middle-of-nowhere South Dakota. Now this?

Dad handed me the tire gauge. The left front tire was sixteen pounds low. Must be a nail. I glanced around at the vast prairie. *Lord, we need some help...and I'm exhausted.*

After we got directions, the road wound through a small country town. When we pulled up to a quaint mechanic shop, I felt like we'd driven back in time or perhaps into Mayberry. The mechanic pulled off the tire. The steel belts bulged where the tire must have hit a rock. The rubber had worn off the bulge and was leaking air. It was going to blow out at any moment. *Lord, thank You for saving us from a disaster.*

Shaken to the core, Dad and I retreated to the waiting area. I wanted to nap, but an older farmer struck up a conversation with Dad. He shared that he was the piano player at his church and that God had given him the ability to write hymns. He ministered to us as we waited, belting out a gorgeous song. Then the mechanic came in. He was the pastor of the local church and shared stories of helping kids in the community. God's presence enveloped us.

When Dad and I pulled out, we had more than a new tire. We knew God had protected us from a horrible wreck, given us new Christian friends, and refreshed us for the long journey ahead.

Thank You, Lord, for placing Christians in unexpected places to give me encouragement. Amen.
—Rebecca Ondov

Digging Deeper: Colossians 3:16; Acts 16:22–32

Tuesday, July 30

Listen to me, my children, for blessed are those who keep my ways.
—Proverbs 8:32 (NKJV)

Our much-anticipated fishing trip across the state was a bust. All day in Wallowa Lake, and we didn't land a single fish. "Let's go somewhere else," my husband, Randy, said. We pulled the boat out and packed up our camp.

A young man walked up to us. "I've always wanted a jet boat like that," he said. Randy stopped packing to show off his pride and joy. "How's fishing?" the man asked.

Randy shook his head. "Awful. Do you know about other lakes around here?" The man grinned. "You could say that. My dad's an outfitter. I've helped him ever since I could hold a pole. What are you using?"

"Wedding rings," Randy said. "They're the best for rainbow trout in our area."

"Don't change lakes; change your rigging." The man told us what to get. "They sell them at the hardware store in town." He waved and went on his way.

A guide randomly stopping to give us advice? What were the odds? I looked at Randy. "Is it just me, or was that a God thing?"

He nodded. "Let's unhook the boat and run to town." We purchased what was suggested and returned to our spot on the lake. It was like night and day. We were catching fish so fast we lost count of how many each of us had caught. We limited out in less than an hour. "Now, that's what I call fishing!" Randy exclaimed.

"I think I know how the disciples felt when Jesus told them to drop their nets on the other side," I said, rubbing my shoulder. Randy laughed. "I bet they sprained something getting all those fish into their boat."

*Dear Lord, thank You for showing me that it always works out
so much better when I stop doing things my way and listen to my Guide.*
—Erika Bentsen

Digging Deeper: John 21:3–11

You should have had mercy on your fellow servant, just as I had mercy on you. —Matthew 18:33 (GNT)

I flew down a steep ramp, about to enter a crowded freeway, and as I approached a place to merge, a large truck was riding my rear bumper. The tailgating made me nervous, so when I found a small opening in traffic I shot into it. The driver I merged in front of had to slow to let me in, and he was not happy about it. The young man in a white sports car pulled alongside me, honking his horn madly. He rolled down the passenger window, leaned out, and yelled at me, shaking his fist.

My wife was in the car. "Don't make eye contact," she advised. I had no intention of doing so.

Then the driver pulled in front of me and slammed on his brakes, to teach me a lesson. Anger welled up in me, and I fired off a prayer for God's protection. Soon a state trooper passed by, and the young man pulled off at the next exit, to my relief.

He didn't know it, but the driver indeed taught me several lessons. From him I learned just how ugly people are when they are enraged, and how dangerous they are in that state of mind. Trying to "teach someone a lesson" could be deadly, for both teacher and student. Most of all, I learned that when someone crowds in front of me on the highway, I need to practice mercy. Getting onto a crowded freeway is not easy, and I need to be more patient with drivers who squeeze in front of me.

Lord, I thank You for all I have learned from my enemies,
especially about mercy.
—Daniel Schantz

Digging Deeper: Proverbs 16:32, 19:4

UNDER GOD'S WINGS

1 _____

2 _____

3 _____

4 _____

5 _____

6 _____

7 _____

8 _____

9 _____

10 _____

11 _____

12 _____

13 _____

14 _____

15 _____

16 _____

17 _____

18 _____

19 _____

20 _____

21 _____

22 _____

23 _____

24 _____

25 _____

26 _____

27 _____

28 _____

29 _____

30 _____

31 _____

AUGUST

Thy mercy, O Lord, is in the heavens; and
thy faithfulness reacheth unto the clouds.

—Psalm 36:5 (KJV)

Everything created by God is good, and nothing is to be rejected,
provided it is received with thanksgiving. —1 Timothy 4:4 (NRSV)

A seminary friend, Taryn, and I were having lunch and before we dug into our meals, I bowed my head for a quick prayer. When I finished, Taryn asked me what I'd said in prayer. I quickly rattled it off, half-joking: "Bless this food I'm about to receive for the nourishment of my body in Christ's name. Amen."

"Do you say the same thing every time?"

"Sure, most of the time."

Sensing my embarrassment, she said, "A lot of people do."

"What do you say?" I asked.

"My husband and I start with an examination of our meal and the sacrifices that were made to have that meal. How many people were involved in getting that grain on our plates; were any lives possibly changed as a result? And we give thanks for each and every thing, for each and every part of the process that led to that moment of sustenance and enjoyment. I'll admit it does take a while, though."

I couldn't help thinking about a meditation about prayer by Howard Thurman I'd read. He even thanked the animal that gave its life so he could be nourished. Howard held in high regard every life God saw fit to put on this earth.

I still use quick prayers frequently before I eat, but also quite often, while I prepare my food or once I've started eating, I meditate on all the sacrifices made so that I might be nourished.

God, while I am grateful for a quick go-to prayer, I thank
You for a friend who can help me expand my prayer life. Give me a
renewed awareness of how my life intersects with other forms of life.
—Natalie Perkins

Digging Deeper: 1 Thessalonians 5:16–21

Friday, August 2

You are precious in my eyes. —Isaiah 43:4 (CEB)

My husband and I arrived at Kennedy Airport to find the concourse jammed with disgruntled travelers. Bad weather in the west had delayed scores of flights, including ours. Making good use of the waiting time, John got out his laptop and set it up on an unused stand in the boarding area. Almost at once, a little line formed in front of him.

"My father's waited half an hour for a wheelchair!"

"I bought this ticket six months ago!"

"I have to be in Little Rock at seven!"

John's red jacket, I noticed, looked a lot like the scarlet uniforms behind the ticket counter. Not one of these aggrieved people so much as looked at John as he or she shouted demands. "He's not with the airline," I tried to tell an angry young man who threatened, "I'm a lawyer and I'm suing!"

As a woman demanded that the suitcase she'd checked an hour earlier be retrieved at once, John closed his laptop and fled, followed by a little group of travelers waving boarding passes like flags on a battlefield.

For us it was a glimpse of life behind the counter. Somehow, when you put on a uniform, you cease to be an individual. Suddenly you are "them," with no more feelings than the electronic Arrivals and Departures board on the wall. How many times, I wondered, have I addressed a uniform, without ever seeing the person wearing it?

The line at the counter was a long one by the time our flight was called at last. John took a moment to say to the patient woman tagging our suitcases, "I bet you'll be glad when this day's over!" He received in return her smile of mingled surprise and warm agreement.

Let me overlook no one, Father, whom You bring my way today.
—Elizabeth Sherrill

Digging Deeper: Revelation 3:9

SAYING GOODBYE TO MY VETERANS
A Gift Only I Could Give
Do not neglect your gift. —1 Timothy 4:14 (NIV)

The veterans' Honor Flight Network pays tribute to those who served in World War II, Korea, and Vietnam by flying them to Washington, DC, to visit the memorials built in their honor. I learned, however, that the flight serving veterans in my geographical area had a great need for wheelchairs in good condition to transport them from one point to another.

That was certainly a project in which a greater need and my passions met! There is no group I hold in higher regard than America's veterans. So nearly every Saturday found me combing the classifieds for treasures found at garage and estate sales.

I simply added "wheelchairs for veterans" to my list of things to find.

Early one Saturday morning just before my retirement, I happened upon an unadvertised sale. A gentleman had a wheelchair that had only been used a few times by his mother, who suffered from multiple sclerosis. "It's been in a closet since Mama went to the nursing home," he told me. "She only took it out for doctors' visits and the occasional trip to the hairdresser." When I explained the purpose behind my interest, the man wouldn't take a dime for the chair. "It would give me so much pleasure to know Mama is living on through one of our heroes. My mama was always such a generous soul. This is what she would want me to do."

In retirement, I would have more time to look for additional wheelchairs for the veterans' Honor Flight Network. And I would keep the recipients (and donors or sellers) in my prayers, anticipating what I might find next.

Thank You for helping me discover a gift that only I can give.
It's all for You, Lord.
—Roberta Messner

Digging Deeper: 2 Corinthians 9:7; Proverbs 3:9

Sunday, August 4

He will wipe every tear from their eyes. —Revelation 21:4 (NRSV)

It was my second year as a Bible study children's leader in the infant room, and I felt totally confident. Babies have always loved me, and I pride myself on my ability to win them over.

During my time in the infant room, I entertained fourteen infants under the age of two, with songs, toys, snacks, and bubbles. They liked to toddle up to me for lap rides whenever I sat straight-legged on the floor and bounced my knees. My goal was to provide a safe, happy morning in which no one cried. After the first couple of weeks, we had very few tears.

As part of the assignment of working with the babies, I had to attend weekly training with the other children's leaders. Some lamented about the kids dealing with separation anxiety, having meltdowns, and throwing tantrums. I often offered advice or insight, taking the opportunity to arrogantly remind them all of the bliss I'd created in the baby room.

One morning as I talked with my new coleader, Kim, I once again shared how I measured the success of our classroom by the absence of crying. She thought about that for a moment.

"I feel differently," Kim said. "Crying provides a chance to deepen my relationship with infants. When I comfort them, they learn to trust me. We build a bond. It also allows me to rely on God's strength instead of my own."

Her words sank deep into my soul. I remembered the times that drew me closer to God. They weren't always when I was happy and everything was going my way. They often came when I desperately needed His comfort or guidance.

Instead of trying to be a magnet for the children that morning, I humbly emptied myself to attract His power.

> *Never let me forget, God, that when I do it all by myself,*
> *I miss the opportunity to partner with You.*
> —Stephanie Thompson

Digging Deeper: 2 Corinthians 12:9–10; Psalm 116:1–2

Do not seek revenge or bear a grudge against anyone among your people, but love your neighbor as yourself. —Leviticus 19:18 (NIV)

I was standing in the checkout line at the drugstore, and a woman stepped in line behind me. I looked over and smiled at her, but she didn't notice. She was talking to someone on her cell phone, rather emphatically and loudly.

She seemed oblivious of those around her as she responded to the person on the other phone. It sounded like a difficult conversation; her voice was shaking. I gave her a sideward glance, hoping she'd look up and realize we could all hear her. She didn't notice. I placed my items on the counter.

The clerk asked her, "Miss, would you like to step out of line to finish your conversation?"

She shook her head no as she kept talking. My first reaction was irritation. *Why doesn't she just step out of line?* I wondered.

I took a breath and said a silent prayer: *Lord, bless her and the person she's talking to. Help them hear what each other is trying to say. Amen.*

With that, I finished checking out. As I picked up my bag to leave, she stopped talking for a moment to listen. With a loud sigh, she said to the person she'd been in conversation with, "Thank you. Thank you for understanding. OK, see you later. Bye."

I walked to my car. A moment later she walked past me toward her car. She was smiling.

Thank You, Lord, I prayed, feeling a sense of relief for her. I don't know if my prayer had anything to do with what I'd just witnessed. But I do know I could have stood in line in irritation about her or in prayer for her. I'm really glad I chose to pray.

> *Just as You love me, Lord, so must I love others.*
> —Melody Bonnette Swang

Digging Deeper: Mark 12:28–31; Matthew 5:43–48

LESSONS FROM THE ANIMALS: Corrective Lenses

Dear friends, let us continue to love one another, for love comes from God.
—1 John 4:7 (NLT)

Sometimes on my morning walk with my two-year-old golden retriever, Gracie, we encounter the unmistakable Billy. Billy has a disability. I've never asked him about it, but having grown up with a brother who had Down syndrome, I'm pretty sure that's what Billy has. But Gracie is especially eager and happy to greet Billy when she sees him coming down the street in his slightly awkward gait with arms outstretched and a smile almost as wide.

"Googoo!" At first Billy had trouble remembering Gracie's name, but once I told him we nicknamed her Googoo, he never forgot.

Gracie pulls me off my feet if she sees Billy first. She dives on the ground and rolls on her back, shamelessly exposing her belly, which Billy obligingly scratches. "Are you having a good walk? Today is going to be a good day because you are a good dog!"

While we're in the midst of the moment and the middle of the sidewalk, a jet stream of pedestrians rushes past us. Most are very understanding. Some scowl, but many more smile. It is quite a sight, the two of them. Sometimes I wonder, *Did I fail to notice Billy all that time before we got Googoo? How often did I pass him walking to the subway in the morning? How many times did I fail just to give him a smile?* As I said, he is unmistakable. It seems like I couldn't have missed him.

But my sensitive, loving dog didn't pass him by. She took to Billy right off, the first time she saw that smile and those open arms. Gracie looks up at me from Billy's feet, with that wonderful, sloppy smile she has and seems to say, "This is how you love."

> *Dear Lord, my eyes are often closed even when they are wide open.*
> *Help me see like Googoo does, with love and acceptance,*
> *especially for those most in need of it.*
> —Edward Grinnan

Digging Deeper: 1 Corinthians 8:3

THINGS MY MOTHER TAUGHT ME
Go Out of Your Own Way

Let us not grow weary or become discouraged in doing good.
—Galatians 6:9 (AMP)

While I was dusting an old piece of furniture at home, an ancient picture slipped to the floor. Memories of Jimmie and me. She was the color of the nighttime sky, and I was fair-skinned and freckled.

My mother explained one day, "Mannie, you know Jimmie hasn't been here for a few weeks." I nodded. I'd missed the young girl who cared for me while Mother worked at the bank. "Jimmie had a baby boy!" I squealed with joy. "We're going to see her this afternoon and take her this gift. It's a blue kimono." Mother had wrapped it in blue paper.

"How will we get there?" We didn't own a car.

"We're going to ride your bicycle! You'll have to hold on to me tightly." Mother laughed.

As we rode, children stopped playing to wave to us. We waved back, then came to an old gray house with zinnias in the yard. Jimmie's mother was sitting on the front porch, shelling peas that hot summer afternoon. She hopped up, and Mother ran to hug her. "We've come to see the baby," I announced.

Jimmie was in an iron bed, holding a baby as small as my doll Bonnie Blue. She patted the bed for me to sit. I handed the present to her, and we hugged. She unwrapped it tenderly and read the front and back of the small tag. She let me help dress that tiny baby.

Soon, Jimmie returned to our home to care for me and brought that sweet little baby with her. I liked to pretend he was my brother, carrying him around on my bony hip.

Mother often went out of her way to help someone she cared about, especially that day in 1942.

Father, help remember the joy in doing for others.
—Marion Bond West

Digging Deeper: James 1:27; Philippians 2:4

Thursday, August 8

A little child shall lead them. —Isaiah 11:6 (KJV)

L ogan, do you have everything you want to take with you?"
"Yes, ma'am," our grandson replied. I glanced at the backseat of
the truck, where he sat wedged between markers, coloring books, stuffed
animals, his Ninja Turtle blanket, a bag of snacks, and a small cooler.

Big Red, our extended-cab pickup truck, is a workhorse—old and loud,
but efficient. The long truck bed has a top, so we can pack plenty for a
vacation. Beach chairs, boogie boards, fishing gear, suitcases, and more
filled the truck.

My husband, Chuck, and I had made lists, preparing for the trip. I
sure hoped we'd remembered everything. We both seemed to be getting forgetful, but now we had to think about what Logan needed, too.
Half the stuff was for him—things to keep a child entertained. How
our lives had changed since he'd come to live with us.

Finally Chuck and I climbed into the front seat, and we left. We'd
been on the road an hour when Logan said, "The back window is open."
Had Chuck forgotten to close the rear window above the tailgate?

"That's OK," said Chuck. "I'll close it at the next rest stop."

"I hope our stuff doesn't fly out," Logan said.

"It won't, because the tailgate is shut," Chuck assured him.

"But the bottom part is open, too," insisted Logan.

Chuck and I exchanged fearful glances. The tailgate was down! How
much had fallen out so far? We exited quickly to assess the loss. Miraculously, nothing was missing.

"Good thing Logan noticed," I said. Chuck nodded as he closed the
tailgate. "Guess I forgot to close it. Somebody was watching out for
us." Yes, somebody was. And He used an eight-year-old to help.

Lord, thank You for using children to show us know-it-all adults the truth!
—Marilyn Turk

Digging Deeper: Psalm 54:4, 70:1, 71:12

ENCOUNTERING GOD IN UNLIKELY PLACES
Rich in Spirit

The Lord seeth not as man seeth; for man looketh on the outward appearance, but the Lord looketh on the heart. —1 Samuel 16:7 (KJV)

B abe, I'm sorry I didn't get this mailed yesterday, but I didn't have money for a stamp...." I was reading from a stash of old love letters my mother gave me before she died.

There it was in my father's sprawling script: no money for a stamp! I turned the envelope over. The stamp cost three cents.

I sucked in my breath. I knew he had traveled, manning crews of ironworkers in those World War II years, doing his part for the war effort, but he couldn't gather together three pennies!

I went outside and sat on the porch, letting it sink in. I had only known him as a prosperous man, one whose generosity was a given to everyone who knew him.

Three pennies. It was difficult to think of my daddy as poor. According to the letters, he even had to hitch rides because he wanted my mother to have a car.

Years of plenty marked my life. I never heard a word from my parents about hard times. They were the givers in our family, our church, our neighborhood, and beyond. Yet I couldn't erase those three pennies from my mind. I'd heard plenty of talk from others about "the bad old days," but not from my mother and daddy. Why hadn't they complained?

A soft breeze brought me back to the present, caressing me with a vision of my parents as God must have seen them: young, hopeful, and living in kindness. He didn't look at what they had; He saw only their loving hearts. They didn't look poor at all. In fact, looking through God's eyes, no one seemed richer.

Father, You offer a fortune in wisdom with those three pennies. Like You, let me look past the outward trappings of those I meet, and see only their hearts.
—Pam Kidd

Digging Deeper: Psalm 44:21, 51:10

Saturday, August 10

So do not fear, for I am with you. —Isaiah 41:10 (NIV)

"O-ma! O-ma! O-ma!" the daunting chant grew louder, and I felt the need for bravery stirring inside me. *I can do this!*

Our family was spending a week on the shore of a mountain lake, and one popular activity was jumping off the end of the long dock into deeper water. Each adult and child had been dared to do it, and one by one, most had. Even the youngest, wearing her floaties, had jumped into her father's arms.

Now the whole group was daring. Truth is, my jumping days were way behind me, and I feared disappearing into that murky green water. It wasn't unsafe, just scary.

"O-ma! O-ma!"

It was now or never. This was the last day of vacation. My last chance to prove I wasn't too old to try scary things.

Though fully dressed, I willed my feet to slowly head toward the end of the dock. There was no turning back. I tried to pick up speed, praying for bravery. Just as I took my last step off the platform, I reached back and grabbed a round metal post that anchored the dock to the lake bottom below. I was struck by the shock of the cold water, the muffled sounds of water in my ears, and a jolting pain in my arm. I resurfaced to wild cheers, so I didn't acknowledge my discomfort. I merely took a shaky bow and marched off to change my clothes.

I felt that pain all night long, and more than six months later, I sometimes still felt it, a reminder that when I choose to take a leap of faith, I need to let go of fear and bravely go forward.

> *Lord, doing scary things reminds me that I need to trust You.*
> —Carol Kuykendall

Digging Deeper: Psalm 73:26; Philippians 4:6–7

Do not be anxious about anything, but in every situation, by prayer and petition, with thanksgiving, present your requests to God.
—Philippians 4:6 (NIV)

The morning Jack and I and my sister, Catherine, arrived at Coki Beach in St. Thomas, Virgin Islands, I was stunned to see four men and four women in the water in a big circle holding hands. As we set up our chairs and snorkel gear, I eavesdropped. They were praying joyful prayers.

When they finished, they all walked out of the water and went their separate ways. The oldest man of the bunch walked past us. I said, "Good morning!" hoping he would stop and chat. He smiled and said, "This is such a beautiful and blessed day, isn't it?" He told us how much he loved living on the island.

His words caught my heart, because I often take everything for granted. My easy condo life in sunny Florida. My sweet husband. My good health. My lively friends. I winced because I rarely take time to pray aloud for my daily blessings in a spirit of such joy.

That morning, after Catherine and I went snorkeling, we sat in our beach chairs and watched the animals on land entertain us while two local women, Pearl and One Love, served us cold drinks. We laughed at the chickens, roosters, chicks, Bahama ducks, iguanas, and Diamond the island cat, who all circled around our beach chairs. The day was magical.

Later we snorkeled again and saw five giant sea turtles swimming in front of us. It was a beautiful and blessed day indeed. But watching those people pray in the ocean in the early morning was absolutely the best part, because it reminded me to appreciate my daily blessings as well as those I experience on vacation.

> *Father, don't let me ever start a day without being joyfully thankful for my many blessings.*
> —Patricia Lorenz

Digging Deeper: Ephesians 1:15–20;
1 Thessalonians 2:13

Monday, August 12

Return to your home, and declare how much God has done for you.
—Luke 8:39 (NRSV)

I'm in a period of transition. Actually, I'm about half-crazy, but "period of transition" sounds better.

I'm leaving the University of Pittsburgh, my academic home and employer for most of the last four decades. I've been on campus so long I might need a map to find my way back home. I'm starting a new job, but not right away. Instead, I'm in a weird limbo: not quite here, not quite gone. And it's been a year since my dad died, so my brother and I are selling the family homestead. Oh, and one by one my three daughters are moving out of our homestead.

Half crazed? Make that three-quarters.

For the millionth time in my life, I am reaching back for...whatever, something, anything to keep from wrecking into the hidden sandbars. At times I feel like Dorothy from Kansas, trying to find my way back home. The wizard gives the tin man a heart, the scarecrow a brain, and the lion courage, but I don't think there's anything in that black bag for me.

There are times someone says just the right thing to keep me going. Or I hear larger voices calling, a divine whisper bubble up through the chaos, allowing me to survive another day amid the emotional earthquake around me. It's some relief from the harsh reality of a career change, my dad's death, our empty-nesting, and from life itself.

In those moments, I know I can do it: it'll take smarts, a heart, and courage, but I'll find a way through. I'll find my way back home.

Lord, You are omnipresent, yet often I cannot see You.
Help me see past my myopic human vision and feel Your presence.
—Mark Collins

Digging Deeper: Mark 5:18–19

When you believed, you were marked in him with a seal, the promised Holy Spirit. —Ephesians 1:13 (NIV)

As my birthday approached that year, my dad wanted to offer a gift he thought I could use. "How would you like a new bike?" he asked.

I checked my tire pressure and slung my backpack over my shoulder. "What's wrong with this bike?" I asked. I rested my hand on the seat of my vintage seventies Schwinn. The forty-year-old bike wasn't in mint condition. Rust speckled the fender, but the frame was still strong— built to last.

"There's nothing wrong with it. But a new one would ride faster and smoother." He was right. My bike only had two gear settings, and it tended to squeak and squeal when I rode it.

"A new bike wouldn't have the history this one has," I said.

"You've only had that bike for a year," Dad said.

"I'm not talking about its history with me." I looked at the handle-bars, where a man had engraved his name and phone number decades ago. I didn't know that man, but I knew he had cared enough about his bike to claim it in such a way. Though the bike belonged to me now, it was inextricably connected to its original owner, bound by the aluminum grooves of letters and numbers.

It reminded me of how God has permanently left His mark on me. No matter what I do or what mistakes I make, He has claimed me. He has engraved His name on my heart and sealed me with His Spirit. "Well, just let me know if you change your mind," Dad said. I flipped the kickstand back and slid onto the seat. "Thanks, but I don't think I can let it go. It's priceless."

Lord, thank You for never letting me go.
—Logan Eliasen

Digging Deeper: 1 John 4:4; Isaiah 43:1

PRAYING THROUGH THE PSALMS
The Value of Honest Confession

Do not let any iniquity have dominion over me. —Psalm 119:133 (NASB)

Robin and I have been best friends for forty years. We've shared a lifetime of honesty. Last month, our phone conversation led to a life-changing discovery for both of us. She'd called because two of her tiny white Maltese dogs were sick. Mike, her husband, was taking them to the vet.

"Julie, I'm worried," she said. "Small dogs can dehydrate quickly. I gave Mike a million instructions. 'Don't put them on the floor at the vet's office. It's probably covered in germs. Hold them in your lap. But don't carry them. Use leashes. You might drop them.'"

My husband and I also had butted heads that morning. "Rick's confronting a friend today. It needs to be said, but I'm nervous. Before he left, I passed along a few communication tips. I reminded him to smile, be gentle. I quoted Ephesians 4:15: 'Speak the truth in love.'"

"Julie, do you realize what we're doing? We're trying to control our husbands. And life."

Robin was right. This had been my biggest battle—the fight for control. "I thought surely by now I'd beat it," I said.

"Me, too. Want to pray?"

"Right now? Over the phone?" I asked.

"Sure. Forgive us, Lord," Robin said. "We were trying to do Your job. Again."

"We're letting go. Again," I added. "Forgive my sin of worry."

"We love You," Robin said. Her dogs got well. Rick's conversation went beautifully. Maybe because we turned the sin of worry into prayer.

Lord, worrying is never the right thing to do. In the past I've allowed it to control me, but no more! You are Lord.
—Julie Garmon

Digging Deeper: Psalm 32:7, 119:11

Jesus said again, "Children, how hard it is to enter the kingdom of God!"
—Mark 10:24 (NIV)

My excellent friend Liz is moving. I haven't allowed myself to think about how hard that will be for me. At the moment my job is to help pack. Liz has lived in her apartment for twenty-six years. Her closets are bursting with stuff, her home office strewn with files and books. She owns more shoes today than I have had in my entire lifetime. I admire, trust, and deeply value my friend, but on the matter of clutter we are vastly different creatures. My dream vacation is to send everyone away and rent a Dumpster.

Last night I helped Liz excavate part of a closet. She removed items, we discussed options (move, sell, put in storage, toss, give away), and I transported things to their respective piles. Liz prefers piles. Piles make me twitch. But I am there to be helpful, and being opinionated is of dubious assistance in times of stress. So I squeezed through stacks of belongings, kept a list of what's going to charity, exclaimed over Liz's grandmother's exquisite cloche, and kept our friendship growing by keeping my mouth shut.

Liz's move is hard for her on many levels. It's difficult for me in different ways. At midnight I walked back to my apartment, and the cool night air blowing in off the Hudson River got me to musing. This is hard, but hard is not the same as bad. Hard things can be painful, sad, unpleasant, confusing, stressful, or far more work than we want to do. Yet the cross teaches us quite clearly that hard is not the same as bad. It's not bad at all.

> *Lord, teach me how to do hard things graciously,*
> *lovingly, and with a thankful heart. As You do.*
> —Julia Attaway

Digging Deeper: 1 Peter 2:24

Friday, August 16

Here I am! I stand at the door and knock. If you hear my voice and open the door, I will come in and eat with you, and you will eat with me.
—Revelation 3:20 (NCV)

When I was young, a unique party idea spread like wildfire in our neighborhood. It was called a "Come as You Are" party. Here's how it worked: on the spur of the moment, someone would decide to throw a party, phone and invite others in and around the neighborhood. No matter what you had going on at that moment or how you were dressed, you were expected to drop everything and head over to the neighbor's house, *exactly* as you were.

Once everyone had gathered, the impromptu party began. I don't recall if during those parties everyone brought something to contribute for food or if the hostess supplied the treats. But what sticks in my mind is the great fear I had that someone would throw a "Come as You Are" party while I was in the bathtub! I also remember planning several scenarios of what I would do if such an instance occurred.

It was a silly fear, and the parties were a blast. I'm sorry to say I haven't heard of anyone throwing parties like that in years. We're far too sophisticated now, I suppose. Many of us want to clean up, look our best, dress appropriately, and put on our best "game face" before leaving the house.

Recently, it came to me that Jesus loves a good party, especially the "Come as You Are" variety. He takes each of us into His arms right where we are, whether during an extremely trying time or while celebrating a high point; whether dressed in filthy rags or in prom attire. We can always come to Him. Jesus receives us just as we are.

Lord, You are always in the party mode, and Your invitation
is always open to us.
—Debbie Macomber

Digging Deeper: Romans 6:14

You have turned my mourning into dancing; you took off my sackcloth and clothed me with a garment of joy. —Psalm 30:11 (ISV)

It was a sign from God. Not a burning bush, a rainbow, or a plague of frogs, but a wooden sign tucked in the corner of a folksy gift shop in Bluffton, South Carolina. Bold white letters on a black background proclaimed this: *Welcome to Awesomeville! Population: Me.*

Yep. The sign stopped me in my tracks. After thirty-three years of marriage, my husband had left...suddenly, unexpectedly, and permanently. Newly single, I felt like an awkward adolescent, unsure of what to do with my life. But I wasn't sixteen. I was almost sixty. And I had a choice. I could choose bitterness, anger, and fear as my new companions. Or I could embrace forgiveness, hope, and joy. I could choose to exist in Woe-Is-Me Town or thrive in Awesomeville. I knew where I wanted to reside.

I brought my sign from God home to my new little apartment. It still hangs right by my front door. It's a daily reminder that my circumstances don't have the final say in what my life looks like. My attitude, choices, and faith (or lack thereof) set the tone each day.

That doesn't mean my residence in Awesomeville is painless. Plenty of days my heart still aches, and tears seem to come out of nowhere. But I don't have to live in a permanent state of bliss to continue to love life. Life can be hard, but nurturing a relationship with God doesn't have to be. I may be by myself, but as God reminds me daily, I'm never alone.

Dear Lord, open my eyes to the beauty and blessing of each new day, even the tough ones. Draw near to me in a way that makes Your presence more tangible in my life.
—Vicki Kuyper

Digging Deeper: James 1:1–4

Sunday, August 18

Those that wait upon the Lord, they shall inherit the earth.
—Psalm 37:9 (KJV)

It was a day I can never forget. I was at the Alabama cabin my grand-father built years before. To most, it's a modest place. To me, it's always been paradise. The night before, I sat outside, listening to the call of the owl that inhabited the middle part of the little island where the cabin sits. Long ago, my grandfather chose this spot for its perfect sunset and made a deal with the property owner. As part of the agree-ment, the middle of the island would forever remain common prop-erty for all to enjoy. The deal was sealed with my grandfather's trusted handshake.

Now, at the crack of dawn, I woke up to a terrible noise. I rushed outside and found a crew of workers clearing trees on the common property. "What are you doing?" I shouted above the bedlam.

"We're harvesting the trees for the owner," a man shouted back. "Lots of money here."

I soon discovered the man on the other side of my grandfather's handshake didn't match Grandfather's trustworthiness. He had some-how shifted ownership of the common property to his name.

I had no idea if the owl escaped or where the other wildlife had gone. The island looked like a war zone. My heart felt shredded.

Afterward, I tried to avoid the ravaged wasteland that was once a wild-life sanctuary. Then one day I noticed a little bit of green, then some wildflowers, and finally trees popping up everywhere.

I whispered, "Oh, God, I see You here." Today, the middle of the island is lush once more. Last night as I was walking on the property with my family, I heard it again: the call of an owl. It reminded me that sometimes when everything seems lost, all that's left is to wait...and trust our Father to make things new again.

Father, when I am defeated, remind me to wait for You.
—Brock Kidd

Digging Deeper: Psalm 62:5; Romans 8:25

Beloved, now are we the sons of God, and it doth not yet appear what we shall be. —1 John 3:2 (KJV)

Angelica had run away and left a note behind.
On my way to the rural Illinois camp where I volunteer each summer, I learned the eighteen-year-old left school and was living with a boy. Angelica was obedient, so this was a surprise. After I arrived, I saw her mother, a godly woman nicknamed Tiny. She and her husband had been crying since Angelica left.

I knew it was time to share. "When I was eighteen, I ran away," I told her. "My mother thought all hope was lost. She and my father cried and cried."

I had cried before I left. Angelica probably cried, too. "It's not about the boy. She probably doesn't know how to tell you why she left."

Tears slid down Tiny's face. I imagined my own parents' tears and remembered what I'd done to cause them.

All my young life, I'd heard stories that promised adventure. Going off to college was, I thought, the beginning of my own.

But during my first semester, my chronic tonsillitis flared up, and I returned home for surgery. Once I was home, my mother told me I wouldn't return to school—I would stay home, work, and attend the local community college.

I was taught to be obedient. I tried to make peace with my mother's decision. Instead I left a note saying simply that I loved my parents but couldn't stay. I wanted adventure. My mother wanted to protect me.

Tiny and I hugged, and I shared what I could not tell my own mother. "Every lesson my mother taught me was inside me. Every lesson you've taught Angelica is inside her. She may not be on your plan, but God's still writing the story." We hugged again, and I saw the faintest hint of a smile.

Lord, we trust You with our lives. Give us the courage and wisdom to trust You with our (Your) children.
—Sharon Foster

Digging Deeper: 1 John 3:2; Romans 8:28–29; Jeremiah 29:11

Tuesday, August 20

The one sitting on the throne said, "See, I am making all things new!"
—Revelation 21:5 (ISV)

The stream over the low-water bridge on my run used to be full of crawdads. Now it's full of small white-and-silver sardine-looking fish. They spend the day leaping relentlessly straight up from the water and then splashing back down.

I'm afraid to research them—or what seems to be the apparent emigration, or demise, of the crawfish. I'm certain the Internet will confirm my fears. Earth is warming, melting, changing. It seems the end of the ecosystem as I know it is happening all around me.

I don't know why these changes seem so ominous. In other scenarios, I welcome change. I love when one season morphs into the next, when the sunlit sky curdles into needed or even unneeded rain. Rain—all precipitation, fog, snow, ice—is always wonderful, so full of nourishment and freshness and relief, but I love when it stops, too, and the hot sun returns.

Seasonal changes are cyclical, though. I know the rain or sun will come again. The crawdads' disappearance might not be cyclical. Nonrecurrent change, even change for the good, means loss. I loved when my magnificent infant daughters became women I could talk to, but in the process I lost their tiny, perfect, baby selves.

Losing what is beloved or familiar means entering the unknown, and that's alarming. Part of me shudders when I read John's prophecy of "new heaven and a new earth, because the first heaven and the first earth had disappeared, and the sea was gone" (Revelation 21:1). I love this earth and ocean, these crawdads, my daughters. I don't want any of them to be no more.

But in the new heaven and earth, John goes on to reveal, "There won't be death anymore. There won't be any grief, crying, or pain." I can look forward to losses like that!

Lord Jesus, help me welcome change instead of fearing it.
—Patty Kirk

Digging Deeper: John 14:2; Revelation 21:1–8

Remember those who led you, who spoke the word of God to you.
—Hebrews 13:7 (NASB)

Scattered across my desktop are framed photographs of mentors. Among the photos is one of the 1969 Furman University soccer team. I was a freshman, and the teammate standing next to me was a senior. Though he did not know it, he was a source of inspiration in my fledgling year. He later went to Oxford as a Rhodes Scholar. His example remains vibrant.

There is a photo of my first editor, Floyd Thatcher. I would not be writing today without Floyd's tutelage and guidance. He willed the very best for the young writers he supervised. He even published my first book. In moments when I sought his personal counsel, Floyd would wink and say, "Scott, you will find your way! God is with you."

Next to the one of Floyd is the photograph of my godparents, Bryant and Peggy Hicks. They were missionaries with my parents in the Philippines. When I was fourteen my father died, and Bryant and Peggy adopted me as one of their own children. They gave me the stability to overcome anxiety and insecurity.

Underneath the others is Jack Flanders. His photograph reveals a handsome young man in a leather flight jacket standing by a P-47 Thunderbolt. Jack was a fighter pilot, who survived the ravages of World War II. He later became a Bible scholar, professor, and pastor. In my young adult years, he modeled for me courage and professionalism.

All of us have photographs and memories of people who have shaped and encouraged us. It is important to wipe the dust away and give thanks for the mentors and "angels" God has sent our way.

> *Father, I give You thanks for people who have loved*
> *and inspired me. Amen.*
> —Scott Walker

Digging Deeper: Proverbs 1:5; 1 Thessalonians 2:8;
Proverbs 22:6, 27:17

Thursday, August 22

The Lord's unfailing love surrounds the one who trusts in him.
—Psalm 32:10 (NIV)

I stood in the gate area of the airport, waiting for my flight home. Violence and global unrest blared from the news station on the TV. Turning away, I wanted to cover my ears. I felt hopeless and helpless. *Lord, where is Your love?*

My cell phone chimed, announcing an incoming text from a friend at home. My eyes widened when I swiped it. It was a photo of a mountain in flames! The text read, "Please pray. Forest fire discovered by town. It blew up like an atomic bomb. Hundreds of homes are being evacuated. Several have burned to the ground." My heart pounded.

After the plane landed in Missoula, Montana, I raced to the local Costco store and bought a cartful of groceries. Temporary shelters set up to house people who were displaced from their homes would be in need of food. An hour later I drove up to the Red Cross shelter to discover cases of groceries stacked from floor to ceiling. The workers thanked me and then shook their heads. They didn't have room for more food.

I pulled my car out of the parking lot, amazed. The fire started only hours before, yet my community had already responded with the love of God. Every shelter was stocked. Over the next few weeks, over one thousand homes were evacuated. Churches held community-wide prayer meetings and fed those in need. Almost none of the people stayed in shelters. Families absorbed them—and their horses, cows, dogs, and cats—into their personal homes and ranches.

Although I was heartbroken over the devastation, I had a renewed hope in the power of a community joining together to share God's love.

Lord, thank You for showing me that Your love is alive and well. Amen.
—Rebecca Ondov

Digging Deeper: Psalm 97:10–12, 145:20

God, my shepherd! I don't need a thing. You have bedded me down in lush meadows, you find me quiet pools to drink from. True to your word, you let me catch my breath and send me in the right direction.
—Psalm 23:1–3 (MSG)

The last place you would want to be on a Saturday night is in the alley downtown where they found little Valerie. Valerie is just seven years old. She lives in my neighborhood. One thing I know about her is how much she loves cats. I see hers petting her on her porch most afternoons when I walk by with my dog. I also see Valerie paying attention to other neighborhood cats and animals.

A few Friday nights back, Valerie heard a cat meowing outside her bedroom window. She was concerned, and when her mother wasn't paying attention, Valerie got out of bed, opened the back door to their apartment, and went looking for the kitty. She followed the sound of the animal until she discovered it... trapped in a trash can two blocks away.

My friend Richard found her in the alley holding that terrified cat. This is really a story about courage, because Richard carried both girl and cat (she wouldn't let it go) from door to door until he found where she lived. Valerie's mother hadn't even noticed she was gone. I'm sure she was thankful my friend guided her daughter home.

God is our shepherd, and I sometimes think God also provides shepherds for each of us.

Show me today, Father, whom I can help find the way home.
—Jon M. Sweeney

Digging Deeper: Luke 2:8

Saturday, August 24

Do not merely look out for your own personal interests, but also for the interests of others. —Philippians 2:4 (NASB)

My five-year-old grandson, Isaac, loves me to read aloud Shel Silverstein's classic *The Giving Tree*, the story of a tree that loves a boy and gives of itself to him until there is nothing left.

In the beginning the boy seems to return the tree's affection, but as he ages he becomes a self-centered taker. First the tree's apples, then its branches, and finally its trunk, until all that remains is a stump.

One day Isaac had had enough. Hearing again the boy's "give me" demands, he burst out, "That's rude! You need to take this book back to the library." His tone implied the library could somehow doctor the book—as though it were a hospital for broken stories and could mend the selfish boy.

I know only one book in which broken stories are fixed, and that's the Bible. I don't have to search long before I find myself among its flawed individuals. When Jesus encountered such persons, He reached out to them saying, "It is not those who are healthy who need a physician, but those who are sick" (Mark 2:17). His joy as God's Son was to heal, change, and empower those who recognized what He wanted to do for them.

The boy in *The Giving Tree* and I share a selfish streak. In the story he seems unwilling to acknowledge he needs to change. Jesus, the great giver, by His own life has shown me a giving heart is desirable...and possible.

I want to change for Him.

*Jesus, Your Word says, "I can do all things through Him
who strengthens me" (Philippians 4:13).
Help me believe that with You I can make good changes.*
—Carol Knapp

Digging Deeper: Luke 9:23, 19:1–10; 2 Corinthians 5:17

THINGS MY MOTHER TAUGHT ME: Just the Way You Are

Remember the former things of old. —Isaiah 46:9 (ESV)

Math has always confounded me. A mystery as are instructions, directions, and recipes. I've felt insecure in these areas all my life. And never done well in them. Failure is more like it.

A counselor explained to me a while back as we talked in her office, "Marion, do you know you have a photographic memory?"

I didn't. "How far back can you recall?" she asked.

The answer was easy. I'd relived and loved the memory all my life. I wasn't yet twenty-two months old. I know because my daddy died when I was that age.

"I stood barefoot in our very small bathroom with the black-and-white tiny tiles on the floor. My view was from below everyone's knees. A man in khaki pants and brown lace-up boots stood in front of me. Thomas Marion Bond, my father, held something strange in his hand. All their voices were high above me. Their words meant nothing. I wore only my diaper. My mother was to the right of me, wearing a dress. My daddy faced me, just inside the door.

"Of course, I didn't know colors or identify names of people or descriptions. My mother filled in those blanks when I described the memory to her many years later. I'd flushed a diaper down the toilet. She said I was barely able to reach the handle. As the event unfolded, she'd laughed. Bless her heart. I understood laughter."

I like to imagine that my father leaned down, picked me up, and gave me a kiss.

Now I feel, well, almost good about not understanding certain things in life. It's okay. God created me this way. With an intense love for colors, emotions, and humor.

Thank You for sweet memories. Father, help me not ponder unpleasant ones.
—Marion Bond West

Digging Deeper: Proverbs 10:7; John 14:26

Monday, August 26

We are God's handiwork, created in Christ Jesus to do good works, which God prepared in advance for us to do. —Ephesians 2:10 (NIV)

The phone rang as I pulled bread from the bread box. It was my husband, Lonny. "Let's spend the lunch hour down by the river," he invited. "Crews are replacing the ties on the railroad tracks. Meet you in fifteen?"

I usually held a no-slack schedule for homeschooling, but the day called for grace. Warm sun. Cool breeze. And my two youngest sons were crazy about trains. Soon we sat on the grassy riverbank, eating honey-and-banana sandwiches from Superman lunch boxes made of tin.

"All this so the train can run," my ten-year-old Gabriel said.

Lonny and the boys talked mechanical things, like how a big claw lifted old planks and about the machine that shot spikes into the new ones. My focus was different. I noticed the flow of activity. It seemed orchestrated. The pulling up and putting down of railroad ties worked because each man behind a machine had a specific job. A part of the process. He knew what to do and did it. Watching this brought a longing to my heart. God's Word tells us He has specific work for each of us—work He's predestined for us. His holy hands reach for ours.

What a glorious thing!

The Lord Most High considered my abilities. My passions. My shortcomings and His own strength. He allows me to be part of His beautiful plan. No matter how grand or small, He calls me to do specific work-of-the-Spirit.

"What do you think?" Lonny asked, handing me half of his apple. I wasn't sure if he meant the machines, the day, or the beauty of our sons. But I thought about how much God must love me.

"I think," I said, "that it's amazing."

Lord, give me keen discernment and a willing heart. Amen.
—Shawnelle Eliasen

Digging Deeper: Jeremiah 1:5; Psalm 138:8

There is no fear in love. —1 John 4:18 (KJV)

Don't forget," Sharon said to me at breakfast, "we are going to the open house today for that new business in town. There will be lots of important people there."

My stomach tightened. Meeting new people is hard for an introvert like me.

On the way to the open house, I watched a small plane land at our airport, and my mind drifted back to my childhood. I lived in the village of New Antioch, Ohio, just south of the Wright-Patterson Air Force Base. A steady flow of aircraft flew low over our house every day, and for some reason it frightened me. The big transport planes sounded mournful, crawling across the sky, and the jets arrived with a boom that startled me.

My father must have sensed my fear, because one day he pointed to a transport plane and said, "That's a Gooney Bird, a DC-3. One of the best planes ever built." The next day he brought me a picture book of airplanes, and I tried to identify the planes that flew overhead. The more interested I got in airplanes, the less I was afraid of them.

"Here we are," Sharon said, pointing to the entrance of the open house.

Drawing on my memory, I approached the strangers with interest instead of anxiety, probing them with questions: "Are you folks new to Missouri?" "Are your children getting adjusted to school?" "Exactly what do you do here?"

Turns out, I had a good time and actually made some new friends.

I am learning that it's hard to be interested in people and afraid of them at the same time.

> *Lord, You made me shy, but You gave me a good heart.*
> *Help me always to listen to my heart.*
> —Daniel Schantz

Digging Deeper: Isaiah 58:10; Luke 2:46

Wednesday, August 28

*Jesus said, "Father, forgive them, for they do not know what they are doing." —*Luke 23:34 (NIV)

My husband and I made the mistake of taking along our Australian shepherds, Sage and Montana, when we visited our son, daughter-in-law, and grandchildren. They keep chickens in their backyard, and Montana thinks a chicken is just another stuffed toy, something to hold between his teeth and shake. Montana is a loving dog and would never intentionally hurt anything. He just likes to play and doesn't understand that chickens aren't playthings. Suffice it to say, it wasn't long before there was one less chicken. Of course, it turned out to be Yellow, our five-year-old grandson Wyatt's favorite.

I felt terrible. I tried to explain to Wyatt that his loss was the result of a very sweet dog who thought he'd found a very fun toy. We talked about forgiveness, and I asked him if, when he was ready, he'd forgive Montana. He said he would try.

The next morning, Wyatt sat, knees clutched, in the far corner of the yard next to Yellow's grave. I watched for several minutes, then went out and put my arm around him. Neither of us spoke.

Later that day I looked out on the porch. Montana was sleeping. Lying next to him, head to head, was Wyatt, his arm gently petting our dog.

> *Lord, thank You for my grandson's tender heart and for putting the gift of forgiveness in it.*
> —Kim Taylor Henry

Digging Deeper: Matthew 6:12, 18:21–22

Children are a heritage from the Lord, offspring a reward from him.
—Psalm 127:3 (NIV)

I woke up to the sound no one wants to hear: someone getting sick in the bathroom. I called out, "Who's in there?"

"It's me," said a weak voice, my son Solomon's.

I looked at the clock: 2:02 a.m. I wasn't sure how much I should intervene, how much a teenage boy wants or needs, but I erred on the side of mothering and opened the door.

I wasn't prepared for what I saw. Solomon was very sick and the bathroom was a mess.

In a flash, a million thoughts went through my mind. Confusion. Worry. Disgust. Love. Mothers. Mothers all around the world, I imagined, were up right at this moment caring for their loved ones, some with just the stomach flu, others with illness the depths of which I don't want to imagine.

Maybe it was divine, the way these thoughts stitched together in flashes. Immense love surged inside me—mother love and God's love collected, and came through me right in my very own bathroom.

It was almost three in the morning when I stood in the darkness by Solomon's bed and asked if he wanted me to stay awhile.

"Nah, I'm all right," he said, but I sat down anyway, thinking that's what I would want, but not necessarily say, if I were a teenage boy sick in the middle of the night.

I woke hours later. My legs and back ached from sleeping on his narrow single bed, but I wasn't tired. I was filled with gratitude.

Heavenly Father, how blessed I am to feel love born of middle-of-the-night dramas and traumas—these moments, it seems, help root our love for one another and for You.
—Sabra Ciancanelli

Digging Deeper: 1 John 4:19; 1 Timothy 5:8

Friday, August 30

I have put before you life and death, blessing and curse. Choose life.
—Deuteronomy 30:19 (JPS)

Every year I get an invitation to my high school class's annual reunion. My classmates are very enthusiastic, enough so that they don't want to wait for five or ten-year intervals. I haven't ever gone to a reunion, though, because the reunions are near Philadelphia and I've been on the West Coast since about ten years after I graduated. Still, they keep me on the list, probably because I invariably let them know I can't attend.

This year the invitation arrived on schedule, but it came with a new wrinkle. In addition to the standard information about date, time, and location of the get-together, the event organizers thoughtfully included a list of all my classmates who would not be attending the reunion because they'd passed away sometime between graduation and now.

That was sobering. I knew my best friend would be on the list. I drive her car every day, since she left it to me in her will, and I see her pictures in carefully chosen frames on my bookshelves. Another of my friends was also on such a list, because her funeral had been only a few months before. But I discovered the name of a boy I'd worked with on the senior play, and the boy who'd sung at graduation, and people I'd been in clubs with. So many names of people I remembered.

Slowly I realized I'd outlived a great many of my classmates. There had to be a reason for my still being here, that my survival couldn't just be random, and I knew I would not be able to figure it out without God's help.

> *Show me what You want me to do, God of my days.*
> *I'll try my best to do it.*
> —Rhoda Blecker

Digging Deeper: Proverbs 15:22; Isaiah 30:18; Habakkuk 2:1

Lord, let your faithful love surround us because we wait for you.
—Psalm 33:22 (CEB)

I really hate to be late, but then again I hate to be early, too. I like to time it so I arrive at the theater just as the curtain is going up or at the meeting just as the PowerPoint is being presented or at the dinner party not a moment before the canapés are served.

The downside of my behavior is a willingness to cut things a little too close. This often translates into an impatience with *anything* that goes awry. Why is that car in front of me going so slow? Where did this traffic come from? Why is the subway train taking forever to arrive? Did I just miss the previous train? Somehow I forget that patience is one of God's spiritual gifts, not a present to be squandered.

My friend Mark gave me a helpful perspective on this the other day at our church men's group. "If I'm stuck waiting in a subway tunnel and get bent out of shape," he said, "I always remind myself there's another train coming." As simple as that: another train coming, another chance. Instead of biting my tongue or pounding the steering wheel with my fist, I can do as we're reminded again and again in Scripture: wait. All good things come to those who wait . . . and truth be told, to those who don't insist on cutting it too close.

> *I pray in patience for the gift of patience and*
> *the ability to see the goodness of God's time.*
> —Rick Hamlin

Digging Deeper: 1 Corinthians 4:5; Micah 7:7

UNDER GOD'S WINGS

1 _____

2 _____

3 _____

4 _____

5 _____

6 _____

7 _____

8 _____

9 _____

10 _____

11 _____

12 _____

13 _____

14 _____

15 _____

16 _____

17 _____

18 _____

19 _____

20 _____

21 _____

22 _____

23 _____

24 _____

25 _____

26 _____

27 _____

28 _____

29 _____

30 _____

31 _____

SEPTEMBER

*The Lord is my rock and my fortress and
my deliverer; My God, my strength, in
whom I will trust; My shield and the horn
of my salvation, my stronghold.*

—Psalm 18:2 (NKJV)

Eli answered and said, Go in peace: and the God of Israel grant thee thy petition that thou hast asked of him. —1 Samuel 1:17 (KJV)

I met Stacey the first summer her twin daughters, then eight years old, attended Bible Witness Camp in Pembroke Township, Illinois. Now, Stacey volunteers each summer to help make the experience special for all the girls.

One day when we were decorating the camp dining hall for a special evening, I noticed how her daughters had grown.

"Beautiful young ladies," I commented to Stacey. She beamed. "They are very special girls." She went on to share something very personal.

"My husband and I tried for so long to get pregnant. I miscarried several times, and then we tried in vitro. We had a number of viable fertilized eggs. But they were placed in my womb, and I miscarried again." She told me she had prayed and prayed.

As she shared I realized I never understood the weight she'd carried. I knew Stacey owned a nail salon. I knew she was kind, but knew nothing of her struggles.

"I had given up. Then one of my nail clients told me she would carry my baby for me. Who could ask anyone to do something like that? I wouldn't even ask my sister to carry a baby for me. I thanked her but never really considered her offer."

Stacey's face was full of wonder as she continued. "My client called me and said, 'What are you waiting for?' She felt like the Lord wanted her to carry my baby." She glowed as she told the story. "It was unbelievable, but I stopped resisting. My husband and I had three viable eggs left. The doctor implanted them. She carried my babies to term. I told them this year at their birthday party." Tears formed in Stacey's eyes. "They said, 'You really wanted us!'" The twins are thirteen now and very special girls indeed.

> *Lord, thank You for all the very special people*
> *You carefully place in our lives.*
> —Sharon Foster

Digging Deeper: 1 Samuel 1:27, 2:7–8; Luke 1:45

Labor Day, Monday, September 2

Whatever you do, work at it with all your heart, as working for the Lord, not for human masters. —Colossians 3:23 (NIV)

When Luis first walked into my "English as a Second Language" class at the church, his smile and humble attitude immediately warmed my heart.

I learned he was a "day laborer," one of the men who gathered in a parking lot each morning in hopes of being hired to do construction work or landscaping.

Since I was in the process of putting my house on the market, I offered to hire Luis to clean up my large yard, and he eagerly accepted. He started as soon as he arrived, laboring all day in the hot southern sun and only accepting water I offered, nothing else.

My oldest son, Jason, came over and met Luis, attempting a conversation using the Spanish he'd learned in school. When he discovered Luis had no transportation and walked everywhere, Jason offered to drive him home. But he never saw where Luis lived, because Luis asked to be dropped off at a street corner.

One day Luis arrived to my house extremely upset. He had been robbed the previous evening. Jason called the credit card company to help Luis cancel his card, but the stolen cash was irretrievable.

We discovered Luis put his daily earnings in the bank, then wired it to his wife in Mexico, who lived there with their young son.

Luis's unselfish, sacrificial attitude and excellent work ethic humbled us. His desire to work and not accept handouts was a refreshing contrast to the world we knew.

> *Lord, thank You for introducing me to Luis,*
> *who showed me an appreciation for work.*
> —Marilyn Turk

Digging Deeper: Psalm 90:7

SAYING GOODBYE TO MY VETERANS: Never Alone

Do not be afraid...for the Lord your God will be with you wherever you go. —Joshua 1:9 (NIV)

During my last week of work at the VA Medical Center, Joyce, the soft-spoken lady in the office next door, stopped by. She carried a large Hefty bag, which I assumed she wanted to dispose of in my trash can.

But Joyce had come to wish me well, and in the bag was a present. The gift was special: a picture Joyce had painted for me. The subject was the beloved log cabin I call home, and the rendering was gorgeous. Coworkers from up and down the hall gathered to see it. "I didn't know you could do anything like this, Joyce," they said, shaking their heads.

Folks knew Joyce as a specialist in credentialing, a woman who loved God and talked about her family. But no one knew she could paint.

In the painting, Joyce had focused in on my love of antiques and flowers. She remembered how I succumbed to the charms of the falling-down-perfect place when I happened upon it two decades before. Like God had found me, I discovered the achingly charming former hunting lodge and purchased it "as is." Joyce knew I loved it for its sweet imperfections and that I adored fixing it up in my "thrifty chic" style.

Joyce also knew my sheer terror in owning that property after my divorce. The old place needed a furnace, air-conditioning, new wiring, a roof, and who knew what else? Armed with nothing but hopes and dreams, I felt alone with only myself to depend on.

But I learned God is with me every step of the way. Now, because of Joyce's reminder, I knew I wouldn't be alone in retirement, either. And in retirement I would have much time to hang pictures!

> *Thank You for friends, Lord, who point Your way.*
> —Roberta Messner

Digging Deeper: Isaiah 40:31, 43:2; Psalm 55:22

Wednesday, September 4

PRAYING THROUGH THE PSALMS
God Is With Us—Always

I am always aware of the Lord's presence; he is near,
and nothing can shake me. —Psalm 16:8 (GNT)

Iattended a Christian speakers' conference, hoping God would fix my fear of public speaking. I had no idea He'd do a much deeper work.

I arrived on Wednesday and quickly bonded with the thirty-five ladies in attendance. We laughed, prayed, and worshiped together. During teaching sessions, I jotted down new topics to share. On Friday I thought, *So far, so good. If I can just survive tomorrow.*

The next day, we'd give five-minute speeches while being videotaped.

Before the first conferee began, the leaders instructed us to note comments during the presentations. As each lady spoke, my panic level rose another notch. These women would be critiquing me...and they were incredibly talented!

I made the mistake of comparing myself to my new friends. Then it was my turn. To my horror, I realized I wouldn't have time to use all my teaching aids, which were stacked beside the podium. I talked too fast and skipped important points. Afterward, I had no idea what I'd said. Only that I'd bombed.

I texted a friend back home and explained the situation. She texted back: "Julie, focus on God. He was with you when you spoke. He's there now. He's your Redeemer. Deliverer. Savior. Counselor." I read the text. Out loud. Over and over. She was right.

Taking a deep breath, I headed back to the conference room. To my amazement, the ladies gave me an envelope full of encouraging comments. Weeks later, the link to my video arrived. Gathering my courage, I clicked it. When I watched myself speaking, I forgot about my blunders and noticed only one element: God's unfailing love shining in my eyes.

Lord, when I remember You're with me, nothing can shake me.
—Julie Garmon

Digging Deeper: Psalm 118:6, 121:5

The Lord is close to everyone who calls out to him, to all who call out to him sincerely. —Psalm 145:18 (CEB)

You've probably noticed it: people staring at their phones. Almost everywhere I go—at the mall, in a lobby waiting for an elevator, in a parking lot, at the doctor's office, or even walking down the street—people are constantly gazing at their cell phones. One morning on the subway platform, my fellow commuters were glued to their mobile screens, and I wanted to shout, "Hey, everybody, look up! Stop staring at your phones!"

Of course before I said anything, I took my own phone out of my pocket, ready to check messages before logging on to my favorite Bible app. But all at once, the urge to stare at my phone seemed less dominant. And I saw the scene before me differently.

I imagined strings coming out of all those phones and pictured where they might be going. A text sent to a spouse, an email to a daughter, a link to a fascinating article, a connection to a Bible verse. I pictured all those strings reaching up and out of the subway tunnel, creating a web that puts us in touch with loved ones, knowledge, literature, the arts, updates on the weather, God's Word—and OK, maybe some news scandal. I clicked on the app for today's Scripture reading.

As I read the psalm, I gave thanks for the countless ways God gives us to connect with one another and with Him.

Dear Lord, connect me to Your love and to all those You love.
—Rick Hamlin

Digging Deeper: Philippians 1:7; Psalm 42:1

Friday, September 6

When I am afraid, I put my trust in you. —Psalm 56:3 (ESV)

Mom, will you please tell Coach I can't make the meet Friday?" eight-year-old Isaiah asked. His swim team had just finished practice at the pool. Water dripped from his bright blue cap. His eyes were ringed red from goggles.

"It's your first meet, Isaiah," I said. "Why?"

The next swimmers, teenagers, stretched poolside as Isaiah's group sloshed to the locker room. But he sat next to me, pulling his towel over slumped shoulders. "I'm afraid," he said. "I can dive off the blocks here, but I don't want to try at a different pool."

"I see," I said. Isaiah had watched his brothers swim competitively for years. It was finally his turn. I ached to see uncertainty squelch his excitement. Yet I could relate: I'd recently been asked to lead a women's retreat. I'd never done that before and wasn't sure how. What if I couldn't manage one more thing?

Isaiah and I sat quietly as the older swimmers finished stretching and formed lines behind the blocks. One by one, they climbed onto the blocks, dived in, and sliced through the water with elegant strength. Soon the lanes pulsed with the rhythm of smooth, even strokes. My small son breathed deep. "If I want to swim like that, I'm going to have to just do it," he said.

"I'm sure of it," I said. "After all, when we're out of our comfort zones, we're still in God's. There's no perimeter on the Lord's goodness and grace."

Isaiah smiled, plucked his cap from his head, and pecked my cheek. He headed off for the locker room, a bounce in his step, wet footprints leaving fresh marks on the concrete all the way.

> *Father, when I have a dream but doubt my own capabilities,*
> *remind me of Yours. Amen.*
> —Shawnelle Eliasen

Digging Deeper: Psalm 13:5, 115:11; 1 Peter 5:7

If we walk in the Light as He Himself is in the Light, we have fellowship with one another. —1 John 1:7 (NASB)

What began as a fun, adventurous five-mile hike in northern Arizona was now downgraded to a grit-my-teeth trudge up a mountain. The occasional ponderosa pine and juniper tree did nothing to shield me and my husband, Kevin, from the relentless sun in a cloudless sky. The complaint in my calf muscles was nothing compared to the grumblings coming from my mouth.

"When will we get back to the car?" I whined, taking another step up the sharp incline.

He glanced at his watch. "Soon."

"By 11:15?" Another bead of sweat dripped to my waistband.

"Probably 11:45."

I winced. "Your idea of soon is different from mine."

He grunted. "True."

I took another sip of water and licked my salty lips as I hitched my backpack higher on my shoulders. Soon. We will get back to the car *soon.* The rocky trail contained one prominent shadow—the outline of my husband. I moved closer beside him and let his tall body shield me from the heat. Step after step we continued up the mountain.

> *Words and expectations often get me into trouble. Jesus,*
> *help me walk in step with those around me today.*
> —Lynne Hartke

Digging Deeper: 2 John 1:6; Ephesians 5:1–2

Sunday, September 8

Bless those who curse you, pray for those who mistreat you.
—Luke 6:28 (NIV)

"Can you believe her?" said Michael as we changed clothes that Sunday afternoon. "She dissed you in the church lobby."

It wasn't the first time that woman had made a mean-spirited comment to me. Over the past year, I'd tried to ignore her digs because our daughters were friends. But now my easygoing husband was riled up.

"That's it," I said. "I'm going to confront her."

The rest of the day, I mulled over the paragraph I'd text her. By bedtime, I'd formulated a new plan. I'd give her a piece of my mind in person. Tomorrow morning.

I decided to text one sentence so she'd know I was really mad: "We need to meet today." She'd see she couldn't talk to me that way. I'd send it at 7:00 a.m.

Getting breakfast for Micah the next morning, I imagined the exchange—she'd say this, I'd say that. I couldn't wait to tell her off. Minutes before seven, the Holy Spirit interrupted my musings: *Your daughters have been best friends all year, and you don't know anything about her. Get to know her. Listen.*

My indignation melted. I sent a text, but the tone was considerably friendlier. "Are you available to chat sometime?" She responded immediately.

The next day, we lingered over lunch. I learned that she felt isolated and was just beginning to be interested in God. A quiet knowing washed through me. I didn't need to set her straight; I needed to be the Christian friend she lacked in her life.

Lord, when I think it's time to speak my piece, send me Your peace.
May I listen to Your wisdom, instead of that negative voice inside my head.
—Stephanie Thompson

Digging Deeper: Matthew 18:21–22; Colossians 3:12–15

Blessed are the merciful: for they shall obtain mercy. —Matthew 5:7 (KJV)

In a moment of inspiration, or insanity, I outfitted the back of my twenty-four-year-old pickup with old toboggans placed upside down. I had to remove the tailgate to make them fit. Trouble was, I needed the tailgate to keep things from sliding out of the bed of the truck.

Then the idea struck me, so hard it almost left a bruise: a wooden sled! Not a toboggan, but a regular old lie-on-your-stomach sled, hung horizontally across the back as a faux tailgate. *Perfect.*

Then things sorta went haywire. Two o'clock in the morning, I was staring at a photo on Craigslist of the same kind of sled my twelve-year-old sister rode when she hit a tree and broke her neck. The accident left her a quadriplegic for the next forty-five years. It altered the course of my family's life. Nothing would ever be the same. And here I was, thinking of installing to the back of my vehicle a constant reminder of that awful day—almost taunting me.

The truck project took a breather while I regrouped. Finally I bought the sled, a sheer act of defiance against fate. My sister's life was formed and changed by her paralysis, but not defined by it. She eventually took orders as a tertiary Carmelite in the Catholic Church, where her charge, her mission, was to pray for others... which she did until her dying day.

Others. Think about that. Someone who couldn't help herself prayed to help you.

The sled is on the truck. I had to use brute force to make it fit, but no way was I was going to let a sled—any sled—defeat me.

> *Lord, have mercy on me. Allow me to see past what*
> *I cannot understand.*
> —Mark Collins

Digging Deeper: Psalm 18:25; Proverbs 11:17

Tuesday, September 10

ENCOUNTERING GOD IN UNLIKELY PLACES
Happy Service

Neither are your ways are my ways, saith the Lord. —Isaiah 55:8 (KJV)

We had been involved in outreach to Zimbabwe for many years, providing children orphaned by AIDS with a loving home at Village Hope. My mother joined our work, giving generously, writing letters, and sending gifts. When a vulnerable newborn came to our Village Hope family, Paddington, the wise father of our projects, chose to give the baby my mother's name: Arlene.

I longed more than ever for her to travel to Zimbabwe to see our progress and meet her namesake. But her traveling days waned, and she passed away, leaving me with a sad regret. She would never see Village Hope.

Then an email arrived from Paddington....

"Before I received the news that Arlene is no more, I had a dream, a vision of three ladies all with gray hair. Two of them stood well dressed in white on either side of a chair, where the third one was sitting. I was told that the one who was seated was Arlene, who had come to see us at Village Hope. This surprised me very much. I woke up and talked to my wife about the dream. I told her directly that something is not well with Arlene. Surely on the following day, we received the sad news that Arlene had passed on. Yet even on her last day, I knew she had visited Village Hope."

As I read Paddington's word, my vision of God cleared. Why did I think He would let my mother leave earth without seeing the good she had done? Within the great mystery that separates us from the life after this, how could I doubt that God would find a way to let me see my fondest wish for my mother fulfilled?

Father, how likely is it I would find You, Your promise of life everlasting, and my mother's final triumph all in one email?
Maybe it's just as likely as I believe it to be. Thank You.
—Pam Kidd

Digging Deeper: Isaiah 64:8; Haggai 1:13

God, who commanded the light to shine out of darkness, hath shined in our hearts, to give the light of the knowledge of the glory of God in the face of Jesus Christ. —2 Corinthians 4:6 (KJV)

My oldest was in my belly the year 9/11 became more than a number. The day we watched in horror as one plane struck and then another. My husband and I were both released early from work. At home we glued our eyes to the television, bracing for another attack when we learned about the Pentagon and the crash in Pennsylvania. The satellites went down, and I put my hands on my stomach as if I could protect the growing baby from the news that advised us to stock up on supplies, water, and other nonperishable goods.

I lay in bed awake that night, looking into the darkness, afraid of what the world had become and wondering what on earth that meant for us and the baby I was carrying. My sons ask, "Where were you? What happened exactly? Why on earth did they do it?" They ask about the people who perished. They ask about the heartbreaking posters of the missing that were everywhere.

I tell them prayer was on everyone's lips and radiating from our hearts. Prayer that somehow healing could come, that we were protected and loved, and that through the grace of God we'd get through this.

I tell them the answers to prayer came again and again in every kind deed, every selfless act. How even the next day strangers asked me about the baby growing inside me and meant it. Coworkers banded together in efforts to send supplies, start prayer chains, and find ways to help. I tell them that what happened after 9/11 is proof of God's love right here on earth and the power of the human spirit, selflessness, and courage.

Heavenly Father, on this day of remembrance, heal our aching hearts with Your infinite light, which will always outshine darkness.
—Sabra Ciancanelli

Digging Deeper: Psalm 9:9; Isaiah 40:31

Thursday, September 12

THINGS MY MOTHER TAUGHT ME: One Step at a Time

Nevertheless I must walk to day. —Luke 13:33 (KJV)

My husband, Gene, and I drove to the hospital in heavy silence. Jeremy, my grown son, had been in another serious car wreck. No other people were involved.

I didn't think I could walk into another emergency room. I'd lost count of the accidents. When he decides to go off his bipolar prescriptions, horrible things happen. Usually he's driving, taking nonprescribed drugs.

A memory surfaced while on this familiar journey. Early morning. Freezing cold. Heavy rain. I watched my mother dress for work. We didn't have a car at that time. I was about eight, and someone would pick me up for school. I stood at the window. "Mother, you can't walk in this weather."

"Hogwash. Of course I can, Mannie." She was smiling, almost laughing. "When I was a little girl, I walked two miles to school and Sunday school. I'll walk today and be fine." She put on her heavy brown coat and tied a plaid scarf around her pretty dark hair.

I took my mother's counsel. *I'll walk into this emergency room today and be fine.* In the emergency room, Jeremy lay under a clean white sheet pulled up to his chin, as a physician sewed a long gash on his forehead. Without taking his eyes off Jeremy, he told us, "He has a broken right hip and broken left femur."

Jeremy stuck a grimy hand from underneath the sheet. "You don't love me anymore, do you?" Tears slid through the dirt on his cheeks.

"Hogwash, Jeremy. I can never stop loving you."

Sweet Jesus, You walked up that horrible Via Dolorosa.
I ask You to walk with readers of this devotional today.
—Marion Bond West

Digging Deeper: James 1:2–4; 2 Corinthians 3:4–6

Whenever I am afraid, I will trust in You. —Psalm 56:3 (NKJV)

Trust. That was what God had been teaching me.

I searched the tack room, but I couldn't find Jack's bridle anywhere. After four years, I'd forgotten which one was his. Someone at the ranch had been using his bridle on another horse, but which one? Nobody I could ask was around.

I'd never gone more than a month without riding, until I'd suffered career-ending back injuries. I was hurt while fighting a wildfire on the ranch, where I'd lived for twenty years. Trust God through that? It took four painful years after the first surgery failed before my lesson climaxed and I underwent spine reconstruction. Six months and one day after that successful surgery, my doctor gave me approval to ride—but here I was, without a bridle.

I walked to the horses grazing on the hillside. Jack thrust his nose against me. "We have to wait a little longer," I said, rubbing his forehead. I must trust God in this delay, too.

Jack snorted. My hand trailed along his neck as he started to move off. Then he stopped below me, my hand on the crest of his shoulder, his back waist-high. He waited. It wasn't planned. My leg swung up, and I was on. For a moment the pain, the heartache, and the uncertainty of the past four years was gone. It was just me and Jack.

He tensed. I stiffened. Had I made a mistake? Should I have waited? Would he buck? *Trust.* I let go of fear. We both relaxed. Jack trotted to the other horses and dropped his head to graze. God was and is in control. I could look confidently at the world once again and know that through His grace I am healed.

> *Praise You for making me rely on You—not on myself.*
> *I trust You, especially when I cannot see the way ahead.*
> *I am safe in the shadow of Your wings.*
> —Erika Bentsen

Digging Deeper: Psalm 73:28; Proverbs 3:5

Saturday, September 14

Give, and it will be given to you. Good measure, pressed down, shaken together, running over, will be put into your lap. For with the measure you use it will be measured back to you. —Luke 6:38 (ESV)

She doesn't know my name anymore. She doesn't even recognize me. I'm "that girl." That girl who came into the house without knocking. That girl who tried to give out hugs. That girl who would probably steal food.

It stings.

Especially coming from the one who taught me to make yeast doughnuts and pepper cookies. The one who walked hand in hand with me across the fields on her farm while we picked apples and blueberries and wildflowers. The woman who told me stories of growing up in a one-room house in Finland. The one who helped me push out fresh cider from the press and produce fresh butter in the churn.

The one who once loved me, cherished me, and protected me.

Now it's my turn. My turn to love even when she shows little gratitude. To be patient, kind, and longsuffering. To place my hands over hers to help her knead dough since her hands have forgotten how. To help her snip rosebuds to put in the vase beside her bed because they remind her of her own mother. To rinse the blueberries and put them in a china bowl, and to spread butter on her bread.

To serve as Jesus served.

Not because it's easy. Because serving one who is angry, berating, and unkind is never easy.

But He did it first.

Lord, You seek me, love me, cherish me, and protect me
even when I am angry, berating, unkind, and undeserving.
Help me do the same for others. Amen.
—Erin MacPherson

Digging Deeper: Deuteronomy 16:7; Proverbs 3:27

Wear shoes that are able to speed you on as you preach the Good News of peace with God. —Ephesians 6:15 (TLB)

I woke up late Sunday morning and dressed quickly. I slipped into my shoes and drove the seven miles to town. I felt a bit unsteady but didn't figure out why until halfway through Sunday school: my left shoe was black with a round stacked heel, the right one brown with a buckle and smaller, lower heel. My classmates got a chuckle, but since I'd be at the organ during church I doubted anyone else would notice.

Just before worship started, however, Pastor Javier asked, "Would you please do the Children's Time? No one signed up for today." Children's Time is when someone offers a special message to the kids in the congregation in front of the entire church.

My mismatched shoes would be on full display, but children are important to us, so I said yes. I breathed a prayer for inspiration as I sat down on the chancel steps. As I looked at my feet, God answered that prayer.

"I made a mistake today," I said, sticking my feet straight out in front of me. "Can anyone tell what it was?" The kids didn't spot it at first, but when they did, they laughed along with the congregation. When it was quiet again, I shared a precious part of the good news of peace with God: "Jesus loves us. Jesus loves and forgives us when we make mistakes and when we do wrong things. Jesus loves us forever."

Lord, You must have a sense of humor! Thank You for
using my shoes to help our children and me understand
Your good news that You offer forgiveness and love.
—Penney Schwab

Digging Deeper: Matthew 6:28; John 8:8–11; Romans 3:23–26

Monday, September 16

Abram left Haran as the Lord had told him....Abram took his wife Sarai, his nephew Lot and everything they owned. —Genesis 12:4–5 (ICB)

The road sign flashed a warning: Freeway Closed Ahead. We were just a few hundred miles into our eight-hundred-mile journey, and now we'd add a seventy-five-mile detour...on a two-lane road... through no-man's land...following a U-Haul. Lovely. If rolling your eyes while operating a vehicle is an unsafe driving practice, I should have turned on my hazard lights.

But I could only keep driving. Besides, my son was driving the U-Haul, which was filled with my stuff. As I stared at the same truck bumper mile after tedious mile, two thoughts repeatedly ran through my mind: *Why do I own this much junk?* and *The only thing of any value in that truck is the one driving it.*

There's nothing like packing up everything you own to make you realize how much you really have. Sure, in my new home I could use a bed to sleep in, clothes to keep me warm, a few dishes to eat off of, and a chair to sit on. But what about all my "treasures"? The shells I've collected from all over the world? The cast-iron mermaid? The piranha head I brought home after staying in a survival camp in the Amazon?

These were just trinkets that commemorate happy memories. My son, Ryan, was the only true treasure, to me and to God. When I later unpacked my boxes and found the tail feathers broken off my favorite ceramic bird statue (the one wearing red tennis shoes), I wasn't heartbroken in the slightest. Instead I thanked God that my son and I had arrived safely, all in one piece.

Dear Lord, help me treasure what You treasure—people, not things.
Teach me how to be content with what I have instead of
indulging my desire for "more."
—Vicki Kuyper

Digging Deeper: Matthew 6:19–21; Luke 12:33–34

Let us not become weary in doing good, for at the proper time we will reap a harvest if we do not give up. —Galatians 6:9 (NIV)

My nine-year-old son glanced at the television set as he walked by to get a snack. I was planted on the couch, enjoying *The Voice*, a reality TV show that's also a national vocal competition. "Mami, you sing like that," he said. "You should be on that show."

Music has always been a part of my life, and I believe singing is a gift God has given me. But I've never done much to share that gift.

I continued to watch the show, thinking about my son's comment.

He recognized my gift and was basically telling me to get off the couch and do something about it.

The next day, I applied online for a preliminary audition. It was an easier process than I'd imagined. Two months later, I took a bus from New York to Philadelphia and stood in line with thousands of others.

"I'm here!" I said as my son's face popped up on my phone. I showed him the crowd and was proud to be an example of someone no longer watching but doing.

Soon it was time to audition. Ten of us were led into a large room, and we each had a turn to sing in front of one judge.

None of us made it to the next round. My son was crushed.

"I wanted you to win," he said, near tears, when I came home.

"I'm disappointed I didn't move on, too," I admitted. "But I'm actually really proud of myself for trying. And I'm proud you encouraged me to be that person." Rejection is hard, but we can't let that stop us from trying. "And guess what," I said. "In six months, I'm going to try again."

Thank You, Lord for the strength to reach for our life goals and the courage to get back up even in the disappointment of perceived failure.
—Karen Valentin

Digging Deeper: Psalm 37:24

Wednesday, September 18

Be of good courage, and he shall strengthen your heart, all ye that hope in the Lord. —Psalm 31:24 (KJV)

O ne of my students asked for help editing his psychology paper. As a writing tutor at a community college, I had done this hundreds of times, everything from helping young writers focus their topics to proofreading—what I call the "beauty treatment" for developed ideas. Though I had the edge on grammar, my students, especially refugee, taught me about living.

That day he presented a paper describing his rationale for a support group for refugee youth and why he should lead it. From previous conversations, I gleaned that he had fled from Tanzania to the US. After ten years in New Hampshire, he had graduated from my mother's alma mater and now worked at a Boys & Girls Club. But he wanted to do more. "I know a refugee's fear and the guilt of leaving family behind. I want to give kids hope," he said.

I began to read his paper: "These are the people I have lost my grandmother, my grandfather, my brother." *Good Lord, how can I teach colon placement when his family has been murdered?* I paused and looked at my student. He was smiling, as he usually does. Punctuation could wait.

"I'm terribly sorry this happened to you. Yet you want to give back. How can you keep smiling?"

His grin dimmed but did not go out as he considered my question. "I believe in God and better days ahead." He again flashed his irrepressible smile, a beacon of hope for us all.

> *God of all hope, may I ever learn from students who*
> *have passed through the shadow of death.*
> —Gail Thorell Schilling

Digging Deeper: Psalm 116:12; Acts 3:6

*Grace and peace be yours in abundance through the knowledge
of God and of Jesus our Lord.* —2 Peter 1:2 (NIV)

I woke up this morning, my head full of worry. Nothing obvious
was at the root of it. Just a generalized angst, pressure in my chest
and behind my eyes, the soles of my feet slightly damp, my breathing
shallow.

Who isn't stressed out these days? My friend, author and motiva-
tional speaker Jon Gordon, claims he's too blessed to be stressed. I wish
I could say that.

My stress engine always seems to be idling, waiting for a reason to
rev up. Work deadlines, the economy, politics, health issues, or just
waiting in line at the grocery store.

Another friend says stress is a fundamental force of nature. Without
it, the world would come to a dismal standstill. Nothing would ever
get done. Society would crumble. We would be lost. Yep, stress is a
great motivator.

But a constant state of stress is harmful. Researchers agree that pro-
longed stress levels contribute to just about every health condition you
can name. That kind of stress is corrosive to the soul. It breaks us down
and distances us from grace. Grace and stress are antithetical.

We all need reminders of that. I say the Serenity Prayer. That's what
I did this morning. Nothing banishes anxiety like putting the focus on
God and concentrating our thoughts on His love for us.

It also helps to have a golden retriever jumping up on your bed first
thing in the morning and licking your chin. Did I mention my golden's
name? It's Grace.

*Father, I am quick to worry, to forget Your presence in every moment of
my life, in the midst of every challenge and joy. Help me stay out of my
own head and remain in Your loving arms.*
—Edward Grinnan

Digging Deeper: Jude 1:2

Friday, September 20

You lifted me out of the depths. —Psalm 30:1 (NIV)

This was a very different trip to the hospital. Four years earlier, driving there for the birth of their first son, they'd broken the speed limi. This time they drove slowly, and neither Sondra nor her husband said much. When they'd learned they were expecting a second boy, they named him Peter after Sondra's dad. Three weeks before the delivery date, however, little Peter's heart stopped beating. They were on their way to the same hospital to meet the same doctor in the same delivery room. But nothing was the same.

The hospital staff was wonderful, Sondra told me afterward. She was wheeled after the delivery to a private room at the very end of the maternity floor, out of earshot of joyous visits to happier rooms. On her door was the picture of a falling leaf, a silent reminder to nurses and Welcome Wagon volunteers.

Her husband was in the room, and he and Sondra embraced in silence. The door opened, and a nurse wheeled a bassinet into the room. Little Peter was swaddled in a tiny white gown, a blue blanket tucked snugly around him. "He took my breath away, he was so beautiful!" Sondra said.

His parents took turns holding him, kissing him, and telling him how much they loved him. Four-year-old Jimmy had sung "Twinkle, Twinkle, Little Star" and "Itsy-Bitsy Spider" to his little brother "in Mommy's tummy." So they, too, sang to Peter.

They made plans for Peter's funeral, for a gift to the hospital in his name, and for a yearly remembrance on this date. Somehow, she said, those few hours of holding their son, talking to him, and welcoming him into their family made it possible to release him into the arms of the Father Who loves him even more.

> *Remind me, when I embrace those I love, Father,*
> *that a hug isn't finished till You let go.*
> —Elizabeth Sherrill

Digging Deeper: Psalm 3:3, 25:2

How good and pleasant it is when God's people live together in unity!
—Psalm 133:1 (NIV)

My colleague Bill, director of development for Guideposts, asked me to join him for a luncheon in Boca Raton, Florida, to meet with donors and subscribers. A week before the event, I looked closely at the guest list. I couldn't believe it. Tony, Marguerite, and their son, Michael, were attending. Seeing their names on the list made me think back to my early days as an interim minister at Gilead Presbyterian Church in Carmel, New York.

Marguerite and her son, who was ten years old at the time, were members of the church. I knew her well as a member who regularly attended the weekly Bible study, and she always brought Michael along with her. I don't know how the little guy managed to sit through these long adult discussions, but he did. After they moved to Florida, we lost touch. I could not wait to see them again, especially Michael, who was twenty-seven years old now and living in Colorado.

The reunion was totally delightful. The first thing Tony said was, "Where's Elba?" I explained that my wife wasn't able to join me on this trip, so he asked that we come visit them. The family and I caught up and discussed old memories. Michael even shared stories with the group about my preaching at church when he was a child. As he spoke, I realized how much my words had impacted him. He shared sermons that refreshed my memories. I felt blessed.

After lunch we all took a picture together, and then Michael asked for one with just him and me. Sometimes I forget the impact and influence I have on others.

Lord, thank You for the people You allow us to
impact on our journey. Bless them.
—Pablo Diaz

Digging Deeper: Galatians 6:10; Hebrews 11:7

Sunday, September 22

Let us lift up our hearts and our hands to God in heaven.
—Lamentations 3:41 (NIV)

My usual ability to slog through difficulty wasn't working. Weariness over family difficulties had mixed itself up with sadness, and the two crashed over me in wave after wave. I sat in church, stuck in my sad funk, while the service moved forward.

I had no idea how to make anything better in my life. I praised God with my lips, because I knew how to do that. I stood up, sat down, and knelt at the right times, because I could do that as well. But I only half-listened to the sermon.

By the time we were encouraged to, "Lift up your hearts," instead of responding, "We lift them up to the Lord," I muttered, "No! You do it!" *You gave me emotions, Lord,* I pouted. *If You want me to figure this out, You're going to have to unclog my heart.*

I reached into my purse for tissues, suddenly needing them. Tears washed away the aching question of what to do, and I thought instead about what kind of person I want to be. Mess or no mess, I am the Lord's. Sure, I'd rather draw near to Him with a quiet heart and peaceful life, but since that apparently wasn't an option right now, I would have to serve Him in the midst of my situation. I took a deep breath and lifted my heart to God, giving it to Him as if for the first time.

"Go in peace to love and serve the Lord," the pastor said.

"Thanks be to God," I replied...and meant it.

> *Jesus, I would rather be happy today. But if I cannot be,*
> *I know that I am Yours always.*
> —Julia Attaway

Digging Deeper: Philippians 3:20

Jesus replied, "Foxes have dens and birds have nests, but the Son of Man has no place to lay his head." —Luke 9:58 (NIV)

There are chapters in my life when I have felt the pain of feeling lost and without a home. When I graduated from college, I felt particularly homeless. My father had died, my mother had sold our house and moved to another city, my college buddies were scattered, I had broken up with my girlfriend, and my new job involved constant travel. I was soon depressed.

During that time, an understanding friend gave me a book, *A Place for You,* by a wise counselor, Paul Tournier. This book touched my soul. Tournier helped me understand the importance of having a "place" for healing. It would still be months and years before I "settled down," owned a house, was married, and had a long-term job. However, I learned that feeling "at home" comes in many forms.

I have an old padded leather chair that has been my close friend for decades. The chair has moved with me wherever I live. The chair and I have read books together, slept together, dreamed together, and watched television together. My chair is "a place for me"!

Beth and I have lived in five states and six cities during forty-two years of marriage. But home is mostly found amid scattered friendships and vital memories that span those years. We intentionally stay connected to "old friends."

Above all, I try to create a place in my soul to be at home with God. God is the one consistent and loving presence that spans all chapters of my life. Wherever I am, I have a place called home because God is near.

Dear God, may I be at home with You today. Amen.
—Scott Walker

Digging Deeper: Luke 10:38; Mark 10:29

You shall accept gifts for Me from every person whose heart so moves him.
—Exodus 25:2 (JPS)

The problem is too much advertising." Yoshi's statement was not at all what we usually hear at Torah study. The rabbi asked Yoshi to explain his startling remark and what it had to do with the building of the tabernacle, which we were studying that morning. Yoshi referred to God's request that the gifts He wanted the Israelites to bring were only requested from those "whose hearts are so moved," and maintained that in today's online and television noise, advertising muddies up individual choices so we can't hear our hearts any longer.

Another person in the group disagreed (as almost always happened), and the discussion went on for quite a while with more people chiming in. While they talked, I thought back to an experience I had while working for Young & Rubicam, an advertising agency headquartered in New York City.

One of the agency's interns was a young man from a small village in Austria, and over lunch his first week with the company, he told us he really didn't understand what good advertising achieves until his first visit to an American supermarket. "There isn't just one kind of anything here," he said. "The shelves are full of choices you have to make. At home we never had to choose, because if you wanted crackers, there was only one kind of cracker. Or olive oil. Or cleanser. Advertising helps you to pick."

Now, listening with half an ear to the ongoing discussion, I realized what he had really been telling me. Our advertising means we are blessed with abundance in America. The line "God shed His grace on thee" is more than just lyrics. With such abundance we should also be moved to give.

> *Your lessons may come in many strange forms, Lord,*
> *but I try to recognize them...eventually.*
> —Rhoda Blecker

Digging Deeper: Exodus 35:10; 2 Chronicles 18:1

When you pray, go to your room, shut the door, and pray to
your Father who is present in that secret place. —Matthew 6:6 (CEB)

It's a beautiful fall morning in the park, the sun peeking out from behind a veil of clouds, the maple leaves turning their first blush of copper, and the roses in the garden holding up their heads. I smile at the other runners who pass me by: "Morning. . . . Beautiful day. . . . Keep it up."

But inside my head, I'm muttering, *I don't ever remember this hill being so steep. How am I ever going to make it? What's that ache I feel in my shins? I'm exhausted. Whoever said running is fun?*

This inner monologue often goes on when I'm praying. My eyes closed, I might look serene as a saint, and yet here's what I'm saying: *God, I wish I did a better job on that project at the office. . . . Why can't I remember that person's name? . . . I want to think of You more during the day, but then I get busy. . . . I don't know if our bank balance will cover that check I just wrote. . . .* The psalmist said God knows the secrets of our hearts, but does He really want to hear all this stuff? Sure He does.

Then comes the moment in my run when I round the corner and turn into our driveway, ready to hurl amens at heaven's loving listener.

"Good run?" a neighbor asks.

"Yeah, it was great," I say. God and I have our little secrets, and I'm sure glad He can keep them.

Father, You see what we do in secret and reward us.
Hear our prayers.
—Rick Hamlin

Digging Deeper: Psalm 56:8; Mark 1:35

Thursday, September 26

Sitting down, Jesus called the Twelve and said, "Anyone who wants to be first must be the very last, and the servant of all." —Mark 9:35 (NIV)

It was Leadership Day, and my colleagues and I were spending the day learning about the work of local charities. It was part of Leadership Northshore, an organization that builds future community leaders.

We visited a food ministry that raises money to cook, prepare, and deliver hundreds of meals to shut-ins every day. I met Miss Dot, who helps cook the meals, and Mr. Tom, who spends most of his day driving around town delivering the meals.

We visited a shelter that provides housing for homeless men and also runs a store selling used clothing items. Miss Betty spends hours cleaning and sorting items to sell at bargain prices.

I met Sue, who runs an organization that provides shelter for battered women. She's on call twenty-four hours a day to arrange a safe haven for wives and oftentimes their children.

We visited a day-care center for low-income families, where Joni and Mary worked with young children to create art using construction paper, crayons, and markers donated by people in the community.

We finished our excursion by helping build a Habitat for Humanity home for a family. I climbed up on scaffolding and nailed siding to the house.

At the end of the day as I drove home, I thought about the acts of love I'd witnessed. I blinked back tears, overwhelmed by the generosity. Joan, who serves on the board for Leadership Northshore, had begun the day by telling us, "You will see many earthbound angels today." Indeed we did.

Lord, may I serve You by serving others with the goodness, compassion, and gentleness You show me.
—Melody Bonnette Swang

Digging Deeper: Colossians 3:23–24; Mark 10:45

The steadfast love of the Lord never ceases, his mercies never come to an end. —Lamentations 3:22 (NRSV)

I walk down the long hospital hallway, heading for room 145. I've been here many times in the last two weeks. My friend Juanita has ovarian cancer; she is dying.

I'm an ovarian cancer survivor who has lived way beyond my life expectancy, and I often spend time with people who are walking where I've been. Juanita is younger than I am and was so full of life, riding her bike over high mountain passes with her husband. Her dying doesn't seem fair.

"Hi, sweet Juanita," I say as I enter her room.

She smiles, and I sit down by her bed. Her eyes look large, and her body looks small.

We talk for a while, and she tells me how she appreciates everyone's prayers because she has trouble praying for herself. I take her hand, and we pray. We pray she'll trust God in this journey and that He will get the glory for the good things He has done. That has been her constant prayer request.

"I love you, Juanita," I say, and blow her a kiss. She returns the gesture. It's our parting ritual.

Driving home, I feel profoundly sad about the painful reality of cancer in so many lives. The ache grows, and before bed, I step out into the silent darkness on the back porch, breathing in the fresh air. Suddenly I hear a meadowlark's beautiful song. In awe, I remember the first time I walked alongside a friend with cancer years ago. A meadowlark often sang outside our kitchen window in the morning. Since then, a meadowlark's song has come to me in times of grief, reminding me of God's faithful presence. But in all these years, I've never heard a meadowlark sing in the dark. Until now.

Lord, thank You.
—Carol Kuykendall

Digging Deeper: Psalm 16:11; 2 Corinthians 1:3–7; Zephaniah 3:17

Saturday, September 28

The Lord is my shepherd, I shall not want. He makes me lie down in green pastures; he leads me beside still waters; he restores my soul.
—Psalm 23:1–3 (NRSV)

"It's quiet," Jan exclaimed. "Thank You, Jesus." My housemates and I often observed how much noisier it seemed here on this beautiful resort island than back home in New York City, which is known as "the city that never sleeps."

We were all there for a two-month contract, and as performers we had schedules much different than a regular nine-to-five. The noise of lawn maintenance at 9:00 a.m. on our single day off each week—Monday—resulted in grumpy actors and not-so-silent protests for an end to all lawn mowers.

We also found other ways to deal with the discomforts of being away from the familiar. I had shipped my scooter to myself before leaving and took a great deal of delight in scooting to work every day. As part of my daily show warmup, I put in my earbuds, unfolded my scooter, and pushed myself the almost two miles to the theater, following the bike trail and belting along with the R&B divas who sang in my ears. I might have disrupted the golf game of more than a few golfers, but they all greeted my gaze with smiles and waves. The wind caressing my face, the warmth of the sun kissed my arms, and the trees and flowers all bowed a sweet hello. And for thirty minutes of my day, I had my own private heavenly escape.

> *Creator, what a blessing to experience Your creation every day! I pray for an awareness that allows me to always seek solace, comfort, and peace in what You have placed all around me. Thank You, Holy One, for these gifts here on earth. Amen.*
> —Natalie Perkins

Digging Deeper: Isaiah 55:12; Matthew 6:1

*He Himself… might free those who through fear of death were subject to
slavery all their lives.* —Hebrews 2:14–15 (NASB)

As I walked down the sidewalk to church, I spotted a squirrel
lying in the grass of someone's front lawn. I knew something was
wrong, for I was almost upon him before he tried to move toward the
safety of a nearby hickory tree.

I stopped to watch him. Was he injured? Could I help? He stood
in the lawn, wavering on his little brown legs. He closed his eyes. His
body sagged a little toward the grass. Then, smelling my nearness, he
opened his eyes and tried again to run to the tree. Instead he carved a
wobbly circle in the grass, his head tilted to one side as if the weight
were too much to bear.

He's dying, I thought. *Maybe he's been poisoned.*

"It's OK, little guy," I whispered, stretching out my hand in a parting
blessing. "Lay it down."

The image stayed with me all day. At night, as I lay back against the
pillows, I was seized with fear of dying. *Will it hurt?* I thought. *Was that
squirrel in pain? Did he know he was dying? Was he fighting it? Will I?*
My heart raced. My breathing grew shallow and my chest tight. I was
having a panic attack. I couldn't go to sleep. It felt too much like dying.

I prayed for the feeling to pass. I prayed that great comforting psalm:
Psalm 23. My heart slowed. My soul quieted down.

I do not know if death will hurt. I do not know if I will fight, like
the squirrel, or lay my soul down readily. But in faith, I believe God
will not let me walk that journey alone. Trusting in that belief, I'll find
freedom from the fear of death.

> *God, death is not my enemy; fear of death is.*
> *Give me courage in my hour of need!*
> —Amy Eddings

Digging Deeper: Psalm 23:4, 31:5; 1 Corinthians 15:22, 51

Monday, September 30

My help comes from the Lord, Who made heaven and earth.
—Psalm 121:2 (NASB)

Autumn in Idaho—my favorite time of year. Crisp air tinged with wood smoke and the promise of coming holidays.

And I was miserable. I had firewood to split and stack, but with surgery looming and a crushed disk in my spine that felt like knife blades, the pile of logs in front of me might as well have been Mount Everest.

"Don't worry—it'll get done," my wife said.

The very last thing I was prepared to do was watch my wife stack wood while I stood helpless.

A car door slammed. Then another. Chris, my brother-in-law, strode into the yard, followed by more family. With a quick hello, they all jumped in and made fast work of the pile.

I was so grateful for the help. I also hoped they wouldn't see the embarrassment burning in my cheeks. I tried to hide it by making coffee for everybody. I stammered a million thanks, all the while mentally kicking myself for my inability to do the work myself.

You see, I'm happy to be the helper, but being helpless makes me want to crawl under a rock. I like to think I'm strong, but God has shown me a different name for it: pride.

Are you like me? Do you find yourself fighting your weakness? Even when you know the answer is to let go and let Him?

Sometimes I think I finally have it down, and then He takes me to the end of myself and there I am again, sitting in the front row of Leaning on God 101.

Funny, even now I find writing this difficult. A good reminder I still have a lot to learn. I guess I'd better go; I'm late for class.

Lord, please strip me of me, until nothing remains but You.
—Buck Storm

Digging Deeper: Psalm 115:15, 124:8

UNDER GOD'S WINGS

1 _____

2 _____

3 _____

4 _____

5 _____

6 _____

7 _____

8 _____

9 _____

10 _____

11 _____

12 _____

13 _____

14 _____

15 _____

September

16 _____

17 _____

18 _____

19 _____

20 _____

21 _____

22 _____

23 _____

24 _____

25 _____

26 _____

27 _____

28 _____

29 _____

30 _____

OCTOBER

The Lord is my helper; I will not be afraid.

What can mere mortals do to me?

—Hebrews 13:6 (NIV)

Tuesday, October 1

Clothe yourselves with compassion, kindness, humility, gentleness and patience. —Colossians 3:12 (NIV)

"Don't hand me anything," the woman commanded, crossing her arms.

I had attempted to show her the colorful flyer of an upcoming fund-raiser benefiting cancer patients I was distributing at a business function. "It's a family event."

She bristled, "I refuse to have anything to do with cancer."

"But it's—"

"Millions have been donated already, and in the meantime, they cut out body parts and drip poison into bodies while patients lie helpless in hospital beds." She spat the words louder and faster with each syllable.

In the uncomfortable silence that followed, I fought the urge to tell her I was a cancer survivor and that the organization had helped not only me but also my family.

Instead I watched, concerned, as the woman bent over a cup of coffee, the hot liquid doing nothing to warm the walled chill that surrounded her.

Resisting the urge to back away, I chose to step closer. Hadn't others listened to me in the difficult sharing of my story?

"Who did you know who died from cancer?" I asked.

Her voice dropped to a whisper. "My brother."

I crouched lower and looked in her crumbling face. "I'm so sorry."

Give me ears of compassion, Lord, to listen without judgment to the difficult realities of those around me.
—Lynne Hartke

Digging Deeper: 2 Corinthians 1:3–4; James 1:19; Psalm 18:6

ENCOUNTERING GOD IN UNLIKELY PLACES:
Not So Different After All

Thy kingdom come. —Matthew 6:10 (KJV)

In a poor village in Appalachia, where David and I began our marriage while serving as missionaries, we were shocked to learn that our little Presbyterian congregation had a fear of Catholics. I wondered, *How do you reeducate those taught by a trusted minister to fear people who are different from themselves?*

David realized the congregation needed to meet some Catholic people to readjust their views, so he reached out. He invited Catholics, who were serving at a mission site on the other side of the mountain, to a joint ice cream social. The ice cream was churned, the tables were set, and the Catholics arrived.

Not one soul from our congregation came.

Soon after, some women in our congregation were chatting about how they had always wanted to learn to knit.

One phone call later, I had signed up a plainclothes nun to teach a knitting class. The church ladies gathered, amid yarn and needles, and fell in love with the kindly woman they fondly called "Teacher." I waited as we progressed to shawls and sweaters, for the reveal.

"Did I ever tell you... Teacher is a nun from the mission?" Silence.

Then, "Teacher, can you show me that last stitch again?"

And there, at that mission site, a small group of Appalachian women, as Presbyterians and Catholics, bonded in mutual love.

There You are, God.

Father, Your kingdom keeps coming in unexpected ways.
I am humbled to find You in the midst of it all.
—Pam Kidd

Digging Deeper: Matthew 6:10–13

Thursday, October 3

For all the animals of the forest are mine. . . . I know every bird on the mountains, and all the animals of the field. —Psalm 50:10–11 (NLT)

We buried Trixie among the sagebrush on the hill above the house. BlueDog and Stubby the cat were in attendance as we lowered her, wrapped in her blanket, into the earth. I tossed in her bone and a shed horn she loved to chew on. BlueDog lost a friend. Stubby gained relief, I think. Trixie tormented cats.

I wiped tears from my eyes. We'd have to face many firsts: the first time we would feed one dog instead of two, the first night without her on guard by the sliding door, the first pickup ride without her.

She was my husband Randy's dog. Trixie tested my patience when I first came into his life. She was the dominant dog, and she often reminded my BlueDog that she was boss. Trixie sometimes turned half-mauled ground squirrels loose under my chair on the deck. Now at the end, I can remember only her sweetness, her soft fur, her border collie kisses on my hand, and the way she would "sing" with me at dinnertime. She was a better singer than I am.

The house seems empty without her. I choke back a sob. *Please be in heaven now, Trix.* How can God find sin in animals? Then I think of Stubby the cat and pray that God grades on a curve. Dogs have to go to heaven. Surely He wouldn't create such a warm, caring masterpiece and condemn it to such a short life on earth alone. The Bible is vague on the subject, but that's where faith comes in.

Please take our dog into Your care, Lord. Please protect her and keep her with You until I can get up there and see her again.
—Erika Bentsen

Digging Deeper: Proverbs 12:10; Ecclesiastes 3:18–19

LESSONS FROM THE ANIMALS: Pleasing the Master

And this is love: that we walk in obedience to his commands. As you have heard from the beginning, his command is that you walk in love.
—2 John 1:6 (NIV)

I was struggling with a decision. A friend had asked me to commit to service for a spiritual fellowship. I felt it would be a burden to say yes. My schedule was already packed. I'd done service many times before, so it wasn't as if I always said no. In fact, I rarely said no. But this time I wanted to.

I wrestled with this dilemma early one morning as I walked to Lower Manhattan. I passed a section of street cordoned off from vehicular traffic between the Stock Exchange and the Federal Reserve Buildings, and I saw a young dog, a black Lab, with a uniformed man. The man had a K-9 patch on his upper sleeve and was putting the dog through paces, presumably so it could qualify as a sniffer dog or in some other security role. Dogs can learn to do amazing things, such as protect us from unknown threats.

This dog was new at it. The trainer rewarded it for going over to a nondescript gym bag in the middle of the street. Praised it more for sitting calmly next to it. But the third step, lying down beside the bag, eluded the dog. It was clearly confused and anxious, getting up, and pacing around, and then sitting again, seeking the trainer's approval. When the trainer finally got it to lie down next to the bag, the dog was ecstatic at the praise received. How it found joy in obedience!

This of course struck home. Had I lost the joy of obedience? Especially spiritual obedience? To say yes even when no was easier?

I quickened my step. I wanted to get to the office and call my friend back.

Lord, never let me forget the joy of being obedient to
Your will when I am called.
—Edward Grinnan

Digging Deeper: Deuteronomy 13:4

Saturday, October 5

He has made everything beautiful in its time. —Ecclesiastes 3:11 (NIV)

As I walked my dog, Kemo, through the neighborhood this morning, I stooped to pick up a bright red oak leaf from the sidewalk. I loved the shape and color. I looked for a yellow leaf, a different shape from a different tree. Then a brown one. This ritual is familiar. I do it every autumn. I bring home a colorful collection of leaves and lay them out on a paper towel on the counter. I place another paper towel over them. Finally I pile on some heavy books, including a Bible.

Surely this habit goes all the way back to my childhood, when my kindergarten teacher helped us gather leaves at recess. Then to my season of doing this with my own young children, hoping they would love pretty leaves in autumn and carry on the tradition with me. And more recently, on walks to the park with my grandchildren. I've loved how they love our hunt for pretty leaves.

This morning, it was just Kemo and me as I picked up leaves.

Why do I do this? I simply can't *not* do it. Autumn awakens something in me. I savor the brilliant beauty and unique shapes of freshly fallen leaves, the crunchy sound of walking through already dried leaves. I want to gather and carry the colors into our house, dry them, and then place them on the windowsill, where I can see them when I make chili.

I do it because it's my way of celebrating and lingering over the spectacular colors of autumn, thanking God for His gift of changing seasons.

Lord, thank You for the colorful markers of this season.
—Carol Kuykendall

Digging Deeper: Genesis 1:14–19

As these men were going away, Jesus began to speak to the crowds about John, "What did you go out into the wilderness to see? A reed shaken by the wind?"—Matthew 11:7 (NASB)

Jesus, in the midst of preaching, tells two disciples the imprisoned John the Baptist was the one prophesied to come. I love how Jesus reminds His astonished audience of the way they had once journeyed into the desert in droves to hear John the Baptist's message.

It's as if He senses their doubts.

It reminds me of the delusions I harbor in my own discipleship, especially when my faith is tested.

I left a high-paying, high-profile job in New York City to move to a small rural town in Ohio. The move put me closer to my family, and it also gave me the opportunity to learn that I am more than my paycheck and job title. Three years later, our finances are low, my relationships with family members haven't developed the way I'd imagined, and I've struggled to make friends in a place where my career path can appear foolish and self-indulgent.

Yeah, I wanted a new purpose for my life, but I didn't think it'd go like this.

What did I come into the desert to see? Did I think spiritual growth was a spectator sport, a walk in the wilderness along a well-marked trail?

No, I came into the desert because of the promise that, as Jesus reports to John's messengers, "the blind regain their sight, the lame walk, lepers are cleansed, the deaf hear, the dead are raised, and the poor have the good news proclaimed to them."

God, I really do want to grow closer to You, but my expectations get in the way. Help me set aside everything I think I already know, so I may have a new experience of You.
—Amy Eddings

Digging Deeper: Luke 7:24–28; Matthew 3:1–5; John 16:33

Monday, October 7

I, even I, am he who blots out your transgressions, for my own sake,
and remembers your sins no more. Review the past for me, let us
argue the matter together; state the case for your innocence.
—Isaiah 43:25–26 (NIV)

I watched in court as the parents cried and the judge prepared to make his decision. Those of us sitting in the gallery were silent. We were all there to support the family. My friend's son was facing the first crisis of his young life. The boy—and he really was just a boy—stood with his lawyer and appeared unmoved.

Just seventeen years old, he was on trial for drug possession. Police had found pot in his car during a traffic stop. He had been coming from a basketball game. He told the judge that was the very first and only time he had ever smoked pot. I know he was telling the truth—and thank God, the judge believed him.

"We all make mistakes," the judge said to that terrified boy standing before him. "I'm giving you another chance. The court forgives you." The judge actually said those words!

Mercy was handed out in a way it often isn't in courts these days, I am told. The judge who heard my friend's son make his plea before the court is a Christian, one who knows what it means—and actually feels like—to be forgiven. Thank God.

I am tired, Lord. But when I pause to be with You,
as I will today, I will find rest.
You are my second (and third and fourth) chance.
—Jon M. Sweeney

Digging Deeper: Psalm 147:5

How can you say to your brother, "Let me take the speck out of your eye,"
when all the time there is a plank in your own eye? —Matthew 7:4 (NIV)

I was on my third errand of the day when I got a call from the bank
teller. Making a cash deposit had been my first errand of the morning.

"I'm so sorry, but I miscounted your deposit," the young man
explained. "I put on your receipt ten dollars more than you actually
gave me. I recounted my drawer several times to make sure. It's an inex-
cusable mistake, and I am so sorry and hope you won't hold it against
the bank." I stopped him and assured him he needn't worry. "Really?"
he asked incredulously. "Are you sure?"

I laughed. "You're talking to a woman who waited tables in grad
school for less than a month," I said. "I lasted twenty-one days before I
quit. And do you know why I quit?"

"No, ma'am."

"Because I was accidentally paying for my customers' meals. We had
to make our own change. At the end of my shift, I had just ten dollars
in my pouch. I'd walked in that morning with twenty. You couldn't
have picked a better customer for this mistake. If anybody can understand miscounting money, you're talking to her!"

I heard the relief in his voice as he laughed along with me.

Now every time I stop by the bank, the tellers know me by name.
They also know me by my secret identity: the Lady Who Can't Count
Money.

Father, it feels good to let someone off the hook, just like
You always overlook my mistakes. Help me to do it more often.
—Ginger Ruc

Digging Deeper: Matthew 23:4; Romans 2:1–5

Wednesday, October 9

Unless you change and become like little children, you will never enter the kingdom of heaven. —Matthew 18:3 (NIV)

Sondra and her husband had released their stillborn son into God's care. Four-year-old Jimmy had not. "He can't understand why the little brother he was so excited about can't come home," Sondra told me when I phoned to see how she was doing. They told him baby Peter had gone home to heaven instead, and that he and Jimmy would play there together someday. "But of course, at four, he can't have much concept of heaven."

Every day, to coax a sign of enthusiasm out of him, Sondra tried giving him something he especially liked. An icecream cone with sprinkles. A miniature car for his collection. "Never a smile."

"He used to love balloons," I suggested.

Sondra tried my idea, but that didn't work either. She'd found a big red balloon with a smiley face. "He simply took it without a word." What really worried her, Sondra said, was what happened after they left the store. "We were nearly at the car when Jimmy somehow lost his grip on the string!" Of course the balloon sailed away. "He didn't even cry, didn't react at all. Just stood watching it go up, up, out of sight."

I shared Sondra's worry and told her so. Which is why, that evening, she phoned again. All afternoon, she told me after they returned home, Jimmy sat watching the front door. "I wondered if he was afraid his father might not come home."

When his dad arrived, though, Jimmy jumped up and ran to meet him. "Daddy! Daddy! Mommy and I gave Jimmy a balloon!"

Four-year-olds have a better concept of heaven than we think.

Give me a child's trust, Father, in Your invisible reality.
—Elizabeth Sherrill

Digging Deeper: Matthew 18:4; Mark 10:15

SAYING GOODBYE TO MY VETERANS: A Lesson Learned

Teach me your way, Lord. —Psalm 27:11 (NIV)

Dave worked in the VA mail room, and he was having a hectic day when, at the close of our shift, I took him a package to overnight. "This is high priority," I emphasized. "A couple of us nurses are hoping to do a presentation at a major research meeting. This is our abstract. It absolutely has to be in Chicago first thing in the morning."

At noon the next day, I checked to make certain we had indeed met our deadline. But the abstract committee had seen neither hide nor hair of it. I was furious.

When I got to the mail room, I gave Dave a piece of my mind. Actually, several large pieces.

Dave's face grew red, and he apologized profusely. But I ignored him. "Don't you understand?" I seethed. "My colleagues and I have worked months on this project. Now it's not going to happen. I depended on you!"

After that, every time I encountered sweet, wonderful Dave at the hospital, I was utterly embarrassed. I'd look away, strike up a conversation with somebody else.

I pleaded with God to let Dave know how sorry I was. Finally, I mustered the nerve to tell him myself. "Please forgive me," I said. "I'm so sorry. Anyone could have had such an oversight."

Years later, Dave moved up and was the IT person who helped me with my computer. More than that, he silently taught me that words spoken in angry haste can't be erased. For the next thirty-three years, I took care to not let my tongue get the best of me. I had gracious Dave to thank for that.

In retirement, help me to remember all the lessons I learned on the job.
—Roberta Messner

Digging Deeper: Psalm 25:5, 86:11

Friday, October 11

I will hope continually and will praise you yet more and more.
—Psalm 71:14 (ESV)

"Hey, Mom, want to hear what I've been working on?" my son asked. I nodded, and we headed to the family room. He took a seat on the piano bench, as I sat on the sofa by the fireplace, and he began to play.

This music wasn't a song yet, just a melody. But the rhythm reached my soul. I watched my boy. He was near adult age, and the growing years also grew distance between us. We've struggled. And when one member of the family hurts, all do. We're connected by love.

As I listened to my son play, I noticed his hands. I remembered when they laced with mine. When his fingers first curled around a pencil and later the steering wheel of my car. I admired his profile. With a few notes, the years washed away. I was looking at my robust, full-of-life little boy.

This invitation was everything. It was more than the beginning of a song. Finally, my son had invited me into a tender part of his life. The place where music lives and creativity runs free. A gentle place. A place of peace. I closed my eyes and thanked the Lord for this goodness. I thanked Him for this moment when worry was suspended, and His love penetrated like heat from the hearth. God was reaching into my son's life. Pursuing him. Drawing him. That night the Lord allowed a glimpse of His presence. A moment to breathe and be warmed by His glory.

The Lord loved this child. This child was His own.

My son stopped playing. I wanted to fill the space with a thousand words, but I shared only two.

"It's beautiful."

He smiled and moved his fingers over the keys again.

To me, this was the sound of hope.

Lord, You are the pursuer of hearts and saver of souls.
In You is every hope. Amen.
—Shawnelle Eliasen

Digging Deeper: Romans 12:1, 15:13; Psalm 33:18

They are like a breath of air; their days are like a passing shadow.
—Psalm 144:4 (NLT)

The text from my first cousin was brief and direct: "Hey, cuz. They are recommending hospice for Dad." I had just woken up and checked my cell phone. This news was unexpected. I knew my uncle's health was declining, but not this rapidly.

I responded with encouragement and a promise to pray fervently for him. I was grateful for the curtain of technology between us. Through a text message my cousin could not hear my voice crack or see the tears roll down my face. She could not discern that her news transported my mind back to two years ago, when I lost my dad after a short illness and my mom exactly three weeks later.

After exchanging a few texts with my cousin, I went on with my typical Saturday routine—cleaning the house, managing my children's chores, and doing a little grocery shopping. I moved mechanically through the day, feeling weighed down by emotional heaviness.

Late that afternoon I took my young daughters, Joelle and Jada, to my goddaughter's high school dance program. I watched in awe of the dancers' beauty, energy, and youthfulness. They moved with an ease and poise teenagers possess, twirling and swirling through "Hallelujah," "Salvation," and "Bridge Over Troubled Water." We applauded for each dancer and went wild when my goddaughter danced near the end.

I marveled at God's timing. Watching these young people dance onstage with vitality and vigor reminded me that life indeed goes on. We are each blessed with seasons of life. My uncle was once blessed with youth and vitality. My parents were as well. This life is truly a passing shadow, but eternity is forever. I am grateful for life, but more important, for eternal life.

Lord, help me appreciate the preciousness of life while looking toward the glory and beauty of heaven.
—Carla Hendricks

Digging Deeper: Job 8:9; Psalm 39:5; James 4:14

Sunday, October 13

Greater love has no one than this: to lay down one's life for one's friends.
—John 15:13 (NIV)

"Would you like to have dinner together sometime?" a woman asked after making a beeline toward me after church. "We'd like to get to know you and your husband better."

I hardly knew her, but I said, "Sure!" I felt that was the right answer to such an invitation.

"I'll call you soon!" she responded cheerfully.

As I walked away, I thought, *"Soon" doesn't always happen so soon.* At least that's what I hoped. Truth is, I felt overwhelmed with responsibilities, relationships, and deadlines on my calendar.

A few days later, I had a message on my voice mail, "Are you free Saturday night? Let's have dinner."

Even though I admired her prompt follow-through, I had that overwhelmed feeling again. But we had nothing planned for Saturday night, so I called back and said, "Let's do it!"

"This feels kind of like a couples' blind date," I admitted to my husband, Lynn, as we drove to the restaurant. Soon the four of us were settled into a cozy booth, and before we ordered, they thanked us for coming.

"We like to think of a few people we'd like to get to know better, and you're on our list," she said. I smiled, admiring their intentionality.

Over dinner, we talked about their family, the beginnings of their relationship, the differences in our faith stories, and even the dogs in our lives. By the time the check came, we felt known by each other. Sunday morning at church, we greeted one another warmly. As friends, chosen and valued.

> *Lord, inspire me to pursue new friendships*
> *with intentionality and to follow through.*
> —Carol Kuykendall

Digging Deeper: Colossians 3:12–17

THINGS MY MOTHER TAUGHT ME: Give It a Try

Forget the former things; do not dwell on the past.
See, I am doing a new thing! —Isaiah 43:18–19 (NIV)

In 1974 I entered the Guideposts Writing Contest, thinking I might have a chance. After mailing my submission, I practically lived at the mailbox. Finally I received a "thank you for entering but" form letter. Disappointment surged through me like an illness. *Why did I ever think I could write?*

In 1976 I toyed with the idea of entering again. Speaking on the phone with my mother, I asked what she thought. I could tell she was smiling.

"Go ahead, Mannie. Give it a try. Do you remember when you were about nine and wanted to enter a short poetry contest? You were afraid then but decided to enter. The prize was an entire box of Peter Paul Mounds, and the assignment was to write about them. Sugar was still scarce then from the war. Even one candy bar was amazing."

I had prayed, "Dear God, please help me with the words." I had written carefully and threw away many attempts. Finally I'd handed my entry to Mother to mail.

Peter Paul Mounds are simply great/Sold for a nickel in every state/Put them in the stocking for Christmas joy/Chocolate and coconut/Boy, oh boy!

I won! And sure enough, the mailman delivered a two-layered box of candy to me. I saved the wrapping. Even though the box plainly stated there were twenty-four inside, I carefully took them out, counted them, and stacked the candy back in the red-and-white box.

In 1976, again asking for God's help, I worked hard on another entry to the Guideposts contest. Lo and behold, I became one of twelve winners.

Trusting You for help, Father, is the big thing. Even bigger than winning.
—Marion Bond West

Digging Deeper: Psalm 37:23; Proverbs 3:5–6

Tuesday, October 15

This world is not our permanent home; we are looking forward to a home yet to come. —Hebrews 13:14 (NLT)

The sun hung low over Iowa corn, and the truck stop glowed in the gathering dusk. There was an island outpost, where truckers, pilgrims, and families packed into minivans could stock up on fuel and soda before hoisting anchor and setting sail down another empty stretch of American highway.

The young man next to me in the coffee line offered a smile.

I glanced at the trucking company logo on his shirt. "Where're you from?"

"South Texas," he said.

"Long way from home."

He nodded. "Can't wait to see my family. My run's over, and all I have left to do now is drive south."

We wished each other safe travels.

Back on the highway, the darkening landscape wrapped itself around me. I sipped my coffee as weariness tugged. A three-week concert tour had brought me far. My porch light and family were still fifteen hundred miles west. I switched on my headlights and drove toward the last remnants of the dying sun.

I thought about that driver's words. *Can't wait*... Desire for hearth and home is something ingrained deep within all of us, isn't it? What a joy to know one fine day this longing will find its ultimate answer. To know that, no matter how many rough trips or, wrong turns we take, when the needle hovers on empty and winds of discouragement threaten to blow us off the road, there is a heavenly house where we are expected and loved, and the porch light never burns out.

> *Lord, thank You for eternal hope—*
> *those beautiful words, "Welcome home."*
> —Buck Storm

Digging Deeper: Hebrews 11:10–16

I will both lay me down in peace, and sleep. —Psalm 4:8 (KJV)

S*leep.* The word to me is almost like a poem. When I was a child, bedtime rituals were a sweet prelude to sleep. Poems like Eugene Field's "Wynken, Blynken, and Nod" sent me floating off to dreamland in a wooden shoe, and spoken rituals such as "Night-night," "Sleep tight," and "Sweet dreams" made me snuggle in safety.

When my son, Harrison, came into my life, I wanted to give him a unique bedtime tradition. Singing "Jesus Loves Me" as I tucked him in continued into his middle school years.

Now with two young girls, Mary Katherine and Ella Grace, we've added yet another nighttime custom: programmable pillows! Every night after bedtime stories and prayers, each girl gets her turn. They tell me what they would like to dream, and together we make a big show of programming their pillows for the dreams ahead.

Sleep is a subject of great interest these days. Sleep doctors, sleep clinics, and entire industries have grown around our country's sleeplessness. I wonder if maybe we've strayed away from something simple in this crazy world in which we live.

My mother had a little sign on her bedside table: "God tucks mothers in at night." The truth is, no matter our age or stage in life, we all need someone to tuck us in. Here's another truth: God, as our Father, vows to be our refuge (Psalm 46:1), give His angels charge over us (Psalm 91:11), and keep us from evil (2 Thessalonians 3:3). The list continues through the Bible.

Can sleep really be a poem of peace? Suppose God is standing by, like a Father, waiting to program our pillows with His best promises. Why not call on Him and see what happens?

> *Father, tuck us in at night. Let us rest in Your promises.*
> —Brock Kidd

Digging Deeper: Psalm 4:8; Isaiah 54:13

Thursday, October 17

Weeping may last through the night, but joy comes with the morning.
—Psalm 30:5 (NLT)

I was sitting at a table with other authors at the International Latino Book Awards. My book was up for an award, and my publisher had flown me to California for the ceremony. The whole trip felt surreal. Just days before, I was busy with my two little boys and endless housework, but now I was in an elegant venue, wearing a fancy dress, eating a delicious meal, and waiting to hear if my book had won. I was grateful and excited for everything—the peaceful flight from which I watched the incredible changing scenery below the clouds, the beautiful hotel room, and the relaxing indoor swimming pool down the hall. I felt important. It amazed me that all this came from having written a book about feeling unimportant. I felt happy and realized this happy moment came from writing my story of grief.

I straightened up in my seat. My category was up, and the presenter opened the envelope. "And the first-prize winner for Best Family Book goes to…Karen Valentin for *The Mother God Made Me to Be!*"

I jumped up and made my way to the podium to accept my award. I gave thanks for such an honor and closed by saying, "This moment is filled with incredible joy, but know that this moment was born from incredible pain. I wouldn't be accepting this award without first experiencing the hard stuff. So I dedicate this award to anyone who is in the midst of pain, because joy is on the way."

Thank You, Lord, for Your promise of hope and joy. Help me
stand on that promise in the depths of my sorrow and pain.
—Karen Valentin

Digging Deeper: Jeremiah 29:11

Love never fails. —1 Corinthians 13:8 (NIV)

Ican't get the words right. I try typing "I had cancer" for an article I am writing, but my fingers have another plan of their own. "I hate cancer," my fingers tap out. I backspace to erase the unintended word and begin again.

"I hate cancer." Again, the wrong words and then the backspace. I have to stop the rhythmic typing and peck out the letters, one by one: *h. a. d.*

But my heart agrees with the truth my fingers spelled.

Getting nowhere with my typing, I close my laptop, grab a fresh cup of Earl Grey, and settle into the glider on the back porch. Back and forth, I swing under the shaded ramada covered with cat's claw, a drought-resistant vine. One yellow flower remains, trumpeting the end of spring in the desert.

The cancer has moved to her lungs.

The doctors say I need surgery.

He has run out of options.

My mind replays the personal messages from three different friends as a redheaded house finch with its matching throat enjoys a breakfast at one of my backyard bird feeders. A sparrow joins it, and seeds scatter in all directions, some landing next to a garden tile propped against the fence, a tile with the words *Love never fails.*

Bodies fail. Insurance systems fail. Love never fails. Doctors fail. Treatment plans fail.

Love never fails. I fail. You fail.

Love never fails.

My hope is thin today, Jesus, and my faith hangs by splintered fingernails. Thank You for Your unfailing love that is bigger than cancer.
—Lynne Hartke

Digging Deeper: 1 Corinthians 8:2

Saturday, October 19

Yes, everything else is worthless when compared with the infinite value of knowing Christ Jesus my Lord. For his sake I have discarded everything else, counting it all as garbage, so that I could gain Christ.
—Philippians 3:8 (NLT)

I finally mustered the willpower to weed through my overflowing bookshelves. I gathered the books I no longer wanted, or never wanted in the first place, into four paper grocery sacks and headed to the used-book store. Even though I'd had most of them for decades and never read them, my instinct was to keep them. It's always been hard for me to let go of stuff—even when the items are meaningless to me.

A rusted-out Ford was parked in front of the bookstore. The poor condition of the faded blue sedan didn't attract my attention as much as its contents. Backseat piled high with plastic bags, paper sacks, discarded boxes, and black lawn bags. Garbage stacked so high the driver couldn't possibly see out the rearview mirror. The front passenger seat had huge pieces of cardboard, used fast food containers, and too many magazine circulars to count. The tower of trash piled up to the headliner.

I stood, mesmerized. Nothing of value inside, just worthless waste. This was the car of a hoarder.

Inside the bookstore, she stood out easily. Vintage hat, layered shirts, sweaters, and a jacket, she displayed three purses on the same shoulder. My heart went out to her.

I understand hoarding is a mental illness, but the image served as a visual reminder of how senseless it is to save that which is useless.

With renewed vigor, I vowed to relieve myself of unnecessary possessions and clean up my act.

Lord, help me fix my eyes on You and to keep only what I need.
—Stephanie Thompson

Digging Deeper: Matthew 6:19–21; 1 Samuel 12:21

Surely I am with you always, to the very end of the age.
—Matthew 28:20 (NIV)

Our church prayer list is really long, filled with the full range of personal struggle. During the weekly Bible study I attend, the question came up, "How do people get through it all?"

Ken spoke up. "I think when you have been through storms, you have a confidence. Not that you can't have faith until you've been through storms, but experiencing God's help in one gives more confidence." I believe the confidence Ken described comes when God's presence is personal to us.

As I pray the prayer list, in addition to their needs, I pray for all of them to experience God's presence in their pain and know he is with them…guiding, helping.

I first became aware of God's presence during a struggle to stop taking a medication prescribed for stress during graduate school. I kept getting it renewed, until a doctor said, "You don't need this. I will only renew it for thirty days. If you need it after that, seek professional help." I asked God to help me overcome this difficulty and, for the first time, surrendered the outcome to Him…even if it required counseling. I never needed further help or the medication again. The memory of that, and other experiences in which God worked out something for me that only He could have done, is all the proof I need to know He is alive and active in my life.

Paul, who is also in the Bible study and battling a chronic disease, was asked how he was doing. Paul said, "When I see the power of God lifting me to deal with each day, and how He is using others to help me, I can say it's not all that big a deal."

Dear Lord, keep growing Your presence in our everyday life so when we're in a storm, we can say, because you're with us, the storm is not so big.
—John Dilworth

Digging Deeper: Psalm 23:4; Philippians 4:13

Monday, October 21

What makes you so confident? —2 Kings 18:19 (JPS)

"Look," said my friend Dee, "there's supposed to be a partial lunar eclipse tomorrow night, and Bellingham's in the viewing zone." I groaned inwardly. For years, Keith and I had faithfully set the alarm and gotten out of bed at 1:00 or 2:00 a.m. or even earlier to try to see the northern lights or a comet, or an eclipse of the moon in whose path the news said we lived. Every effort had been futile because of cloud cover. Even if the nights before the phenomenon were supposed to be clear, clouds always rolled in. It was frustrating, but we never gave up trying. For some reason, I became convinced that Keith wouldn't die until after he got to see the aurora, something he wanted very much, but I was wrong about that.

Ultimately I decided I really didn't want the hassle of getting up in the middle of the night to be foiled again when looking for a celestial natural wonder. I vowed that it didn't matter what was supposed to happen in the sky—I was going to sleep through it. But when Dee mentioned the partial eclipse, even after I assured her that was "interesting but not irresistible news," I set the alarm for 2:30 a.m. I supposed it was really silly, but I was still somehow hopeful it would pay off.

Wrong again. The night was completely clouded over. I went back to bed quickly, certain I should have known better. By morning I admitted to myself that I would probably do exactly the same thing the next time a comet came by or the northern lights were supposed to be in the sky. I realized I believe that, just because I haven't seen them before, it doesn't mean I might not see them sometime later.

Help me to keep trying, Lord, because I would very much
like to see Your glory as well as I believe in it.
—Rhoda Blecker

Digging Deeper: Psalm 111:2, 144:5

A good tree cannot produce bad fruit. So then, you will know them by their fruits. —Matthew 7:18, 20 (NASB)

For a hundred years the Magnificent stood over our little town's parsonage. A stunning silver maple, she whispered her secrets at its upper-story windows, sheltered it in storms, and in summer shaded its big front porch.

Driving through town one day, I was shocked to see the tree in huge amputated chunks on the ground. Having been the preacher's kid in the parsonage during my teenage years—and visited the tree many times since—I couldn't let it become firewood.

Several weighty chunks were brought up the mountain road to the home where I live with my husband, Terry. I knew our friend John—a craftsman in wood—could unlock the hidden beauty in the grand old tree.

Months later I was not disappointed. John gifted us with stunning bowls made from the Magnificent. He remarked on the beautiful swirls in the grain being very unusual.

As I sat one morning looking at the bowls, I was reminded of a Bible passage about vessels. In his letter to Timothy, the apostle Paul writes of a house having vessels of gold, silver, wood, and earthenware—some honorable, others not. He urges followers of Jesus to be "a vessel for honor, sanctified, useful to the Master, prepared for every good work" (2 Timothy 2:21).

The story of the Magnificent made perfect sense to me in that moment. A tree which for decades had faithfully sheltered the home of small-town pastors was preserved now as a vessel of honor in the home of one pastor's daughter. It continues to teach of "being useful to the Master."

Jesus, make of me a "vessel of honor" in useful service for You.
—Carol Knapp

Digging Deeper: Psalm 1:1–2; John 17:17–20; Romans 12:1

Wednesday, October 23

The heart knows its own bitterness, and no stranger shares its joy.
—Proverbs 14:10 (ESV)

It was the first day of the administrators' conference, a three-day event for school leaders in the district—about two hundred to be exact. The conference marked the beginning of the new school year. Principals and supervisors greeted each other, catching up after summer vacation.

I noticed a lady sitting by herself at a table in the back of the room. I didn't recognize her. *She must be new,* I thought. After our lunch break, she still sat alone. I was just about to walk past her when I recalled a painful memory. It was in this same building about fifteen years ago, when I was at my first administrators' conference. I didn't know many principals yet, and they didn't know me. I sat by myself at an empty table in the back of the room for the entire day. I recalled how awkward and uncomfortable I'd felt.

I knew what I needed to do. I walked over and introduced myself. "Hi," she responded with a nervous smile. "I just got hired. I'm the new internal auditor." She looked around. "I was told to come today, but I'm not sure where to go or what to do."

"No problem," I said, smiling. "Come with me."

I led her over to a table and introduced her to employees from the business department. "Join us!" one offered. Another pulled out a chair for her. She sat down, and within a few minutes, she was laughing and talking with her new colleagues.

I walked a way smiling broadly. A difficult memory had just been replaced with a much better one, simply by helping someone else in a similar situation.

It's truly a point of grace, Lord, that helping others can also heal me.
—Melody Bonnette Swang

Digging Deeper: Ephesians 4:31; Psalm 51:10

At once he was able to see, and he began to follow Jesus, praising God.
—Luke 18:43 (CEB)

On my morning jog, I often see the same people: folks heading to work, taking their kids to school, walking their dogs, or going for a run. Mostly, I don't know their names, just recognize their faces. Sometimes they or I say something passing. "Morning.... Beautiful day.... How ya doing?" But I was stumped by the comment one fellow made as he walked by: "Six years, and it's finally gone."

"Great," I said, perfectly clueless. *What is he talking about?*

But after I passed him, it became clear. *That was the guy who used to walk with a cane.* He always had a very jaunty walk, confident, a sure step in his business suit, and I'd wondered about the cane. He hardly used it. I guess I'd mentioned in passing, "You're walking well," or something like that. And now he just told me he didn't need the cane anymore.

There was so much I didn't know. The years of physical therapy, the accident or illness that led to the cane, the reason for his improvement—it was all a mystery. But he wanted to share the good news with me.

When Jesus healed the lame and made the blind see, He often told them not to share the good news—advice they mostly ignored or found difficult to follow. And for good reason. When your life has been turned around, you want to celebrate. It can be a moment of praise and thanksgiving.

Next time I passed the man I told him, "Congratulations!" Thanksgiving grows when it's shared, even with perfect strangers on a morning jog.

Help me, Lord, to see Your good news and celebrate wherever it's seen.
—Rick Hamlin

Digging Deeper: 2 Chronicles 5:13; Psalm 9:1

Friday, October 25

When I am afraid, I put my trust in you. —Psalm 56:3 (NIV)

W e fear many things, such as death or loneliness. But perhaps one of the most pervasive anxieties is the question, "Will there be enough?"

I remember when Beth and I were newlyweds and had just moved to Louisville, Kentucky, to attend graduate school. After unloading our rental trailer and carrying our few possessions into our apartment, we drove to the grocery store. We counted our money and had $29.53.

Bringing our groceries to the cashier, I realized I had not carefully counted the cost. I was filled with anxiety. I did not want to be embarrassed by not having enough money. When the bill was tallied, I had less than a dollar to spare!

That was forty-two years ago. Since then we have worried about whether we would have adequate funds to cover medical needs, buy our first small house, pay our taxes, support three children through college, and amass adequate retirement funds. It seems that in every chapter of life, many wonder, *Will there ever be enough?* No matter how much we earn or save, this fear is central to the primal human quest for survival.

Jesus knew what it was to feel fear and anxiety. Yet He taught His disciples, "Do not worry about tomorrow, for tomorrow will worry about itself. Each day has enough trouble of its own." This does not mean danger is not real or that provisions are not sometimes depleted. What Jesus promises is that we will find a way to deal with today. And God will guide us through the new chapter of tomorrow.

> *Father, may I walk with You through this day confident*
> *You will provide for my true needs. Amen.*
> —Scott Walker

Digging Deeper: Psalm 55:23

Give thanks in all circumstances; for this is God's will for you in Christ Jesus. —1 Thessalonians 5:18 (NIV)

Grimacing at the hamper of dirty clothes, I glanced at the clock on the basement wall. It seemed laundry was all I did lately. Reaching into the washer, I lifted a pair of wet jeans. Something about them sent my mind back to a time when my husband, Jim, and I were worse than broke—paying off large debts accumulated while we started our business. When our washer died, we couldn't afford another, so Jim's grandmother's old Maytag wringer washer was pressed into service. Kept as a remembrance of her, it was something we never expected to actually use ourselves.

At first, running it was a novelty. That wore off quickly, though, and the process became work. A lot of it. Each article of clothing had to be handled multiple times per washing: once when it was added to the soapy water, again when it was put through the wringer (beware your fingers!), then when it went back into the tub, of rinse water this time, and yet again as it was fed through the wringer once more. Jeans were always the most challenging—heavy when dripping wet and difficult to make flat enough to fit through the wringer. It was a relief when a more modern, new-to-us washer finally fit in our budget. I looked again at these jeans I'd handled only twice—when I'd dropped them, dirty, into the washer, and when I'd taken them out, clean. Suddenly I realized what a gift Grandma's washer had been—showing me how God's gift of gratitude can be found anywhere—even in a pair of easily washed jeans.

Thank You, Lord, for my challenges. Help me remember they're often opportunities to recognize Your blessings.
—Erin Janoso

Digging Deeper: Ephesians 5:20

Whoever dwells in the shelter of the Most High will rest in the shadow of the Almighty. —Psalm 91:1 (NIV)

Hey," ten-year-old Gabriel said. "That space would make the perfect man cave!"

"Yes!" eight-year-old Isaiah agreed.

The afternoon was set aside for cleaning closets—some of the many secret spaces in our 1864 home. We'd just purged the area my boys coveted, open-front cabinets that line the lengthy wall of a hidden hallway.

Within the hour, my boys moved in. They used a rope and basket to lift a battery-operated lantern, sleeping bags, a stack of books, board games, playing cards, a brown bag of magic tricks, and a shoe box full of Goldfish crackers. When I climbed up to visit, they rolled out regular hospitality. They were as happy as I'd seen men be.

"I love it," I said.

I understood my boys' desire to sneak away, to be removed from routine and rush. It's dear to create and claim a place of peace. I feel this way about where I meet the Lord. In my bedroom is a wingback chair. My Bible and a blanket are near, and a table for my tea. It's the place I go to find solace, to get away and get lost in God's presence. My soul has soared in that chair. My heart has also broken wide. Both are OK. When I'm there, away from the world, I feel the serenity of His shelter. The chair provides a physical place to rest under His wings.

Later that evening, I climbed the ladder again with a plate of peanut butter sandwiches. A sign had been taped to the wall. It read *Man Cave* in round, little-boy letters.

Claiming refuge.

I could support that.

> *Lord, I long to be in Your shelter. Amen.*
> —Shawnelle Eliasen

Digging Deeper: Psalm 36:7, 61:4

The heavens and the earth were completed in all their vast array.
—Genesis 2:1 (NIV)

White canvas tents filled the park. My friend and I strolled by them, sometimes moving in for a closer look but mostly just glancing as we ambled along. We'd stumbled onto this weekend event by chance and were curious to see what it held. Tents brimmed over with paintings, pottery, wood carvings, sculptures, handmade jewelry, and eager artists. The aisles were people-filled, the air music-packed.

It was a fun diversion, but nothing really caught our attention until brilliant flashes of color diverted our eyes. A man in a T-shirt and shorts stood surrounded by a crowd, three huge parrots perched on his arm and shoulders.

They were magnificent, sleekly feathered in indigo blues, iridescent greens, and intense scarlets. Lemon yellow encircled their coal-studded eyes. Turquoise wings flapped, revealing vibrant orange. The birds looked near surreal in their rainbow beauty. They cocked regal heads and jutted black curved beaks as they took in the oohing and aahing crowd.

I made my way closer, to confirm they weren't hand-painted. That's when it hit me. Had they been hand-painted, they wouldn't have been, couldn't have been, so glorious. Their artist is a master—the Master, Whose handiwork no one and nothing can equal. Those parrots drew more attention than the art-filled tents, for they exhibited a beauty only God can produce. Try as they might, humans will never match the magnificence of God-created wonders. God, I decided, won the artistry award that day, hands down.

Lord, thank You for the breathtaking beauty of all You have fashioned.
—Kim Taylor Henry

Digging Deeper: Psalm 9:1, 104

Tuesday, October 29

Therefore encourage one another and build each other up.
—1 Thessalonians 5:11 (NIV)

It's as if Andrew's not really there," I told a friend, haltingly. "I'm living with his depression instead." My husband's illness left him wrung out and lifeless, unable to do much other than leaf through magazines or surf the Internet.

It wasn't just that Andrew couldn't take on parenting or household responsibilities. His illness was an emotional black hole that threatened to suck me and the rest of the family into it. The hardest part of having him there-but-not-there was that it had been years since I felt like I existed. I knew he loved me. But he could barely find himself, never mind see anyone else.

I sought ways to stay strong while keeping the door open for a real relationship. I prayed about it constantly. "Teach me how to love this man," I prayed. "Show me how to be the wife You want me to be to him."

It was years before Andrew showed signs of life. It was all simple stuff: occasionally he emerged from the bedroom or did the dishes before 11:00 p.m. It wasn't much, but it was a start.

Relieved but wary of disappointment, I said nothing. More accurately, I said nothing positive. Suddenly, seemingly out of nowhere, my patience grew shorter, my complaints longer. It took a while to figure out that since Andrew was stronger, I assumed he could now take a bit of negative feedback. He could, but he needed encouragement, too. I searched my heart and came up with no words of kindness to share with a man I hadn't seen in half a decade. My love was there-but-not-there.

Fortunately when words don't work, we still have actions. I brought him coffee when I poured a cup for myself. I made him a favorite meal. It wasn't much, but it was what I could do. Slowly, we staggered toward healing.

Jesus, move my heart forward from the place it is stuck.
—Julia Attaway

Digging Deeper: 1 John 3:18

I will take refuge in the shadow of your wings until the disaster has passed. —Psalm 57:1 (NIV)

Cue the *Ghostbusters* theme. My granddaughter tosses a white, fuzzy blanket over her head and runs helter-skelter around the kitchen, making eerie-sounding moans and groans. "I ain't afraid of no ghosts!" she shouts. Then, sliding the blanket onto the floor, she adds quietly, "Except sometimes..."

I appreciate her honesty. I certainly know the feeling. Although a fear of the supernatural doesn't rank high on my list, plenty of other things go bump in the night, or at least bump around in my overactive imagination, to set my heart racing and make me want to hide under the covers. I think that's why I watch police procedurals and a few semi-creepy television shows. I want what I fear to be contained, explained, and have everything come out OK in the end. Preferably in under an hour.

However, watching reruns of *Sherlock* or *The X-Files* isn't the most effective strategy when fear creeps into my life. In Psalm 56:3, David captures God's solution rather simply: "When I am afraid, I put my trust in you." Figuring out how to trust God in concrete, practical ways isn't always that simple. It doesn't mean I turn a blind eye to my fears and hum "Amazing Grace." It means I face my fears, head-on, trusting that God is by my side.

In truth, most of my deepest fears stem from my own insecurities. They creep in from the inside. That's when I need to take refuge in the shadow of God's wings through honest prayer. It's like hiding under a blanket that provides the courage I need to face what I fear most.

Dear Lord, You're my sword and shield, my refuge and strength.
Help me trust in You more than in my own abilities.
—Vicki Kuyper

Digging Deeper: Psalm 34:4, 118:6–7

Halloween, Thursday, October 31

You were once darkness, but now you are light in the Lord. Live as children of light. —Ephesians 5:8 (NIV)

Holidays are magical when kids are around.

The first year we carved a pumpkin, my kids were not impressed. The innards were sticky, the stringy parts were gooey, and everyone was over it by the time I stenciled on the face.

When we were ready to light the pumpkin, I called the kids back over. Looking at the empty eyes, dark smile, and pile of pumpkin guts, the kids backed away slowly. This was the fun Mom called them over to enjoy?

"Just wait," I told them. They watched Dad light the candle and then tuck it safely inside the hollowed pumpkin. Suddenly the grim face shone brightly in the dimming daylight. Where once a scary grimace leered, now a pumpkin shone bright, casting a goofy grin on my front steps.

In our house, we talk a lot about being good-hearted, being your best person on the inside and out, and, of course, letting your light shine for Jesus. Sometimes, when our light is hidden from the world, we can appear callous, harsh, and unwelcoming. But with the help of God's light, our hearts and kindness can shine.

For our family, Halloween isn't a day of ghosts and ghouls; in fact, it's more princesses and cartoon characters. That's fine by me. Ahead of my kids is a whole world in which they can find the dark corners and scary moments. For now I'll actively show them the light, God's light, wherever I can.

Lord, renew my strength each morning to shine my light
so those in my home are blessed by my spirit
and find strength to shine theirs.
—Ashley Kappel

Digging Deeper: Colossians 1:9–14; Isaiah 60:1

UNDER GOD'S WINGS

1 _____

2 _____

3 _____

4 _____

5 _____

6 _____

7 _____

8 _____

9 _____

10 _____

11 _____

12 _____

13 _____

14 _____

15 _____

October

16 _____

17 _____

18 _____

19 _____

20 _____

21 _____

22 _____

23 _____

24 _____

25 _____

26 _____

27 _____

28 _____

29 _____

30 _____

31 _____

NOVEMBER

Whoever dwells in the shelter of the Most
High will rest in the shadow of the Almighty.
I will say of the Lord, "He is my refuge and
my fortress, my God, in whom I trust."

—Psalm 91:1–2 (NIV)

Friday, November 1

We do not lose heart. Though our outer self is wasting away,
our inner self is being renewed day by day. —2 Corinthians 4:16 (ESV)

Growing up, I waited inside the house for the school bus to come. The bathroom window faced the road and gave a clear vantage point, so I had just enough time to race out the front door. For most of elementary school, I spent every morning beside my mom. She stood in front of the bathroom mirror, getting ready for work. The flowery smell of her Oil of Olay filled the air as she glided her fingers across her face. Once I asked, "What does it feel like to be old?" She was thirty-five at the time.

Mom smiled. "Inside, I feel exactly like I did when I was your age."

"You do?" It was an answer I couldn't believe. It seemed nearly impossible, like a mind-bending puzzle. I wanted to ask more, dig deeper, and understand.

The bus rounded the corner, and I ran outside, thinking the entire ride to school about what she had said. *Is it possible? Will I still feel young when I'm old?*

Mom's answer and that moment stays with me. It comes to mind at different points in my life, certainly when I notice a gray hair or two.

This morning when my youngest child boarded the bus, I looked at him. He's just about the age I was when I asked Mom that question, and I realized what Mom meant. The little girl I was is still in me. How can this be? How is it that each of us has this extraordinary ability to carry around our childhoods inside us, never losing who we were amid what we've become?

Dear God, aging is amazing! Thank You for the gift of memory . . .
and sparks of recognition that take us back to
incredible moments that shape our lives.
—Sabra Ciancanelli

Digging Deeper: Psalm 73:26; Proverbs 10:7

ENCOUNTERING GOD IN UNLIKELY PLACES
God Knows My Name

I am with you, saith the Lord. —Haggai 1:13 (KJV)

My husband, David, and I were sitting in a trendy café, sharing a dessert that cost more than an average meal. A grassy green park was on the other side of the street, and as I gazed out the window, a man caught my eye. He was waving as cars passed by. There was a dignity about him, even though he wore several layers of rumpled clothes.

No one else in the café seemed to notice him. That is, until I saw David quietly fold a twenty-dollar bill he had slipped from his wallet.

"I'm going with you," I said. We knew each other well, and I already anticipated that he would find a way to pass some money to the man.

Soon, we were out in the street. "What's your name?" I asked the man. He was big but seemed gentle. "They call me Homeless Homeboy," he answered, looking out into the night air.

"No." I touched his hand. "I mean your real name."

His big, soft eyes met mine. "Kevin. My name is Kevin."

He went on to share with me that he made a mean gumbo and loved to cook. And he wanted to set up an online site to sell his tie-dyed shirts.

Most people passing by ignored us as if we were invisible. But one well-dressed man stopped and said, "He's one of the best people I know."

Back in the café, amid patrons with their eyes set straight ahead, I looked through the meticulously clean glass once more. I seemed to float to that place on the street—so near, yet so far. Kevin was looking up at the stars. For a moment, I was perfectly sure I saw God there, too, holding Kevin's big hand.

> *So, Father, here You are again, in Kevin's big eyes.*
> *I'm grateful for the chance to see You there.*
> —Pam Kidd

Digging Deeper: Job 12:10; Ephesians 4:6

Sunday, November 3

Let the peace of Christ rule in your hearts. —Colossians 3:15 (NIV)

I lowered my head into the palm of my hand as the young soloist forgot the entry to the second verse of her song. *What else could go wrong?* I was so excited when my friend Kathy agreed to visit our church, but now I was embarrassed. *Why did she come on this Sunday of all days?*

The morning was one mishap after another. First, the air-conditioning had come on, instead of the necessary heat to ward off the winter chill. Second, the opening video failed to play, upsetting the plans of the worship team. Then the words were incorrect for a worship song in English and Spanish. The video tech had typed *pastry* instead of *paz* (for "peace"), and *Joe* instead of *Jesus.*

The soloist was the final straw. I knew my friend would never come again. After the service, I approached Kathy with an apology.

She met me with a smile. She couldn't stop talking about the good humor of the congregation in the midst of minor mishaps and how everyone had cheered on the young soloist.

"My heart was encouraged as the pastor shared the message about peace," she continued. "I've been so worried about my daughter in Paris after the terrorist attacks in Europe."

"But Joe's pastry," I began.

"Peace," she corrected me with a laugh. "I only saw the peace."

Open my heart, Lord, to choose peace in the midst of
small inconveniences and major concerns.
—Lynne Hartke

Digging Deeper: Philippians 4:6–8; Psalm 29:11

Call to me and I will answer you. —Jeremiah 33:3 (NIV)

The sound track of my life plays on repeat: "Mom? Mom. Mom!" I hear the call from morning to night, and it doesn't bother me, because I recall the days of doing the same to my mom. And when she responded by asking what I needed, I would reply, "Just checking!"

My four-year-old understands the notion that one must leave some air in order to hear a reply. "Mom!" she calls from the kitchen, then pauses, leaving me a moment to respond, but my two-year-old, Jake, hasn't mastered the pause.

"Mom!" he cries out from the living room. "Yes, Ja—" I begin, only to be cut off by a more urgent shout. *"Mom!"* The cycle repeats until I am right in front of him, down on my knees, asking what he needs. Only then does he realize I've been listening and responding to him the entire time.

During this stage of my life, working full-time, wrangling two kiddos, and managing other day-to-day life things, I often pray as I go. Like Jake, I call out for help over and over without leaving a moment for God to answer. The Bible tells us repeatedly to be still, because there is grace and teaching in the moments between my asking and God answering.

While I can't always take time to step away from life to pray to God, because dinner might literally burn down my house, I have learned to petition Him in my prayers, then to pause and listen so I can actually hear His response.

Someday Jake will learn to take a beat after he calls out, so he can hear my answer, but for now I'm thankful the soundtrack to my day is a reminder to be present, be mindful, and be still in God's grace.

Lord, help me to listen, and to really hear Your voice.
—Ashley Kappel

Digging Deeper: Jeremiah 29:12; 1 John 5:15; Psalm 18:6

Now these three remain: faith, hope and love. But the greatest of these is love. —1 Corinthians 13:13 (NIV)

It was a beautiful fall day in New York's Hudson Valley. The chairs were lined up perfectly in two rows, forming an aisle for the bride to walk down. The artistic display of God's presence was all around us. The weather and setting couldn't have been more ideal.

I had the pleasure of officiating the wedding. I've been delighted to do so for many weddings before, but this one was very special. The groom was Taun, my future son-in-law, and the bride was my beautiful daughter, Christine. As we walked down the aisle, tears of joy ran down her cheeks. I kept my composure, as my daughter had asked. She warned me that, if I got emotional during the ceremony, she would cry. But the joy and promise of the day were enough to inspire her tears. I knew once she started, there might be no return. When she was growing up, I witnessed this many times. But I maintained my promise and showed great self-control throughout the ceremony, fulfilling my pastoral and parental role at the same time.

I knew this day would come, but it once seemed so far away. I still have memories of holding her in my arms when she was born and praying I would be the best dad for my baby girl. In every season of her life, her mom and I prayed for her well-being, future decisions, safety, life mate, and more.

Yes, I have officiated many weddings but never one like this.

On my office desk at home is a picture of me praying for the couple on their wedding day. I continue to ask God to give them a long, healthy marriage and that they remain faithful to each other throughout all the seasons to come.

> *Lord, thank You for the gift of love and marriage.*
> —Pablo Diaz

Digging Deeper: Jeremiah 29:6; Song of Songs 8:6

Sin shall no longer be your master, because you are not under the law, but under grace. —Romans 6:14 (NIV)

The house wasn't ready.

"Someone pick up these shoes," I yelled. "Dust the piano. Grab the vacuum. The rug is covered with hair from the dog!"

My sons and husband helped, but it wasn't enough. Lonny and I were hosting and teaching a Bible study that evening. We'd done both many times, but the mess, the preparation. We finished cleaning only after I melted down. Anger swelled, and ugly words fell free. Our home was tarnished quickly.

An hour later we sat in the living room. A scented candle burned. Soft music beat a rhythm of peace. Four couples sat in a circle, ready to share learning, loving, and life. We chatted. Then Lonny asked me to open in prayer.

The words wouldn't come. I was ashamed. I'd gone through the mechanics of opening my home, but my soul was sealed tight. After my antics, I felt embarrassed to pray out loud. Unworthy to lead. How could I encourage others to live in the Lord when my own living had fallen so short?

I looked around the room at all the faces, all the friends, and I couldn't speak a word.

Lonny reached for my hand. His hand, worn and warm, covered mine. He squeezed tight. I pulled back, but he didn't move. I was held in his love. He had seen my sin and offered forgiveness.

It was tangible grace.

My eyes met my husband's, and there were new words now. They were unspoken, but they were soulful. God, too, was there.

Lonny and I could welcome our friends. We could study the Lord's Word. I could serve because of the sacrifice from God's own.

Embracing this, I opened my mouth to pray.

Lord, where would I be without extravagant grace? Amen.
—Shawnelle Eliasen

Digging Deeper: Ephesians 4:7; 1 Peter 4:10

Thursday, November 7

Children are a gift from the Lord; they are a reward from him.
—Psalm 127:3 (NLT)

I sat in the back of the classroom, stapling homework packets as the first-grade teacher read a book to the class. I worked part time as a teacher's assistant in my son's school, because I liked being close to him and thought it would be fun. It wasn't. School is no fun. I was reminded of this as my days were spent listening to teachers tell children to sit still and be quiet. The hyper child in me who spent years frustrated in school seemed to return with incredible empathy for these boys and girls. The teacher came to a part in the book about a cow and read "moo" aloud. Of course, as I suspected, the children wanted to *moo*, too, and with smiles and giggles proceeded to do so.

"Excuse me!" the teacher said sternly, giving them the death stare until they quieted down. *Why can't they moo?* I screamed in my mind. *Can't you just let them moo their very best moo, and then continue with the story? Can't a kid just moo?*

Why are we always trying to shut down childhood? I wondered. "Sit still, be quiet, be careful, don't open that, stop climbing, get down, you ask too many questions, stop being silly, stop daydreaming, leave that alone!"

Our children will have time enough to sit down and be quiet, to worry and stress, to stop believing anything is possible and be void of fascination and wonder.

What if we let them live this fleeting gift of childhood? We might wake the child hiding inside us all.

> *Dear Lord, help us to treasure children and their gifts as You do.*
> *Help us to be patient and loving as they grow in our care.*
> —Karen Valentin

Digging Deeper: Matthew 19:14

Are you tired? Worn out? Burned out on religion? Come to me. Get away with me and you'll recover your life. I'll show you how to take a real rest.
—Matthew 11:28 (MSG)

I don't like to wait for anything. I have a habit of praying when I have to stop at a red light. It makes the time go by faster. Sometimes I pray for the people in the cars around me or crossing the street. Several times, I've offered prayers on behalf of homeless people. Once I prayed for a dog, which appeared lost.

But this day, I had no prayers to offer for others. I needed prayer. I was tired physically because of health problems and age, feeling overwhelmed, depressed. I whispered a very familiar Bible verse, but God seemed to stop me and suggest a new way to pray it.

Come: "Yes, come on. Move toward Me."

Unto me: "Only to Me; there's no other way."

All ye: "It's not only you, Marion. So many are hurting."

That labor: "Physically, mentally, spiritually."

And are heavy laden: "You don't realize the burdens others carry."

And i: "I. The Great I Am. Look unto Me."

Will give: "Gladly give. I have so much to offer you. You don't have to beg or manipulate. I love to give My children good gifts."

You: "Yes, dear one—you. My beloved. As though you were My only child."

Rest: "For your body and soul. Blessed peace in your thoughts. Rest now, child."

I took a deep breath, and as the light turned green, I left behind the sharp, accusing thought: *You think God speaks to you at red lights?*

> *Oh, Father, help me keep my faith childlike.*
> —Marion Bond West

> *Digging Deeper:* Mark 6:31; Psalm 55:6;
> Genesis 2:23; Isaiah 14:3–4

Saturday, November 9

Don't you realize that in a race everyone runs, but only one person gets the prize? So run to win! —1 Corinthians 9:24 (NLT)

I sat on the bleachers at the indoor soccer arena while Micah had her third private session. At twenty dollars an hour, we were lucky to find Coach Thomas. Others charged twice that.

Fee structure wasn't the only thing that set him apart. Instead of starting a stopwatch and promptly ending when Micah's hour was up, Thomas had a list of skills he wanted her to master at each session. He practiced alongside her, rather than standing and instructing. He exuded passion, intensity, and love for the game.

At the end of each lesson, Micah handed him the payment, then met me outside the Plexiglas. Instead of flushed cheeks this day, she had tears in her eyes.

"He won't take the money," she whispered, sniffing. "He said he didn't earn it."

Perplexed, I walked through the penalty box gate. Thomas was packing his soccer balls. I smiled and held out the cash. He shook his head adamantly.

"If a player doesn't give me a hundred percent, I didn't do my job."

"You still put in the time," I replied. "It's not your fault if she didn't train her hardest."

His dark eyes flashed. "I won't accept. I didn't earn it."

Our drive home was somber. "I feel so guilty," said Micah, "like I cheated him."

Then the principle of Thomas's action hit me. "When we don't try our hardest, we cheat not only ourselves but others, too," I told Micah.

That session was free, but the lesson Thomas instilled was priceless.

Father, help me remember that giving my best effort honors You.
—Stephanie Thompson

Digging Deeper: Ecclesiastes 9:10; Colossians 3:23–24

Let heaven and earth praise him. —Psalm 69:34 (RSV)

It's happened again. At the end of an otherwise nothing-special day, I'm drawn outside by an impressive sunset, this time after clearing off the Sunday dinner table. I walk around the block, first heading west, to catch the brief best view of the popcorn-puff clouds.

Considering the day of the week, the time of day, I grow nostalgic for my childhood, when churches, including ours, welcomed worshippers for a Sunday evening service. You could find my family sitting under a stained-glass window, buoyed by singing and heartening testimonials. I've forgotten every evening sermon preached by my pastor-dad, but the nourishing songs remain, hidden in my heart, ready to be Spirit-bidden to the fore.

Now I can almost hear my father's strong voice leading the congregation through his favorite evening hymn, "Day Is Dying in the West." The poetic lines bridge two realms: day and night, heaven and earth, maybe life and death. As I turn and head north, I remember a more specific scene. The night before my dad died, a parishioner visited his hospital bedside. "I brought a hymnbook," she said, before singing all the verses of this very song: "Day is dying in the west; heaven is touching earth with rest." And, "Gather us who seek thy face, to the fold of thy embrace." And, "Lord of angels on our eyes, let eternal morning rise." All followed by a biblical refrain: "Holy, holy, holy, Lord God of Hosts! Heaven and earth are full of thee. Heaven and earth are praising thee."

Inspired by the sunset, back home I light a candle and open a hymnbook. I imagine myself sitting next to a stained-glass window, ready to worship with song.

> *Lord, in the evening and the morning, with the*
> *heavens and the earth, I praise You.*
> —Evelyn Bence

Digging Deeper: Jeremiah 23:24; Psalm 121

Veterans' Day, Monday, November 11

They loved not their lives even unto death. —Revelation 12:11 (RSV)

It's a cold November day in Arlington National Cemetery. The honor guard at the Tomb of the Unknown Soldier wears a heavy scarf, gloves, and a long wool coat. I can see the winter skyline of our ruling city.

I am strangely warmed by emotions stirring within me....

Reverence: There's a hush here stronger than the roar of war. Tourists speak in whispers. Sightseeing buses snake slowly, silently, through the trees. The only sound is the signature *click* of the guard's heels as he turns on his rounds. Nasturtiums, still blooming along the walkway, remind me that this wooded cemetery is a quiet garden, where we plant our loved ones to bloom in the resurrection.

Honor: Four hundred thousand veterans rest here, and I feel profound respect for them. Large monuments are engraved with names, like Pershing, Marshall, and Patton. Smaller stones list more common names, like Smith, Brown, and Rodriguez, but all are honored here. I see the colors of our flag in the red maples, white stones, and blue sky. The glory of the sun reflects from the guard's brass buttons and from the polished marble monuments.

Gratitude: The veterans who lie here loved their country above themselves. I grieve the many who suffered, but I would grieve a lot more if evil men had prevailed in their attempts to take our freedom. These soldiers have gone on to their reward, but they left us with a season of peace in which to rear our children.

To all veterans living among us or resting, thank you for serving God and country.

I am humbled, Lord, by this rare collection of brave men and women who purchased our peace. May we keep the peace with the same devotion.
                                        —Daniel Schantz

Digging Deeper: Romans 8:18, 13:7

I will pray with the spirit, and I will also pray with my understanding. I will sing praise with the spirit, and I will also sing praise with my understanding. —1 Corinthians 14:15 (CSB)

I've told this story before: years ago the bathtub backed up. With one tub and three young daughters, I was forced into action.

I did the normal dad repair sequence: swearing, a drain snake, chemicals, then more swearing. Nothing. I had but one option: knock out part of the ceiling in the powder room below, then awkwardly reach up with two hands to cut the pipe with a hacksaw and pray I was at the right place to find the problem.

I was greeted with a rush of water—a heady mix of soapy mess and liquid lye. I still have the scars.

After rinsing off and bandaging up, I felt around inside the newly severed pipe to locate the blockage. There it was: a tiny troll doll covered in all manner of hair, scum, and who-knows-what-else.

What I took away most from that experience was realizing how one tiny misplaced item caused all that havoc. I'm remembering this story now because recently my life has become clogged. I don't know where the jam-up is or how to unblock it. I've tried swearing and chemicals—nothing.

This time I can't blame the kids. A hacksaw won't help. I have but one option: awkwardly reach up with two hands and pray I'm at the right place to find the problem.

> *Lord, drain away my anxieties. I know*
> *Your wisdom leaves no scars.*
> —Mark Collins

Digging Deeper: Ephesians 5:19; Colossians 3:16; James 5:13

Wednesday, November 13

He took the children in his arms, placed his hands on them
and blessed them. —Mark 10:16 (NIV)

I had a writing deadline, and no words were coming to mind. I squinted at the screen, willing the words to come, and that's when my son came out of his room. Again.

"What is it?" I snapped. "I'm trying to work! Please just go to sleep."

He shuffled toward me. "I can't," he whined. "Can you snuggle with me for a little bit?" I huffed in exasperation, seeing his sad and adorable face.

"I have to get this done," I begged.

"Please?" he pleaded back.

I finally caved and agreed to go into his room in fifteen minutes, and with that he happily went back to bed. Five minutes passed, and the words were finally flowing.

"Is it fifteen minutes yet?" he yelled from his room.

"No," I shouted back, typing.

As the screen filled up, my ideas grew. I was on a roll.

"Now?" he shouted.

"Not yet," I barked.

I typed and typed until my piece was finally done. "Yes," I hissed in victory as I closed my laptop and stretched.

I'd forgotten about my snuggle promise and did the dishes, tidied up, washed my face, and brushed my teeth.

"Tyler," I gasped, and quickly opened the bedroom door.

His sleeping cherub face pressed against his pillow broke my heart in a thousand pieces.

Lord, help me balance my responsibilities and time with loved ones.
Help me not only to be mindful of my relationships
but also to forgive myself when I fall short.
—Karen Valentin

Digging Deeper: Romans 8:1

I am fearfully and wonderfully made. —Psalm 139:14 (KJV)

U p, two-three-four! Down, two-three-four!" I mimic the fitness instructor and thrust my puny two-pound weights toward the ceiling. Already my arms burn from exertion. I feel a dew of perspiration on my forehead. I laugh. The instructor smiles and thinks I'm feeling endorphins. Actually, I'm feeling embarrassment. I'm in the "old lady class" I avoided for years. I can barely keep up.

For most of my adulthood, I enjoyed wellness classes: aerobics, stretching, Zumba, Pilates. I kept pace with the women thirty years younger by slightly modifying the routines. But that ended seven years ago, when my schedule changed and fitness classes didn't fit. Sure, I swam, but the workout didn't challenge me.

I might have avoided the "old lady class" indefinitely but for a conversation on a bus bound for Boston. I spent an hour visiting with Billie, an acquaintance from my knitting group. She was headed to Boston to fly to Scotland for what sounded like an arduous trekking vacation. After her overnight flight, she would hike *only* three miles the next morning. "Then I'll hike five to eight miles a day."

"Five to eight miles a day? I couldn't do that!"

She continued. "Well, I've been getting in shape for a year. I swim, walk every day, and take the senior fitness class." The old lady class! "It's made a huge difference." When she disclosed her age, well into her seventies and seven years older than I am, I revisited my notion of "old lady."

So here I am, in senior fitness, toning up my muscles…and toning down my arrogance.

> *Yes, Lord, I am wonderfully made.*
> *Please help me keep up my maintenance.*
> —Gail Thorell Schilling

Digging Deeper: Job 12:12; Psalm 90:10, 92:14; Proverbs 29:23

SAYING GOODBYE TO MY VETERANS: Always a VA Nurse

Your restoration is what we pray for. —2 Corinthians 13:9 (ESV)

As I steered my cart through my neighborhood Kroger, a somewhat familiar man approached me.

"Aren't you a nurse at the veterans hospital?" he asked. I nodded and smiled. He told me he'd just been discharged after receiving treatment for congestive heart failure, and that while he was in the hospital, his blood pressure was dangerously elevated.

"When I left the VA, my doc told me to cut down on sodium," he told me.

I encouraged him to eat fresh vegetables and other foods with no added salt.

"I'll get me some of that salt substitute," he said, smiling. "My neighbor uses it."

"Be sure and check with your doctor first," I cautioned. "Some salt substitutes contain potassium, and that can interfere with your heart medication."

He paused. "I can't read, Nurse," he whispered, leaning closer to me.

I had a thought. "I'm friends with some dietitians at the VA. How about if I arrange an appointment for you? They are the real experts and can make this a whole lot easier."

A smile spread across his timeworn face. "That would be perfect, Nurse. My great-grandkids are coming to visit, and I'd like to be home to enjoy them."

It occurred to me then that I'd been mistaken about retirement. I didn't have to say goodbye to my veterans after all. I would always be a nurse who cared for America's heroes. I'd just be doing so at different locations.

The word retirement *isn't even mentioned in the Bible, Lord.*
Thank You that when we work for You, we always have a job to do.
—Roberta Messner

Digging Deeper: Psalm 23:3, 51:12

Therefore encourage one another and build each other up.
—1 Thessalonians 5:11 (NIV)

"You have arthritis in your left hip," the doctor said, pointing to the X-ray. "Eventually, you'll need surgery." I'd worn the joint out, probably from years of biking and hiking.

"Why the left hip?" I wanted to know. "It could be this," he said, tapping the spot on the X-ray where the left side of my pelvis was fractured when I was hit by a car while on my bike as a kid. It surprised me that a decades-old injury, long forgotten, had come back to haunt me. Could that also be true, I wondered, of other injuries I suffered—spiritual and emotional injuries as well as physical? As we grow older, battered and bruised, are we just a collection of our wounds?

No, a loving God wouldn't do that to us. I remembered the two months it took for my pelvis to heal, flat on my back in bed. People from church and our pastor visited often. My friends congregated daily outside my window. A few years later, on crutches after a skiing accident, I got a permanent seat on the school bus (to say nothing of the attention from girls). Much later when I broke my arm playing on the Guideposts softball team, New Yorkers waited to hold doors for me and surrendered their cabs. Bank tellers filled out my deposit slips, and friends cut up my food.

What about the emotional and spiritual wounds? Then, too, people were there to love me when I couldn't love myself. Never could I have gotten sober without the collective strength of my support group. Every moment of pain in my life has a corresponding moment of kindness and compassion. Yes, we might be a collection of wounds, but we are even more so a reservoir of the love that has healed us.

Lord, You bind up our wounds through the love of others. Let me
be a wounded healer, helping to love others through their pain.
—Edward Grinnan

Digging Deeper: 2 Corinthians 12:19; Ephesians 4:29; Jude 1:20

Sunday, November 17

You know when I sit and when I rise.... You are familiar
with all my ways. —Psalm 139:2–3 (NIV)

Icouldn't remember ever being so ready to sit down! My husband,
John, and I were visiting Venice, renting a room in a private home
away from the sky-high prices in the center of town. We agreed, when
we set out that morning, to meet back at the room at 6:30 that evening. John, I imagined, had headed for the nearby open-air market,
but I made the half-hour walk to the Basilica of San Marco.

After three hours wandering about that glorious Byzantine church, my
legs ached, but right next door was the Doge's Palace! Once the residence
of Venice's rulers, it's now a fabulous museum. I kept meaning to sit and
rest, but room led to lavish room. Up the Golden Staircase. Down to the
prisons. Sculptures, maps, paintings, inlaid ceilings, armor, tapestries…

I was startled when museum guards began herding visitors toward
the exit. How could it be six o'clock! In the Piazza San Marco, scores
of small round tables had been set up with chairs placed beckoningly
around them. I longed to sit, my legs actually shaking with exhaustion,
but there was no time. I'd be late joining John.

Then I saw him walking toward me! I must have told him where I'd
planned to go today.

"Tib! What are you doing here?"

John said he had just gotten off the ferry. He'd gone out to the Lido
and spent the day at the beach. "I must have walked ten miles! Would
you mind very much if we sat for a while?"

That the ferry terminus, I was thinking, happened to be nearby. That
John took a boat that arrived just as the museum closed. That I hadn't
left five minutes earlier…

"No," I said. "I wouldn't mind at all."

> *How intimately You know us, Father! How tenderly You guide!*
> —Elizabeth Sherrill

Digging Deeper: Psalm 44:21; Isaiah 66:18

Let the words of my mouth and the meditations of my heart be pleasing to you, Lord, my rock and my redeemer. —Psalm 19:14 (CEB)

When I retired I thought my worst duty—laying off employees—was forever behind me. But since I now serve on a civic board and a couple of church committees, I'm occasionally asked to help deliver that same unwelcome news. Once it was to a pastor who hadn't met educational requirements. Another time we asked a treasurer who was struggling with financial statements to let someone take her place. Both people responded with grace.

I went with a friend to speak with a longtime volunteer whose heart was in the right place but whose physical condition had become a safety issue. We expressed appreciation for the volunteer's past contributions, outlined clearly why she couldn't continue, and tried to assure her she was valued and loved. But she was too angry to hear and responded by attacking our motives and character. The gift we'd brought in recognition of her services seemed to make her pain even worse.

I've delivered unpleasant news, and I've received it. I will no doubt receive it again. My first reaction may also be injured feelings and bitterness. I might feel tempted to lash out in anger. So to remind myself of what my attitude and speech should be, I keep these words from John Wesley's Covenant Prayer tucked in my Bible: "Let me be employed for thee or laid aside for thee... exalted for thee or brought low for thee.... I freely and heartily yield all things to thy pleasure and disposal."

> *Lord, make my words tender and kind*
> *in whatever life situations I face. Amen.*
> —Penney Schwab

Digging Deeper: Ephesians 4:15;
Philippians 4:11–13; James 1:19–20

Tuesday, November 19

The Lord is good to those whose hope is in him, to the one who seeks him.
—Lamentations 3:25 (NIV)

"Mom, Calvin's gone!" my daughter, Kendall, told me tearfully in an early-morning phone call.

"What happened?" I asked. I pictured the kitten they had gotten recently because their three young children seemed old enough for a cuddly friend.

"He must have gotten out last night," she said. "I've looked all over."

"I'll come help," I said.

We made posters and walked the neighborhood, calling for Calvin, while I kept eyeing the field behind their house where coyotes roamed. By the third night, I gave up hope and prayed for acceptance of the loss.

At five the next morning, my phone rang. "Mom, I found him! He's in the storm drain under the street. Policemen are on their way to get him out!" Kendall explained that she woke at four and felt God nudging her to look one more time. In darkness, she walked up and down the sidewalk and spotted some bushes hiding a storm drain she'd never noticed.

"Here, kitty," she called into the drain and then heard a distant muffled sound. "Calvin?" she called again, and this time, there was no mistake. *Meow!*

The sun was coming up as I neared their house. Two policemen huddled over an uncovered storm drain on the sidewalk. Kendall had descended into the small space with a flashlight, calling Calvin, who was trying to find his way out of the maze of drains under the street.

"I see his eyes!" she exclaimed, and then shone the flashlight on her face so Calvin could see her. He came running! Soon she emerged with the kitten in her arms.

Calvin is just a kitty, but for me, he's also a visual aid for hope. One I can hold on to even when things feel seemingly hopeless.

Lord, thank You that Kendall did not give up hope.
—Carol Kuykendall

Digging Deeper: 1 Peter 1:3

O give thanks to the Lord, call on his name, make known his deeds among the peoples. —1 Chronicles 16:8 (NRSV)

Why can't they get this right?" I fumed, watching CNN's *Finding Jesus*, a special presentation that was (supposedly!) based on biblical, historical, and archaeological findings. My friend Cathy shrugged, her eyes fixed on the screen.

She just doesn't get it. I smoldered, now to myself. *This just isn't as important to her as it is to me. I know what's in the Bible!* And clearly, CNN's "experts" didn't.

The segment focused on the boy Jesus remaining in Jerusalem to discuss Scripture at the temple while his parents, not knowing he'd stayed behind, journeyed on. After three days of desperate searching, they found Jesus among the teachers at the temple. But according to CNN, Jesus "got lost" in the Jerusalem Passover crowds, and couldn't find Mary and Joseph before they departed.

I couldn't keep silent. "Can't you see?" I groused to Cathy. "They're making it look like He didn't know what He was doing!"

Her eyes on the scene of Mary reuniting joyfully with her young Son, Cathy answered, "Well, He was just a boy. Isn't it amazing how He ended up teaching the teachers! I never knew that."

I stopped myself. Cathy was learning something, and she was caught up in the deep drama of the family story. She was experiencing the Jesus story, while I was nitpicking the details. Thousands, perhaps millions, of viewers were watching, learning, and being deeply moved, while I was acting like...well, a Pharisee. I settled next to my friend for the rest of the program, determined to keep my eyes and heart open, and my mouth closed.

Jesus, help me be open to everything You have to teach me in whatever form You offer it.
—Marci Alborghetti

Digging Deeper: Psalm 15:1–4

Thursday, November 21

Do not neglect to do good and to share what you have, for such sacrifices are pleasing to God. —Hebrews 13:16 (ESV)

My doorbell rang while I was in the middle of folding laundry. I opened the door to find my three-year-old niece, Alma. She lives next door and often comes to visit. "Hi, Auntie. I'm here for a paydate with Kate."

"Oh, baby, Kate's at school, so she can't do a playdate."

"OK, Auntie. Then I do a paydate with you."

I looked at the pile of laundry on my couch and dirty dishes piled up in my sink. Then I looked at her hopeful blue eyes.

"Sure, Almie. We can have a playdate."

She clutched my hand and led me to the cabinet where I keep my paper and crayons.

"We can color rainbows!"

I took the orange and drew an arch. Alma drew the yellow, and I drew the green. Ten minutes later, we had a beautiful rainbow picture, complete with tiny turquoise clouds and a bright yellow sun.

Alma stood, held up her page, and smiled. "I love you, Auntie. I go home now."

She was off, toddling back home. I went back to my laundry, a smile on my face.

Sure, I lost ten minutes of work time, but in those ten minutes, I gained a moment of sunshine, a bit of laughter, and a smile that lasted the rest of the day.

Lord, I want to take the time to stop and feel Your presence
throughout every day, whether it's in a beautiful sunrise,
a moment with a child, or simply ten minutes with You. Amen.
—Erin MacPherson

Digging Deeper: John 15:12; Luke 6:38

Whatsoever you do, do it heartily, as to the Lord. —Colossians 3:23 (NKJV)

Seven people worked behind the counter in the Centre, Alabama, Waffle House. They moved in perfect synchronization. No efficiency expert on earth could have directed them in a more seamless fashion. As soon as a waitress called out an order, the eggs were cracked, the bacon sizzling, and the hash browns steamed. Each person seemed to be a specialist at an assigned task. One made perfect waffles, another produced flawless eggs. Something in their moves said, *When it comes to toast, waffles, or frying sausage, nobody does it better!*

Sitting at the counter, I was mesmerized. "You are amazing," I said to the waitress as she refilled my "America the Beautiful" coffee cup. "How do you work so well together?"

She laughed. "We love it here," she said, taking my order. "Now, if you order number five, it has the same thing…but it's cheaper."

Background music gave the waitresses a certain sway. One belted out a few bars of a song, and everyone laughed.

"Some of us have three jobs," she said, looking back at me. "Others have two. It's worth the other jobs to work here."

The truth was there. These seven people found happiness in serving. They found joy in working together. They took pride in a job well done. God surely danced with them.

People were waiting, so reluctantly I gave up my stool. I was almost to the car when the waitress caught up with me. "You forgot your jacket," she said, grinning.

In the car, I noticed that in her haste to catch me, she had left a fingerprint on the sleeve of my jacket. I smiled, hoping mine was as broad as hers. I touched her sticky fingerprint, willing it to stay. I want to be more like the waitresses in the Waffle House.

Father, I see Your face in those who serve.
Let me be equally hearty in my service to others.
—Pam Kidd

Digging Deeper: Ecclesiastes 9:10; Romans 12:11

Saturday, November 23

My heart rejoiced in all my labour. —Ecclesiastes 2:10 (KJV)

The maid who sweeps her kitchen is doing the will of God," is the beginning of a Martin Luther quote I'm particularly drawn to. No matter that a bit of Googling tells me Luther never actually spoke the words; its significance lingers on in my mind.

My family has always embraced the dignity of work. From picking up pine cones when I was three to walking into my office today, lighting up my computers, and following the financial markets, the satisfaction of work is deeply ingrained in me.

As I advanced from the pine cones to mowing lawns, hauling bricks, making pizza, and so on, I have always found joy in work. In high school I became enamored with investing and following stocks, bonds, and other financial investments. That's when I knew what I wanted to do. It was the perfect way, as I saw it, to follow my family's tradition of serving others. Helping people invest their earnings and devising ways for them to save for their kids' college, a home, and a good nest egg seemed like a worthy ambition. Almost daily, I feel a sort of excitement as I drive to work. Sometimes I feel fairly amazed that I am doing just what I felt called to do, when I was a kid.

I've read that the word *vocation* means "to call." The end of that non-Luther quote fits in well here: "... because God likes clean floors."

Since I love the vocation I was called to, I can also see every laborer in this same light. From the woman at the to-go window offering coffee, to my assistant, Jeannine, who is sincerely dedicated to our clients, I see a spark of God rejoicing in the labor He has called each to do.

Father, remind us of our call. Let us see Your delight in our "clean floors."
—Brock Kidd

Digging Deeper: Ecclesiastes 5:12; 1 Corinthians 3:9

This is my command—be strong and courageous! Do not be afraid or discouraged. For the Lord your God is with you wherever you go.
—Joshua 1:9 (NLT)

My heart was heavy as I sat in church next to my friend. She'd just confided in me that her son, Chad, was in jail. "He was arrested last night because he failed a mandatory drug test as part of his drug diversion program," she said.

I reached over and took her hand. "Oh, Debbie, I'm so sorry." We'd prayed often for Chad. "Let's pray right now before the service starts," I whispered. I placed my hand over hers. "Debbie needs Your comfort, Lord. Give her faith to trust in Your divine plan for her son. Amen."

"Amen," she whispered. "I'm just praying to find a way to accept this. The thought of him sitting behind bars is just too much to bear." She looked away, tearfully.

The service began. Pastor Steve preached about how God puts us in situations as opportunities for us to grow. "Sometimes God has to slow us down or even stop us," he said. "Sometimes we're forced to sit still because that's the only way we're going to listen."

Debbie looked over at me, nodding in agreement. After church, we walked out together. "As much as it hurts, I think Chad is where he needs be right now, isn't he?" she asked.

"I think so, Debbie," I replied.

"I have to admit," she said, "when I woke up this morning, I wanted to just run away. I had to decide whether I was going to turn to God or turn away from God." She hugged me. "I'm sure glad I chose to come to church. I heard just what I needed to hear."

*Only when I turn to You, God, can I see the difficulties
in my life from Your divine perspective.*
—Melody Bonnette Swang

Digging Deeper: Zechariah 1:3; Ecclesiastes 3:1–8

Monday, November 25

Shepherd of Israel, listen! You, the one who leads Joseph as if he were a sheep. —Psalm 80:1 (CEB)

We call it the boys' room, even though it's been more than a few years since either of the boys lived there. How old are they now? Let's see.... William just turned thirty, and Tim is twenty-seven. Yes, we can say they are happily out of the house and living on their own, forging ahead in adulthood, with jobs, apartments, and girlfriends. So who are the ones acting like children now? A pair of empty nesters who still insist on calling a room with two empty beds, a bookshelf of children's books, and a dresser "the boys' room"?

Their cousin Kirk used the room for a couple of months when he was looking for a position as a New York City schoolteacher, but he moved out when he got a job. William was here for ten days at Thanksgiving, and no telling when Tim might drop by—although they both live a couple of thousand miles away. Moving the kitty litter box into the room might mean we call it our cat "Fred's room," but I'm not sure that nomenclature would stick.

Rooms get remembered for what has happened in them, no matter how much time passes. Would the owner of the Upper Room ever forget the transforming event that occurred there? Someday we'll take down the Grateful Dead poster in "the boys' room" and winnow through the old books. We'll give away the bats, balls, and mitts, but the space will remain sacred as the place where two rambunctious boys argued and slept, the walls still echoing the bedtime prayer we sang, "Tender Shepherd." We can always marvel at how the Shepherd, without our quite noticing it, transformed them into two extraordinary young men.

Come into our rooms, Good Shepherd, and lead us to Your home.
—Rick Hamlin

Digging Deeper: John 14:2; Mark 14:15; Acts 20:8

Physical training is of some value, but godliness has value for all things, holding promise for both the present life and the life to come.
—1 Timothy 4:8 (NIV)

Nine months after knee surgery, I was still experiencing discomfort. Talk about discouraged! Trying to walk after sitting for more than twenty minutes was painful for the first dozen or so steps. Getting in and out of a car was touchy, since one of my knees still only had a ninety-degree bend. I wished desperately I could turn back the clock to years earlier, when I was much more active and had no pains.

One day as I checked my Facebook page, one of those boxes filled with inspiring quotes popped up. It read, "The Best Six Doctors Are: sunshine, water, rest, air, exercise, diet." I read the list again. It was all there. Simple gifts from God. Everything I needed to feel better. The six best doctors. And, of course, time to heal. My surgeon told me it often takes two years to fully recover after double knee replacement.

Right then I promised myself that every day I would either go for a walk or get back on my bike in the glorious Florida sunshine. I started drinking more water. A thirty-minute nap became part of my daily routine on most days. I changed my diet and worked hard to lose weight to help improve my overall health.

Sunshine, water, rest, air, exercise, and diet. I decided I needed to add "patience" to that list. But the fact remains, nearly everything we need to be healthy is simple, easy, free, and available.

Within a couple of months, I felt like a new woman. I felt healthier, more energetic, and happier. What a healer God is!

Lord, remind me when I get discouraged to step back, take a deep breath, and remember that all I need has already been given to me.
—Patricia Lorenz

Digging Deeper: James 5:14–15; Revelation 22:1–5

Wednesday, November 27

The greatest of these is love. —1 Corinthians 13:13 (NIV)

Our fortieth wedding anniversary was approaching. My husband, David, and I hadn't a clue what to give each other. We finally decided to just go to a nice restaurant, delighted that since it was Thanksgiving week, our youngest, Rachel, would be flying from Oregon to Colorado to join us.

The night after she arrived, Rachel told us she was leaving to meet a friend. Back home two hours later, she joined us as we watched TV. There was a noise at our back door. "What's that?" she said.

"Hello!" familiar voices called to us. In walked our son, Kirk; daughter-in-law, Courtney; and their three sleepy children. My hands flew to my mouth. Tears flooded my eyes. They'd flown in from Tennessee. Rachel had picked them up from the airport!

"Lauren and Chris couldn't get off work to come," Rachel said. While we'd certainly miss our daughter and son-in-law who lived in Washington, DC, we were thrilled to have so much of our family with us.

The next morning, we were all trekking through the fresh snow around our home when we saw a car on our driveway. My jaw dropped. Chris and Lauren!

Several days and many beautiful memories later, David and I stood in our home, renewing our vows of forty years ago—another part of the surprise! With us as bridesmaids and groomsmen were our children, son-in-law, daughter-in-law, and grandchildren. They wore our wedding colors, and had even duplicated our wedding flowers and cake! I wore my original wedding dress, David a tux. Forty years earlier, we didn't known what the future held. Now here it was. An amazing family, standing as one, affirming the love that led to them.

God provided the greatest gift—our family and friends and their love, expressed through this stunning surprise.

> *We're together, Lord. We could ask for nothing greater.*
> *Our hearts overflow with love and gratitude.*
> —Kim Taylor Henry

Digging Deeper: Genesis 2:24; Psalm 4:7

Give thanks in all circumstances; for this is God's will for you in Christ Jesus. —1 Thessalonians 5:18 (NIV)

Our Thanksgiving plans with extended family are often shaped by what's happened within the year leading up to the holiday. In the past we've gathered at my brother's house, but he had open-heart surgery recently and is still recovering. My daughter-in-law lost her stepfather a month ago, so her family is having Thanksgiving with her newly widowed mom. Our smaller group is gathering at my daughter's house today.

I've been feeling sad about these circumstances and my own loss of a couple of friends to cancer this year. So a few days ago, I tried some closet-cleaning therapy and came across three large cardboard figures of pilgrims I used to put on the wall every Thanksgiving when our kids were growing up. After they left home, I stashed the figures in a hanging garment bag because I couldn't bear to throw them away.

It's been years since I thought about real-life pilgrims at Thanksgiving, but I feel they had lots to be unthankful for. In November when they arrived at America's shores, they had to find shelter and resources for food. By that first winter, they'd lost roughly half the people who began their trip across the Atlantic in the *Mayflower*. Yet a year later, they didn't dwell on their losses. Instead they gathered with the Native Americans in the region to thank God for the blessings of their first harvest of corn and barley. Their prayerful gratitude shaped the thanks giving purpose of the holiday we celebrate today.

After my closet cleaning discovery, I tacked those pilgrim figures to our wall. Now on Thanksgiving morning, as I make mashed potatoes and green bean casserole, they again remind me of the people who endured many losses but chose to focus on thanking God for what they had.

Lord, as our family gathers today, may we find
and focus on our many blessings.
—Carol Kuykendall

Digging Deeper: Psalm 100

Friday, November 29

I am sure of this, that he who began a good work in you will bring it to completion at the day of Jesus Christ. —Philippians 1:6 (ESV)

My family had spent over an hour inspecting rows of Christmas trees. Dozens of cars left the lot with balsams strapped to their roof racks, but our search for the perfect tree continued. "We aren't going to find a tree we all like," my fourteen-year-old brother, Samuel, said. "There are seven of us. We need to just pick one."

For me, the trees had lost their distinguishing features as the November chill seeped into my boots. "How about this one?" I asked. "It has a straight trunk, and it's skinny enough to fit in the corner of the living room."

Several heads nodded in relief. But my ten-year-old brother, Gabriel, crinkled his brow. "I don't like it," he said. "Its branches are spindly." Sighs. My eyes drifted over a sea of pines.

"I'm sorry, Gabriel," Dad said. "I think you're outvoted. But you can help me cut it down."

Dad offered Gabriel a bow saw, but he pushed it away. "No, thanks."

As Dad's saw bit into the tree, I came alongside Gabriel. "I know you don't like this tree now," I said. "But try not to look at the tree as it is. Imagine the tree as it's going to be."

As we watched the tree shiver to the tune of the saw, I thought about how glad I was that God chose me despite my flaws. I make mistakes; not every part of me is appealing. But God knows I'm worth His time. He sees who I'll be when He finishes His work in me.

"Do you think the tree will look wonderful on Christmas morning?" Gabriel asked.

"I believe it will."

> *Father, thank You for beginning Your work in me*
> *and promising to complete it.*
> —Logan Eliasen

Digging Deeper: 2 Corinthians 3:18; 2 Thessalonians 2:13

Jacob... said, "Surely the Lord is in this place, and I did not know it."
—Genesis 28:16 (ESV)

Every Saturday morning, an energetic young neighbor comes over. I often whisper a generic, ancient prayer: "Lord, have mercy..."

Preparing for Advent, I set out a basket of small figurine candles and introduced a new theme. "You can make a Christmas scene," I told her. She quickly assembled a crèche crowd: Santa, snowmen, angels, and trees encamped in a circle around lambs peering into a manger. "Baby Jesus is missing," she reported.

Hmm, the manger's underside did look like an empty cradle. I turned it over. "Hey, He's here. We just didn't see Him." So far so good. Mercies evident.

Later that morning, we took the girl's grandmother to a nearby food bank. Nearing the charity, as I prayed for new mercies, I saw a couple standing on the sidewalk with a toddler and a few full totes. They didn't look like the usual clientele, but I figured they were. I drove, then walked, by them. I passed them again with my young friend at my side. This time the strangers approached us. "Are you coming from the food bank?"

I gestured toward my sidekick. "I dropped off her grandma."

"Here, for you." They handed me a big bagged lunch, which I passed along to my young neighbor. They insisted, "Another, take it, for you."

I couldn't refuse the meal. "Thank you, thank you," I repeated even to the toddler. Suddenly teary, I wondered if we'd found the holy family focused on their morning merciful task.

During this Advent and Christmas season—may you find them, or they you.

Merciful Lord, give us glimpses of
Your presence here with us and among us.
—Evelyn Bence

Digging Deeper: Luke 18:35–42

UNDER GOD'S WINGS

1 _____

2 _____

3 _____

4 _____

5 _____

6 _____

7 _____

8 _____

9 _____

10 _____

11 _____

12 _____

13 _____

14 _____

15 _____

16 _____

17 _____

18 _____

19 _____

20 _____

21 _____

22 _____

23 _____

24 _____

25 _____

26 _____

27 _____

28 _____

29 _____

30 _____

DECEMBER

But be sure to fear the Lord and serve him faithfully with all your heart; consider what great things he has done for you.

—1 Samuel 12:24 (NIV)

A child is born to us, a son is given to us. . . . He will be named Wonderful Counselor, Mighty God, Eternal Father, Prince of Peace. —Isaiah 9:6 (CEB)

About forty years ago, our pastor decided the church needed an Advent candle wreath and a tall stand. He hoped an emphasis on Advent would help us understand December isn't meant to be a whirlwind of shopping and a headlong rush into Christmas. Instead, it is a time to prepare our souls to receive the coming Christ.

Pastor asked Bob, a church member, if he could make a stand. Bob could and did. He fitted a discarded 1958 Ford air filter on a pole and stood the pole on a base. He closed the holes partway to make them into candleholders and painted the whole thing gold.

Each Advent season since, the stand has held five candles nestled in a wreath of evergreens. Four of the candles are purple, symbolizing gifts of Jesus: hope, love, joy, and peace. The fifth candle is taller and white, reminding us that Christ is the light of the world.

Today, we will light the candle of hope. We will hear the ancient prophesy of Isaiah, and we will begin our journey toward the fulfillment of Christmas Day. Yes, we will give and receive gifts, bake cookies, and perhaps gather with family and friends. But we will also remember that our hope is in Christ, and that hope should not get lost in the business and busyness of the season.

With all we have to anticipate, we can be thankful that we, like the Advent stand, can be transformed to reflect His glory.

As we await Your coming, Lord, prepare our hearts
to receive Your gifts of hope and transformation.
—Penney Schwab

Digging Deeper: Matthew 4:12–17; 2 Corinthians 3:18, 5:17

Monday, December 2

Simeon... said to his mother Mary, "This child is destined for the falling and the rising of many... and a sword will pierce your own soul too."
—Luke 2:34–35 (NRSV)

It happens at the beginning of every winter, around the first week in December. Between the cold air outside and dry heat inside, my skin seems more fragile. The same tiny cut opens up near the nail on my right thumb. I'm amazed at how something so small can be so painful and annoying. It seems every single thing I do requires this thumb, from tying my shoes in the morning to flossing my teeth at night. When I complained to my mom, she responded, "Oh, I know! That happens to me, too. I offer it up."

I'm not proud of this, but normally I cringe at phrases like, "Offer it up," and, "Let go and let God." I guess I think I shouldn't bother the Lord with the small stuff.

I teased Mom, "You think the Lord cares about our thumb cuts?"

She gave me the Mom look. "It usually happens during Advent, right? When I was little, we gave up chocolate during Advent to show we cared about the sacrifice Mary and Joseph were making. You think that trip from Nazareth to Bethlehem was easy? I offer up the small aggravation and hurt from the cut to show I'm remembering the pain and fear they must have felt."

Mom is no religious scholar. She doesn't study Scripture. I doubt she's read the New Testament through even once. But she'd just given me one of the simplest and most extraordinary ways to honor the holy family and what Jesus's birth meant to them.

"Offer it up" perhaps isn't quite as generic as I'd thought.

Father, thank You for a mother who knows
the true meaning of CHRIST-mas!
—Marci Alborghetti

Digging Deeper: Matthew 2:13–14; Luke 2:1–7

To console those who mourn in Zion, to give them beauty for ashes, the oil of joy for mourning. —Isaiah 61:3 (NKJV)

For forty years, I've valued a beautiful blue handmade pottery bowl. Not that I used it often or even displayed it. But I frequently noted its presence in the cupboard among other small serving dishes. It was the first gift given to me by a dear friend—Christmas 1979.

Last Monday, on the anniversary of my friend's death, a neighbor girl asked for a bowl so she could make fruit salad. When I couldn't find the "usual suspect," I handed her the blue beauty. *Oh, be careful with this,* I thought but didn't say.

Not thirty seconds later, I heard the shatter, followed by a familiar line, "I'm so sorry." And, "It just slipped."

Prompted by the Spirit, or maybe the popular song lyric, I "let it go," though I didn't deny my sadness. "It's OK, but it was special because it reminded me of my friend, whom I miss."

Later in the day, without a clear reason, I pulled the ten or so chunks out of the trash can. My brother thinks he can glue the dish back together. A friend suggests a Japanese finishing technique that accentuates the breaks with gold lacquer. But repair—having an imperfect bowl that reminds me merely of what used to be—doesn't appeal to me.

This morning I hammered the larger pieces into thirty-odd shards. For now, I've sealed them (they're sharp; I've already cut myself) in a bailed canning jar. Set on the corner of my desk, it strangely comforts me. In the jar of shards I see the potential of a newly designed piece—a mosaic hot pad or set of coasters. The first gift transformed into the last—another blue beauty.

> *Lord, help me see the possibilities... of creating beauty out of brokenness.*
> —Evelyn Bence

Digging Deeper: Isaiah 30:14–24; Jeremiah 18:1–4

Wednesday, December 4

Cast your burden on the Lord—he will support you! God will never let the righteous be shaken! —Psalm 55:22 (CEB)

I have a way of keeping anxiety as a close companion, not willing to let it go. I invite it in for just a moment and then give it the run of the house. A worry floats into my head, and instead of batting it away or even putting it into God's capable hands, I build it up, feed it tidbits of more worry, and soon the worries have multiplied, putting me in a stranglehold.

The other day I was feeding anxiety with more anxiety, trapping myself in a prison of my own making. Then I recalled something my son, Tim, in his senior year of high school said to my wife, Carol. It was a Sunday night, and he had a project he needed to get done, deadline looming, and his mother asked one time too many about its progress.

"Mom," Tim said, "your anxiety is not making me get it done any faster."

Ah, the unexpected wisdom of a teenager, puncturing the allure of anxiety. How often since I've used those words to myself. *Rick, your anxiety is not helping you get things done.* Then I ask the worry to leave, kick it out, send it packing, slam the door, and wish it a fond farewell. After all, how much good does my anxiety do? "Here, God," I can say, "take this worry. I've had enough of it." It's gone.

Dear Lord, I gladly pass along today's worries.
I suspect I'll have more for You tomorrow.
—Rick Hamlin

Digging Deeper: Proverbs 3:5–6; Matthew 11:28

Listen to God's voice today! —Psalm 95:7 (CEV)

My Christmas rush resembled a tornado. I whirled through town, finishing my last-minute shopping. Before going home, I stopped by the office and picked up the money pooled to buy gift certificates for the office staff. We'd present them tomorrow.

I walked toward my car, holding tightly to the envelope, which contained more than fourteen hundred dollars. *Where am I going to keep this until tomorrow morning, when I go to the Chamber of Commerce to pick up the gift certificates?* I lived in the country and didn't want to forget it at home. I thought, *Maybe I should lock it in the dash?* But something grated inside my spirit, like it wasn't a good idea. I brushed it aside.

I parked the car in the driveway. *The dash or the house? Do I have a key to the dash?* When I purchased my used car, it came with only one key, which wasn't an original. I slid the key into the lock and got an ominous feeling. This time I reasoned the feeling away. I stuffed the fat envelope in the dash and locked it.

The next morning at the Chamber of Commerce, I slid the key again in to the dash lock, but it refused to budge! For fifteen minutes I twisted, pushed, and wiggled, but the key wouldn't open the lock. I even called our only locksmith in town, but he was gone for a week! I slumped in the driver's seat. *God, You tried to tell me, but I kept brushing You aside. I'm sorry. What do I do now?*

The answer to my blunder was time-consuming. I drove an hour to a dealership to have them make an original key, which worked! I barely made it in time for the office party. It would have been faster to listen to God's still, small voice... especially when I'm busy.

Lord, thank You for Your unfailing love that gives me plan B. Amen.
—Rebecca Ondov

Digging Deeper: Psalm 32:8; Proverbs 4:11

Friday, December 6

I needed clothes and you clothed me. —Matthew 25:36 (NIV)

I'd found nothing at the department store's "Giant Pre-Christmas Sale." Crowds of shoppers. Harried saleswomen. *Why did I bother to come?* I thought, heading for the exit. Then I stopped. The young woman was standing in the children's department, exactly where she'd been when I arrived almost an hour earlier, She was still flicking through the offerings on a rack marked, "Final Clearance: 30% Off Already-Discounted Merchandise." She pulled out a small pink snowsuit, looked at the ticket, put it back, and took out a little girl's coat with a furry white collar.

Afraid she'd see me watching her, I sat down (oh, the glories of a walker!) and pretended to study the store flier. The young woman wandered to a nearby display of children's shoes but soon was back at the clearance rack. Apparently, even with the double discount, she could not make her purchase.

Should I offer to help? What could I say without offending her? I was rehearsing various lame-sounding speeches—"I don't have a little girl to shop for, may I shop for yours?"—when a harried saleswoman stepped up to the rack.

"Lucky you!" she said to the young woman. "This rack has just been discounted again! Everything's sixty percent off now."

The shopper stared at her, scanned the rack again, and drew out the fur-collared coat. "I'll go with you to the checkout," the saleslady said. I stood up and pushed my walker to the desk in time to see a beaming young woman depart with her prize, and a tired saleslady pull her own pocketbook from under the counter and drop some bills into the register drawer.

I knew why I had come to the Giant Sale.

In what unexpected place, Father, will I see You at work today?
—Elizabeth Sherrill

Digging Deeper: Isaiah 58:7

I pray that the eyes of your heart may be enlightened in order that you may know the hope to which he has called you. —Ephesians 1:18 (NIV)

Constellations of snowflakes whipped past our family van as we drove toward the Christmas light display. This was a yearly tradition, so I knew what we'd see. A two-story Christmas tree decked with multicolor bulbs. Santa's sleigh with double rows of reindeer. A simple nativity scene. Normally, I enjoyed our traditions. But this Christmas, I wasn't feeling it. It had been a tough year. I was halfway through law school, and the daily pressure was overwhelming.

Before we reached the display, my dad pulled into a gas station to fill the tank. While gas guzzled, he headed toward the complimentary window cleaner. I wondered why. The glass seemed fine to me.

My dad sprayed cleaner on the window and ran the squeegee down. The clean portion of glass was as clear as air, and the grime on the rest of the window was obvious: salt and dirt collected from months of driving. He dipped the squeegee back into the nuclear-blue solution and finished the rest of the glass.

My family could have seen the Christmas lights through the windows despite the collected debris. But my dad wanted us to see clearly. Uninhibited. Just like another Father Who knows when my vision is clouded. Who wants me to see Him fully, not through the crust that creeps onto the windshield of my life.

I had become jaded, bogged down with the wear of everyday living. But if there was a time of year to change the way I looked at things, it was the season celebrating the Almighty God becoming a vulnerable child. My dad clicked his seat belt into place, and we drove off. Ready to see a manger scene with unobstructed sight.

Lord, help me see You without distraction.
—Logan Eliasen

Digging Deeper: Psalm 119:18; Hebrews 12:2

Second Sunday of Advent, December 8

God so loved the world that he gave his only Son, so that everyone who believes in him won't perish but will have eternal life. —John 3:16 (CEB)

The Bible doesn't provide many details about Jesus's birth. According to Luke, Joseph traveled to Bethlehem to be enrolled on the tax list, accompanied by Mary. Luke says, "She gave birth to her firstborn child, a son, wrapped him snugly, and laid him in a manger, because there was no place for them in the guestroom."

Over the centuries, songs, art, and traditions have portrayed Jesus's birth as serene and effortless. But mothers likely don't believe that. Mary was in a stable, so she probably labored to the sounds of bleating sheep and perhaps a braying donkey. She surely longed for her mother or another woman to help her deliver, but Luke says nothing about help. Joseph was no doubt troubled he couldn't find more suitable lodging. Even as Mary was still recovering, the family had company. Shepherds arrived, telling how angels had appeared and announced the Savior's birth. It was certainly a labor of love.

Today we light the candle of love. At my church we sing Christina Rossetti's carol "Love Came Down at Christmas."

We are thankful for the love and care Joseph showed for Mary and Jesus. We are thankful for Mary, mother of Jesus. And most of all, we are thankful for Jesus, Love Incarnate, the most precious Christmas gift of all times.

With all my heart, Lord, thank You for Love.
—Penney Schwab

Digging Deeper: Matthew 5:43–45; 1 John 4:7–13

If you want to stay out of trouble, be careful what you say.
—Proverbs 21:23 (GNT)

I lost my voice. Now a scratchy, hoarse sound came out when I tried to speak. One more thing to pile upon my stress—a sick voice. I replayed the events of the night before. I should have said no. I attended a community meeting in hopes of lending a hand, maybe baking cookies for a bake sale, and I'd been put on the spot to run an upcoming huge event.

I sat in my chair, trying to find a way to back out. I was busy. It was a lot to take on. All of my objections went unheard, with reassurance I would have a lot of help and gratitude for my being there. I blinked, and the meeting was over, the job mine. All night long I lay awake, thinking how I felt bamboozled. I looked for a way out—could I email someone and say I couldn't do it? All the while I knew I had to do it, because I never back out of a commitment.

When I got out of bed to start the coffee, it was still dark. I went into the living room and sat in my favorite chair, thinking that if nothing else I really learned my lesson. I should have spoken up.

I closed my eyes, took a deep breath, and silently prayed, *You'll help me, right?*

Thank You, God, for knowing what's in my heart even when I don't speak it, but mostly for being there to listen to my panicked stresses, my random crazy worries, and finally my plea for help.
—Sabra Ciancanelli

Digging Deeper: James 1:19; Proverbs 15:4 (NIV)

Tuesday, December 10

Let the words of my mouth and the meditation of my heart be acceptable in Your sight. —Psalm 19:14 (NKJV)

I say inappropriate things at inappropriate times. Not sure what compels me. Maybe I'm nervous. In any case, the reviews are mixed. At my friend Steve's third marriage, I joked to the stranger next to me, "I was going to skip this one and make the next one." Turns out the stranger was Steve's new mother-in-law. She smiled weakly. *Nicely done, Mark.*

My dad and I once rebuilt a '74 Volkswagen, but we had to take a time-out when he self-amputated the top third of his ring finger. In the emergency room, I told him, "Great news! The doctor says you can still play piano!" My father (a) has never played a musical instrument, and (b) was not amused.

My former student Jennifer lost her sister recently. I've been to sadder funerals—oh, wait. No, I haven't. At the wake, amid the numbing heartache of a young woman's early death, I leaned over to Jen and said, "Your cousins all look exactly like you. It's like watching *The Stepford Wives* but all in black."

Jen laughed. "I know, right?" she said. "It's creepy!"

This time my comment had a purpose. I most assuredly wanted to break the mood, to take Jen away just to make her smile. Inappropriate? I don't know. The Bible tells the story of an angel who tells an elderly childless couple they're going to have a baby...and Sarah laughs. Laughs! At a messenger from God! Inappropriate?

Take a minute to consider the sheer absurdity of such an idea. And when the child does come, name him Isaac.

Isaac is Hebrew for "laughter." Ha!

> *Lord, use my nervous habit for wisdom...and*
> *please comfort my friend and her family.*
> —Mark Collins

Digging Deeper: Psalm 18:2, 31:5, 104:34

The Lord is your keeper; the Lord is your shade at your right hand. The sun shall not strike you by day, nor the moon by night. —Psalm 121:5–6 (NKJV)

"Red next to yellow, friendly fellow!" I recited the old rhyme to my kids after we spotted the five-foot-long red, yellow, and black snake slithering across our driveway.

We ran inside to get our camera, creeping up close to get a good picture.

"You see, kids, a really dangerous snake called a coral snake looks just like this. But the rhyme tells us a snake that has red stripes next to black stripes is dangerous and that a snake like this with the red next to yellow is a nice, harmless king snake."

Later that night, I showed my husband the pictures, and he looked at me like I was crazy.

"Erin, the rhyme says, 'Red next to yellow kills a fellow,'" he shouted. "You let the kids get that close to a coral snake!"

Thankfully no one got hurt, and we all now know that when a snake has red stripes next to the yellow stripes, it is not a friendly fellow. It's a fellow we should run away from very, very quickly.

We also now know that putting our trust in old nursery rhymes—rhymes we might not remember correctly—puts ourselves at risk.

Just as when we put our trust in anything of human origins.

While we as humans fail daily—we remember things wrong; make silly mistakes; we get angry, forgetful, tired, or frustrated—God never fails.

He always protects. He always watches.

He never forgets us even for a moment.

In His arms, we are safe. Even if we don't have the insight to understand the danger.

Father God, thank You for protecting me even when I can't protect myself and for loving me even when I fail. Amen.
—Erin MacPherson

Digging Deeper: Psalm 28:7, 91:1–16

Thursday, December 12

As iron sharpens iron, so one person sharpens another. —Proverbs 27:17 (NIV)

For the first time ever, my lifelong girlfriends and I were going on a weekend getaway. It wasn't anything fancy, just a home on a lake an hour north of town, but it was a guaranteed forty-eight hours with the women in my life who are such good influences, godly examples, and wonderful mothers. I already felt the lightness and fun of the weekend, and it was still a week away... or so I thought.

The Friday before my calendar' big "Girls' Weekend" block, I started getting text messages about departure times, weather updates, and plans for the weekend.

Wow, I thought, *everyone is as excited as I am!* Then the next text arrived. "See you all tonight!"

"Wait," I typed back, "is it this weekend? Do I have my dates wrong?" In a panic, I looked back through emails. Even though every exchange said it was this weekend, I'd written it in as the next weekend on my calendar.

"Don't kid, Ashley," one girlfriend wrote back.

"I'm not," I said, "but I'll be there!"

Normally, I start prepping for trips about a week before I head out. I do laundry, pick up last-minute items at the store so there's food in the house, and write up a list of activities to make it easy for my husband, Brian, when he has both of the kids alone.

This time, I called Brian and told him the situation. "Go," he said. "We'll be fine."

I ran home, threw clothes in a bag, and left. I like to think God knew how badly I needed that girls getaway. It was the perfect gift, one that left me feeling refreshed and ready for life back at home, and I couldn't be more grateful.

Lord, thank You for the blessings You sneak into my life. May I always recognize and be thankful for them.
—Ashley Kappel

Digging Deeper: Ecclesiastes 4:9–10; Proverbs 18:24, 27:9

Give thanks to the Lord, for he is good; his love endures forever.
—Psalm 118:1 (NIV)

I was visiting my daughter, Rachel, in Portland, Oregon. We'd been shopping at a favorite boutique, and were chatting and laughing as we headed back to our car, which was parked on the other side of a four-lane street.

In Oregon, cars are required to stop for pedestrians in a crosswalk, so when a car halted in the lane next to us, we glanced in the opposite direction and, seeing no cars, started to cross. Rachel was about three feet ahead of me. I saw a blur from the left and yelled her name. Thankfully she saw it, too, and stopped in her tracks as a car zoomed by her in the lane next to the stopped car. Going probably twice the twenty-five-mile-per-hour speed limit, it missed my daughter by about a foot. I couldn't stop thinking about what would have happened if she'd walked even one step farther. When we reached our car I cried tears of gratitude for her safety. How instantly joy can turn to despair. One second we can have everything, and the next lose it all. I've always known this, but her close call had just made it vivid.

I believe God protected Rachel that day, that He paced her steps perfectly. He used what could have been a tragedy, for good—a lesson of gratitude for every minute we have, reinforcing that we should never take anything for granted.

Thank You, God, for Your divine protection and for
reminding us how precious every moment is.
—Kim Taylor Henry

Digging Deeper: Colossians 2:6; Psalm 116:12

Saturday, December 14

When troubles of any kind come your way, consider it an opportunity for great joy. For you know that when your faith is tested, your endurance has a chance to grow. So let it grow, for when your endurance is fully developed, you will be perfect and complete, needing nothing. —James 1:2–4 (NLT)

I've gained some experience with physical therapy after having left hip replacement surgery. The first time I'd been on the operating table was when I had my tonsils out at age six. I was in the hospital for a couple of days after saying goodbye to those tonsils. After hip surgery I was booted out the next morning, and only because it was too late to release me the night before when the anesthesia wore off.

Two days later I was walking my golden retriever, Gracie, leash in one hand, crutch in the other, gesturing for people to make way. Within a week or so, I was paired up with Dublin-born Rachel, the physical therapist who soon became an unexpectedly significant part of my life. The first thing she said to me was, "You probably think this is going to be easy, don't you?"

I lied and said no. My attitude said something else. In fact, it was easy...at first. Rachel warned me not to push myself. Within a few weeks though, she was saying, "You've got to do ten of those, Edward. That was only eight." When I muscled the last two out, Rachel said in her lovely Dublin brogue, "OK, let's do them again, this time with proper form."

But I learned the harder it got, the stronger I got. There is a faith lesson for me in that. It's easy to have faith sitting in church on Sunday. When things get hard, my faith, like an underdeveloped muscle, is challenged. Those challenges push me and make my faith stronger even through the pain.

Lord, my faith is challenged each and every day. Let me meet that challenge and grow stronger in my love for You.
—Edward Grinnan

Digging Deeper: Matthew 5:12; James 1:12

The angel said, "Don't be afraid! Look! I bring good news to you—
wonderful, joyous news for all people. Your savior is born today in
David's city. He is Christ the Lord." —Luke 2:10–11 (CEB)

Christmas is supposed to be the most wonderful, joyous time of year. But for many people, it's a time of acute sorrow. A close friend's longed-for grandson was born too early to survive. Another friend's dementia has reached the point where she hardly recognizes her husband. Our church is again without a pastor since ours left to be closer to family. And in July, two of my grandchildren unexpectedly lost their father to a massive heart attack.

Our world has been torn by bombings, shootings, and acts of violence. Natural disasters—fires, hurricanes, floods, and earthquakes—have devastated thousands. Families have been broken by death or troubled relationships. Financial strains and job concerns cause stress. For many, it will be painful to hear or sing songs of celebration. It will be difficult to think about giving and getting gifts. And it will be impossible to hold back tears of grief in the face of the year's overwhelming losses.

Yet this morning we light the candle of joy. We remember the angel's message of "wonderful, joyous news." We can rediscover the joy of knowing Christ. His promise is true: "God himself will wipe away every tear from their eyes. There will be no mourning, crying, or pain anymore, for the former things have passed away" (Revelation 21:4).

God of Joy, help me be sensitive to those who mourn during this holy,
holiday season. Let me speak a word or do a deed or share a tear
that point to the joy found in You.
—Penney Schwab

Digging Deeper: Psalm 96:11–13; Isaiah 12:6; Romans 15:13

Monday, December 16

The Lord will be between me and you, and between my descendants and your descendants forever. —1 Samuel 20:42 (NASB)

I had an unexpected awakening when our daughter Brenda, whom I hadn't seen in a year, flew in from Alaska to visit her ninety-year-old grandmother. She wanted to spend as much time with her as she could. Her dad and I, residing an hour away, shared a hotel room with Brenda, near where her grandmother lived. We wanted as much "Brenda time" as we could cram in.

After my daughter returned to Alaska, I relished the wonderful memories we'd made. She and her sister Tamara, who lived locally, had attended an art event, bringing back beautiful painted canvases they showed off to me and my husband, Terry. We looked after Tam's children so the girls could spend an evening together.

When Brenda couldn't decide which bakery cake to choose for her grandma's ninety-first birthday party, she bought all four—Oreo cookie, raspberry, peanut butter, and caramel. Other family joined us until the small apartment was bursting with laughter and chatter.

As I relived Brenda's visit, already looking forward to "next time" it suddenly struck me that one of my unalterable griefs is no longer being able to add meaningful new memories with loved ones I've lost. What I have in my storehouse is what I must go back to time and again.

Jesus embraced making memories with others. In just three years of public ministry, His disciple John wrote of Him that if all the things He did (read: with and for people) were written in detail, "even the world itself would not contain the books that would be written" (John 21:25).

Brenda's visit left me with a deep urge to create new ways of being with friends and family near and far. I want my memory storehouse bursting its seams.

> *Lord, keeping in touch is such a tremendous privilege.*
> *Bless my efforts. Build my memories.*
> —Carol Knapp

Digging Deeper: Hosea 10:12; Ephesians 5:1

Pray for us, too, that God may open a door for our message.
—Colossians 4:3 (NIV)

I'd been stressing over my writing career, finances, home logistics, and the endless to-do list for the last few days. And instead of sorting my bills, washing the pile of dishes, or wrangling my ninja warrior boys, I sat on the couch with a tub of ice cream, trying to block everything out.

In just one week, I was scheduled to speak to a group of mainly single moms. *How can I stand up in front of them,* I asked myself, *and encourage them when I can't even encourage myself right now?*

Days later I reluctantly changed out of my pajamas and into a sharp outfit with high heels. I headed to the event. I entered with my book and notes, and even smiled as the attendees welcomed me with applause. I read excerpts from my book, about my brokenness from divorce, my struggle with being a single mom, and the night I entertained the idea of harming myself. I spoke about my decision to let go of my grief so I could better hold on to my children, life, love, and adventure. "How," a woman asked during the Q&A, "did you let go of the pain?"

I quoted my pastor, who'd told me, "You can change your attitude like you change your coat. It's a choice. You don't have to wear it." I told them about my recent struggles. "Small choices move you forward, even in the midst of adversity. I could have stayed in my pajamas and my discouragement this morning, but I chose to be here and share my heart with you."

Lord, thank You for giving me the strength and courage to take off the negativity in my life and put on something that pleases You and also moves me toward becoming the person You purpose me to be.
—Karen Valentin

Digging Deeper: Exodus 9:16

Wednesday, December 18

We fix our eyes not on what is seen, but on what is unseen, since what is seen is temporary, but what is unseen is eternal. —2 Corinthians 4:18 (NIV)

"Kiss Avery for me," I tell my mom. She's staying with my thirteen-year-old niece while my sister and brother-in-law vacation. Avery is one of the greatest joys in my life. She lives a thousand miles away, and I wish she lived closer. As she's the only child of my only sibling, I've tried to establish a close bond with her. I make sure we see each other in person several times a year. I send cute cards for holidays. On birthdays, I go overboard with surprises. During the Christmas season, I choose gifts she wants or I think she'll like, along with presents that point her to Christ. I hope she feels God's eternal love through the attention I lavish on her.

We're close, but Avery's now a teenager, school and sports dictating her schedule. Last year we got together only twice. I worry she'll forget about me and how much I love her.

But I learned something that made me feel a bit better about our relationship. During the first night of Grammy's visit, Avery and my mom slept in the same bed. As she snuggled between the sheets, she fanned out a plush designer blanket on top of the bedspread.

When she crawled into bed with Grammy the next night, she shook out that same blanket and carefully arranged it on top of the covers.

"Is that your special blankie?" Mom asked playfully. "Do you sleep with it every night?"

Avery nodded. "Aunt Stephanie gave it to me."

I no longer worry that Avery will forget. After all, she's covered with God's love and mine.

> *Lord, thank You for reminding me that the seeds of love*
> *I plant in another heart always grow.*
> —Stephanie Thompson

Digging Deeper: Psalm 91:4; Isaiah 51:16

*The eyes of all look to you, and you give them their food at the
proper time.* —Psalm 145:15 (NIV)

I don't remember eating in restaurants when I was a kid. My parents,
brother, sister, and I sat around the old wooden table in the kitchen
and ate home-cooked meals every night, often made with foods picked
from our garden. I remember being in a restaurant only after high
school football games when my friends and I visited the local truck
stop diner for cinnamon rolls.

I cooked meals at home for my kids when they were growing up as
well. But now that Jack and I are retired, we eat out at least a couple of
times a week.

Once during a visit to my folks in Rock Falls, Illinois, when Dad
was ninety-six and my stepmother, Bev, ninety-one, these names
punctuated our conversation: Arthur's, Candlelight Inn, Eggs In Paradise, Family Table, Froggy's, Gazi's, Maid Rite, Mom's Diner, Pre-
cinct, Wagon Wheel, and Willy's. In my ten-day visit, we actually ate
at all eleven restaurants.

For Dad and Bev, staying in their own home in their nineties meant
giving up certain ways of doing things. Instead of relying on Bev's delicious home-cooked meals, they discovered that eating out was easier,
faster, less stressful, and often more economical than cooking at home.
When we kids visited, we joined right in, restaurant after restaurant.

I learned from Dad and Bev that there are solutions to growing
older. New things to try. New ways of doing things. When Dad and
Bev joined the YMCA in their nineties to get some exercise in a safe
environment, they taught me that I'm never too old for change in
God's ever-changing world.

> *Lord, thank You for food no matter where I get it.*
> *Help me to make healthful choices.*
> —Patricia Lorenz

Digging Deeper: John 4:27–37; Psalm 22:26; Proverbs 30:8

Friday, December 20

It is better to be patient than powerful. It is better to win control over yourself than over whole cities. —Proverbs 16:32 (GNT)

"Mimsy, do you still like me?" My four-year-old granddaughter's question filled me with shame.

"Of course, I do," I replied with a sigh, aimed directly at myself. "I not only like you—I love you. And I love spending time with you. That's why I feel so sad this afternoon. Today it seems like nothing makes you happy."

It had been a rough day, for everyone. It began with a wild-winded blizzard depositing snowdrifts several feet high. My plan was to sit by the fire in my slippers, work on a writing project, and sip hot cocoa. Then my son texted. He was sick, hadn't slept, and was home alone with his two young daughters. Would I help?

When the roads cleared enough for me to venture out, I was on my way. But my heart stayed planted right in front of the hearth. In its place, a pesky little grudge settled in. So when my eldest granddaughter threw a full-on screaming fit every time her little sister touched a toy, I looked at her askew or didn't respond to her demands, I felt like throwing a fit of my own. I tried time-outs (for her, although I needed one, too!), reasoning with her, and ignoring her. But she was four and wanted control. I was sixty and wanted the very same thing. Neither of us had it.

The only thing in life I can control is myself. Even with God's help, it's an ongoing battle. But I have learned to thank my granddaughter and everyone else who doesn't acquiesce to letting me have my way. God continues to help mature the four-year-old in me.

Dear Lord, do whatever it takes to help me grow in love
and self-control.
—Vicki Kuyper

Digging Deeper: Galatians 5:22–23; James 1:19

Mary kept all these things and pondered them in her heart.
—Luke 2:19 (NKJV)

A Christmas thought. It has to do with dek hockey.
Our dek hockey team is, um, old. Old and not good. We play in the D league—only because there's no E or F league. And because we're on the bottom rung, we're an afterthought for scheduling. Last night the playoffs began. We played at 6:30—if we lost, we'd play again at 9:30. *Do they have any idea how old we are? That's when I take my Geritol.* As fate would have it, we lost the 6:30 game. Some guys couldn't stick around for the 9:30 game, so we were down to five guys and Sue, the goalie. It was like the Charge of the Light Brigade. And—Christmas Miracle—we won. We had no business playing, let alone winning.

After the game, I felt a weird peace. It was some ineffable gratitude—genuine thanks just for the ability, the mere chance to play, to be active, to be. It wasn't thanks for the game; it was thanks for everything—friendship, a job that allowed for leisure time, the sense that I can still do things like write a note like this to people who understand and appreciate...everything. "A tree, a rock, a cloud," said writer Carson McCullers. Joy in the face of reason. Joy in the face of the season.

Lord, I am made in Your image.
Help me appreciate the gifts I've been given,
especially the Gift we await this season.
—Mark Collins

Digging Deeper: Psalm 119:11; 1 Samuel 21:12; Luke 2:51

Fourth Sunday of Advent, December 22

Because of our God's deep compassion, the dawn from heaven will break upon us, to give light to those who are sitting in darkness and in the shadow of death, to guide us on the path of peace. —Luke 1:78–79 (CEB)

Every Sunday, our congregation participates in "Passing the Peace" as part of worship service. Some church members exchange the traditional words, "The peace of Christ be with you." And then, "And also with you." Others use the time to welcome guests or share news and needs: "So glad you are worshipping with us! Can you stay for the soup lunch?" "Susan's knee replacement went well." "My cousin has lost his job and is struggling to pay bills." "A young man was seriously injured in a rollover north of town." Later in the service, the whole congregation prays for these and other joys and concerns. After church, those prayers set in motion plans for follow-up to help people with their needs. In many ways we continue to pass the peace after worship.

Today we light the candle of peace. We hear the angel's words to the shepherds: "Glory to God in heaven, and on earth peace" (Luke 2:14). We remember that when Jesus appeared to the puzzled and terrified disciples after His crucifixion and resurrection, He said, "Peace be with you" (John 20:21). We embrace Jesus's call for us to share His peace with others.

Lord, may we seek and share Your peace this Christmas and always.
—Penney Schwab

Digging Deeper: Matthew 5:9; John 14:27, 16:33

ENCOUNTERING GOD IN UNLIKELY PLACES
Beauty for Ashes

Ye thought evil… but God meant it unto good. —Genesis 50:20 (KJV)

When Christmas approaches, my heart bursts with the urge to give. I'm driven by a passion to make sure no one is left behind. So when a major Nashville charity announced that refugee kids would not be included in their toy giveaway, I was devastated.

"What can we do?" I wailed to my husband, David, fighting back tears. David responded with, "We can get some toys," which soon turned into a big idea. I organize a group of progressive people who meet monthly to hear speakers. Why not ask them to help?

We plotted and planned, and convinced a priest at a local church to help with the giveaway.

We overwhelmed him with piles of toys.

The next year, people shoped in earnest, and it was clear we needed a better plan.

I knew where to turn: Spruce Street Baptist, an inner-city church, the oldest African-American church in the area.

Soon, our toy project became as efficient as a well-oiled machine. The ladies of the church took charge. Now they start early each year, scouting the area for homeless children, refugees, and those in need. They welcome them. They usher the children into a huge room transformed into a toy store. No one is ever turned away.

Looking for God at Christmastime, I find no better place than this. A modest building, a long line of parents and children bused in from the shelter, a room filled with toys.…Who needs pipe organs and stained-glass windows when you can bask in the glow of unconditional generosity?

Father, only You can take a heartless act and turn it into a mighty
fine party. Thank You for inviting me to Your dance.
—Pam Kidd

Digging Deeper: Psalm 107:9; Galatians 6:10

Christmas Eve, Tuesday, December 24

The grace of God has appeared that offers salvation to all people.
—Titus 2:11 (NIV)

We arrived home from church with a clatter. My boys bolted upstairs. I hung my coat and started lunch. To my surprise, on the kitchen counter beside the cookie jar was a blue plastic star. No note. Just the star. I knew where it had come from.

Earlier in the week, my friend Judy had visited and brought her heirloom tablecloths. After years of shepherding souls by holding tea parties, she wanted to pass the linens along. Judy is close to my mother's age, and we share a love for days gone by. She noticed my vintage, light-up Christmas tree first thing. Her fingers fluttered over green ceramic. "I have my mama's," she said. "I wanted one for years," I said. "My grandmother had one. This one's similar. They're hard to find."

The tree had been hiding on a high shelf in a dusty antique shop. I bought it quickly. One of my boys carried the box to my van, and another held it on the ride home. It was fragile. That evening, we decorated the tree with colored pegs from a worn paper bag.

"It's wonderful," Judy said. She smiled. "But you're missing the star." "The star?" I asked. "Why, yes. The Christmas star. See here? Where you have this yellow peg." We'd chosen the yellow peg for where the star would be. I'd modeled this tree after my grandmother's and didn't remember her tree having a star. "Oh," I said. "Guess the peg will have to do."

But then Judy brought a star. My boys were as excited as I was! We pulled the peg and placed the star on the treetop right away. "It's beautiful," one son said. I thought so, too. Joy swelled in my spirit. My friend had given this gift with quiet, gentle grace.

Like a Savior babe in a manger.

God's gift when we didn't know the need.

Thank You, Father, for Jesus. My salvation. Gift of grace. Amen.
—Shawnelle Eliasen

Digging Deeper: 2 Peter 1:2; Ephesians 2:8–9

Thank God for his gift that words can't describe! —2 Corinthians 9:15 (CEB)

"What did your husband give you for Christmas?" a friend asked after I admired her sparkly bracelet.

"Don gave me floor mats for my car," I told her, "and he also had the interior and trunk cleaned."

My friend laughed. "Wouldn't you have preferred a romantic surprise wrapped in pretty paper with a bow on top?"

Floor mats certainly aren't romantic, and neither gift was a surprise. I'd driven the car to the shop for the cleanup and had seen the receipt for the mats. "No, I actually got exactly what I wanted," I replied honestly.

The conversation led me to think about the first Christmas. There were moments of surprising glory—a magnificent angel chorus, a bright star, and gifts of gold, frankincense, and myrrh. But other events surrounding Jesus's birth were less glorious. He was born in a stable that might also have housed donkeys and sheep. His crib was a feeding trough. His first visitors were humble shepherds. When Jesus was presented at the temple on the eighth day, His parents gave the sacrifice required of the poor: "a pair of turtledoves or two young pigeons." He was recognized as the promised Messiah only by prophet Anna and devout man Simeon. He was worshipped briefly by kings but then lived as a refugee in Egypt.

The greatest gift of all time was both divine and human, glorious and humble. He is the perfect gift for my sparkly friend, my practical self, and indeed the whole world.

Thank You, Jesus. Thank You. Amen.
—Penney Schwab

Digging Deeper: John 3:16–17, 4:10–13; Philippians 2:6–11

Thursday, December 26

Cast all your anxiety on him because he cares for you. —1 Peter 5:7 (NIV)

I watched my husband, Chuck, walk away from us at the Sydney Airport, my stomach in knots. *Lord, please help me do this.*

We'd traveled to Australia to celebrate Christmas with Chuck's son, his wife, and their two boys. Logan, the seven-year-old grandson who lived with us, accompanied us on the trip. But he had to return to school soon afterward, so I agreed to take him back home by myself. Chuck wanted to stay longer and spend more time with his family he hadn't seen for two and a half years since they moved.

We'd never been to Australia before, and Chuck handled all the arrangements in our multileg journey navigating our way there. Now I was traveling back without him, and I was worried about the trip because I had to look out for Logan as well as find our way through several busy airports. Fear of getting separated from the child had my nerves on edge.

Logan pulled on my hand, and I peered down at his inquisitive face. "Where are we going now, Grandma?"

Not wanting to show him my anxiety, I told him to search for the number of our gate. I pointed to the various signs posted overhead. "It's on one of the signs that says, 'Departures.'"

"There it is!" Logan pointed to a screen to our left.

Sure enough, he'd found the correct one. I was amazed at how much his reading skill had advanced in second grade. From that moment on, I asked him to help me find every sign we needed to navigate through the airports, and he did quite well. He even insisted on pulling the heaviest suitcases to show how grown up he'd become.

Halfway home, I realized I was no longer nervous about our trip and that I didn't have to look out for Logan. He was looking out for me.

> *Lord, help me remember that I don't need to worry*
> *since our lives are in Your hands.*
> —Marilyn Turk

Digging Deeper: Luke 12:25–26

The beginning of wisdom is this: Get wisdom, and whatever you get, get insight. —Proverbs 4:7 (ESV)

For months now I've been sorting and culling household goods. Shredding professional files. Donating worn towels to an animal shelter.

I felt ambivalent about tackling the stash of hand-scrawled journals hidden away in the corner of a large trunk. Was I afraid of what I'd find? Looking back over several decades, would I see molehills described as mountains? Would I be repulsed and want to burn every page? Or find value in every paragraph and throw nothing away?

Last week I sensed the Spirit's nudge: *Do it. Sit down and review the ruminations. Discard inconsequential pages. Keep what's important.* As I read, over the next few days, a few passages brought up painful memories. But I gratefully gained understanding of recurring themes: *Why do I welcome guests at my table? Why do I rarely vacation?*

I also discovered notes from a spiritual exercise I started several times but too quickly dropped. Every day I'd write down a grace or blessing—an affirming thank-you from a client, an unexpected smile from a stranger, a few cookies from a neighbor.

I've reclaimed the practice, this week noting a fortuitous estate sale find, a fair-weather sky, an apt Scripture to ply.

Reviewing and savoring the best of my past has set me on a new path of gratefulness, present tense. As for the underlying downsizing goal, I succeeded in cutting the passel by half. All the worthy pages of my journal are tucked back in the corner of the old trunk, saved for a future read.

Lord, as I sort through my possessions and memories, help me draw out and dwell on the positive—the best—insights.
—Evelyn Bence

Digging Deeper: Philippians 4

Saturday, December 28

Turn ye not unto idols, nor make to yourselves molten gods:
I am the Lord your God. —Leviticus 19:4 (KJV)

I was thrilled to pieces when I discovered an antique cast-iron patis-serie table for a song. The only problem was, my treasured find was missing its marble inset. I searched for something that might work in its place, and not long after, while out of town, I found a slab of antique marble at a tag sale. The price was unbelievably reasonable, and I couldn't wait to get it cut to size for my new table. I already had visions of it functioning as an island in the kitchen of my log cabin.

When I took my project idea to a local shop that specialized in fabri-cating marble, the wizened old man who ran the place wanted to look at both the table and the marble. They were sequestered in the backseat of my car, wrapped in an old quilt.

The man shook his head and looked me over as if sizing me up. "That's not even marble," he said, almost laughing.

I was sure his next words were going to be, "It's a very heavy plastic, ma'am." Or maybe, "This here is faux-painted poplar. Once a table leaf, I'd say." But instead he said, "What you've got here is granite. Granite doesn't crumble when cut like marble does. Now I can agree to the job." The man studied the table's lacy ironwork and almost grinned. "Well, I haven't seen one this fine in years. From the twenties, I'd say, or maybe Victorian."

After I left the table and grayish brown granite in his care, I congrat-ulated myself for being such an astute antique sleuth. It was virtually all I could think about. I was about to be the proud owner of an authentic patisserie table, and I hadn't even traveled to France to procure it.

> *Dear Lord, when I start worshiping my possessions,*
> *please stop me. Quick.*
> —Roberta Messner

Digging Deeper: Deuteronomy 5:8; Exodus 20:4

Heal the sick, raise the dead, cleanse those with skin diseases,
and throw out demons. —Matthew 10:8 (CEB)

I felt like an imposter, sitting there in a circle with a dozen other people at church, all of us training to be healing ministers. Not that I had the slightest notion of having any sort of healing gifts. Would that I could touch someone with my hands and make a cold disappear or a fever fade away. I once asked a minister who clearly had such powers to pray for me, and as he did, his hands trembled with heavenly medicine surging through him. I had no such illusions about myself.

In my recent readings of the Gospels, I kept noticing how often Jesus healed and how He expected His disciples to do the same, actually charging them to "heal the sick." Today we have fine doctors and hospitals equipped with the latest technology to do just that, but I didn't see how that lets the rest of us off the hook. I could think of too many people, in medical situations, who'd been glad for prayer.

So here I was, getting trained and feeling completely inadequate for the task. Various healing prayers were suggested, questions were posed that we as healers might want to ask, a gentle hand on the head was recommended while praying. But how would I do any of it? It was so far beyond me. And then the woman training us put it all into perspective. "God is the One Who heals," she said. "It's not what you do; it's what He does."

Not what I do but what He does. That sounded just right.

Oh, Great Physician, be with me and all those who need healing.
—Rick Hamlin

Digging Deeper: Mark 16:15–18; Matthew 28:18–20

Monday, December 30

Human one, listen closely, and take to heart every word I say to you.
—Ezekiel 3:10 (CEB)

Abright, talented friend of more than forty years has been diagnosed with dementia. She no longer drives, doesn't always choose appropriate clothing, and often forgets the names of family members.

She still loves to eat out, so my friend Glenda and I treated her to lunch at her favorite Mexican restaurant. We talked about good times, like the night we ate an entire carrot cake, digging into it while we talked about families, God, life, and death. We remembered kids' swimming lessons and ball games, and our New Year's Eve tradition of playing charades.

As we drove back to her house, I opened my mouth to give my friend some helpful advice about coping with her disease. But before I got the first word out, Glenda gently asked her, "What one thing would help you most?"

"Getting together with people like me," our friend replied without hesitation. "I need to talk to people who know how frustrating it is when you can't remember. Everyone talks about our problems, but no one listens to us."

Glenda followed up: "What one thing can your friends do for you?" Again, the answer was "Listen."

We've planned future lunches and visits. Our friend is blessed with a loving family and church that provide support. Glenda is exploring ways to facilitate peer-to-peer interaction. I'm working on something different: learning to listen, truly listen, with my heart as well as my ears.

Lord, I am so quick to give advice and so slow to hear and understand real need! Help me listen to Your voice before I open my mouth.
—Penney Schwab

Digging Deeper: Ecclesiastes 3:6–7; Matthew 13:13–16

I have learned by experience that the Lord hath blessed me.
—Genesis 30:27 (KJV)

Ever since I was a child, I've had this perfect New Year's Eve scenario, undoubtedly from some old movie, floating around in my head. A festive room is crowded with people in evening gowns and tuxedos. There are glittery hats and noisemakers, and the band strikes up "Auld Lang Syne" at the stroke of midnight. Of course there are lots of kissing and streamers and balloons as the crowd cheers in the new year. Everyone's deliriously happy.

Since then, I've been to plenty of New Year's parties, and none have risen to my early expectations. At the beginning of my career, I actually tried to put together a party like the one in my imagination. That's when I discovered that life...is not a movie.

After I married Corinne, New Year's Eve took on a whole new meaning.

Each year we reserve the evening for dinner at a favorite restaurant. We always ask for a paper menu we can take home. On the back of that menu, Corinne takes notes as we talk quietly, remembering the year that was and anticipating the one to come. We break down our resolutions into categories. How can we improve our spiritual life, our family life, our professional and social lives? Are there ways we can be better to each other and to each of our children?

To Corinne and me, there's no finer way of welcoming the coming year. It's nice if strains of "Auld Lang Syne" happen to waft through the restaurant, and of course I'd never turn down a New Year's kiss...but who needs a party when God's best blessing is the person who is sitting across the table and looking forward with me?

Father, my past experiences magnify Your blessings. Thank you.
—Brock Kidd

Digging Deeper: John 9:25; Psalm 35:9

December

UNDER GOD'S WINGS

1 _____

2 _____

3 _____

4 _____

5 _____

6 _____

7 _____

8 _____

9 _____

10 _____

11 _____

12 _____

13 _____

14 _____

15 _____

16 _____

17 _____

18 _____

19 _____

20 _____

21 _____

22 _____

23 _____

24 _____

25 _____

26 _____

27 _____

28 _____

29 _____

30 _____

31 _____

Marci Alborghetti of New London, Connecticut, notes that the past year has been challenging for the world, the nation, and so many individuals. "Our family is no exception, and we are relying more than ever on God's help and grace," she writes. "My husband, Charlie, ended up in the hospital with a serious, drug-resistant infection that spread to his blood. After a frightening week, he was released with a month's worth of IV and oral antibiotics. Thank the Lord, he continues to recover. We lost Charlie's youngest sister this year as well, giving us even more reason to place ourselves at God's feet and wait upon the Lord."

"It was a long year, the kind made of three-inch binders of medical claims and more doctor appointments than ought to be allowed," says **Julia Attaway** of New York City. It was also, she tells us, a year of healing and growth, of realizing that the shadows that seemed so dark were also the shadow of His wings. "I seem to keep relearning the same lesson: that the goal is to love God in all circumstances, rather than ask Him to get me out of the situations I don't like."

Evelyn Bence, of Arlington, Virginia, looks back on a year filled with the joys of family. "Last spring, my sisters met for several days in Gettysburg to celebrate my birthday. Then in August, we enjoyed a larger gathering in northern Pennsylvania, joined by our brothers and various spouses. We reminisced and 'caught up.' We laughed, sang hymns, and prayed together. We returned to our work-a-day world spiritually and relationally renewed."

Erika Bentsen of Sprague River, Oregon is embracing her second chance at ranch life. A year and a half after the surgery that ended her four-year battle with crippling back pain, her life is as active as ever. "I savor every moment of God's grace," she says. She's adding salmon fishing to her long list of favorite things to do. "I caught my first one ever. I had no idea how exhilarating it is. But once word gets out that you have fresh salmon, it's amazing to find out how many friends you have!"

"I've been working five different jobs," **Rhoda Blecker** of Bellingham, Washington, says. I teach fiction writing and inspirational writing; do spiritual direction; do research and referencing for an executive recruiter; edit other people's books, both fiction and nonfiction; and—oh yes—write for *Daily Guideposts*. I also serve on three synagogue committees, study with the rabbi, belong to the sisterhood, and give sermons or lead Torah study when the rabbi is out of town. In my copious (hah!) spare time, I am working on needlepoint and spoiling the dog and the cat."

Sabra Ciancanelli of Tivoli, New York, says, "This year has been full of challenges and blessings. My nephew's death knocked me to my knees in every sense—but amazingly, the darkness of grief has a bright side of strengthening my faith. My sons are growing and becoming, surprising me, delighting me, and making me laugh along the way. As I write this, our dog and cats are all sleeping together at my feet in one big lump of love. Life, it seems, is sometimes hard, but always beautiful and every moment is filled with meaning."

"Something wild happened this past year," writes **Desiree Cole** of Olathe, Kansas. "My husband, our golden retriever, and I left New York City. After eight years, we moved back to my hometown. I'd had a grand plan of becoming a successful newsroom journalist after college. The plan was working, but something about my spirit was off. Then, Jesus started meeting me in my dreams at night. His eyes were warm. His heart was tender. A thriving career quickly lost its appeal. Those encounters with Him transformed my heart. Now I know what I really wanted to chase: God's heart. I was captivated by it. I was ready to love others like that, starting with my family."

"Here's advice I've given many times to many students," notes **Mark Collins** of Pittsburgh, Pennsylvania. "'Take time to take stock, to carefully consider your future.' Of course, I never followed such wise counsel myself; recent circumstances have forced me to confront, perhaps for the first time, who I am and where I'm headed. They say God works in mysterious ways—this isn't one of them. God knows I understand irony, and God has made such irony clear to me: follow your own advice. Be mindful, Be thoughtful. Be kind to yourself and others. Maybe I'll start by apologizing to all of my former students for providing advice that I hadn't first tested on myself."

Pablo Diaz of Carmel, New York, quotes writer Leonard Cohen, "Pay attention to the cracks, because that's where the light gets in." As he nears his sixties, Pablo says, "I'm more attentive to the light that shines into my life through the changes and opportunities. Often, Elba and I travel to Detroit to visit our son, Paul, where we have gained a newfound appreciation for the city. Our daughter, Christine, and her husband, Taun, moved closer to our home, which allows for more family time. We are grateful for all of God's blessings."

John Dilworth of North Canton, Ohio, writes, "This year Pat and I celebrated our fortieth wedding anniversary and forty years of reading *Daily Guideposts*! Before retiring, I was concerned about how I would spend my time. I prayed for opportunities to work with youth, stay involved with business, and encourage others in their faith. Multiple doors have opened in all three areas. I am deeply grateful for days packed with opportunity and filled with meaning.

Amy Eddings is a writer who lives with her husband, Mark Hilan, in rural Ohio. They continue to enjoy welcoming bed-and-breakfast guests to their 1900 Victorian home. In 2017, Amy returned to public radio, taking a job at WCPN in Cleveland hosting NPR's *Morning Edition*. She and Mark are "feeling and praying their way into this new season of their lives."

"This was a year of learning," says **Logan Eliasen** of Port Byron, Illinois. "I expected that, since I was rounding off my first year of law school and starting my second. But what surprised me was that I didn't just learn about Miranda rights and constitutional standing doctrine. God constantly taught me about who He is and how His identity shapes my own as His child. And even when I've long forgotten some of the intricate legal theories I've studied, I'll still remember how God sustained and restored me over this last year."

"This year, the Lord is teaching me about trust," says **Shawnelle Eliasen** of Port Byron, Illinois. "It's my nature to want to hold life tightly and to resist change. But I'm understanding that if I live with my fists curled around gifts that the Lord has given, my hands aren't open to receive the fresh grace and goodness that He brings." Shawnelle and her husband, Lonny, live in a rambling Victorian with a houseful of boys and a yellow labrador named Rugby. Shawnelle tells us that she has discovered change is an opportunity to move to a deeper faith-place. "It's an invitation to trust in the Lord and find rest in the shadow of His wings."

"It has been a challenging year, though it's also been a blessed one," says **Sharon Foster** of Durham, North Carolina. "Chase, Lanea, and I continue to do the work God has assigned us; we each love what we do, even when it is challenging. Two friends were diagnosed with cancer this year, but I am to be able to report that they are now cancer free. Thank You, Jesus! I've lost several elderly relatives, including an uncle who passed away. I am also grieving the loss of my spiritual father, Bishop Howard Oby. He taught me so much about faith, about being assured of God's power.

"Every year I choose one word to be my theme," says **Julie Garmon** of Monroe, Georgia. "This year, it's love. In the past, I've focused on joy, enough, surrender, follow, dance, and simple, but love has turned me inside out. No other word compares to love. Love rearranges my schedule, my ministry, and most of all, my heart. The Lord is teaching me that nothing—not one single thing—matters more than loving Him and loving others. Sure, writing's still important to me, but putting words on paper doesn't outshine taking a meal to a friend who's lonely, being quiet long enough to listen, or simply making a pot of soup and praying over the chairs in my den before our small group arrives. My priorities have shifted. I have a new goal in life: To Love Well."

"It has been a busy and joyful year of family, life, and ministry," says **Bill Giovannetti** of Santa Rose, California. "For the first time, I'm the parent of a driver! This has been a wonderful adjustment, as Josie is a wise and careful teenager. She has fallen in love with graphic design and Photoshop and friends. My son, Jonathan, turns out to be an excellent mathematician and skilled tennis player. My wife, best friend, and lawyer, Margi, has been busy leading huge teams, designing gorgeous sets, and orchestrating special projects at the northern California church I pastor. She also teaches business law and ethics classes at a local college. It has been an incredible blessing to see two special edition magazines I have written hit the shelves nationwide, one on Christmas and the other on Easter. Could there be better topics?

"It was a year of incredible change," says **Edward Grinnan**, Guideposts editor-in-chief and vice president of Guideposts Publications. He spent a good deal of time this past year promoting his newest Guideposts book, *Always by My Side: Life Lessons from Millie and All the Dogs I've Loved*, including an interview with Robin Roberts on *Good Morning America*. "Robin is a great friend to Guideposts and a true lover of dogs," says Edward. Speaking of dogs, Edward and his wife, Julee, are busy keeping up with their newest dog, a golden retriever named Grace, who turned three. "She keeps us young, that's for sure," he says. "And she is a great source of inspiration for my devotions. I think God uses our animals to teach us lessons in life and love. If you agree with me, check out our newest Guideposts publication, *All Creatures, The Animals Who Share Our Lives*. It's packed with stories of how our relationship with God's creatures inspires us and helps us grow in our faith."

"I always feel like I don't get any older.... It's just my kids who seem to age," says **Rick Hamlin**, executive editor at *Guideposts* magazine. His oldest son, William, just got married. ("My wife, Carol, is thrilled to finally have another girl in the family.") And his younger son, Timothy, might well be next. Rick and Carol continue to sing in their church choir. Rick is also an enthusiastic volunteer at the church's Saturday soup kitchen. "I love leading the guests in song," he says. "They sound great on 'Amazing Grace.'" This spring Guideposts will publish Rick's book about his spiritual journey.

Lynne Hartke says she often hears the Sonoran Desert where she lives described as "'a desolate place, even god-forsaken.'" At one time, Lynne would have agreed with that statement. But after three decades of exploring desert trails with her husband, Kevin, and rust-colored mutt, Mollie, she has encountered the beauty found in barren places, a beauty enjoyed by the couple's four grown children and three grandchildren. An author and breast cancer survivor, Lynne receives inspiration from other survivors at the cancer organizations where she volunteers—individuals who have taught her to celebrate life despite challenging realities.

For **Carla Hendricks** of Franklin, Tennessee, the past year was filled with a series of twists and turns, a relocation, and a career shift. She tells us, "As an adoptive mom and child advocate, I know the lows of walking with vulnerable children and families. I also witness the highs of emotional and spiritual healing in those children and families. While traveling the winding road of justice ministry, I find joy and refuge during family movie and game nights with my husband, Anthony, and four children, during cherished moments of writing, and most of all, while connecting with the loving heart of the Father."

Kim Taylor Henry of Elizabeth, Colorado, says the highlight of her year was a trip to the Holy Lands. Being baptized in the Jordan was a thrill. Another thrill this year was the publication of her first solo book, *Making God Smile, Living the Fruit of the Spirit One Day at a Time*. Kim tells us, "It's for those of you who, like me, want to live a life of love, joy, peace, patience, kindness, and more, but find ourselves acting in unloving ways, irritable, unkind, harsh, losing self-control, and lacking peace." Kim would love to have you join her on a journey to living life as God intended. Check it out at kimtaylorhenry.com.

Erin Janoso writes, "We said goodbye to my grandmother, Nanny, in August of this year. I feel her loss deeply, but also rejoice with her in her spirit's newfound freedom. As I write, my husband, Jim, our five-year-old daughter, Aurora, and I are preparing to leave our home in Roundup, Montana, to spend the winter in Alaska. I recognize Nanny within me as I look forward to this coming season of rest, snow, and the Northern Lights. I'm grateful for this opportunity to share Nanny's zeal for life with my own daughter. I cannot imagine a richer legacy."

"What a year!" says **Ashley Kappel** of Birmingham, Alabama. After welcoming a third child, Beau, to the family, she says she "has enjoyed transitioning from a man-to-man defense to a zone defense with her husband, Brian. In spite of the challenges a newborn can bring, Beau has instead filled the house to overflowing with love." Ashley continues to work full-time in publishing, learning daily how important it is to find strength, satisfaction, and reward in her faith, not in the things of this world.

"Our house is full," reports **Brock Kidd** of Nashville, Tennessee, "but we are preparing for my son Harrison to spread his wings and experience his next adventure at college." In addition to Harrison, Brock and his wife, Corinne, have Mary Katherine, six, Ella Grace, five, and baby David, who just turned one. "I'm the only guy I know who has gone on a college visit and then returned home to change a diaper!" Brock continues to enjoy his professional life in wealth management and he and Corinne still manage to travel somewhere together once a year.

Pam Kidd of Nashville, Tennessee, writes, "When I consider how this year has unfolded, I seem to see God's fingerprints in every happening. Our work in Zimbabwe keeps taking marvelous turns, 'Can I build a library at Village Hope?' a friend asks. Imagine: a library where people living in mud huts can learn to read, check out books, and in essence travel the world. Sadly, we lost my brother. But he departed our world in perfect peace, having come full circle, surrounded by the love of his wife, Carol, and their daughters. We see the same touch of God in the lives or our grown children, Brock and Keri, who have a remarkable knack of finding joy in their work, their homes, and in giving to others. David and I continue to work as a team in our many endeavors, and honestly only God could have engineered our lives to be this happy."

It was another quiet year of teaching and writing for **Patty Kirk.** She tells us, "after abandoning Pokémon Go—too hard to hatch eggs on the updated versions!—I returned to my favorite pastimes with new vigor. I put in a fall garden for the first time and stepped up the speed on my regular twenty-one miles a week of jogging." She also submitted well over a hundred checklists to the Cornell Lab of Ornithology's *eBird* database. "A small contribution to our collective knowledge," she says. "Does anyone really care about bird distribution in my smidgen of eastern Oklahoma? But it makes me feel like a scientist."

Carol Knapp of Priest River, Idaho, says, "I think my husband, Terry's, back and other surgeries the past three years, including a kidney out for cancer last spring—and then last fall being put on a helicopter Life Flight for cardiac arrest—finally caught up with me. I found myself feeling anxious and unsure. And it didn't help that our north Idaho winter had days and days of fog. It was a season for gathering under God's wing—because that's the only place I feel truly protected and made strong."

Carol Kuykendall of Boulder, Colorado, writes, "This has been a full-circle year! I revised my book, *Give Them Wings*, written more than twenty years ago when our three kids were leaving home. Those three have grown and married and now have kids of their own. My daughter-in-law, Alexandra, whose oldest is in high school and will leave home soon, wrote the foreword. Also, my daughter, Lindsay, who lives next door on our hilltop where she grew up, brought two horses to live in our empty barn where her horses used to live. Her youngest, Peyton, has become an avid horse lover. Full circles all around us."

This year, after her son and daughter-in-law adopted their two foster daughters, **Vicki Kuyper** packed up all her belongings and moved from Phoenix, Arizona, to Colorado Springs, Colorado. "Love will lead you places you never expected to go," says Vicki. When she isn't hanging out with her grandkids, Vicki spends her time writing, having authored more than fifty books over the past thirty years. One of her latest projects is a devotional for grandparents, entitled *Off My Rocker and On My Knees*.

"Near the end of 2017, eleven people in my life died, starting with my beloved ninety-eight-year-old father," says **Patricia Lorenz** of Largo, Florida. "As hard as it was, I felt blessed to be there with Dad during his final days. The other deaths were friends and neighbors, some of whom died well before their time. Since then, whenever an opportunity arises, I hear myself saying, 'Life is short, let's do it now.' More time with family and friends, more volunteering, more travel, more walks on the beach, more phone calls with my children and grandchildren. More quality time with Jack. 'Let's do it now' is a philosophy I intend to use for the rest of my life because without a doubt, life *is* short."

"It's truly been a year of experiencing 'how wide and long and high and deep' God's love is for me and for my family, and I pray that you, too, will encounter the same," says **Debbie Macomber,** *New York Times* #1 best-selling author. Besides her beloved novels, Debbie has published three cookbooks, numerous inspirational nonfiction titles, as well as two acclaimed children's books. Debbie serves on the Guideposts National Advisory Cabinet, is the international spokesperson for World Vision's Knit for Kids, and serves as a YFC National Ambassador. A devoted grandmother of eleven, Debbie lives in Port Orchard, Washington, with her husband, Wayne, and writing companion, Bogie.

"This year really was a scorcher for me," says **Erin MacPherson** of Austin, Texas, "both literally—I do, after all, live in Texas—and figuratively. With my grandmother still holding on to a few precious memories while declining rapidly and my oldest son becoming a preteen, I realized that there are times in life where it seems impossible to escape the heat. Except *Under the Shadow of His Wings,* I still found rest—contentment, even. In His shadow, I found myself resting in little moments, surrounded by people who love me and love Him."

This year marks the first year of retirement from a thirty-eight-year nursing career with the Department of Veterans Affairs for **Roberta Messner** of Huntington, West Virginia. "A few years ago, one of my veterans' wives asked me to join her in praying for her husband, Jack, who was getting older but had never asked Jesus into his heart," Roberta says. "I gave Jack past and current volumes of *Daily Guideposts* and drove past their cozy home every evening for the express purpose of praying for him. This year, Jenny wrote me the most exciting news: Jack had joined the family of God and been baptized. Now, I'll never have to say goodbye to my beloved veteran-friend," says Roberta, "in this life or the next."

Rebecca Ondov of Hamilton, Montana, had a jam-packed year between her day job, irrigating her hay field (her golden retriever, Sunrise, faithfully swam in the ditches), and helping her family. Often, she would launch her kayak in the cool of the morning before the sun rose. She felt like she was dwelling under the shadow of His wings as she slipped through the water, watching the world wake up. Another highlight has been working with a coach to create audio books. She invites you to connect with her via her Website: http://www.RebeccaOndov.com and on Facebook.

Natalie Perkins of New York City says she sees each day as a constant choice to try to order her steps in the way God would have her to walk. Along the journey this past year, Natalie was fortunate to lecture on early Christian texts in Irvine, CA for a Jesus Seminar on the Road with the Westar Institute, sing in Japan for the USO, and spend two whole holidays in a row with her family in Indianapolis. You can follow her on Facebook at Diva Does Divinity, on Twitter at @DivaDoesDiviniT and on Instagram at @divadoesdivinity.

"No good deed goes unpunished," jokes **Ginger Rue** of Tuscaloosa, Alabama, who complicated her family's life considerably this past year by rescuing a puppy from the local animal shelter. "Our best guess is that she's part black lab and part pit bull, but whatever she is, she loves to chew! She has made it her mission to destroy everything we own!," says Ginger. "I remind myself that God made her to be a puppy, and she's just doing what puppies do. Also, I find it so dear that all she really wants is just to be wherever we are. What a beautiful daily reminder to me that I, too, should delight in the true Master's presence and spend more time with the Lord."

Daniel Schantz, professor emeritus of Central Christian College, gave the sixtieth anniversary commencement address on May 12, 2017. He began his career there as a student, graduating with two degrees in 1966. Then he was called back to teach at his alma mater. During his forty-three years in the classroom, he has seen many changes in students. "One thing has not changed," he notes. "Students still trust God to be their 'shield and refuge' as they move into an ominous future. Their faith inspired me every day."

Gail Thorell Schilling of Concord, New Hampshire, was thrilled when all of her family, plus the new grandbabies, gathered for our daughter's wedding. Son Tom played guitar, daughter Trina served as matron of honor, and son Greg escorted the bride down the aisle. Thanks to her new hip and "miraculously restored mobility," Gail could navigate cobbled streets in Quebec City with Trina and family. With Tom and family, she comfortably trekked miles to attractions in Baltimore and Washington, DC. Back in Concord, Gail spends time with her family, church, tai chi class, and memoir writing groups.

"Transition describes our lives," writes **Penney Schwab** of Copeland, Kansas. "Son Patrick and his wife, Patricia, moved back to Kansas; son Michael and his wife, Jeri, adopted Haylee and Naomee as sisters to Caden; grandson David received his wings as a marine helicopter pilot; and grandson Mark graduated from college. We experienced grief and loss in the death of grandchildren Caleb's and Olivia's father. Grandson Ryan and Paige moved to Colorado, as did Caleb. My husband, Don, and I remain on our farm, and Rebecca is still in Topeka. Through it all, we've relied on God's promise in Psalm 91:4: 'His faithfulness is a protective shield.'"

Elizabeth (Tib) Sherrill and her husband, John, met aboard ship traveling to Europe, and continued traveling throughout their seventy-year marriage. This year, Tib says, they made the greatest journey of all. When emergency surgery for John, at age ninety-four, led to repeat hospitalizations, they opted instead for home care with hospice. "It's the new sights and sounds of any trip," says Tib, "the hospital bed in the living room, a bench in the shower, the gurgle of the oxygen compressor." Their trip diary this time, she says, records mostly gratitude: for their marriage, for family and friends, for the faith they found along the Way that is Jesus. John passed away at the couple's home in Hingham, Massachusetts.

Buck Storm grew up in Yuma, Arizona—a true son of the American Southwest. He is a critically acclaimed touring singer/songwriter and the author of two novels—*Truck Stop Jesus*, and Selah Award finalist *The Miracle Man* (Lighthouse Publishing of the Carolinas/Heritage Beacon)—as well as his nonfiction work, *Finding Jesus in Israel: Through the Holy Land on the Road Less Traveled* (Worthy Publishing). His short story, "A Waffle Stop Story of Love and Pistols," was featured in *21 Days of Grace: Stories That Celebrate God's Love* (BroadStreet Publishing). Whether in lyrics or prose, Buck says that he "writes about this mixed-up, out of control, beautiful cacophony we call humanity that God loved so much He gave his own Son to die for."

It's been a wonderful year filled with God's blessings for **Melody Bonnette Swang** of Mandeville, Louisiana. Melody and Cary just celebrated their first year of marriage. Their combined family now totals twenty-three. That includes Cary's daughter, Catherine, and Cary's son, Lawrence, and his wife, Clare. "Twenty-three blessings and twenty-three opportunities for prayer," says Melody. "From praying for son Kevin as he juggles working full-time while returning to college to prayers for sixteen-year-old grandson, Indy, as he assumes a leadership role in his high school JROTC class, covering my family with daily prayers keeps me connected to God and to the ones I love the most."

Jon M. Sweeney and his wife adopted a teenage daughter last year. They also moved back to the Midwest, leaving Vermont for Milwaukee. "It's been a year of changes and blessings," Jon says, with gratitude. He's the author of thirty books, including *The St. Francis Holy Fool Prayer Book*, published last year, and his first book for children, *The Pope's Cat*. He's a busy father and husband, and also the editor-in-chief at Paraclete Press.

This year's *Daily Guideposts* theme, "In the Shadow of Your Wings" is right where **Stephanie Thompson** says she is now. "For the past year I've watched a family member struggle with wrong choices. The deeper I feel my heart aching, the tighter God pulls me under the shadow of His wing. Because of His faithfulness, I trust He will work this situation for His good." Stephanie and her husband, Michael, live in an Oklahoma City suburb with their teenage daughter, Micah, a pug named Princess, Missy, a "Schweenie" (shih tzu/dachshund mix), and a tuxedo cat named Mr. Whiskers.

Marilyn Turk of Niceville, Florida, tells us, "My journal is entitled '*A person who follows God is always moving in the right direction.*' God continues to lead me into new paths, and I follow, often with self-doubt about my own ability. But I've learned that God's got me covered. What I can't do, He puts others in my path who can. Recently, He led me to direct a Christian writers' retreat, something I'd never done before. But God was faithful to finish the work; the retreat was an amazing event. In the same way, He continues to lead my husband and me in parenting our grandson."

Karen Valentin of New York City shares, "I brought in the new year with a painful kidney stone, alone in the emergency room. It was just a hint at what my year would look like—career roadblocks, financial issues, tough challenges as a mother. *How did I get here?* I wondered. Last year I was on top of the world. But as always, despite my feelings, my two little boys motivated me to keep pushing forward. This is my journey. It's not always how I want it to look, but my experiences both good and bad, are shaping me, teaching me, and bringing me to all the places God needs me to be."

"This year has been a year of joy and storm," reports **Scott Walker** of Macon, Georgia. "In August, our son, Luke, married Jessica, a wonderful young woman from Brazil. The wedding was a beautiful moment of celebration. Two weeks later, hurricane winds tore through Georgia. A massive cedar slowly leaned onto our wooden house built in 1847. A branch slammed through a bedroom window, narrowly missing Beth and me. Yet, the house was not destroyed and we were not hurt. Faith is renewed through the broad range of our experiences and emotions. Beth and I reaffirm that God is with us in all seasons and events of life."

Marion Bond West of Watkinsville, Georgia, shares, "Gene and I were jubilant when Jeremy graduated n April from TAC (Training and Accountability Court), a two-year judge-ordered tough-as-nails program. He qualified because of addictions and bipolar diagnosis. In mid-November, one gloomy morning, my heart felt like lead. Jeremy was off his prescriptions and using again. I wasn't certain he was alive. I pulled up old Bill Gaither songs from my iPad. Gene awoke, joining me. I moved from my lonely chair and plopped onto the floor, between his knees. He placed his hands on my shoulders. I reached for them. For nearly two hours we sat silently, absorbing, as one might from blood transfusions, powerful music—'Let's Just Praise the Lord,' 'No One Ever Cared for Me Like Jesus,' 'The Old Rugged Cross Made the Difference.' In our pajamas, we were gathered up by God's Holy Spirit, who transformed us into His glorious victory."

Jacqueline Wheelock writes, "The youngest of five girls, I have struggled this year with the loss of Gloria, the last sibling I had. I had never imagined sole survivorship, but I have found solace in the reminder of the cycle of life via four-year-old Selah, my first grandchild, whom Gloria got to see and adore. As I observe her joy, I see a faint image of the new life Gloria and all Christians will one day experience. My fiction writing has helped, too, as I immerse myself into the lives of characters whose journeys reflect an array of God's children."

SCRIPTURE REFERENCE INDEX

Scripture Reference Index

Authors, Titles, and Subjects Index

Authors, Titles, and Subjects Index

Authors, Titles, and Subjects Index

Authors, Titles, and Subjects Index